A Century in Uniform

A Century in Uniform
Military Women in American Films

STACY FOWLER *and*
DEBORAH A. DEACON

McFarland & Company, Inc., Publishers
Jefferson, North Carolina

ALSO BY DEBORAH A. DEACON AND PAULA E. CALVIN

*War Imagery in Women's Textiles:
An International Study of Weaving, Knitting, Sewing,
Quilting, Rug Making and Other Fabric Arts* (2014)

BY PAULA E. CALVIN AND DEBORAH A. DEACON

*American Women Artists in Wartime,
1776–2010* (2011)

ALL FROM McFARLAND

ISBN (print) 978-1-4766-7713-2
ISBN (ebook) 978-1-4766-3797-6

LIBRARY OF CONGRESS AND BRITISH LIBRARY
CATALOGUING DATA ARE AVAILABLE

© 2020 Stacy Fowler and Deborah A. Deacon. All rights reserved

*No part of this book may be reproduced or transmitted in any form
or by any means, electronic or mechanical, including photocopying
or recording, or by any information storage and retrieval system,
without permission in writing from the publisher.*

On the cover from the top: *Down Periscope*, 1996, 20th Century–Fox; *Serving in Silence*, 1995, NBC television film; 1951 musical *G.I. Jane*, Murray Productions

Printed in the United States of America

*McFarland & Company, Inc., Publishers
Box 611, Jefferson, North Carolina 28640
www.mcfarlandpub.com*

To all who have served their country
bravely and honorably.
Thank you.

In every time of crisis, women have served our country in difficult and hazardous ways ... women should not be considered a marginal group to be employed periodically only to be denied opportunity to satisfy their needs and aspirations when unemployment rises or a war ends.
—John F. Kennedy

Table of Contents

List of Acronyms — ix
Preface — 1
Introduction — 3

ONE. The Early Days: 1910–1939 — 15
TWO. You Can Do It! The 1940s — 25
THREE. Now What? The 1950s — 44
FOUR. The Times They Are Changing: 1960s and 1970s — 64
FIVE. Great Expectations: The 1980s — 85
SIX. Wish Fulfillment—Almost: The 1990s — 104
SEVEN. All That You Can Be: The 2000s — 131
EIGHT. Shattering the Camouflage Ceiling: The 2010s — 148

Conclusion — 171
Appendix A: Filmography by Year — 175
Appendix B: By the Numbers — 195
Chapter Notes — 199
Bibliography — 207
Index — 211

List of Acronyms

ABC	American Broadcasting Company
AOC	Aviation Officer Candidate
AOCS	Aviation Officer Candidate School (Navy)
APC	Armored Personnel Carrier
AST	Aviation Survival Technician
ATS	Auxiliary Territorial Service (British)
AWOL	Absent Without Leave (Army, Air Force)
CID	U.S. Army Criminal Investigation Command
CRT	Combined Reconnaissance Team
CSA	Confederate States of America
DACOWITS	Defense Advisory Committee on Women in the Services
DEA	Drug Enforcement Agency
DEFCON	Defense Readiness Condition
DI	Drill Instructor
DMZ	Demilitarized Zone
DOPMA	Defense Officer Personnel Management Act
GRU	Glavnoye Razvedyvatelnoye Upravleniye (Soviet Military Intelligence)
HBO	Home Box Office
HUAC	House Un-American Activities Committee
ICBM	Intercontinental Ballistic Missile
IED	Improvised Explosive Device
IMDb	Online database of information related to films, television programs, home videos, video games, and internet streams
JAG	Judge Advocate General
MASH	Mobile Army Surgical Hospital
MiG	Russian Military Aircraft
MOS	Military Occupational Specialty (Army)
MP	Military Police (Army, Air Force)
NASA	National Aeronautics and Space Administration
NBC	National Broadcasting Company
NCOC	Naval Covert Operations Center
NFO	Naval Flight Officer
NORAD	North American Aerospace Defense Command
NVA	North Vietnamese Army
OCS	Officer Candidate School (Army, Navy, Marine Corps)
OTS	Officer Training School (Air Force)

List of Acronyms

OWI	Office of War Information
PDA	Public Display of Affection
POW	Prisoner of War
PTSD	Post-Traumatic Stress Disorder
RAF	Royal Air Force (British)
ROTC	Reserve Officer's Training Corps (Army, Air Force, Navy, Marine Corps)
RPG	Rocket Propelled Grenade
SAM	Surface-to-Air Missile
SAS	Special Air Service
SEAL	Sea, Air Land (Navy)—Navy Special Forces
SERE	Survival, Evasion, Resistance and Escape Training
SHAPE	Supreme Headquarters Allied Powers Europe
SPAR	*Semper Paratus* (Always Ready); U.S. Coast Guard motto and nickname of World War II era women in the Coast Guard Reserves
UAV	Unmanned Aerial Vehicle
UN	United Nations
USAF	United States Air Force
USCGC	United States Coast Guard Cutter
USN	United States Navy
USO	United Services Organization
USS	United States Ship
VA	Veterans Administration
VCR	Video Cassette Recorder
WAAC	Women's Army Auxiliary Corps
WAAF	Women's Auxiliary Air Force (British)
WAC	Women's Army Corps
WAF	Women's Air Force
WASP	Women Airforce Service Pilots
WAVE	Women Accepted for Volunteer Emergency Service
WESTPAC	Western Pacific
Wren	Women's Royal Navy Service (British)
WOPR	War Operations Plan Response
XO	Executive Officer
Y2K	Year 2000

Preface

This book is the result of the authors' shared interests in military women, war and film. We met at the 2017 Southwest Popular American Culture Association Conference in Albuquerque, New Mexico, where Stacy presented on a number of films that featured military women and discussed the history of legislation regarding American women in the military, a topic of longstanding interest to Deb. We quickly compared notes about films on the subject and found common ground.

Once we agreed to combine our efforts into a book, we began uncovering treasure troves of American films, many of which have been forgotten or are unknown to contemporary film fans. Movies included in this volume include theatrical releases in the U.S., films that were released as direct to video productions, and a number of made-for-television movies. We intentionally excluded television series and science fiction works, as well as foreign films, with the intention of looking at those in subsequent projects. We agreed to limit our film selections to those that only feature military women, so Red Cross workers, guerrillas, and militia members are also excluded. Additionally, all films analyzed within these pages have been personally viewed by one or both of us; there are a number of films we were unable to locate, so those have not been included.

We discussed the idea that film portrayals of military women could be examined from a number of perspectives, such as the ways in which the women are portrayed, including their sexuality, race, maternal and marital status; their leadership skills; actual jobs performed; whether the film was set in time of war or time of peace; the accuracy of the depiction of military women and their roles in the military; and whether the women were featured in starring/costarring roles or just as minor characters. The "types" of women (Madonna, whore, masculine, feminine) as depicted in various genres could also be explored. We considered several formats for structuring the book and ultimately decided to explore the films by decade produced, which provided us with the opportunity to examine the ways in which social issues of the times, such as women's place in the home and in society, as well as the actual status of military women throughout the twentieth and early twenty-first century, could be incorporated into the film analyses.

We are extremely grateful to the many people who have made this book possible through their kindness and generosity. The book required a significant amount of archival and Internet research as we attempted to find films to include. Rosemary Hanes from the Moving Image Section of the Library of Congress was particularly helpful in sorting through their huge film holdings. The staffs at Rare War Films, Zeus DVDs, Pre-Code Classics, and Robert's Videos were also extremely helpful in locating old and rare films.

A number of scholars and friends made us aware of their favorite films, which we gladly added to our list. These include Dr. Steffen Hantke from Songang University; Dr. Robert W. Matson from the University of Pittsburgh; Bill Howard from the Asian Arts Council at the Phoenix Art Museum; Ben Peterson; Dr. Philip Stewart, Captain, USAF, and Dr. James Thurman, who helped put some of the depictions of war into perspective; and CDR D.L. Tate Walker, USN (Ret.), for her perceptions on the experience of military women. Many thanks go to Dr. Sherry Harlacher, Iris Cashdan-Fishman, and Shelly Dessin, who sat through numerous war films and willingly listened to our research headaches. Linda Hirshman generously shared her research and thoughts on gays in the military. David Curd from Harrison Middleton University kindly provided research funding, and Lauren Guthrie provided technical assistance. And a special thanks to Tracey Boisseau of Purdue University for her kind words of encouragement.

Special recognition must also be given to Melanie Brown, Christine Clayberg, Lisa Dooley, Pete Freeland, Whitney Hamilton, Kevin McMahon, Rebecca Murga, Lauren V. O'Connell, Amber Patton, Edward Hicks, Donre Walker, David Witt, Vivian Wong, and Tania Zee—thank you all for speaking with us and for sharing your inspired films.

We would also like to sincerely thank our families, who have suffered through our obsession with this subject for a number of years. It is only with their tremendous understanding and support that we have been able to explore the changing ways which women's contributions to warfare and nation building are portrayed in theatrical and television films and examine a century's worth of changing social norms regarding women's accepted place in the home, military and society at large in the United States.

Introduction

Warfare has been a fundamental aspect of human existence since the beginning of history. Its importance has been heralded and lamented in song, literature, theater, and art for millennia—and in film since its beginnings in the late nineteenth century. Traditionally, warfare has been seen as a gendered activity that affects the men who fight, not the women who have been relegated to the safety of the home front, a situation that has been frequently reinforced in theatrical war films. Yet the reality is quite different—women have served as Red Cross nurses and ambulance drivers on the front, as civilian nurses and volunteers, and as members of the military in most of the wars in which America has been involved. From the earliest days of this nation's history, they have served as unofficial and official members of the military fighting force. And from the earliest days of motion pictures, the contributions of women to the military cause have been depicted in Hollywood films.

A significant amount of scholarship has been devoted to depictions of women in war films. These range from depictions of wives, daughters, and mothers on the home front to military and Red Cross nurses at home and in times of war to non-medical military women, as well as fictional adaptations of the lives of actual women who participated in a wide assortment of military conflicts in one way or another. In most cases, previous scholarship has focused on a few popular films such as *G.I. Jane*, *Courage Under Fire*, and *A Few Good Men*, exploring issues associated with gender, femininity, and/or the social norms affirmed or violated by the women in question. Others have explored the social interactions and social mores exhibited by groups of female nurses in films such as *Cry 'Havoc'*, *So Proudly We Hail*, and *MASH*, noting the women's emphasis on love and romance rather than teamwork and abilities. Few consider women's roles in early war films, and even fewer consider military women's roles in non-war films. This book is the first to explore the ways in which military women of the Air Force, Army, Coast Guard, Marine Corps, and Navy have been depicted in American theatrical and television films beginning with the earliest films from the turn of the twentieth century through contemporary films of the first two decades of the twenty-first century. It includes movies about the American Civil War, World Wars I and II, Korea, Vietnam, the Gulf War, Iraq, and Afghanistan, as well as films that concern the day-to-day life of military personnel in times of peace.

In order for a film to be included in this book, the film must have at least one military woman with a speaking role as a member of the cast, whether credited for the role or not. The survey includes theatrical releases as well as films released directly to video or initially created for television, but not television series or mini-series. It also does not include military women depicted in science fiction films, fantasy films, or documentaries, nor does it include non-military women such as Red Cross workers, contract and volunteer nurses, and ambulance drivers who were so important during World War I but not official members of the military.

The book explores depictions of military women in a wide range of genres beyond the typical war film, including comedies, disaster films, dramas, mysteries, romances, thrillers, and action films, comparing these depictions to the realities under which actual women in these positions functioned in society at the time of the conflict or time period depicted. Films often reflect public opinion about social issues, and many of these films mirror America's ambivalence toward, support of, rejection of, and acceptance of a variety of social issues relevant to the status of women in the military. The portrayals of military women in these films cover a wide variety of professions as well, ranging from nurse to lawyer to aviator to spy, and the analysis discusses the realities of the women's position in relation to their experiences in the military, the laws impacting their service, and the social norms to which they have been subjected. It examines the challenges the women faced as they broke through the barriers that prevented their full military service, the tropes used to depict a variety of character types, ways in which depictions of military women varied by film genre, and the ways in which non-traditional female characters were accepted by the viewing public. A complete filmography can be found in Appendix A.

History of Women in the U.S. Military

From the earliest days of western civilization, war has been considered to be the realm of men, and the exploits of military heroes have been lauded in literature and mythology in such works as Homer's *Iliad* and *Odyssey*, the poems of medieval bards and the plays of William Shakespeare, and the stories of comic superheroes like Captain America and Sergeant Fury. In such works, the military hero displays heroism, courage, self-sacrifice, exceptional strength, and endurance, all characteristics generally associated with men. While female warriors are found in Western history and literature, such as the Amazons, Artemisia, Boudicca, the Valkyrie Brunhilde, and Joan of Arc, they are typically portrayed as being motivated by a traditional female goal—the desire to be reunited with or saved by a spouse or lover who has gone off to war.[1] Yet these women are also predecessors of today's military woman, serving as role models for those who have come after them. And some of them have been depicted in film, although they are not necessarily discussed in this book.

In the U.S., hundreds of women have disguised themselves as men to fight for their country in the American Revolution (a film about Deborah Sampson, for example, is discussed in Chapter Four), the War of 1812, and the Civil War (several of the earliest films discussed in Chapter One include cross-dressing women whose exploits occurred during that war), unmasked only when wounded or killed, and many received pensions for their military service.

Official military service did not begin for American women until 1901, when Congress authorized the establishment of the Army Nurse Corps, followed closely by the creation of the Navy Nurse Corps in 1908. Although these units were called the Army and the Navy Nurse Corps, they were considered to be working *with* the military and not actual military personnel; these units were always classified as separate from the "real" Army and Navy.

In 1917, with the impending entrance of the U.S. into World War I, Secretary of the Navy Josephus Daniels came up with an ingenious solution for filling the manpower shortages that he knew were coming—using an accidental loophole in the Navy Act of 1916, Daniels authorized the recruitment of women other than nurses into the Navy. Loretta Walsh became the first woman to be sworn into the Navy in a non-nursing capacity on March 21, 1917. By the time the U.S. officially declared war on Germany three weeks later, more than 200 women had followed suit. Unlike the two Nursing Corps, these women were considered to be actually in the military, and they were given the same "rank, responsibilities and benefits as men, including identical pay of $28.75 per month."² In total, more than 13,000 women served in the Navy, Marine Corps, and Coast Guard during this time period; most were quickly mustered out following the end of the war.

Through various laws that were passed during the inter-war period in America (1919–1941), military women slowly began to accumulate some rights. Public Law 62-95 awarded women equal benefits when stationed outside the continental United States. Public Law 67-235 gave female nurses equal treatment with regard to housing and subsistence, and Public Law 67-294 granted service pensions to those nurses who had served with the troops during the Spanish-American War, the Philippine Insurrection, and the Boxer Rebellion, even though they were not considered to be military at the time.

When the U.S. declared war on Japan in 1941, men flocked by the thousands to join the military. By 1942, World War II had created such a manpower shortage at home that the Army decided to fill these shortages with women. Hence Congress passed Public Law 77-554, establishing the Women's Army Auxiliary Corps (WAAC). For the first time, Army women were allowed to work in capacities other than nursing, but they still were not considered as part of the official Army. They were barred from combat service, and a limit was set on how many women could enlist. Due to the overwhelming need, however, that limit was raised less than a year later by Executive Order 9274.

Other branches of the service soon followed with women's units of their own. In 1942, Public Law 77-689 was amended to allow women, nicknamed WAVES, to serve in the Naval Reserve. As was the case during World War I, these women were considered to be actual members of the Navy, rather than an auxiliary unit. As with the WAAC units, however, many restrictions were put in place, including minimum age requirements and severely limited duty assignments. There was also a section stating that female personnel killed in the line of duty would be treated as civil servants for the purposes of benefits rather than receiving the same consideration as male active duty personnel. Also in 1942, Public Law 77-773 was enacted, which established the women's reserve of the Coast Guard; female personnel were nicknamed SPARS. This law changed gendered language to allow women to enlist, but it specifically restricted where women could serve by stating the reservists "shall not be assigned to duty on board vessels of the Navy or Coast Guard or in combat aircraft and shall be restricted ... within the continental United States only."

In 1943, just one year after the Women's Auxiliary Army Corps was established, its effectiveness was questioned, so a new law was passed to remove the word "auxiliary" and to equalize treatment somewhat. Women were slowly starting to be able to spread their wings, but in reality, not much changed. It was not until 1948, several years after the end of the war, that the first real step toward gender integration in the regular military became official. Public Law 80-625, known as the Women's Armed Services Integration Act, finally made the women's divisions of every service branch fully integrated with the men's divisions, but the majority of restrictions remained. During the first two years, the number of women who could be in the service was limited to approximately 8100. After the initial integration period, a 2 percent limitation would apply, meaning that not more than 2 percent of total American military personnel could be women.

The codification of Title 10 of the U.S. Code, which covers all federal laws pertaining to the Armed Forces, also included many restrictions on women in the military, explicitly spelling out where and in what occupations women were *not* allowed to serve. According to a 1981 report by the United States Commission on Civil Rights, even as late as 1977, "73 percent of all authorized military slots were closed to women entirely."³ The military claimed to have maintained those exclusions because women were prohibited from combat, but 30 percent of those jobs were not combat-related. Things had stalled as far as advances for military women were concerned, but during the 1970s, many changes were coming, several due to lawsuits filed by women in the military.

These lawsuits worked to garner military women greater control over their own lives and military careers. Captain Susan Struck, an Air Force nurse serving in Vietnam, got pregnant and was given honorable discharge orders; she did not want to separate from the military, so she appealed the decision. The case eventually went before the Ninth Circuit Court of Appeals, and she lost her appeal.[4] She was then granted a writ of certiorari at the Supreme Court level, but before the case could be heard, it was rendered moot when the Air Force changed its regulations to allow pregnant women to remain in the service if they wanted to; the other branches soon followed suit, and pregnant women were no longer automatically discharged from the service.

Sharon Frontiero was an Air Force lieutenant whose husband did not automatically receive dependent benefits. Section 1072 of Title 10 of the U.S. Code stated that military men's wives automatically received military benefits, but military women's husbands had to prove financial need before receiving those same benefits. Frontiero believed this to be discriminatory, and she proceeded to file suit. In U.S. District Court for the Middle District of Alabama, the Court found against her, stating that the law was justified because there were many more male servicemembers, and if those men's wives were made to establish need, it would cause the government "a substantial administrative burden." The Court further stated that an affirmative finding would mean "any classification established ... must operate ... without providing any[thing] not equally available to members of all classes." The Court seemed to think that would set an unreasonable precedent, but the wording essentially says that people should be treated the same regardless of who or what they are—which was what Frontiero was suing for in the first place. The case was eventually argued in front of the Supreme Court with Ruth Bader Ginsberg as amicus curiae, where the Court ruled eight to one in Frontiero's favor.

Finally, the finding of the 1978 class action lawsuit *Owens v. Brown*, which was filed by several female officers and enlisted women, directed the Navy to "move forward in measured steps" toward gender integration aboard naval vessels not involved in direct combat, which became law with the passing of Public Law 95-485. The same law also caused the Women's Army Corps to cease as a separate entity, stating that assimilating women more fully into the Army structure would be helpful in eliminating feelings of separateness.

The 1970s also saw women become eligible for entrance into the military service academies. In 1975, Public Law 94-106 mandated the "orderly and expeditious admission of women to the academies, consistent with the needs of the services." As a result, 119 women entered West Point the following year, along with 157 into the Air Force Academy, eighty-one into the Naval Academy, and three into the Coast Guard Academy, who were actually appointed before the legislation had passed.

The next twenty-five years were basically spent defining what combat was and why women could not serve in combat units. As late as 2005, Congress was still passing laws on the subject. Those laws primarily dealt with the Army and Marine Corps—the Air Force and Navy had nearly all of their military specialties open to women for many years. One of the last areas to open up to Navy women was submarine duty, which has only been authorized since 2010.

Finally, in 2013, the last stone fell. Secretary of Defense Leon Panetta announced the elimination of the ban on women in combat. Each branch was allowed to request that exceptions be made for particular military specialties, and each was told to submit such requests, along with the justification for the exclusion, by May 2015. Early in 2016, however, Secretary of Defense Ash Carter announced that no exceptions were to be allowed; if a woman could pass the same training as the men, she would be allowed to serve in any specialty for any branch, including the Army

Rangers and Navy SEALs. With the limitations on women's military service finally eliminated, every servicewoman can now truly be all she can be.

A Short History of War in Film

Film is an international language, and from the medium's earliest days, it has exposed the world to American culture and helped bring world culture and events to America. It can serve as pure entertainment or as a form of propaganda, helping to shape public opinion on a variety of issues, including war. It can humanize or dehumanize concepts of war and those who engage in it by creating grand narratives on the subject.[5] While director George Stevens asserted that all film is propaganda, film historians John E. O'Connor and Peter C. Rollins have noted that film can provide an interpretation of an historical event, serve as evidence for social or cultural history, or provide evidence of an historical event by using actual footage of an event.[6] In the case of war films specifically, it is often the way in which many Americans learn about and understand the military. Unfortunately, films are not always accurate in their representations of military culture.

War has been a popular subject of movies since the industry's beginnings; countless films have covered every war, real or fictional, since the dawn of man. The Thomas Edison Company created a number of silent film shorts based on events of the Spanish-American War, for example, including *Love and War* (1899) and *U.S. Troops and Red Cross in the Trenches* (1899), both of which include depictions of Red Cross nurses. D.W. Griffith's controversial epic *Birth of a Nation* (1915) explored the Civil War and the roots of the Ku Klux Klan, but it did not include women as soldiers.

One of the earliest propaganda films that advocated for America's entrance into World War I was Windsor McCay's animated drama *The Sinking of the Lusitania* (1918), which opens with a live-action sequence before switching to an animated depiction of the ship's sinking.[7] McCay's was not the first animated film to look at the fighting in Europe—in 1916, comic favorites Mutt and Jeff joined the fighting in the European theater in the animated short *The Outpost*, one year before the U.S. officially entered the war.[8] Live action films made shortly before and during the war, like *Pro Patria* (1915) and *The Lighthorsemen* (1917), tended to demonize the "evil Hun" in an effort to dehumanize the enemy and laud allied bravery and efforts during the war.

While the majority of the films produced during the nineteen months of U.S. involvement in World War I were not war related, the number of films about World War I made during the 1920s and 1930s increased dramatically and fall into two categories—those that glorified the war, which typically included battle scenes using innovative visuals and editing techniques, and those that advocated for peace and against the horrors of war.[9] Among the former are the Academy Award winning *Wings* (1927), *The Dawn Patrol* (1930), and *The Eagle and the Hawk* (1933), and while some of these films do feature women in roles as nurses or ambulance drivers, the primary focus of the films is on the flying sequences; the women are merely included as love interests. The world's fascination with flight and the elegant aerial ballet of dogfights glamorized the exploits of these early pilots, and filmmakers were quick to tell their stories. At least twenty-six aviation war films were made between 1927 and 1938.[10]

Films that reflected disillusionment include *All Quiet on the Western Front* (1930), which did not feature any female military characters, and *The Mad Parade* (1925), aka *Forgotten Women*, whose protagonists, female canteen workers and ambulance drivers, experience the horrors of war firsthand. Later films focusing on the horrors of World War I include *Johnny Got His Gun* (1971) and *Regeneration* (1997), both of which focus on the "shell shock" experienced by soldiers, a continuing problem now better known as post-traumatic stress disorder (PTSD). While such films realistically portrayed the destruction of the land and the difficulties and sacrifices made by those who fought, no military women were featured in these films. In fact, for the more than 340 films surveyed in this book, only two depict a woman serving in the U.S. military during World War I.[11]

By the late 1930s and early 1940s, American filmmakers watched as the world again hurtled towards global war and soon began producing films warning of the suffering experienced by Europeans as Hitler expanded his control. Once America entered the war, the American film industry began churning out numerous propaganda films in support of the war effort. In fact, Donald Fishman noted that between 1941 and 1945, "the motion picture industry became the pre-eminent transmitter of wartime policy and a lightning rod for public discourse."[12] These films gave the people on the home front the opportunity to vicariously experience the hardships encountered by the American fighting man; in many cases, women were excluded from the stories altogether or were included only as love interests, typically in traditional social roles of wife or nurse. In these stories, the hero is the center of the film, standing up and accepting the challenge with pride and a sense of honor when duty calls, serving as a model for others, no matter the consequences. These heroic traits, however, were rarely attributed to women, who were often portrayed as helpless and dependent on others for help. However, as can be seen in Chapter Two, a number of the films included military women—nurses, other medical personnel, or administrative personnel—from all services, roles which often required women to throw off these assumptions and rise to the occasion when confronted with the realities of war. These were new roles for many women and certainly new for many moviegoers. While many women were shown working competently at their appointed jobs and in precarious situations, many were again included as love interests for the films' protagonists.

Along with live action films, American film studios began producing cartoons, geared up in support of the war effort.[13] In addition to producing animated shorts like *Out of the Frying Pan, Into the Firing Line* (1942), which encouraged housewives to save cooking grease, and *Cinderella Goes to a Party* (1942), where Cinderella goes to work in a factory, the Walt Disney Company designed characters for military unit insignia and aircraft nose art. Most of the animation shorts that looked specifically at the fighting man included popular animation characters such as Donald Duck, Popeye, and Porky Pig and did not include depictions of military women, with the few exceptions noted in Chapter Two. These cartoons, along with a ten-to twenty-minute newsreel, were shown before the main feature in the local movie theater.

The U.S. military commissioned a number of animated training films designed to educate primarily enlisted men in the do's and don'ts of military life. The most famous character from these films is Private Snafu,[14] a hapless, immature, narcissistic Army private who served as a negative role model for enlisted men, who were primarily young and white. Military women and minorities were not represented in the films, with one exception—in the episode "The Homefront" (November 1943), viewers are told in a song about how civilians at home are helping the war effort and that Sally Lou, Snafu's girlfriend, has joined the WACs. She is only onscreen for eighteen seconds of the four-minute episode.

In the years following World War II, a number of films were spoofs of military life. These comedies presented a nostalgic look at the service, the result of audience familiarity with military life. They remained popular during the early years of the Cold War, and film served as a battlefield of ideas, promoting patriotism, heroism, and dedication to the American cause. These comedies, however, did not extend to films about the Korean War, about twenty of which were released during the war years. Many of these films reflect the disillusionment and frustration experienced by Americans as the result of the failed war. While military nurses served both in Korea and Japan, few are represented in the films about the war; their service, like that of the men who served during America's "forgotten war," was barely noticed.

The angst produced by the lack of resolution of the Korean War rose to new heights as America became involved in the war in Vietnam. Initially, filmmakers began depicting the war in much the same way as they had World War II. Films like *The Green Berets* (1968) offered preachy propaganda in support of the war in a movie supported by the U.S. Army. As objections to the war increased, however, Hollywood began to allude to the war in films like *MASH*, rather than to confront it directly. It wasn't until several years after the war ended that Hollywood began to tell the story of the war. Films like *The Deer Hunter* (1978), *Apocalypse Now* (1979), and *Platoon* (1986) gave the general public its impression of the war; despite the fact that 11,000 women served in Vietnam, none are depicted in these films.[15] As discussed in Chapters Four and Five, the few Vietnam War movies that did include female servicewomen feature only medical personnel, despite the fact that several hundred non-medical military women served in theater during the war.

Films from the late 1980s and 1990s changed their focus and began to explore issues of global terrorism, often using spies and Special Forces personnel rather than the typical soldier as the hero. While a few of these films include women characters, as discussed in Chapter Six, those that did primarily focus on their personal and/or professional isolation, frequently portraying as them victims of sexual violence rather than productive members of a military team.

The focus of war movies shifted again in the wake of 9/11, and Hollywood quickly began portraying stories of individual male heroes in theatrical films like *The Hurt Locker* (2008) and *American Sniper* (2014), most of which do not include military women in combat situations or even in the cast, despite the fact that women have been integrated into military units in both Iraq and Afghanistan since the onset of those wars. In fact, many of the films discussed in Chapters Seven and Eight show that women's role in today's military is actually central to military operations, yet the women are generally not given status as primary figures in these films, and many Americans fail to recognize their contributions to the war efforts.

Military Women in American Films

The idea of women warriors has been part of the culture and literature of the West for millennia. Probably the most famous woman soldier is Joan of Arc, the young French peasant who led French troops to victory over the British in the fifteenth century. The Maid of Orleans has been portrayed in literature and film numerous times, but primarily in European films. She does appear in one film in this survey, *Joan the Woman* (1916), which is discussed in Chapter One.

Women have unofficially served in the U.S. military since the colonial period, often dressing and living as men. Stories about these cross-dressing women, often purported to be written as autobiographical tales in books such as *Female Marine: The Adventures of Miss Lucy Brewer*, were popular during the early nineteenth century, as were cross-dressing women theatrical performers who frequently portrayed boys on stage. This trend continued in films of the early twentieth century, and several of these early films featuring cross-dressing women are discussed in Chapter One.[16] In the decade following World War I, however, attitudes about cross-dressing women in film changed, and they were now seen as threatening socially acceptable concepts of male and female identities. Implementation of the Hays Code of 1934, which prohibited films from depicting anything that would "lower the moral standards of those who see it," effectively ended portrayals of nudity, homosexuality and cross-dressing in film.[17]

While cross-dressing women have been seen as threatening to social conceptions of "proper" female attitudes, military women in general have also been considered a threat to social norms about femininity, often seen as deviant, controversial, loose—or even traditional. Seen as "the Other," women are treated as being separate from and unequal to men, even a distraction from their wartime duties. Traditionally, women in war films were shown as being passive, subject to social expectations in terms of their life choices and appearance. Frequently serving as a foil for male characters, they labor in traditional roles such as wife and mother; if a woman joins the military, itself a radical idea that blurs gender lines, she works in a traditional job such as nurse, which still allows her to show her nurturing side and perform an important function. Often portrayed as a "girl" who is just working at a non-traditional job temporarily to help with the war effort, her focus is on the time after the war, when she can return to wearing feminine clothing, find a husband, and have children. Silent, passive, and sensitive, she serves as an inspiration for the fighting man, who often places her on a pedestal (often referred to as "the Madonna," the embodiment of the maternal) and fights to keep her safe.

The "loose" woman provides temporary satisfaction for a man far from home. She behaves like a man by actively seeking sex and power, and her behavior is often threatening to both men and women. Brandishing her lipstick tube as a weapon of strength and defiance, she typically pays the ultimate price, either voluntarily or not, for her indiscretions and serves as a warning to other women who choose to deviate from social norms.

For many Americans, until very recently, the image of the military woman is that of a mannish individual who rejects all aspects of femininity, able to competently act under the pressures of war without giving consideration to her appearance or what people think. She, too, often dies in a war film, usually heroically, recognizing that she has no place in peacetime society. But are these stereotypical portrayals of women actually accurate?

As previously noted, while women have historically participated in war, they have largely been omitted from the historical record, and their relative absence from films about war leads people to think that women have not been involved in any meaningful way. Hollywood films tend to depict war as a man's job, unsuitable for women, yet women have played a valuable and official role in the military since World War I. While the military woman has been seen as problematic because she "violates traditional norms, exercises autonomy, travels widely, and demonstrates great flexibility in her determination to master her environment," she also serves as a sign of modernity.[18] Today's military women work in jobs ranging from the traditional nurse and secretary to those considered to be more "masculine," such as pilots, jet mechanics, and shipboard engineers. And many of those roles are reflected in films of the twenty-first century.

The military woman also has been depicted as a hero in films. She frequently is a woman living life on her own terms who finds herself in a situation usually encountered by a man, performing well in that situation. While she may deemphasize her femininity, she usually has a healthy relationship with the men around her and with other women as well. She is focused, organized, and capable—and she exists in real life as well as in the movies, as can be seen in the films discussed in this book.

Each chapter of the book addresses a specific decade of film production and reveals the film genres, types of characters, jobs they performed, the rules under which women in the American military operated in the real world at that time, and how they were received by the film viewing public. The first chapter, The Early Days: 1910–1939, sets the stage for the rest of the book by examining the earliest war films, those made between 1910 and 1939. Created in black and white by filmmakers in America, the earliest were silent films that featured women in traditional roles as contract and military nurses or ambulance drivers, caring for the wounded and often falling in love with the hero. For the most part, these women were "good girls" who followed the social norms of the day; those who did not typically died to atone for their transgressions. One interesting trope that began with the earliest of these films was that of women dressing as military men and serving on the front lines. Despite the fact that more than 13,000 women joined the U.S. military during World War I, serving in the Navy as yeomen (F), the Marine Corps as Marines (F) and the Army as Hello Girls, this military service has not been depicted in film at all except for one short film discussed in Chapter Seven.

As the U.S. entered World War II, there quickly became a manpower shortage at home as wave after wave of men joined the military. This provided a great opportunity for American women, allowing them to serve in roles not traditionally available to them at that time. This included military service. Chapter Two, You Can Do It! The 1940s, examines the roles of military women during World War II. With the passing of Public Law 77-554 in 1942, Congress established the Women's Army Auxiliary Corps (which became the Women's Army Corps a year later); this act was quickly followed by legislation establishing women's units for the Navy, Marine Corps, and Coast Guard as well. With so much going on, it is not surprising that Hollywood took full advantage and produced a greater quantity of films, many of which depicted women in the military in a much wider variety of roles, especially those that were released post–World War II. During the war years, many films, like *Corregidor* and *Cry 'Havoc'*, for example, chronicled the experiences of nurses assigned overseas. There were also a number of films centered on basic training, including *Never Wave at a WAC* and *Keep Your Powder Dry*, which were generally vehicles for the decade's most glamorous screen stars to be able to do their part for the war as well.

As both World War II and the Korean Conflict faded into memory, life in the U.S. began to transition to a somewhat normal state. Chapter Three, Now What? The 1950s, looks at the status of military women in the 1950s. Women were expected to just return to being housewives, but that became problematic. Many of these women had gotten their first taste of independence, and many of them did not want to give up that independence so easily. At that time, however, Hollywood generally chose to portray military women in a much more traditional light, with few films of this decade doing much to showcase the ever-increasing role of women in the military and society at large. Some notable exceptions were films that focused on the burgeoning Cold War, such as *Jet Pilot* and *The Iron Petticoat*, both of which featured female Soviet fighter pilots who were considering defecting to the West. Comedies also became much more common during this decade, but many films continued to portray women in the more traditional scenario of military nurse as love interest for her male co-star.

During the 1960s and 1970s, changes occurred throughout all aspects of society, and those changes are explored in Chapter Four, The Times They Are Changing: The 1960s and 1970s. By the 1960s, American military leaders recognized that female military members had made significant contributions during World War II and the Korean Conflict, and while the number of military women had been dramatically reduced after those wars, those who remained continued to show that women could make a difference in the military as they worked to open new jobs and opportunities for women in all branches of the service. War films from this time period continued to primarily feature World War II as their settings, but rather than just focusing on dramatic events, many, like *The Horizontal Lieutenant* and *Wake Me When It's Over*, depicted more humorous aspects of military service, reflecting the ebullient mood of the country at the time. That cheerful mood soon turned dark in both society and film as America's involvement in the Vietnam War geared up in the late 1960s and early 1970s. While they used the setting of previous wars, films like *MASH* and *Catch-22* were actually commentaries on the Vietnam War and reflected society's growing desire for peace. At the same time, Cold War films such as *The President's Plane is Missing* and *Warhead* reflected growing fears about terrorism, the Cold War, and the possibility of nuclear war.

As the horrors of the Vietnam War faded from the public's consciousness, Hollywood filmmakers felt the time was right to revisit the war, producing films like *Hamburger Hill*, *Platoon*, and *Apocalypse Now*, which showed the experiences of the men who fought and died during the war. While the majority of these films did not feature military women as part of the story line, several did, including *Full Metal Jacket* and *Purple Hearts*. The end of the military draft meant a shortage of men to fill military manpower requirements, eventually leading to increased positions for women in the military—and to films like *Private Benjamin*, *A Time to Triumph*, and *She's in the Army Now*, which explored the trials and tribulations women experienced as they adapted to military life. Chapter Five, Great Expectations: The 1980s, examines these increased opportunities as well as issues of gender discrimination and sexual harassment, which were increasingly being talked about as more women joined the military. The need for the military to address these issues and adapt to change were addressed on the screen as well, in movies such as *Lethal Woman* and *Opposing Force (Hellcamp)*. Many of these issues would continue to be explored and developed by both the military and filmmakers in subsequent decades.

The 1990s saw increased public interest in the idea of women in the military and of women serving in non-traditional military roles, the result of the ever-shifting front lines that occurred during the conflict in Grenada and during Operation Desert Shield/Desert Storm. As seen in Chapter Six, Wish Fulfillment—Almost: The 1990s, films such as *Courage Under Fire*, *Fire Birds*, and *By Dawn's Early Light* feature women aviators as key figures and as heroes. Other films, such as *A Few Good Men* and *Inflammable*, also show strong military women in a positive light. The decade also saw filmmakers look back to women's roles in previous wars, in such films as *The English Patient*, *In Love and War*, and *Paradise Road*, and to continue to explore important issues of gender discrimination and sexual harassment. The role of women in the military and the bending of gender roles even entered the world of children's films in Disney's *Mulan*. Like the military, commercial filmmakers also began to address the issue of gays in the military in films such as *Serving in Silence*.

Since the turn of the twenty-first century, films featuring women in the military have become standard Hollywood fare. While other decades tended to look back, less than one-third of films from the 2000s are about historical conflicts. As seen in Chapter Seven, All That You Can Be: The 2000s, filmmakers now prefer to talk about the present as well as to look ahead to what the military woman has and will become. During this decade, military members themselves began making their own films, reflecting their personal experiences and the issues of importance to themselves and their compatriots.

Since 2010, decisions allowing women to serve on submarines and to serve in combat units have been implemented, and Hollywood has adjusted accordingly. Today's films, which are examined in Chapter Eight, Shattering the Camouflage Ceiling: The 2010s, show servicewomen in a much greater variety of roles. For the more than 120 films in this survey that were released between 2000 and 2018, only eight have a nurse as the primary military female character, and five of those portrayals are about World War II. This contrasts sharply with the forty-seven films made during the 1940s, in which almost half feature nurses as the main female military character(s). Exploring the ever-present topic of PTSD has also become more prevalent, and films such as *Blood Stripe* and *Stand Down Soldier* address all aspects of how combat affects the soldiers of this generation.

While warfare is still considered to be the realm of fighting men and their military exploits have been the subject of American film since the medium's beginnings, women have also answered the call to defend their country, and their story deserves to be told as well. Women's military service has received recognition in film, but not to the extent of the men's. Their depictions, measured against what was officially authorized at the time of the film's release, are discussed in the following chapters.

ONE

The Early Days
1910–1939

From the dawn of the American film industry in the late nineteenth century, war has been a subject of interest for filmmakers and audiences alike. War provided filmmakers with easy, popular, and predictable plots and could also be used to inform and persuade viewers. When audiences clamored to know what war was like, early filmmakers like Thomas Edison showed them in film shorts like *Love and War* (1899) and *U.S. Troops and Red Cross in the Trenches* (1899), which featured reenactments of scenes from the Spanish-American War.[1] These early war films established the conventions found in war films to the present day, including aggressive masculinity as the ideal in war heroes, the idea of the "team," and the fact that the hero always gets the girl.[2]

While most early war films showed heroic actions by American military men, the few women who appeared in them were relegated to roles as wives, mothers, or nurses—all "appropriate" roles for women. In real life, the nurses who cared for American troops during the Spanish-American War were contract employees of the Army and Navy since military service was not considered appropriate for a woman. The nurses' outstanding performance during the war helped change such perceptions, and in 1901, the Army Nurse Corps (Female) was founded. The Navy Nurse Corps followed in 1908.[3]

As the threat of World War I loomed, military planners searched for ways in which to solve manpower shortages. They ultimately agreed to enlist women to fill clerical positions in the U.S., freeing men for combat. Young women across the country answered the call; most were white, middle- and upper-class women seeking good pay and adventure as well as a way to show their patriotism. The Navy yeoman (F), Marine Reservists (F), and Coast Guard recruits earned the same pay and allowances as men of the same paygrade. While thousands of women served during the war in roles other than nurses, filmmakers for the most part have ignored their service and have not depicted them in war films.

Action Films

Action films are exactly as they sound—films that feature a lot of excitement, activity, and adventure on the part of the characters. These films typically have good character development, minimal plots which involve a quest, and lots of action. They have been favorites since the beginning of the film industry, providing viewers with the thrills missing from their own lives. The roots of action films can be traced to silent era comedies like the Keystone Cops and Laurel and Hardy, as well as early cowboy movies, all of which feature frenetic displays of excitement, energy, and adventure.[4]

As previously noted, while women were not permitted to officially serve in the U.S. military until the twentieth century, women have fought in all of America's wars—often disguised as men. The idea of female cross-dressing was not unheard of in Western culture. Such characters are found throughout Western literature, from Greek times through the works of Shakespeare to modern times. While cross-dressing women, imaginary or real, were known, they presented a problem for early twentieth century society, disrupting social norms and questioning sexually assigned roles.[5] In some cases, the women were seeking greater opportunities that were denied to them as women; others joined the military to escape from abusive relationships or for greater financial security or just for the adventure. Many were well educated, spoke multiple languages, and were familiar with firearms.

But cross-dressing is also subversive. Combat is seen as the ultimate test of masculinity, and if a woman performs well in combat, her conduct threatens the definition of masculinity. As Stacie Robyn Furia has noted, "Women making war shatters quintessential categories of gender and family, most fundamentally the notion that men fight and women nurture."[6] To counter this threat to the American social order, filmmakers in later decades tended to depict non-medical military women as either super-macho Amazons (think Warrant Officer Ripley in the *Alien* franchise), often of questionable sexual orientation, like Private Vasquez in *Aliens*, or as being frail and needy, requiring a man to save them, like Joan in *She Goes to War*, which is discussed in this chapter. This was not true, however, of the earliest filmmakers.

Not all cross-dressing characters appeared in war films. In fact, many were featured in early films set on the American frontier, where the cross-dressing woman was able to successfully navigate the hazards presented by the harsh western landscape. Through her riding, roping, and shooting skills, she embodied the American ideal of physical ability and courage, mastering the harsh environment like those who colonized the West.[7] These characters were seen as positive figures by American viewers. Some feminist scholars have presented them as representations of the "New Woman," independent and engaged with the world outside of the woman's traditional sphere of home and family. Other scholars have seen them as subversive, operating outside the boundaries of civilization as a result of their athleticism and skills. These early films, made primarily between 1908 and 1921 during the golden age of female action heroines, were used by the American moving picture industry "to help the [film] medium become respectable and appeal to audiences of all classes."[8] The ploy worked—the women were seen as positive figures of nationalism appealing to both working class fans of dime store novels and more sophisticated middle class theater goers.

One of the key features of these early action frontier films was a chase scene, typically on horseback. Laura Horak describes "the cross-dressed chase sequence, which showed off a woman's physical vitality within the types of landscape that had mystically forged her. Disguised as men, white female characters could get into dangerous situations and demonstrate their bravery, while their white and female identity generated pleasurable anxiety for audiences who feared for their safety."[9] There is a formula to the chase scene. The woman appears first, riding across the screen. When she is out of sight, the men chase after her. After they clear the screen, the woman is seen again in a new location. This alternating between the woman and men in different scenes continues several times, and the chase ends when the male pursuers ride past her hiding place or she reaches safety. The chase sequence is a key scene in these films, showing the woman's ingenuity, dedication to completing her mission, and skills in riding and shooting.

The early war films that feature cross-dressing women are primarily set during the Civil War and share similar plots and storylines with frontier films. While scholars such as Horak and Richard Abel have noted the existence of these films, there is not much significant scholarship about them, perhaps in part due to their lack of easy availability. Each film features a chase sequence, and in most cases, the woman is not unmasked. Cross-dressing in these films is also tied to location. In many instances, the woman must leave the confining location of home in order to escape the roles forced upon her by society so that she can show her true self as a heroic individual.

Women disguised as men fought on both sides of the Civil War, and both sides also used female spies, who did not typically cross-dress, but early filmmakers appear to have focused their attention on Confederate women rather than Northern women, emphasizing the sacrifices made by the former throughout the war. Northern women sacrificed their sons and husbands to the cause, showing their loyalty through "womanly" pursuits such as knitting clothing for the troops, sending care packages to the wounded, and holding fundraising events. They tended to see themselves through the lens of supporting a "just war."[10] They also were not threatened as much by the actual fighting as Confederate women were.

Southern women, on the other hand, saw their sons and husbands as fighting to defend their threatened way of life, gladly giving them to the Confederacy.[11] Their deep hatred of the North led them to a form of determined militancy and an identification with the women of Sparta, who were well known for their own strength in the face of adversity. Like their Northern counterparts, Confederate women knitted for the troops, sent care packages to the wounded, and raised money for the cause. But since so much of the fighting occurred in the South, they were subjected to having their crops destroyed, their homes occupied by invading Union troops, and physical danger from the fighting that occurred nearby. Long after their defeat, Southern women worked tirelessly to raise money to erect monuments to commemorate the heroes of the Confederacy. This love of the Confederacy and dedication to the cause were captured by early filmmakers in films that featured cross-dressing women.

The Girl Spy before Vicksburg (1910) is the third episode in the *Girl Spy* series of shorts produced by the Kalem Company.[12] Shot in Jacksonville, Florida, the fourteen-minute silent film stars Gene Gauntier as Nan, the girl spy. Initially seen as a traditional young woman at home, attired in a white hoop skirted dress, when Nan receives a message from a Confederate general who needs her help, she comes to the rescue, donning a short wig and a Union enlisted uniform and riding into the Union camp under false papers. Despite her lack of military training, her disguise is good enough to allow her to be mistaken for a young male soldier. Almost captured in an act of sabotage, she escapes on foot, chased through a swamp by Union troops.

The pursuit scenes follow the pursuit script of frontier films, with Nan easily moving through the picture frame from right to left, followed by the men, who experience difficulties navigating the treacherous landscape. The same sequence is repeated twice more as they race through the woods and then to a lake where she hides among the reeds until they give up the chase. The men never gain ground in their pursuit, and Nan is able to safely report her success to the Confederate general before returning home. The film ends without Nan returning to her female attire, an indication that she is prepared for yet another call to action.

In 1912, Anna Q. Nilssen starred as fictional Confederate spy Agnes Lane in *Darling of the C.S.A*. The loyal agent is first seen in decidedly feminine attire—a long dark dress with a white collar and cuffs and a large cavalier's hat with a jaunty white plume, her long dark hair in "Shirley Temple" curls, seated sidesaddle on a horse. On her way to deliver a dispatch to a Confederate camp, she spots a Union flyer offering a reward for her capture. Never one to resist a challenge, she decides to turn herself in, hoping to be able to gather information for the Confederate cause. She dresses in a Union officer's uniform, pins up her hair, then puts a dress on over the uniform and rides to the Union camp, where she is arrested. When left unguarded, she quickly sheds her dress, steals important Union papers, tucks her hair under a cap, and escapes—after writing "Thank you" on the tent wall. She successfully returns to the Confederate camp with her stolen information, but that is not the end of the story. Union soldiers, eager to avenge her escape, attack the camp where she has returned to a more traditional feminine pursuit of tending the wounded. As men die around her, she decides to end the fighting by surrendering to the Union troops, which she does, leading the Confederate soldiers to rally and save her.

Nan and Agnes are very different depictions of the cross-dressing heroine. Where Nan is young and cute, effecting a daring mission and escaping unscathed, Agnes is a mature woman who is effective as a spy but who needs to be rescued by men. Nan's disguise as a young soldier, which she wears for more than half of the time she's onscreen, is fairly convincing; Agnes is too beautiful and voluptuous (and has too much hair) to be mistaken for a man, except at a distance. Her appearance is not that much of a disadvantage, however, as she only needs the disguise to escape from the Union camp. She spends the majority of her four minutes onscreen dressed in feminine attire, signaling to filmgoers that her work as a Confederate spy is merely a means to an end, not a rejection of her femininity.

Drama

A dramatic film is one that presents an exciting or emotional series of events. From the beginning of the film industry, dramatic films have been audience favorites, and their popularity increased even more as films moved away from shorts toward full length feature films between 1911 and 1914.[13] By the second decade of the twentieth century, movies had become part of the American social fabric and powerful social influences, no longer seen as a fad or low-class entertainment. War films fit nicely into the drama category, as they tend to exaggerate serious elements of fighting and feature an increased intensity of emotion while downplaying the boredom of "down" time that comes between periods of fighting.[14]

The idea of the cross-dressing woman also works well in film dramas, as the need to cross-dress is frequently the result of a dramatic event in the story. One of the best known American silent dramas which is set in the Confederate South and features a cross-dressing woman is the short film *The House with Closed Shutters* (1910). The film, whose story features a young woman who wears her cowardly brother's Confederate uniform and races into battle to save her family's honor, did more than merely entertain its audience. In addition to setting some of the standards for cross-dressing women in later films, it serves as a morality tale for viewers. None of the characters except the brother has a name—star Dorothy West's character is listed merely as "His Sister" in the credits and intertitles, and the others are also listed by their role. This gives them an air of "everyman," representations of universal figures with whom the audience can identify.

The film opens with Sister sewing a Confederate flag, which she proudly shows off to her family.[15] She is a proper Southern young woman, attired in a white lace skirt, dark bodice and white caplet, bow in her long dark hair. She is proud of her brother's service until he returns home to hide from his Union pursuers, having failed to deliver an important dispatch to the front lines. Horrified by his behavior, she springs into action, donning her brother's uniform. In a dramatic moment, she lops off her long hair, that symbol of feminine virginity, and rides off to complete his mission. This cutting of a woman's hair, which is carried forward in later cross-dressing movies, is symbolic, a liminal experience which marks the woman's transition to that of a warrior with a mission.

On her way to the front lines, Sister encounters a Union patrol, which she outsmarts after following the standard pursuit scripted in action films, arriving safely at the front. Overcome with emotion from the battle raging in front of her, she races onto the battlefield to rescue a fallen

Confederate flag and is killed. Sister's disguise is not uncovered—Mother receives a telegram reporting the death of her "son," for which she berates Charles, ordering the house's shutters closed and her son to never again show his face to the daylight. While Sister is only onscreen for six of the film's sixteen minutes, her actions are central to the film's storyline, the catalyst for a serious critique of duty and honor.

By the mid–1910s, films featuring cross-dressing women and those focusing on the Civil War fell out of favor, as did war films in general.[16] An exception to this was Cecil B. DeMille's ten reel silent film *Joan the Woman* (1916), in which the ghost of the historical Joan of Arc serves as a muse forا World War I soldier, using her life story to inspire him before a fatal mission.[17] Opera star Geraldine Farrar portrays Joan as confident and capable, even in the face of death. The film opens with an intertitle that states, "Founded on the Life of Joan of Arc, the Girl Patriot Who Fought with Men, Was Loved by Men and Killed by Men—Yet Withal Retained the Heart of Woman," situating the well-known warrior first and foremost as a woman. At a time when women who fought were seen as abnormal, the film serves as a commentary on gender roles; even though Joan was a brave soldier whose life serves as an inspiration to a soldier in the trenches of World War I, the film's overall message is that war is the business of men, and Joan was depicted as an example of true womanhood in advertising aimed at the American public. To enforce this message, in her fifty-six minutes onscreen, Joan is never shown completely clothed in armor, the uniform of fifteenth century warriors. Rather, she wears her metal breastplate and armor over a long, sleeveless white tunic embroidered with gold *fleur de lis*, emphasizing her femininity above her warfighting skills.

The taste for cross-dressing women in film steadily declined after 1915, although they do appear from time to time in later decades. As war loomed in Europe, the American film industry continued to flourish, and many Hollywood stars lent their talents to films that supported the war effort and their names and images to various war relief programs. In 1918, Mary Pickford starred in the film *Johanna Enlists*, the story of a country girl who prays for a lover and instead gets an entire Army regiment which camps in the family's field. Contrary to the film's title, she does not join the Army; however, at the end of the film, Pickford appears in an Army uniform, complete with jodhpurs, boots, Sam Brown belt, and three rows of ribbons, astride a cavalry horse alongside Colonel Ralph Faneuf, Commanding Officer of the 143rd Field Artillery. In the sixteen second piece, both pose at the head of the regiment and recognize its outstanding service during the war. An intertitle identifies her as "Colonel Mary Pickford, Godmother and Honorary Colonel of the 143rd," a position she could not hold by law.

As previously noted, while filmmakers ignored the service of most of the young women who enlisted in the military, they did include military nurses in several films. After the war, military nurses continued to serve at home and abroad, providing healing and nurturing to service personnel and civilians overseas. In the black and white film *Tell It to the Marines* (1926), Eleanor Boardman stars as Navy nurse Norma Dale, who is stationed at U.S. Marine Corps boot camp. The object of affection for both DI Sergeant O'Hara (Lon Chaney) and screw-up recruit Private Burns (William Haines), she resists the advances of Burns and considers O'Hara to be a friend. When the men deploy to Shanghai during a crisis, they find her there as well, part of ship's company onboard the hospital ship USS *Relief*. When the nurses are sent to Hangchow (Hangzhou) to help with an epidemic, the Marines are deployed to protect them from bandits, giving Burns the opportunity to show he has reformed. While Dale wears a uniform for the majority of her sixteen minutes onscreen, at the film's end, she is a civilian, married to Burns and forced to resign her commission.

As the 1920s came to an end, films about World War I became "elegiac in tone, pacifist

Marine Sergeant O'Hara (Lon Chaney) flirts with Navy nurse Norma Dale (Eleanor Boardman) in *Tell It to the Marines* (1926).

in purpose, and cynical in perspective," a reflection of the disillusion felt by combatants and non-combatants alike.[18] Anti-war films had the goal of proving that the ideas about valor and righteousness espoused by war films were merely romantic illusions and that the reality of war was, in fact, death and desolation. The realistic depictions of battlefield deaths and devastation in these films were intended to debunk the idea of heroic warfare, although the hero in an anti-war film is never shown as a coward, so the films do not renounce the idea of courage in warfare.[19]

The silent film *She Goes to War* (1929) begins with a disclaimer stating that the film is not taking sides in the hawk and dove debate. Rather, it is just telling the truth about the realities of war. It notes that the "viewer will find heartache, humor, courage, cowardice, horrid death and high romance, all blended together in this greatest picture of the World War of 1914–1918."[20] In the opening scene, men go off to war by train, leaving behind heart-broken spouses and parents as "Stars and Stripes" plays in the background. Included in the crowd is wealthy socialite Joan Morans (Eleanor Boardman), who follows her drunken boyfriend to a small town near the front in France. There, she is horrified by the suffering, death, and destruction she sees all around her.

When the men in her lover's unit are called to move out to the front, Joan notices that he is not there; he is drunk, and when she is unable to sober him up, she dons his uniform to replace him. Her masquerade goes unnoticed because the men have all donned gas masks, which obscure their faces. Once the gas has cleared, she dirties her face to continue her ruse. The film is known for its exceptionally realistic battle scenes, and Joan experiences the harsh realities of war in the eleven minutes she is onscreen, surviving horrific bombings in a foxhole with two soldiers who make lewd comments when they realize she is a woman, causing her to flee despite the danger.

Untrained in Army tactics, she is a danger to herself and the men around her. As they cross a field, they are subjected to barrel bombing, which sets the field on fire. The men run from the bombs, but she freezes until someone drags her to the safety of an armored personnel carrier (APC). As they advance through the fire amidst continued bombing, the interior of the APC becomes stifling, making everyone miserable. She is not the only person who panics; one soldier runs out into the inferno and is killed. Later, she finds herself in another foxhole with the same soldiers who physically threaten her, causing her to flee again. Her flight takes her behind the enemy lines, where she kills a German soldier with her pistol. Horrified, she screams and faints. The unit's commander later finds her lying in the foxhole with the dead German and, upon removing her helmet, realizes she is a woman. In the film's final scene, weary soldiers slowly walk back to town, the captain carrying Joan on his back. Her head rests on his shoulder, and when she wearily looks up and kisses his neck, he smiles and keeps walking.

A strongly anti-war film, *She Goes to War* also served as a morality tale about women's unsuitability to go to war. Despite her good intentions, Joan was nervous and hysterical when confronted with the realities of war and needed a man to save her. The film also illustrated some of the perils women might encounter when placed in close confines with men. While the U.S. was not actively involved in military conflict at the time the film was released, it served as a warning about the impropriety of women in combat, a warning that was echoed for decades afterward.

Comedies

Comedies were among the most popular of early films, giving viewers the opportunity to escape from the vicissitudes of life and explore ideas about authority within the social structure. While war is a serious business, comedy can help relieve the stress of military life. Comedies, however, do not view war as a laughing matter and do not

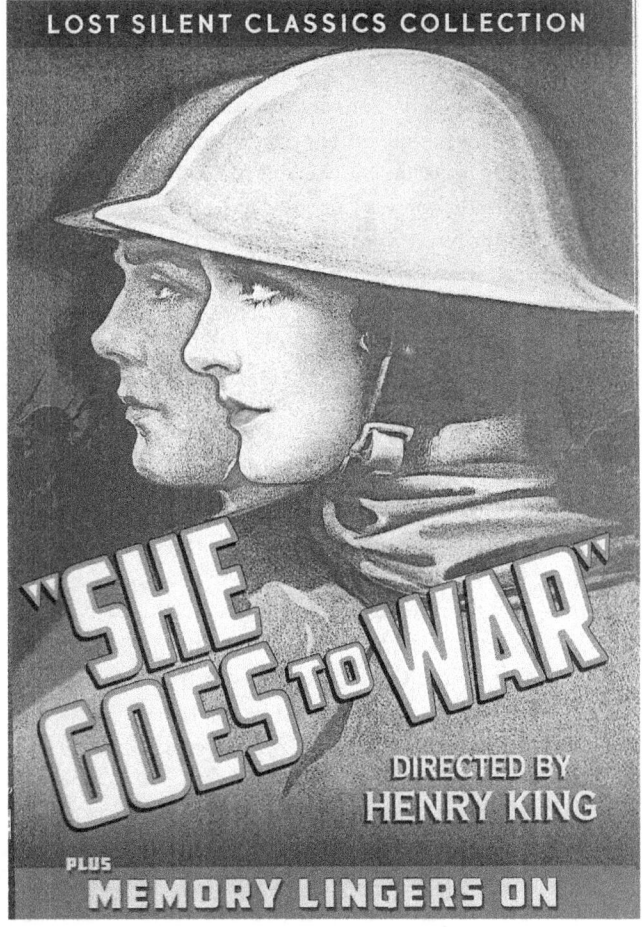

Eleanor Boardman replaces her drunken lover on the front lines in 1929's *She Goes to War*.

satirize the brutality, insanity, and meaninglessness of war.[21] The tradition of military comedy, derived from satires based on the idea of war for political gain, can be traced back to the works of ancient Greeks like Aristophanes.[22] In comedies, characters have more latitude to "misbehave" without significant consequences, and in war comedies, the hero is typically an enlisted man who ignores military etiquette and comments on the foibles of his superiors.[23] Most military comedies are set in boot camp rather than in actual battle, which is seen as sacred.

Perhaps the best-known early war comedy is Charles Chaplin's *Shoulder Arms* (1918). The forty-four minute film features his character The Tramp as a World War I soldier on the front and Edna Purviance as "The Girl" who shelters him as he tries to escape from pursuing Germans and is captured for her efforts.[24] Through some ridiculous antics, he saves her from the advances of a German general, then hatches a plot to kidnap the Kaiser. The Girl's eighty second cross-dressing in a German army greatcoat and cap, complete with a grease moustache, goes undetected by the enemy brass, who fall into the trap. Her unmasking is not shown in the film; however, at some point, she has shed her military clothing, appearing as a proper French woman by the time they arrive at the American camp.[25]

With the advent of "talkies" in 1928–29, audience interest quickly turned to musicals and films with a lot of dialogue, including animated shorts.[26] Fleischer Studios, founded by brothers Max and Dave Fleischer, quickly became a leader in animation, producing numerous iconic characters including Betty Boop, whose round, saucer-like eyes, shapely legs, and sexy figure made her a big hit.[27] In the seven-minute black and white musical cartoon, *There's Something About a Soldier* (1934), Betty dons an Army uniform to encourage men to enlist to fight the giant mosquitoes that are invading the city. Betty's uniform is not quite "uniform"—her short skirt reveals her panties whenever she moves, and she wears her trademark garter on her left leg above her knee-high boots. Betty loves Captain Fred, and when he sends an SOS for help against the enemy, she comes to the rescue with a truck of insect repellant and saves the day. The animated film, made in peacetime, was a precursor of the pending European conflict.

Romance

Many of the films examined in this book treat military women as an afterthought or an appendage of a male protagonist, the love interest to humanize him in an inhuman situation. Typically, these women are Red Cross nurses, ambulance drivers, canteen workers, or local civilians, as seen in films like *Wings* (1927), *The Eagle and the Hawk* (1933) and *The Last Outpost* (1935). While films that feature elements of love and romance have always been popular with movie goers who love a happy ending, few films about World War I include depictions of military women.

The cross-dressing woman in the film *A Fair Rebel* (1914) is not a spy on a mission to save the Confederacy. Rather, she is a woman in love who is forced to take extreme measures to save the man she loves. Clairette Monteith (Linda Arvidson) is a true Virginia Southern belle, clad in a long white dress, white bow in her long dark hair. Her brother Steve leaves West Point to join the Confederate Army at the start of the Civil War, while his best friend Ezra remains loyal to the Union. As fierce fighting rages nearby, two Union officers appear on the Monteith's doorstep, one in need of medical attention. Both are welcomed, despite their enemy status. The younger man is Ezra, and Clairette is soon enamored with him. When Ezra surrenders to his former roommate and is sent to prison nearby, Clairette takes drastic action. While Ezra digs an escape tunnel, Clairette arranges to change places (and clothing) with a young Confederate sentry. Her attire should have aroused suspicion, for the uniform pants and heavy greatcoat overwhelm her slight frame, and her long curls threaten to escape from beneath her forage cap. Yet, the camp commander and other officers do not notice. She is noticed, however, after she has exchanged her Confederate greatcoat for Ezra's even larger Union jacket. Mistaken for the escaping prisoner, she is shot. Her pain is worth the effort when she is reunited with her true love at the end of the war. Like Agnes Lane, Clairette's time as a cross-dresser is short—only three and a half of the eight minutes she is seen onscreen in the forty-one-minute film. But unlike Agnes, she has no reason to transgress social norms again by cross-dressing and will be a lady for the remainder of her life.

The film also contains a thirty-eight second scene that features, according to the intertitle, "Captain Johnny and her home guards," a group of six black children who play soldier in front of the Monteith mansion. Their leader, Johnny, is a girl who wears a Confederate forage cap and jacket over her white dress. The remaining "soldiers" are boys who willingly submit to her authority as their leader, and Johnny exudes military bearing, shouting orders as the "squad" drills smartly. Despite their status as the children of slaves, they are willing to defend their master's plantation against the invading Union soldiers. It will be almost three decades after the film's release before black women are able to officially fight for their country.

D.W. Griffith's short film *Swords and Hearts* (1911) also features a cross-dressing young woman out to save the man she loves. Jenny Baker (Dorothy West) is a poor girl secretly in love with a wealthy Confederate officer. Jenny exhibits all of the traits of a traditional Southern woman—she is beautiful, kind, hard-working, and true to the Confederacy. Unfortunately, Hugh loves another who is Jenny's opposite—beautiful but self-absorbed and shallow, she consorts with a Union officer behind Hugh's back. When a Union scouting party arrives at Hugh's home, quick thinking Jenny dons his uniform jacket and hat and rides off on his horse, drawing them away so Hugh can escape. The standard chase scene is modified here. While Jenny shoots one soldier as she rides away and eventually eludes her pursuers, she is wounded during the chase. Exhausted, she makes her way back to Hugh's, where she recovers and eventually earns her reward—Hugh's love.[28]

In the five-minute comedy short *Navy Blues* (1923), Dorothy Devore stars as a young wife who follows her husband into the Navy so she can be with him on his ship. Both go separately from recruiter to the same ship without attending boot camp. Unlike "Sister" in *The House with Closed Shutters*, she does not cut her hair but just pins it up under her Dixie cup hat after donning a blue jumper, and the antics begin. She floods a berthing compartment in an effort to cool off by opening a porthole that is below the waterline, which results in her being exiled to a storage compartment. Her husband's own antics get him exiled to the same space, where they are joyfully reunited.

One World War I film that includes a romance with a military woman is *Today We Live* (1933), which features Joan Crawford as British aristocrat Diana Boyce, who is in love with an American pilot (Gary Cooper as Captain Richard Bogard) but engaged to a British naval officer (Robert Young as Claude). Fearful of her feelings for Bogard, Diana joins the British Army and is stationed in France with her brother and fiancé. While she is shown in uniform for two-thirds of the forty-five minutes she is onscreen, most of that time is spent outside of her military duties. Instead, she deals with Claude's drinking and subsequent blindness while avoiding her true feelings for Bogard. Ultimately, Claude dies while destroying a German battleship, leaving Diana and Bogard free to pursue their relationship. The film ends with Bogard (in uniform) and Boyce (in civilian clothing) visiting a war memorial that contains the names of those killed during the war, including that of her brother and Claude.

In the 1935 film *Navy Wife*, Claire Trevor is Navy nurse Vicky Banks working at the Naval Hospital in San Diego. Devoted to her patients and her career, she has avoided romantic entanglements due to the pain she suffered from her parents' divorce. The daughter of a naval officer, Banks is comfortable with sailors and with Navy jargon and traditions, and she is shown as a working nurse for about one-third of her forty minutes onscreen. Despite her aversion to love, she falls hard for Navy surgeon Lieutenant Commander Quintin Harden (Ralph Bellamy), a widower with a crippled young daughter. While Harden respects her professionalism and compassion, he still worships his dead wife, with whom Banks feels she cannot compete. Still, she adores his crippled daughter and agrees to marry him for her sake, giving up her Navy career to become a Navy wife, a move that makes her desperately unhappy. Despite her efforts to help her stepdaughter overcome her disability, Harden's apparent flirtation with another woman almost derails their marriage. But as typical for romantic films, he in fact is working "under cover" to derail a spy ring and realizes that he is madly in love with Vicky, resulting in a happy ending for all.

Thrillers

Thrillers are dominated by suspense, linear plots, and significant action. The storylines build anticipation for viewers over the length of the film to its climax. Plots of thrillers center on the hero who must solve the mystery, and there is typically little character development. Among the genres found in thrillers are murder mysteries and spy stories.

In *Navy Secrets* (1939), Carol Evans (Fay Wray) is an undercover investigator for the Office of Naval Intelligence, out to crack a Navy spy ring that is selling military secrets to the enemy. When her initial contact is imprisoned, she works with his "friend," Chief Petty Officer Steve Roberts (Grant Withers), to infiltrate the spy ring. While they are obviously attracted to each other, she does not allow her feelings to interfere with her mission. After a number of twists and turns, the pair successfully foils the bad guys. Each thinks the other was innocently involved in the caper and doesn't want the other to be tarnished. Roberts suggests she disappear for a while so no one can find her, and she recommends he be more careful in choosing his friends. They soon learn that they both are members of Naval Intelligence and are assigned to new cases an ocean apart. Seeing their chemistry, their boss promises them a joint assignment in Hawaii after solving their next individual cases.

Onscreen for forty-one minutes, Carol Evans proves herself to be a capable investigator, nimbly extracting herself from difficult situations and cleverly unraveling clues to solve the case. She wears civilian clothes throughout the movie, while Roberts wears his service dress blue uniform, and she is never addressed by rank, unlike Roberts, who is called Chief throughout the film. The viewer can assume that she is in the Navy since civilian investigators were not added to the Office of Naval Intelligence until 1945.[29] This is problematic, however, since with the exception of nurses, women were not permitted to serve in the Navy at the time, a fact that Hollywood glossed over in this film.

The notion that military service was not a proper occupation for women, coupled with a general anti-war sentiment that resulted after World War I, was reflected in American films during the late 1920s and 1930s, and American films emphasized escapist entertainment during the period. While 1938 was the last full year of world peace, 1939 was a banner year for the American film industry, which released popular films like *Gone with the Wind* and *The Wizard of Oz*. Those war related films released in the late 1930s looked to the historical past rather than to the pending conflict in Europe and Asia, and none of those films featured military women.

Two

You Can Do It!
The 1940s

According to Judith Bellafaire, "Throughout this nation's history, the extent of women's military participation has been directly tied to society's ideas of women's place."[1] Women's place in society, up until the 1940s, was primarily relegated to the domestic sphere. During World War II, however, the idea of societal norms needed to take a back seat to the war effort.

The U.S. entered into World War II following the bombing of Pearl Harbor on December 7, 1941. By the early months of 1942, World War II had created such a manpower shortage at home that the Army decided, as the Navy and Marine Corps had done to a limited degree in World War I, to fill these shortages with women. As Katy Goebel notes, "For the first time in American history, the military services of the United States called for large numbers of women to fill essential positions new to the employment of womanhood ... as well as traditional roles such as those in nursing and secretarial duties."[2] This was accomplished through Public Law 77-554, which established the Women's Army Auxiliary Corps (WAAC). Initially, there was a cap placed on how many women could serve in the WAAC (originally set at 150,000), but that limit was raised a mere fourteen months later by President Franklin Roosevelt's Executive Order 9364, which, in conjunction with Public Law 78-110, abolished the inefficient WAAC and established the WAC (Women's Army Corps) in its stead.

Two months later, the Navy followed suit with Public Law 77-689, amending the Naval Reserve Act of 1938 to allow women to enlist in the Reserves. Unlike the Army's WAAC, these WAVES (Women Accepted for Volunteer Emergency Service) were considered actual members of the Armed Services of the United States. Many restrictions, however, were still in place, including minimum/maximum age requirements and severely limited geographical locations for duty assignments; as Section 504 of the law stated, "Members of the Women's Reserve shall be restricted to the performance of shore duty within the continental United States only and shall not be assigned to duty on board vessels of the Navy or in combat aircraft."

Less than six months later, the Coast Guard also had a women's reserve, nicknamed SPARs for the Coast Guard's motto of *Semper Paratus* (Always Ready). Again, many restrictions were placed on what these servicewomen were allowed to do—Section 404 of this law, for example, made it clear that SPARs would "not be assigned to duty on board vessels of the Navy or Coast Guard or in combat aircraft and shall be restricted to the performance of shore duty within the continental United States only."

Despite the restrictions laid out in these and other pieces of legislation, thousands of U.S. servicewomen did end up serving bravely outside the continental U.S. The belief that women were only intended for certain types of work, however, still limited their choices for job assignments, as evidenced by the fact that "about seventy percent of women who served in the military during

World War II held traditionally 'female' jobs."[3] Despite these limitations, women excelled and thrived in their new military roles, and "although these jobs may have been less glorified than those of the men fighting on the front lines, women were essential in maintaining the bureaucratic mechanisms that are necessary in warfare."[4]

It is notable that at the time, many of these women were regarded as serving *with* rather than *in* the military (this was especially true for the Army). These women who "enlisted" had signed up not for a particular length of time, but for "the duration" of the war, and plans were made to release the women from service as soon as the war ended. Many women wanted to stay in, and there was enough support for this that the service branches and Congress worked to make it a reality. In 1948, with the passage of the Women's Armed Services Integration Act (Public Law 80-625), women would finally find a permanent home in the United States military.

At the same time the military was adapting, so was Hollywood. The films of the early 1940s reflected "a nation newly at war, a nation just recently awakened from the slumber of isolationism, eager to take on the task at hand and conquer the Axis powers of Germany, Italy, and Japan."[5] Nearly 400 war-related films were released in the United States from 1942 to 1945, as President Roosevelt believed that "movies were among the most effective means of reaching the American public"[6]; approximately 6 percent of these films feature at least one woman in uniform.[7] Many additional films in the 1940s also chose to showcase the abilities of America's new crop of female military personnel.

Musicals

The 1940s in film were part of the Golden Age of the Hollywood musical. Following the U.S. entry into World War II, many of those musicals became major propaganda vehicles for the war effort. They were also starring some of the biggest stars of the era, showcasing their talents while paying homage to the thousands of American servicemembers serving overseas and stateside. There were hundreds of musicals made during this decade, but only five include any women in the military, both as primary and secondary characters.

Here Come the WAVES (1944) stars Betty Hutton as twins Susan and Rosemary Allison. Onscreen for fifty-one minutes, the sisters decide to join the Navy in order to "free a man to fight." While at basic training, the sisters perform in a stage show, singing "The Navy Song" as well as the title tune. Rosemary quickly becomes a squared-away sailor, but Susie is much more interested in chasing new recruit Johnny Cabot (Bing Crosby). Despite her original amorous intentions, however, she winds up becoming serious about her service as well, proudly proclaiming, "Even I replaced a man—Susie Screw-Up." Both sisters do end up in romantic relationships before the end of the film, however, in keeping with the social mores of the time—that while women did join the service to help out in the war effort, they would much rather be able to get married, have babies, and become homemakers.

The year of 1944 also produced the wacky *Up in Arms*, which stars Danny Kaye as reluctant recruit Danny Weems and Dinah Shore as Army nurse Lieutenant Virginia Merrill. Also in the film is Constance Dowling as Army nurse Lieutenant Mary Morgan, the object of Weems' affection. Onscreen for twenty-five minutes, Morgan is the consummate professional, taking both her nursing duties and her military service seriously; Weems, however, is only interested in wooing Mary, and those around him have to constantly remind him that "enlisted men don't talk to officers except in the line of duty." When Mary accidentally ends up onboard Weems' ship, she must dress as a man to avoid detection and possible court-martial; these cross-dressing scenes are reminiscent of those discussed in the previous chapter, a trope that is visited several more times in this book.

A third musical from 1944 is *A WAVE, a WAC, and a Marine*. Despite the title, the main characters (Elyse Knox as Marian and Ann Gillis as Judy) do not spend any screen time actually in the military—rather, the title reflects the name of the stage play the stars perform in nightly, dressed as the real thing. Onscreen for twenty minutes each, the majority of the women's time is spent working on a movie deal. Both women do, however, join the WACs at the end of the film, with Judy musing to her deceased husband, "You'll be proud of me, Bill."

In the Navy (1941) features Abbott and Costello as six-year veterans of the Navy and Dick Powell as national singing heartthrob Russ Raymond, who joins the Navy under his birth name to escape the limelight. News photographer Dorothy Roberts (Claire Dodd) makes it her mission to get a photo of Raymond, whose disappearance from the public eye has become a gigantic news story. In pursuit of that photo, she ends up stowing away on the USS *Alabama*, which is headed for Hawaii with Raymond aboard. Discovered by Adams and Watson (Abbott and Costello) but not turned over to the authorities, "Dot" ends up cross-dressing as a second class petty officer in order to remain undetected by the ship's officers. In uniform for approximately two minutes (and onscreen for a total of eleven minutes), Roberts is seen scrubbing the ship's deck while pretending to be a sailor. She is almost unmasked when the boatswain orders all the deck hands to take their shirts off, but an alert sounds, and she escapes detection. As opposed to the majority of cross-dressing women discussed in the previous chapter, Roberts' motives are much more selfish—she does so in order to obtain the "money shot" she needs to become a staff photographer at her local newspaper.

The final musical of this decade is 1946's *Tars and Spars*, one of only four films in this survey that feature a woman in the Coast Guard. Janet Blair stars as Petty Officer Third Class Christine Bradley, onscreen for one-third of the film's run time but basically just a love interest for the film's protagonist (Alfred Drake as Howard Young). Bradley works in communications, and she is efficient and well-trained. Time out from her duties is taken, of course, to perform as lead in the musical production being put on by the Coast Guard to build morale and entertain the troops. Bradley is the only Coast Guard woman portrayed in film for another fifty years.

Drama

In four of the dramas from this decade, a military woman is onscreen for just a very brief time. *The Iron Major* (1943) shows Barbara Hale as new recruit Sarah Cavanaugh during her swearing in ceremony. In *Twelve O'Clock High* (1949), an Army nurse (Joyce MacKenzie) is shown for one minute when General Savage (Gregory Peck) goes to visit a wounded man in the hospital, and in *The Story of G.I. Joe* (1945), Dorothy Coonan Wellman portrays Army nurse Lieutenant Elizabeth "Red" Murphy for two minutes in just one scene—her marriage to a fellow soldier, perhaps included in the film to show that even during war, love survives and thrives. In a more unique role, 1948's *Sealed Verdict* features Olive Blakeney as Camilla Cameron, a newspaper reporter for the Navy. Onscreen for just two minutes, Cameron's duty assignment has her reporting at a war crime trial, which would have been quite unique at that time.

The vast majority of dramatic films with women in uniform, however, show them onscreen much more extensively, albeit primarily in traditional roles. Especially during this time, films played "an important part in setting stereotypes and promoting a limited number of role models" for women.[8] In 1944's *Lifeboat*, for example, Mary Anderson is Lieutenant Alice MacKenzie, an

Army nurse, onscreen for almost 40 percent of the film's run time. Anderson's character is given all the typical "female" qualities of compassion, nurturing, and pacifism, stating at one point, "I don't understand people hurting each other and killing each other." When asked why, then, she is in uniform, she responds, "I'm doing the only thing I can—trying to put them together again when they get hit."

A Yank in the R.A.F. (1941) features Carol Brown (Betty Grable), a club dancer who joins the British war effort by serving as an ambulance driver in the Women's Royal Naval Service (Wrens). Also starring Tyrone Power as anti-hero and ex-boyfriend Tim Baker, Brown works at not falling for his old lines again, but she eventually gives in, despite the fact that at one point, he sexually assaults her by forcing her down and kissing her against her will. This was not an uncommon occurrence in films of this era, but it is something that would not be shown in the movies of today. Brown's eventual capitulation effectively renders her selfless service secondary to her being the standard love interest to the dashingly rakish male star.

Another film which features the female lead falling for the man who forces himself on her is 1944's *The Navy Way*. This film stars Jean Parker as Lieutenant Ellen Sayre, a pharmacist's mate in the Navy, who is chased by Johnny Zumano (Robert Lowery). When he forces a kiss on her, she responds with "I could have you put on report for that." In reality, Zumano would be in serious trouble because he is an enlisted man and Sayre is an officer; no report, however, is ever filed, and in typical Hollywood fashion, Sayre ends up falling in love with Zumano and leaving the Navy so that they can be together.

Boot Camp

The 1940s saw a plethora of films focused on the throngs of men enlisting in the armed forces to do their bit; many of these films center on basic training, including *Buck Privates*, *Great Guns*, and *Caught in the Draft* (all from 1941). There were also quite a few films of this type that used servicewomen as the main characters rather than men. Changing things up like this was not an unusual thing for Hollywood to do; as Jeanne Basinger explains, the idea of "taking a genre and populating it with women instead of men was ... a variation that freshened up the action or gave the studio a chance to work all of its female stars."[9] Several films in this survey fit this mold, and while the films mentioned above featuring men at basic training are all comedies, those focused on new female recruits are more dramatic in nature.

This Above All (1942) features a member of the British upper class (Joan Fontaine as Prudence Cathaway) who joins the WAAF. Her family is aghast, telling her she should have had them get her a commission, but she simply tells them, "I don't want to be an officer until I've learned to be a private." While going through basic training, she and some other women becomes friends, and one (Queenie Leonard as Violet Worthing) introduces her to American Clive Briggs (Tyrone Power), who has gone AWOL. Her training is sidelined for the rest of the film as their romance takes center stage, but Cathaway is still portrayed as dedicated to serving her country and performs her duties with pride.

Ladies Courageous (1944) focuses on the female pilots in the WASP (Women Airforce Service Pilots). For much of the film, the ladies are at training camp, honing their piloting skills while learning the ins and outs of military life. Pilot Roberta Harper (Loretta Young) and the other women volunteered because they "wanted to be part of the Army," and they were upset that they did not get "militarized into the Army Air Force like the other pilots." They are informed that "there are still certain brass hats who aren't convinced that women should accept equal responsibility in the Air Forces," despite the fact that the women had been ferrying ships for six months

WASP ace pilot Roberta Harper (Loretta Young) meets up with her husband Tommy (Phillip Terry) in the 1944 film *Ladies Courageous*.

at that point. Prevailing voices at the time simply could not grasp the concept of female military aviators, so the WASPs functioned under the military but were actually considered civilians—it was not until 1977 that the 1,074 women who served in the WASP program were finally granted veteran status.[10]

Parachute Nurse (1942) is centered on training for a fictional new unit of nurses who will parachute down to injured soldiers that cannot be reached in other ways. The unit is called the Aerial Nurse Corps of America, predecessor to the flight nurses of the USAF, promoted as "the toughest service ever opened to women." The new cadets are considered part of the Army Nurse Corps; if they wash out of their training, they will automatically be "transferred to another branch of the service."

The women's transition to military life is rough at first, including sleeping on bunks that are "soft as a supervisor's heart." Tensions surround the women as they get used to living together in close quarters, and animosity is strong against Gretchen Ernst (Evelyn Wahl), whose brother is in the German army. Ernst is shunned by nearly all the women in her unit, with the exceptions of Dottie Morrison (Kay West) and Glenda White (Marguerite Chapman), who strive to include her as a welcome member of the "hen emporium," their jump instructor's nickname for the unit. Their efforts are not successful, however, and due to the bullying and hatred she endures, Gretchen commits suicide by failing to open her chute during a jump. This causes Glenda much anxiety, and she is subsequently unable to jump. Love conquers all, however, and she finally manages to jump when she thinks the man she loves is in danger, thus saving her from transfer and showing her bravery and selflessness, at least as far as love is concerned.

Women at War (1943), a film short that was shown with the film *Air Force*, centers on the basic training experience of new WACs. Presented in pseudo-documentary style, the narrator states that once on base, the women "quickly became adjusted to the military way of life," but it is also stressed that makeup can be purchased "so a girl doesn't lose her femininity when she dons her uniform." Additionally, the unit sergeant (Marjorie Hoshelle) makes a blatant recruiting pitch, stating that "the WACs offer a great opportunity for every woman that wants to specialize. You'll be serving your country, and, at the same time, you'll be learning something that may prove to be of great value to you after the war."

Three WACs are the film's main focus. Mary Sawyer (Virginia Christine) joins up to take her husband's place after he is killed in action in Africa; Stormy Hart (Faye Emerson) enlists to do her bit for the war effort, and Lorna Travis (Dorothy Day) joins the service to prove her military mettle to her father, Major General "Blood and Thunder" Travers (Robert Warwick), former commander of the now-WAC training camp, who was "really burned when he found out a bunch of women were taking over his old fort." When addressed as lieutenant by Stormy, the general practically turns blue, shouting, "Doesn't this petticoat army know the difference between a lieutenant and a major general?" It is clear he has old-fashioned ideas on the subject of women in the military when he states, "I feel that WACs have no place in a man's war." By the film's end, however, the women have proven how proficient they are at their chosen jobs, and the general admiringly tells his daughter, "You're a pretty good soldier."

Keep Your Powder Dry (1945) stars Lana Turner as Valerie Parks, a former party girl who is promised an inheritance if she straightens up her life; naturally, she begins that journey by joining the WACs. Due to her attitude of entitlement, Parks almost immediately runs afoul of both her fellow recruits and her superiors. When it comes down to it, however, she realizes the importance of serving her country, even foregoing her inheritance in order to stay in the service. Basinger (1993) asserts that due to this turnaround in attitude, Turner's character "makes it as a soldier, proving that World War II really did usher in, however briefly, a new era in which a beautiful sex symbol could find success" in the male-dominated military.[11]

Bands of Sisters

Much like the films about men and women in basic training, there were also many films that focused on military units rather than individual characters. Two movies in this survey focus almost exclusively on women's units stationed in the Philippines during the battles of Bataan and Corregidor. These films helped raise the visibility level of the actual nurses who served in the Pacific theater, many of whom either died or became prisoners of war.

The 1943 film *Cry 'Havoc'* features a ragtag lot of nurses who must pull together to get things done. As the film starts, the narrator informs the audience: "This is the story of thirteen women. Only two of them—Captain Alice Marsh [Fay Bainter] and Lieutenant Mary Smith [Margaret Sullavan]—were members of the Armed forces of the United States. The others were civilians—American women who, until that fateful day in December, knew no more of war than did you or your nearest neighbor." It was this group of civilians that Smith has to train under the roughest of conditions.

Smith is tough on the new volunteers, and Pat Conlin (Ann Sothern) bucks her at every turn; it also doesn't help that Conlin has taken a liking to Lieutenant Steve Holt, to whom Smith is secretly married (military regulations at that time did not allow married couples to be stationed

After completing basic training, WACs Valerie Parks (Lana Turner, left), Ann Darrison (Susan Peters, center), and Leigh Rand (Laraine Day) find out their first assignment in *Keep Your Powder Dry* (1945).

in the same place). After an air raid on the hospital, one girl is missing; she is found alive three days later, but in a catatonic state for having spent those days trapped with the corpses of several soldiers. Successive attacks make it clear that the nurses should leave the area, but as a group, they decide to stay and help.

Smith, meanwhile, has recurring malaria attacks which often leave her incapacitated for several hours at a time. She does her best to hide her medical issues from the other women, remaining staunchly on duty as long as possible. Her dedication is obvious to the other women in the unit, and they respect Smith very much, standing bravely with her as the unit is forced to surrender to the Japanese at the film's end.

So Proudly We Hail (1943) is also focused on nurses stationed on Bataan. Lieutenant Janet "Davey" Davidson (Claudette Colbert) is in charge of a nursing unit that gets rerouted from Hawaii to the Philippines because of the bombing of Pearl Harbor. The unit includes Paulette Goddard as Lieutenant Joan O'Doul, and en route, they pick up some servicemembers whose ship has been torpedoed, one of whom is Army nurse Lieutenant Olivia D'Arcy (Veronica Lake).

Onscreen for almost half the film, Davidson is strong and heroic; at one point, she burns her hands while trying to save people who were inside a hospital that the Japanese bombed, and she insists on continuing to work. Davey has a strong work ethic and is generally a by-the-book soldier, but she eventually violates military policy by secretly marrying Lieutenant John Sumners

(George Reeves), which, in reality, could have gotten her kicked out of the service. Due to this obligatory romantic involvement, the film begins and ends with Davey being shown in a catatonic state because she believes John has been killed in action; despite her bravery in the face of danger while in the Philippines, she quickly reverts back to "acting like a woman" when her heart is involved.

D'Arcy spends much of her early time onscreen making enemies amongst those in Davey's unit, primarily for her surly attitude, eventually explained by the fact that she saw her husband die during the bombing of Pearl Harbor. Throughout the film, however, D'Arcy grows from wanting to kill all Japanese to realizing the value in every human life. She eventually bonds with the other women in the unit and is instrumental in their eventual escape from Corregidor, sacrificing herself by blowing herself up along with several Japanese soldiers.

According to Basinger, a female changes from a heroine to a hero when certain criteria are met. One of her talking points refers to a woman who "forms and maintains a positive sisterly relationship ... or who joins a group of women in an important professional endeavor."[12] When D'Arcy sacrifices herself to allow the others to get away, she crosses over from heroine to hero. For Hollywood, however, D'Arcy's sacrifice is necessary because, as Basinger also notes, "when a male genre is feminized, it allows women a chance for freedom and heroism but also maintains a status quo in which the women themselves cannot, for example, win the war, only wait for the men to win it for them."[13] D'Arcy crosses gender lines by becoming the hero momentarily, and she therefore must die so the women will be eventually saved by men, thus keeping the social order of the day intact.

Claudette Colbert as Lieutenant Janet "Davy" Davidson in 1943's *So Proudly We Hail*.

In *Corregidor* (1943), another film set in the Philippines, the main characters are Dr. Jan Stockman (Otto Kruger) and his recent bride, Dr. Royce Lee Stockman (Elyssa Landi). Jan is in the Philippines doing research and Royce joins him; the next day the Japanese bomb Pearl Harbor, and the two help out when the Japanese start bombing the Philippines next. After their village gets bombed, Jan and Royce travel with some soldiers to the Army hospital at Corregidor. There, they meet "Dutch" (Wanda McKay), an Army nurse who is in love with one of the soldiers escorting Royce and Jan; as Dutch muses, "I want to marry Pinky [Rick Vallin], settle down, and raise a family." Despite the fact that she is a lieutenant and Pinky is a sergeant, they are involved in a relationship and engaged to be married; this would have been strictly against regulations but difficult to enforce. The Japanese soon bomb the hospital, and Dutch is injured while attending to patients. From her hospital bed, she and Pinky get married, but she dies right after that. Onscreen for almost 15 percent of the film's run time, Dutch exhibits great courage and resolve, a true testament to the brave Army and Navy nurses who gave their all for patriotism.

Primarily a star vehicle for two of Hollywood's top draws of the era, 1948's *Homecoming* stars Clark Gable as Army doctor Colonel Ulysses Johnson and Lana Turner as Lieutenant Jane "Snapshot" McCall, an Army nurse serving overseas. Although, as Myra Macdonald asserts, "the media regularly serve a menu of female stereotypes that stimulates misogynistic taste buds,"[14] Snapshot refuses to be one of those stereotypes. After her husband dies in battle, she joins up to serve her country, leaving her young son with relatives while she is stationed abroad. Prior to the late twentieth century, film portrayals of servicewomen with children were extremely rare—of the 147 films in this survey that were released from 1910–1980, *Homecoming* is the only film to explicitly feature a military mother.[15] This is not surprising considering the military's belief at the time was that "a woman who is pregnant or a mother should not be a member of the armed forces and should devote herself to the responsibilities which she had assumed, remaining with her husband and child as a family unit."[16] It was never and has never been suggested that a man should devote himself to those same responsibilities.

Nurse Lieutenant "Snapshot" McCall (Lana Turner) and Colonel Ulysses Johnson (Clark Gable) relax during some rare down time in MGM's *Homecoming* (1948).

When Dr. Johnson finds out that Snapshot has a son, he is quite shocked and asks her, "Why are you here?" All she has to say in reply is, "Because I want him to become twelve." Later, when he tries to deter her from going with him to help some wounded soldiers, she simply asks him, "Is my life worth more than any of the others?" McCall is dedicated and steadfast in her belief as to where her place is in the war—it's in the trenches, because "if they can use a doctor, they can use a nurse." When she dies following a bombing, Johnson notes her dedication and bravery by stating, "She stood up through everything that even men couldn't take."

Phyllis Calvert stars as ex–POW Joan Crews in 1948's *My Own True Love*. A tough loner who is first seen scrubbing floors as punishment for some slight indiscretion, Crews meets Clive Heath (Melvyn Douglas) and begins a relationship with him. Relations get strained somewhat due to her reticence to talk about her time as a prisoner of war. When Clive's son Michael (Philip Friend) comes onto the scene, it is revealed that he, too, was a prisoner of war. This shared experience gives them a bond that Clive cannot understand or intrude upon; he misreads the situation and instead believes that the two have begun an affair. Only time convinces him that there is no romance between them—just the therapeutic cleansing that comes with talking to someone who shares a similar experience, the value of which cannot be overstated.

Another female prisoner of war is featured in 1945's *First Yank into Tokyo*. Lieutenant Abby Drake (Barbara Hale) is a POW of the Japanese, one of the Army nurses taken prisoner at Bataan. She is constantly fending off sexual advances from the Japanese officers, all while trying to run the hospital and care for injured prisoners. This film does not delve into the subject of PTSD like

Clive Heath (Melvyn Douglas) with Private Joan Clews (Phyllis Calvert) in 1948's *My Own True Love*.

My Own True Love did, but Drake, too, will likely have to get some kind of therapy to be able to process her war experience and move on to a productive life back home and out of the service.

International Squadron (1941) features Olympe Bradna as Jeanette Benoit, a youthful French girl who becomes the object of desire for the rakish American pilot Jimmy Grant (Ronald Reagan), who joins the RAF to escape woman trouble in the U.S. Not as naïve as Jimmy might like, Jeanette initially rebuffs his attention, telling him, "It seems wrong to think of ourselves now; there's so much to be done." She views him as just another part of her job, since she is assigned to drive him around. Eventually, however, she warms up to him, and they spend a lot of time together. Rather than becoming just another love interest, however, Jeanette actually makes Grant start caring about something other than himself. Her patriotism and committed service rub off on him, and he eventually echoes her sentiment to do "whatever I can to help" the war effort.

In 1949's *The Red Danube*, Angela Lansbury portrays Junior Commander Audrey Quail, who serves as a general's aide in the British army. She is not, however, subservient to him, telling one soldier, "I am not his servant. Rank: Junior Commander. That's equivalent to Captain." She makes it clear, in no uncertain terms, just how important her job is, illustrated well when she helps plan the covert mission that the film's star (Walter Pidgeon) must undertake. Much more so than onscreen portrayals of American servicewomen working in an administrative capacity, Quail is an integral part of the general's team whose opinion is highly valued, rather than thought of as just a "secretary."

Another strong role for a female can be seen in *A Guy Named Joe* (1943). Tough as nails and full of gumption, Dorinda Durston (Irene Dunne) is an aviator in the WASPs. Although Dorinda is the character tying the film's plot together, a man is the titular character and Spencer Tracy gets top billing. Dorinda is tough and fierce—she even ends up saving Ted Randall (Van Johnson) when she flies a dangerous mission rather than letting a man handle it. Despite the love interest angle of the film, Durston proves she is just as capable as any man when it comes to flying and dedication to service.

Commandos Strike at Dawn (1942) features Anna Lee as Judith Bowen, an ensign in the British Navy. She is initially a civilian, but following the Nazi invasion of Norway, she joins the military in order to make a difference. Onscreen for just ten minutes, her primary role is that of love interest to the protagonist Eric Toresen (Paul Muni), but her upbringing as an admiral's daughter almost mandates that she do her part for the war effort as well, and she honors his legacy adeptly.

Two dramatic films in this decade have particularly interesting portrayals of servicewomen. In 1942's *Army Surgeon*, Jane Wyatt portrays Dr. Beth Ainsley. At the film's onset, she and her husband (James Ellison as Captain Jim Mason) are aboard a naval vessel, shipping out to serve in World War II. Almost immediately, flashbacks take the audience back to their first meeting, when they were again deployed together, only it was during World War I. At their first meeting, Mason makes it clear that he does not think the front is any place for a woman, even a nurse, which is what Ainsley must pretend to be in order for her to be allowed to serve in the military; at that time, female doctors were not accepted for enlistment in the military. Watching Mason treat Beth like a second-class citizen, it is reasonable to assert that "women who are denied opportunities ... or whose demonstrations of value are ignored become the objects of what seems to be justified abuse."[17] When he discovers that she is actually a doctor rather than a nurse, his demeanor and attitude change considerably, and he begins to trust her judgment. The title is particularly interesting because it is unclear as to which army surgeon it refers, since both characters are prominent throughout the film (Ellison does get top billing, however).

Bomber's Moon (1943) also features a female Army doctor, but in this film, the woman is a

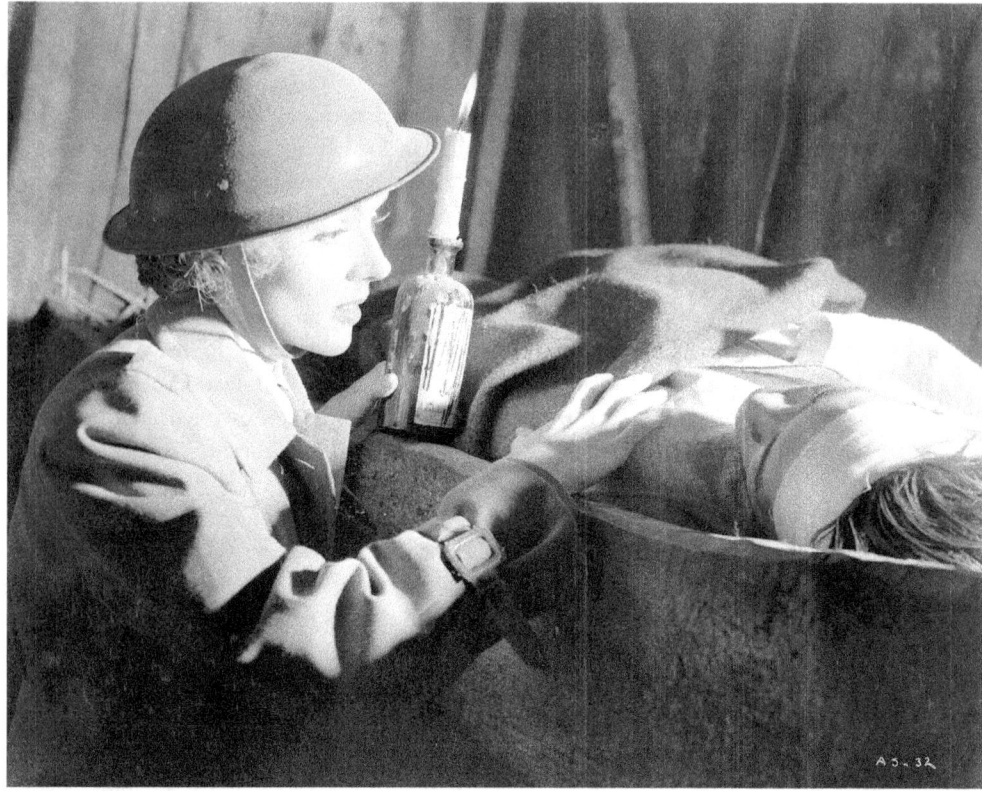

World War I Army nurse Beth Ainsley (Jane Wyatt) tends to her patient in *Army Surgeon* (1942).

lieutenant in the Soviet army. Annabella portrays Dr. Alexandra Zorich, who is being held as a prisoner of war by the Germans. As she tends to the wounds and illnesses of the other prisoners, she is the consummate professional, deftly performing her duties while helping two prisoners plan an escape. Thanks in part to her help, the escape is successful, and Zorich flees as well.

Following the escape, Zorich walks deep into the woods to change into civilian clothes in an effort to ensure the men she is with will not realize that she is female (it is a stretch, however, to think that Annabella could ever really pass for a man); eventually, however, it becomes clear that she has hidden her gender from everyone. When Captain Dakin (George Montgomery) proclaims, "Hey—you're a girl," it is obvious he cannot conceive of her as both woman and soldier; the combination cannot coalesce in his mind. Like many men at that time, he immediately sees her "only" as a woman; she sees herself, however, as a soldier—for her, gender is irrelevant. Zorich even confides to Dakin, "I don't feel much like a lieutenant in these clothes, but I suppose they must do until I can wear my uniform again."

As the obligatory romance starts to form, Dakin tells her, "Just when I thought you were finally turning into a woman, you start looking at the moon through a bombsight," the line upon which the film is titled. He still cannot get past Zorich's gender, but she knows her priorities. She clearly has nothing to reconcile—she is proud to be both soldier and woman. Although she does act more "womanly" as the film progresses, everything she does showcases that Zorich defines herself as a soldier and a doctor; the fact that she is a woman as well is inconsequential.

In a second military role from 1942, Jane Wyatt portrays Myra Mallory in *The Navy Comes Through*, a nurse who enlists in the Naval Reserve to help the war effort. Mallory is a tough, no-nonsense type who is not afraid to stand up for what she believes in. She is aboard a hospital ship when the ship her brother (Pat O'Brien as Chief Petty Officer Mike Mallory) is on sends for a doctor; she comes along to help, simply stating, "I had to come, Mike—it might have been you." Immediately catching the attention of the other men onboard, one comments, "She's not a cruiser; she's a destroyer." The comment just rolls off Myra's back (but not so easily her brother's), and she goes about performing her duties. Although Lieutenant Mallory is primarily included in the film as a love interest, Wyatt's portrayal of a proud Navy nurse who is willing to go the extra mile to perform her duties is overall a positive one.

Several other films also show the dedication of military nurses during World War II. *Seven Were Saved* (1947) features Catherine Craig as Lieutenant Susan Briscoe, an Army nurse. Onscreen for twenty-two minutes, Briscoe is a whirlwind of efficiency. When their plane is hijacked by their Japanese prisoner, she remains calm and keeps the others calm as well, maintaining a sense of normalcy despite the precarious situation. After their crash into the ocean, Briscoe tends to the injured, keeping them in good shape until their eventual rescue. She even helps navigate by the stars, keeping their raft and hope alive. Following their rescue, Captain Jim Willis (Russell Hayden) insists she get some rest; she declines, letting him know that she still has patients to take care of. Though often referred to by her first name or as "Miss" Briscoe rather than by her rank, she is a true military woman, always willing to go the extra mile to get the job done.

In *To the Shores of Tripoli* (1942), new Marine recruit Chris Winters (John Payne) takes a liking to Navy nurse Lieutenant Mary Carter (Maureen O'Hara). Initially, he is dumbfounded at seeing a woman in uniform, saying, "Say, what's this, a gag? A woman lieutenant?" She is attracted to him, but she lets him know that they cannot have a relationship since, "as a Navy nurse, I hold rank equivalent to a lieutenant and that, at all times, I should be addressed in the same manner as a commanding officer." For Carter, the military comes first. Despite Winters' irreverence for the Marines and even after he assaults her by forcing a kiss on her, Mary still ends up in a relationship with him. In the end, however, she does choose the military over him—following the attack on Pearl Harbor, Carter is seen shipping off to overseas duty, confident in her ability to contribute.

Donna Reed as Lieutenant Sandy Davyss also manages to keep both her man and her military career in *They Were Expendable* (1945). She is an efficient nurse, tending to Lieutenant Rusty Ryan (John Wayne) when he is hospitalized with blood poisoning. Despite his initial attempts to boss the nurses around and control the situation, Davyss coolly let him know, "Despite your gold rank, you don't tell us—we tell you," making it clear that Davyss is the one in charge at that time. Although primarily a love interest in the film, Davyss shows she is more than willing to take charge and make sure her patients' care comes first at all times.

Another servicewoman who falls for a soldier but still maintains her military bearing is Lieutenant Ellen Foster (Ruth Hussey), an Australian WAAF featured in 1944's *Marine Raiders*. In a Hollywood case of love-at-first-sight, Foster and Captain Dan Craig (Robert Ryan) meet and get engaged almost immediately. Onscreen for twenty-five minutes of this ninety-minute film (28 percent of the time), Foster says she yearns for the turn of the century and a simpler time, but Dan tells her, "You're meant for now, when they need fighters." When he is unexpectedly shipped back to the U.S., she is stalwart, despite a lack of information on his whereabouts. She understands how the military works, knowing that "it's only a troop movement [that] would be kept confidential." Despite her worry, she carries on, performing her duties at all times. In a comical moment, after seeing a new bunch of young recruits in San Diego, Sergeant Leary (Frank McHugh) comments, "Well, what won't they be taking into the Marine Corps next?" just as a unit of female Marines smartly marches by. Their shocked faces tell just how much of a novelty women in uniform still were at that time. When Craig returns to Australia, they get married in uniform just before he

Lieutenant Mary Carter (Maureen O'Hara) intervenes in an argument between Gunnery Sergeant Dixie Smith (Randolph Scott, left) and new recruit Chris Winters (John Payne) in *To the Shores of Tripoli* (1942).

ships off to fight in the Pacific again. The film ends with her remaining stoic, looking off into the horizon and wishing Dan and his troops a victorious campaign.

A final dramatic film with a military nurse is 1949's *The Hasty Heart*. In this movie, the military nurse is actually not a love interest; that is because Patricia Neal is portraying a Canadian Army nurse who is also a nun. Sister Parker runs the hospital in Burma, near the end of the African campaign; although her rank is not shown, she is onscreen for forty-two minutes, all of it in uniform. Her compassion and caring for her patients often push her to the breaking point, but she maintains composure and keeps everyone alive, often in spite of themselves.

G.I. War Brides (1946) features a WAC for only two minutes, but her role is interesting due to the nature of her somewhat unique situation. The films centers around a group of war brides en route to the United States, but there is also "one lone war groom" aboard ship, whose American wife "sent for him through the regular Army channels that allow soldiers to bring their brides to America." His mere existence causes much confusion, and the military personnel helping the new spouses during their voyage often get confused when calling his name, insisting it must be a typo—until they meet Harold (Patrick O'Moore), which only increases their bewilderment. When their train pulls into Los Angeles, Sergeant Peggy Williams (Maxine Jennings) is there to meet Harold, and they stroll off together. Although her appearance onscreen is brief, it does showcase an interesting situation that many military women had to contend with following the end of the Second World War. This role reversal is something that would be explored much more fully in 1949's *I Was a Male War Bride*, discussed later in this chapter.

Comedies

Before America joined World War II, there were several Hollywood films that worked towards educating the public about the very serious threat looming in Europe, often through a satirical lens. One such film, Charlie Chaplin's magnum opus, is the 1940 anti–Fascist *The Great Dictator*. Interestingly but not historically accurate, Chaplin chose to include some women in the military in the film.[18] As a not-very-thinly veiled Hitler-esque leader named Adenoid Hynkel, Chaplin has several female administrative personnel, and they are all in uniform, clearly part of the army of their country. Of the three servicewomen, one doesn't speak at all, one just says, "No" as Hynkel attempts to ravage her, and the third has just one line as well, offering Hynkel a pencil after he calls the three of them "incompetent, stupid, sterile stenographers," despite their obvious proficiency at their jobs.

A very competent soldier is seen briefly in 1946's *Without Reservations*, a rare comedy starring John Wayne and Van Johnson as Navy pilots Rusty and Dink and Claudette Colbert as a best-selling author. While travelling across country, the three stop by a military airstrip to see if Rusty can borrow a plane to fly the group to San Diego, and a female Navy lieutenant is at the service desk when he arrives. Although she is onscreen for just one minute, her professionalism and proficiency are obvious. She sets him up with a plane immediately, and though he decides not to take it, she performs her duties well.

The comedy team of Abbott and Costello star in *Buck Privates* (1941), which features Jane Frazee as Judy Gray, a camp hostess for the Army. Onscreen for ten minutes, Gray's job is to try and give new recruits "a feeling the camp is their home," and she takes great pride in her duties, fending off romantic advances by simply stating, "I'm on duty." The film also features the Andrews Sisters singing several tunes while dressed in uniform, but they are not truly in the Army.

The comic duo reprised their roles in the 1947 sequel *Buck Privates Come Home*. When they are discovered to have smuggled an orphaned French girl onboard ship, Captain Christie (Don Porter) immediately hands her care over to the only woman around, Lieutenant Sylvia Hunter (Joan Fulton). When Evie (Beverly Simmons) insists she would rather stay with "Uncle Herbie" (Costello), Hunter reminds her why they must follow the captain's orders: "You know the Army—regulations are regulations." She is highly efficient, performing her duties while taking care of the child; she is also instrumental in keeping Evie in the United States when threatened with deportation, deftly handling both the police and immigration authorities. Although Hunter admits that in the Army, "glamor wasn't part of the regulations," she clearly learned organizational and diplomacy skills while serving her country.

Two cartoon shorts in the 1940s also chose to feature women in uniform. *Barnyard WAAC* (1942) has one of the farm's hens joining the WAAC, inspiring the others to do so as well. The girls then leave the farm's rooster a note stating, "We have joined the WAAC. Take care of the kids for the duration," leaving him to navigate the new role of the one left behind to keep the home fires burning. While the hens are shown marching and training, the rooster gets chased by some cats, leaving him and the chicks in danger. Luckily, the hens come around just then and rescue everyone, demonstrating how much the Army has already taught them in the areas of ingenuity and defense.

The Weakly Reporter is a 1944 cartoon commenting on the effects of war on the American people. As the film notes, due to the masses of men signing up to serve in the military, "more and more, women are filling jobs that in the past have been held exclusively by men." These worker shortages extended past the private sector as well, resulting in "even the Army open[ing] its doors to women." Their use of the word "even" in that sentence is somewhat derisive, as evidenced by the depictions of a WAC applying lipstick to her gas mask and illustrating the teaching of "the rough-and-tumble fighting tactics of the commandos," as a free-for-all fight in a clothing store.

In 1947's *Suddenly It's Spring*, Paulette Goddard portrays Army JAG Lawyer Captain Mary Morley, a rising star and relationship guru who, upon returning home after being stationed overseas, finds out her husband (Fred MacMurray) seeks a divorce. Her major concern is not losing her husband—it is, rather, how others will perceive her. She is tough and determined, driven by work ethic rather than emotion, which is evident when she tells her husband, "What do you expect me to do—break down and cry?" Morley is sharp-witted and sharper of tongue, giving her estranged husband more than he bargained for, which makes him realize that they are meant to be together. Able to save face with both her husband and the military, Morley's reputation remains intact as she continues in her marriage and in her upwardly mobile military career.

Where There's Life (1947) features Bob Hope as Michael Valentine, heir to the throne of the fictional Barovia. Hunted by terrorist assassins, he is closely guarded by General Katrina Grimovitch (Signe Hasso), addressed by her fellow countrymen as Your Excellency. She has reached the summit in her military career, aided by the fact that she "fought, ate, and slept with 10,000 men" during World War II. It is obvious that she is viewed as an equal to the men in the Barovian Army, not as a second-class citizen like many U.S. servicewomen were and are. As Grimovitch tells

Captain Mary Morely (Paulette Goddard) poses with her husband, Peter (Fred MacMurray, left), for a publicity photo in Paramount Pictures' 1947 film *Suddenly, It's Spring*.

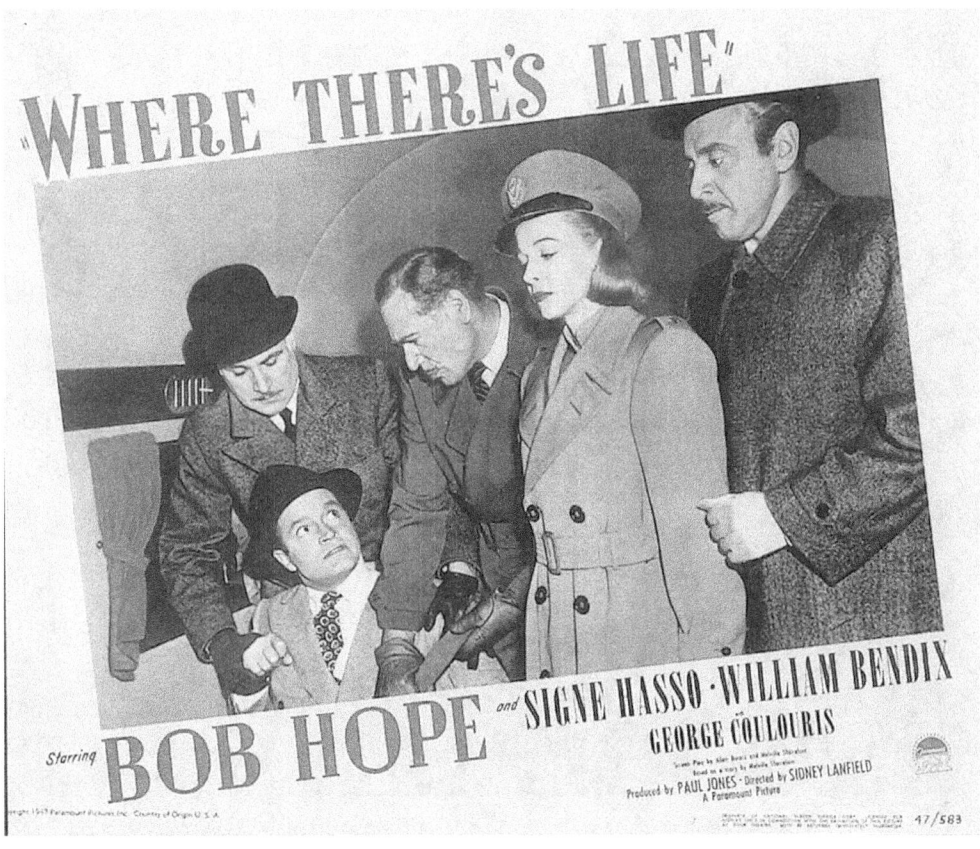

Soviet General Katrina Grimovitch (Signe Hasso) discusses capitalism with Michael Valentine (Bob Hope) in *Where There's Life* from Paramount Pictures (1947).

Valentine, "The Army of Barovia has no such thing as man or women—that's an old-fashioned idea." Gender integration is the norm for Barovia, something the United States is still struggling with seventy years later. As a result of that struggle, it can be asserted that while U.S. "military culture and its emphasis on masculinity may not be solely responsible for ... discrimination against women, the evidence ... suggests that it plays a prominent role."[19]

The Doughgirls (1944) features another foreign woman who is simply seen as a soldier, rather than as a female soldier. Credited with shooting 396 Nazis, Soviet Army Sergeant Natalia Moskoroff (Eve Arden) is proud of her record and of her prowess with a rifle. Moskoroff is onscreen for thirteen minutes, hilariously detailing her exploits as she proves why Russian officials believed that, in women, "the combat intuition is instantly triggered, set by nature ... executed exactly, focused and merciless."[20]

True to the Army (1942) also features a woman with remarkable shooting skills. Judy Canova stars as Daisy Hawkins, a circus performer who witnesses a murder. She immediately goes to see her boyfriend (Jerry Colonna as Private J. Wethersby "Pinky" Fothergill) on post and is forced to cross-dress as a soldier to avoid being found by either the hitmen who want to silence her or by the police who want her to testify. While dressed as a new recruit, Hawkins participates in basic training exercises, winning a marksmanship medal by outshooting every other "man" in the company, proving that women are just as capable as men when given the opportunity to showcase their skills.

Lieutenant Catherine Gates (Ann Sheridan, left), French Army Captain Henri Rochard (Cary Grant), and Lieutenant Kitty Lawrence (Marion Marshall) in 1949's *I Was a Male War Bride*.

I Was a Male War Bride (1949) is arguably the best service comedy to come out of this decade. Ann Sheridan stars as Army First Lieutenant Catherine Gates, a no-nonsense transportation officer serving in France. After she and French Army Captain Henri Rochard (Cary Grant) are given an assignment to complete, the role-reversal antics begin when Gates wears the pants, both figuratively and literally—with no jeeps available, the two are forced to take a motorcycle with a sidecar, and since Rochard does not have a license to drive one, Gates dons khaki pants and takes the wheel, forcing Rochard to ride passively in the sidecar for the entire trip. They banter and argue for much of the film, then predictably fall in love. Unlike many films of this time, however, Gates never gives up her independence or becomes subservient to Henri, and at one point, it is actually Gates who has to rescue Rochard, who has gotten himself arrested.

Following their marriage, Rochard and Gates have difficulty getting Henri, a French citizen, the necessary paperwork needed so that he can travel to America with his new wife. He repeatedly tells military personnel that he is "traveling under Public Law 271," which allowed spouses of American servicemembers to go to the United States with their spouses and did not use gender-specific language. Much like the war groom of 1946's *G.I. War Brides*, the military personnel that Rochard encounters are baffled at his mere existence. Since all the other spouses the clerks deal with were female, no one knows what to do with him. He is ultimately forced to cross-dress in a WAC uniform to get onboard the New York–bound ship with his wife, where Gates tells him, "Henri, remember you're a lady!" Equal rights and benefits for male spouses of female servicemembers were an ongoing issue until 1973 when the decision in the Supreme Court case *Frontiero v. Richardson* finally granted military women "dependents' benefits on the same basis as men."[21]

The 1940s ushered in rapid and lasting advances for women serving in the United States military. Major legislation helped pave the way for a more permanent female presence in the U.S. military; with these changes came more visibility and ever-expanding career opportunities. Hollywood took note, and the films of the next decade feature military women in a somewhat wider variety of jobs and in more prominent roles.

Three

Now What?
The 1950s

Following the end of World War II, the remaining years of the 1940s were a time of relative peace for the United States. In June 1950, however, over 75,000 North Korean troops crossed the 38th parallel to the south, setting off the police action known as the Korean War. The hostilities only lasted until 1952, but the conflict effectively ushered in the Cold War era, which would last four decades.

On the home front, many consider the 1950s an idyllic time to have lived on America. Men were still men, and the majority of women returned to the domestic sphere following the turbulent war years; most servicewomen were released from active duty as soon as feasible, and the majority of the female factory workers were replaced by the men returning home from war. Many, however, did not want to go back to the way things had been—they had gotten a taste of independence and adventure, and they liked the flavor. Society as a whole, however, was ready for things to return to what was considered normal.

Those women who wanted to remain in the service, therefore, had a difficult time in doing so. Despite the Women's Armed Services Integration Act of 1948, those in power did not feel it was necessary for women to remain in the military in any substantial way, and several laws were amended in order to make their separation from the service easier. Not all women were summarily discharged, as medical professionals and administrative personnel were still deemed useful; however, severe limits regarding female servicemembers were kept in place, such as the number of women who could be on active duty, the maximum age allowed, and how many could hold higher ranks simultaneously.[1]

Despite these limitations, women continued to answer the call to serve. As during World War II, there was "an undeniable demand from American women that they be permitted to serve their country, together with the men of America, to protect and defend their cherished freedoms and democratic principles and ideals."[2] In order to help facilitate their service and to give them much needed support, Secretary of Defense George C. Marshall created the Defense Advisory Committee on Women in the Services (DACOWITS) in 1951. Anna M. Rosenberg, Assistant Secretary of Defense for Manpower and Reserve Affairs, was selected to run the committee, whose goal was to provide "oversight and guidance on the entire spectrum of issues impacting women in the U.S. military."[3] The advocacy of DACOWITS helped to "create public acceptance of and respect for women in uniform" and worked toward improving their quality of life in general.[4] Due to the visibility of DACOWITS and aided in part by the manpower shortage caused by the Korean War, leaders in Washington were forced to consider revising official policy towards women in the military.[5]

Hollywood took notice and began expanding the portrayals of servicewomen on film in a variety of ways. As such, this chapter includes discussion on more films than all but one chapter of this book. Fully half of the movies discussed in this chapter feature nurses as the primary women in uniform; the remaining films, however, broaden the spectrum of job assignments portrayed, highlighting the abilities of servicewomen and showcasing the possibilities of what the future could hold.

Musicals

The musical genre continued to be a significant source of entertainment for American moviegoers throughout the 1950s. Major productions of the decade ranged from Gene Kelly in both *An American in Paris* (1951) and *Singing in the Rain* (1952) to 1957's *Jailhouse Rock* starring Elvis Presley. While there were not a lot of musicals that centered on the military, five that did included women in the military in their casts.

In *G.I. Jane* (1951), Iris Adrian portrays Lieutenant Adrian, a squared-away soldier in charge of a unit of WAC trainees. She is also technical advisor for the WAC recruitment film Tim Rawlings (Tom Neal) is working on, letting him know immediately that, "in the Army, we don't mark time that way." Throughout the dream sequence that comprises the majority of the film, Rawlings

Lieutenant Adrian (Iris Adrian) addresses a group of new recruits in the 1951 musical *G.I. Jane* from Murray Productions.

runs into Adrian again after he is drafted, and when trying to get away with something, she chides him again, saying, "It's too bad you're not more familiar with Army procedure." Even though women were not given command over male servicemembers at this time, Adrian's dedication to duty almost compels her to guide Rawlings into becoming a better soldier.

Esther Williams was able to show off her singing and swimming prowess in the star vehicle *Skirts Ahoy!* in 1952. Portraying Seaman Recruit Whitney Young, Williams is initially late reporting for basic training and has to see the unit commander, Lieutenant Commander Staunton (Margalo Gilmore). Staunton quickly sees that Young is well-bred and asks her why she enlisted, to which Young responds, "I wanted to feel useful. I never have." Unlike Jo McBain in *Never Wave at a WAC* (discussed later in this chapter), Whitney wants no special privileges afforded to her because of her background; even though she could have requested a commission, she instead tells Staunton, "I didn't want it made easy." She turns out to excel in the military, becoming recruit company commander in just two weeks and earning the respect of both her peers and her superiors. Through their training, Young and her fellow recruits learn to embrace what their commander tells them—that women "don't have to be dependent, weak sisters."

Sound Off (1952) stars Mickey Rooney as new recruit Mike Donnelly, who falls for Army nurse Lieutenant Colleen Rafferty (Annie James). Rafferty, who wears a European theater ribbon on her uniform and is all business, initially rebuffs Donnelly's advances, letting him know that he should be at attention when addressing her because she "also rates a salute." Predictably, however, Rafferty eventually begins a relationship with Donnelly. This film is the first of the decade to feature a female officer falling in love with an enlisted man—unfortunately, many more would follow.

Dean Martin and Jerry Lewis team up in their fifth buddy film for 1952's *Sailor Beware*, which features two women in uniform. Petty Officer Second Class Hilda Jones (Marion Marshall) is love interest to Seaman Apprentice Melvyn Jones (Lewis). Onscreen for five minutes, Hilda initially meets Jones when he accidentally ends up in the office where she clerks. At first shown acting completely professionally, she soon turns into the typical love interest, acting emotional and getting upset when Jones won't kiss her and when he gets chased by other women.

Additionally, Elaine Stewart portrays Lieutenant Saunders, a Navy nurse who tends to Jones when he is hospitalized. Highly professional and efficient, Saunders deftly deflects a pass by Seaman Apprentice Al Crowthers (Martin), threatening him with "thirty days in the brig," while simultaneously letting the Navy doctor (Alan Dexter) know that if Jones "doesn't cooperate with me, his condition is going to be a lot worse." Because Saunders is all business and clearly not interested in romance, she is disparaged by the Navy men; rather than being admired for her professionalism, they instead describe her as "colder than a deep freeze."

The Broadway musical *South Pacific* became a silver screen attraction in 1958 and features Mitzi Gaynor as Navy nurse Ensign Nellie Forbush. A typical Hollywood musical, replete with corny songs such as "I'm Gonna Wash That Man Right Outta My Hair," the film also carries a strong message about prejudice. This film is primarily a musical romance, however, and Forbush, while onscreen for over half the film's run time, is generally seen singing and dancing rather than performing her duties as a nurse. It is not until the last fifteen minutes of the film that she is shown making rounds in the base hospital, and she is only shown in uniform for a brief time as well. Overall, this film does not do much in the way of positive portrayals of women in the military, as Forbush spends almost the entire film trying to decide whether to stay with her boyfriend (Rossano Brazzi as Emile De Becque) or dump him because her family would not approve. She eventually decides that she loves him enough to embrace him and his children as they are, not as her family would like them to be.

New recruit Melvin Jones (Jerry Lewis) meets Petty Officer Second Class Hilda Jones (Marion Marshall) in the Wallis-Haven production *Sailor Beware*.

Drama

While more than one-third of the films discussed in this chapter are comedies, the decade also produced a number of dramas featuring women in uniform in a variety of roles. Several include only very small roles for military women. In *The Flying Missile* (1950), Commander Talbot (Glenn Ford) is injured and must be admitted into the hospital; a ward nurse who attends him (Helen Brown) is onscreen for two minutes and has just a few lines. *The Hunters* (1958) shows an Army nurse for just a few scenes as well, as do 1951's *Bright Victory* and *The Proud and Profane* from 1956. All of these nurses are onscreen for two minutes or less with a minimal amount of spoken lines, but all are shown performing their duties well, with an efficient bedside manner and a kindly disposition. *Breakthrough* (1950) also shows an Army nurse briefly (Danni Sue Nolan as Lieutenant Janis King), but not while she is on duty. She is standing by her tent in her fatigues as some men pass by on patrol. As they stare and make comments, it is clear she is there as a reminder to the men that women do still exist and may be what they are fighting for. For that brief moment, it also shows that women served overseas during the war as well, voluntarily performing what they considered their patriotic duty.

Two uncredited nurses can be found in 1959's *Never So Few*. Onscreen for three minutes, the ward nurse (Maggie Pierce) handles Captain Tom Reynolds (Frank Sinatra), telling him, "You stay in bed and watch your language—you're not in the jungle." The head nurse (Irene Tedrow) orders him back to bed, and he tells her, "One of these days, I'm going to meet a nurse who doesn't sound like a troop commander," after which she lets him know that she is going to report him to the colonel. Neither is important to the plot, but it is quite the comic scene as they march to see the colonel to complain about the hospital food Reynold's men are being given.

The apocalyptic *On the Beach* (1959) features an Australian Navy lieutenant (Lola Brooks as Lieutenant Hosgood) in several scenes. As secretary to Admiral Bridie (John Tate), she is privy to top-secret information about the coming disaster. When offered the chance to leave and be with family, she insists on staying, wanting to be as helpful as she can be during the national emergency. Her dedication to duty and country comes first, and the admiral's admiration for her is evident.

A final small role is that of Lieutenant Sally Johnson (Andrea Martin) in 1959's *Up Periscope*. She has been tasked with assessing the psychological suitability of Lieutenant Junior Grade Kenneth Braden (James Garner) for a dangerous underwater mission. To be able to observe him without him knowing what she is doing, she "accidentally" meets him one evening. Onscreen for just six minutes, Johnson is with Naval Intelligence, and she observes Braden covertly—he thinks she is just a woman he happened to meet. When he does learn of her ruse, he is dumbfounded, but he does not seem all that upset over the deception, as he has fallen in love with her. She is in love as well, and at the film's end, she is waiting for Braden on the dock as his submarine comes into port.

In 1958's *In Love and War*, Sheree North portrays Lorraine, a third class petty officer who has just recently joined the WAVES. When she meets up with her childhood sweetheart (Robert Wagner as Marine Frankie O'Neill), he is shocked to see her in uniform. In his drunken stupor, he even mistakes her for a man at first, telling her, "Beat it, sailor—this is a private party!" Tough and independent, Larraine quickly lets Frankie know that she is tired of his immature ways, and when he gets a little too fresh, she punches him in the stomach, letting him know that "basic training" is where she learned how to defend herself so well. Onscreen for just nine minutes and not essential to the film's plot, Frankie does at least realize that Lorraine is doing something worthwhile, letting her know, "Hey, sailor, you're really something!"

In *The Young Lions* (1958), Barbara Rush portrays Margaret Freemantle, love interest for Private Michael Whiteacre (Dean Martin) and employee of the Office of War Information (OWI). After being drafted and completing basic training, Whiteacre announces to Margaret that he is being transferred to London; Margaret informs him that she, too, is being sent overseas.[6] When the two meet up in London, he finds her in an Army uniform, making it appear as if OWI employees were in the military, but there is no documentation indicating this is historically accurate. Since she is shown in uniform, however, it is more plausible that she moved on from the OWI in order to enlist. In an additionally confusing scene, when they run into a general that she knows, Margaret addresses him by his first name rather than by his rank, something that would have been highly inappropriate for a subordinate to do. Throughout Freemantle's ten minutes onscreen (four of which are in uniform), she is tough and practical, preferring to voice her disapproval or opinion rather than go around wearing rose-colored glasses, especially when it comes to Whiteacre. With her strong personality and take-charge attitude, she will likely advance quickly through the ranks, if she chooses to remain in the service.

Battle of the Coral Sea (1959) features Lieutenant Peg Whitcomb (Patricia Cutts), a member of the Australian Nursing Corps, who is being held prisoner in Japanese Interrogation Camp #7. Along with many others at the camp with her, Whitcomb became a prisoner due to the fall of Corregidor in 1942. Onscreen for ten minutes, Whitcomb is proud but practical, telling new prisoner Lieutenant Commander Jeff Conway (Cliff Robertson) about the Japanese at the camp: "Tell them whatever it is they want to know—that is, if you care about your men." During her time in internment, she has found it easier to go along and not run afoul of their captors. She eventually regains her sense of duty, however, and she is instrumental in planning and executing their escape to freedom.

Another film focused on nurses who have been taken prisoner is 1959's *Five Gates to Hell*, which features five women in the French Nursing Corps.[7] Along with an Army doctor (Ken Scott), the women are taken to the stronghold of Gung Sa (Benson Fong), one of Indo-China's biggest drug lords, who is in need of immediate medical attention. Once the doctor operates, the rebels decide to continue keeping them all captive, primarily in order to use the women as sex slaves. Joy (Patricia Owens) willingly submits, thinking it will help keep her alive, but Athena Roberts (Dorothy Michaels) refuses and is brutally raped by Sa's right-hand man (Neville Brand as Chem Pamok). Escape plans are hatched, and during their initial attempt, the doctor is killed. The women eventually take up arms and begin shooting all of their captors, escaping in the process. Their tenacity surprises everyone, even themselves; they learn that despite the fact that they are nurses, each of them has persevered and performed "almost like a soldier." As Athena guns down Pamok during the final showdown, it is clear these women are "brave, strong, and intelligent, and they behave as real heroes."[8]

The 1950 movie *Pygmy Island* is the fifth installment of the *Jungle Jim* film series featuring Johnny Weissmuller as the titular character. In this movie, Jim is tasked with locating an Army captain who has gone missing; he is stunned when told the captain is a woman, commenting, "Did you say *she*?" He then learns the captain is named Ann Kingsley (Ann Savage), and she is the Army's top expert in the field of tropical plant research. It is interesting that Jungle Jim takes Captain Kingsley's abilities as a given, evidenced by the fact that at one point he leaves her to stand guard over the boat in case the bad guys return. Later, however, the pygmy wants her to stay put, treating her as a helpless woman and acting as her protector. Additionally, it's Jim who gets caught and used as leverage against the U.S. Army, not the female character as one might expect, since so often Hollywood portrays women as weak and in need of rescuing. It is clear Kingsley is more than capable of taking care of herself; throughout the film, Kingsley does much to promote the capabilities of American servicewomen, handling herself deftly in all situations and saving her plant samples for the advancement of science.

Thunderbirds (1952) tells the story of a primarily Native American National Guard unit that gets called up for active duty during World War II. Lieutenant Gil Hackett (John Derek) is the film's main protagonist, and he is recovering from heartbreak when he meets Army nurse Lieutenant Ellen Henderson (Mona Freeman). They quickly become an item, and as with so many other war films, Henderson's primary role in the movie is that of love interest. She is barely seen performing her duties, but what is shown proves her to be a well-trained, efficient member of the Army Nurse Corps.

In *Force of Arms* (1951), Nancy Olson stars as WAC Lieutenant Elinor MacKay. Onscreen for more than 42 percent of the film, she works in the Army's mail section while stationed in Italy. At the first meeting between MacKay and the film's protagonist, Sergeant John "Pete" Peterson (William Holden), he invites her for a drink; she declines, and he gets offended, telling her, "Oh, I get it—you're taking that sort of big," assuming that Landers says no because she's an officer and he is a sergeant. Following that encounter, the two cross paths again at her duty station—he is trying to help one of his men (Phil Harris as Sergeant Hank Stack) find some missing mail, and she offers to help. Stack's initial reaction is one of disdain, commenting that things are "all flubbed up if women are handling it," but Peterson is quick to remind him, "WACs ain't women ... they're officers and gentlemen. Congress says so."

The next time MacKay and Peterson see each other, he has gotten a battlefield commission to lieutenant, and it is she who then invites him for a drink. When she pays for the drinks, he makes fun of her, stating, "That's what I like about you—you're such a perfect gentleman." It is evident that Peterson doesn't approve of women in the military, as he refers to her as a man several other times as well. He even questions her motives for enlisting, asking her, "How come you joined up?" MacKay's initial flippant answer of "I thought the uniform would match my eyes" does not appease him, so she tells him the real reason: "I'd like to be able to go back [home] and feel that I helped keep this place, this street, free and safe." Her patriotism strikes a chord with him, and despite their initial friction, the inevitable romance blooms, which ends with them getting married.

The 1951 film *Operation Pacific* features Patricia Neal as Lieutenant Junior Grade Mary Stuart, Navy nurse and ex-wife of Lieutenant Commander Duke Gifford (John Wayne). When the two meet up after four years, he is quite surprised to see her in uniform, but he lets her know immediately, "I'm proud of you." It is apparent how much Gifford respects her—when his crew chief (Jack Pennick) addresses her as "Ma'am," he quickly corrects him that she is only properly addressed as lieutenant. Gifford tries to rekindle their old flame, but Stuart is hesitant, letting him know, "I have a life of my own to live." Like many other films, Stuart is included in the cast as the obligatory love interest; their back story makes things a bit more complicated than somewhat similar story lines, but they predictably get back together at the film's conclusion.

The Wild Blue Yonder (1951) tells the story of the early days of the Boeing B-29 Superfortress bomber. The cast includes Vera Ralston as Lieutenant Ellen Landers, an Austrian-born nurse in the U.S. Army, as well as her supervisor, Major Ida Winton (Ruth Donnelly). Landers, on-screen for seventeen minutes, is primarily the love interest of both male leads in the film, but she is tough and completely dedicated to her patients. During an air raid, rather than take cover as ordered, she races to the hospital to help protect her patients.

Winton is a seasoned veteran. Although she wonders aloud "why any sane woman would join the nurse corps," she also says that she stays in the Army because "I'd rather be out here with my 'sons' than back home worrying about them." She looks out for Landers, with whom she has formed a special bond. At one point, when Landers is confused over whether to choose Captain Harold Calvert (Wendell Corey) or

Publicity still featuring John Wayne and Patricia Neal as Lieutenant Commander Duke Gifford and Lieutenant Junior Grade Mary Stuart in *Operation Pacific*, a 1951 film from Warner Brothers.

Major Tom West (Forrest Tucker), Winton does not help her decide, but she does council her to not "miss the boat like I did ... get out, get married, and have some kids of your own." Although she clearly does not regret the decisions made regarding her own career and life, Winton realizes that same road is not right for everyone and that most women probably prefer a more traditional path.

D-Day: The Sixth of June (1956) is ostensibly about the invasion of Normandy in 1944, but the film's primary plot involves two men in love with the same woman—Valerie Russell (Dana Wynter), a member of the Auxiliary Territorial Service (ATS), which was the women's branch of the British Army during the Second World War. Often shown working at her post within the American Red Cross Service Club, Russell is a typical British woman, reserved and proper. Onscreen for almost 40 percent of the film's run time, Russell knows that during war time, "You just take what they give you," and she does so with stoicism. Throughout the film, both men vie for Valerie's affections, and although she loves Captain Brad Parker (Robert Taylor), she stays with Lieutenant Commander John Wynter (Richard Todd) out of loyalty.

The only screen pairing of future President Ronald Reagan and his wife Nancy Davis (as she was then billed) was 1957's *Hellcats of the Navy*, in which Davis portrays Lieutenant Helen Blair. The pair was married when the film came out, and she is cast as a Navy nurse and love interest to Reagan's character, Commander Casey Abbott. Almost all of Blair's seventeen minutes onscreen are shared with Abbott; although she is seen working occasionally, her primary role in the film is as confidant and sweetheart to Abbott.

Purple Heart Diary (1951) focuses on the travels of USO singer Frances Langford, who portrays herself in the film. During a visit to one Pacific island base, Langford ends up rooming with Lieutenant Cathy Dietrich (Aline Towne), an Army nurse stationed there. Another character who is primarily a love interest, Dietrich is more extensively shown performing her duties; she is also severely injured in an air raid and almost loses her life. With her boyfriend aiding the camp doctor, however, she makes a full recovery and returns to her duties. Onscreen for only seven minutes, Dietrich is a minor character in the film, but her grit and determination provide the audience with a positive depiction of the character of military nurses in general.

A scientific experiment gone awry forms the basis of the plot for 1950's *Experiment Alcatraz*. The film features Joan Dixon as Lieutenant Joan McKenna, who is working with Dr. Ross Williams

The only screen pairing of Ronald and Nancy Reagan, seen in this publicity shot from Morningside Productions' **Hellcats of the Navy** (1957).

(John Howard) to try and find a cure for a fatal blood disease that has afflicted her brother. McKenna is hard working and diligent in her quest to help her brother, but a careless mistake leaves her culpable of negligence that results in murder. After a hearing on the matter, Colonel Harris (Kenneth MacDonald) informs McKenna that the board is "willing to forgo court-martial, but we have no choice except to ask you to request release from active duty." She abides by their decision but then works with Williams to prove the validity of his serum. Often putting herself in danger, McKenna eventually finds the clues that bring resolution to the case, clearing her name in the process. Her grit and determination pay off; at the film's conclusion, she is back in uniform and taking her brother for his life-saving treatment.

Korea

Amongst the films of this decade, military women can be found in nine dramatic movies centered on the Korean War (1950–1952); only one is not medical personnel. This is not surprising since most people at that time subscribed to the belief that men were the only ones built for fighting; Hollywood, therefore, produced movies in which "the basic objective of women in combat is clearly seen to be *taking care of men,* not fighting the war itself."[9] The majority of the female military personnel in these films do garner significant amounts of screen time, however, and although the portrayals are overwhelmingly of nurses, the roles still offer filmgoers a look at the perseverance and tenacity of women in the military at that time.

In *Flight Nurse* (1953), Joan Leslie stars as Lieutenant Polly Davis and actually gets top billing for the film. The movie is based on real-life Air Force flight nurse Captain Lillian Keil, who made over 400 combat evacuation flights spanning both World War II and the Korean War and was awarded nineteen medals during her distinguished career; Keil was also a technical advisor for the film. Onscreen for half of the film's run, Davis is the quintessential nurse and soldier, excelling in all aspects of her military duties. During long days of training, she focuses on survival skills, in case of a plane crash. When asked why she is there, she simply states, "This was what I'd been trained for ... this is where I belong." Despite her tough Army training, however, Davis is still feminine—she is constantly applying lipstick, at one point even when the plane she is on is about to crash. As the film ends, the flight nurse's creed is recited: "I will set the very skies ablaze with life and promise for the sick, injured, and wounded who are

Publicity photo of Joan Leslie as Lieutenant Polly Davis in 1953's *Flight Nurse*.

Lieutenant Ruth McGara (June Allyson) and Major Jed Webbe (Humphrey Bogart) take cover during an air raid in the 1953 film *Battle Circus* from MGM.

my sacred charges. This I will do. I will not falter, in war or in peace." Davis embodies this creed and does her best to live up to the ideals it espouses.

In a somewhat lighter role, June Allyson stars as Lieutenant Ruth McGara, who gets sent to a MASH hospital in 1953's *Battle Circus*. Upon arrival at camp, she immediately starts assisting others, offering cigarettes to the wounded and helping a blinded patient get under cover during an air raid. Her acts catch the eye of camp commander Major Jed Webbe (Humphrey Bogart), who asks her, "What are you trying to do—win the war single-handedly?" When given the opportunity, Webbe makes a pass at her, but McGara handily fends him off by telling him she's not interested, only there to be "the best nurse I can." As expected, they do finally get around to the romance part, and as all the other nurses have warned her, he likes his women to stay in "their place." She challenges those notions, however, with her strong sense of duty, and he eventually comes around to her way of thinking.

Torpedo Alley (1952) begins during the waning days of World War II and continues on through the outbreak of the Korean War. The film features Navy Lieutenant Susan Peabody (Dorothy Malone) as a nurse torn between two men. Her long-time beau, Lieutenant Dore Gates (Douglas Kennedy), constantly asks Susan to marry him, but she keeps turning him down, commenting, "Maybe we just don't have that spark that's necessary in a marriage." Lieutenant Bob Bingham (Mark Stevens) doesn't even try to hit on her at their first meeting, causing Susan to comment, "You're the only flyer I've ever known that hasn't tried to buzz the field." Despite her inclusion as a love interest, Peabody is a dedicated nurse who takes her duties and her service seriously. She also provides a little comic relief at times, like when she tells Bingham that he has "more brass than a shell casing" after he and Gates squabble over whose girl she is, letting them both know in no uncertain terms that she will not idly stand by and let them decide her life for her.

In *Jet Attack* (1958), there is an American Air Force sergeant (Madeline Foy) in one scene, shown operating the film projector as her superiors look over some classified information. In a much more substantial role, however, Tanya Nikova (Audrey Totter) portrays a medical aide in the Soviet Army, deployed to North Korea. Highly trained and professional, the North Korean security officer Major Wan (Leonard Strong) seems surprised, telling her, "You are very capable" when she dresses his wound; in response, she notes that, "if it weren't for the war, I would be a doctor by now." Throughout the film, she works as a double agent against the Communists, helping the Americans rescue a captured scientist (Joseph Hamilton as Dean Olmstead) behind enemy lines. She is all business, completely steady and self-assured under pressure, even in the midst of deceiving those for whom she works. Her dedication to the task at hand does help get the scientist rescued, but Nikova dies in the process, paying the ultimate price for her dedication to duty.

Red Snow (1952) features an Air Force nurse (Carole Mathews) who is only referred to by her rank. As in many other films, Mathews' primary purpose is that of love interest; as a first lieutenant, she outranks Second Lieutenant Phil Johnson (Guy Madison), but he still lets her know he's been "wondering what it would be like to kiss a first lieutenant." Onscreen for just four minutes, "Lieutenant Jane" (as she is credited on IMDb) is shown performing her duties competently, attending to several patients while braving the frigid Alaskan weather.

In 1953's *Mission Over Korea*, Audrey Totter portrays Army lieutenant Kate, a MASH nurse seen onscreen for five minutes. Despite Lieutenant Pete Barker's (John Derek) best efforts, no romance ensues. Kate is clearly not interested, telling Pete, "Put it down to my being a nurse—I'm cooled by formaldehyde." Her focus is strictly on healing, letting Barker know, "For everyone that goes, the burden increases for those who stay." She feels the weight of every patient that dies and knows that despite the fact that "they're all great guys, and they all mean something to someone," some are just not going to make it. All she can do, therefore, is focus on the job at hand and take the best care of every soldier who comes her way.

Tank Battalion (1958) features Marjorie Hellen as Army nurse Lieutenant Alice Brent as well as Regina Gleason as Lieutenant Norma "Red" O'Brien. Like many comedies released during this decade, this film also features enlisted men dating female officers. Brent and Sergeant Dunne (Don Taylor) were a couple prior to enlisting; despite the fact that Captain Caswell (Mark Sheeler) reminds Dunne "to keep in mind that she's not only a woman but an officer as well," the two never let their ranks hinder their romance.

O'Brien is a little older and much more cynical. Although she claims to have joined the Army to snag "a millionaire soldier boy, nurse him back to health, and ... live happily ever after," she bucks military regulations by going out with Private First Class "Skids" Madigan (Frank Gorshin), telling the well-bred Caswell, "Tonight's my night for the enlisted men." Even though the captain is clearly the type of man she claims to be hunting for, she never even goes out with him and predictably falls for the lower-class Madigan. Onscreen for about eight minutes each, the nurses are just included as love interests, only shown performing their duties in one short scene.

Army nurses who get taken prisoner is a subplot of 1959's *Battle Flame*. First Lieutenant Frank Davis (Scott Brady) is in love with Lieutenant Mary Ferguson (Elaine Edwards), the nurse who attended him while he was in Japan recuperating from wounds received in battle. When the plane transporting Mary and her unit crashes, she and the other nurses are taken prisoner by Chinese Communists. When Ferguson complains to the unit commander about the conditions under which the nurses and other prisoners are being held, he quickly offers to make Ferguson's stay more comfortable for sexual favors, but she slaps him instead; he is set to retaliate, but he does not get the opportunity as Davis and his crew show up to rescue them right at that moment. She gets emotional and cries when Davis' unit arrives to save them, and he tells her, "I know this wasn't in your contract." It is obvious that despite the fact that women were not officially allowed in combat, Ferguson and her squad have seen more than their share. She is battle-worn and somewhat inured to men dying around her, even stating at one point that she "was so busy, I forgot where I was," but Davis lets her know, "You've been wonderful, Mary—really. All of you have."

Time Limit (1957), the plot of which focuses on a potential court-martial, features Dolores Michaels as Corporal Jean Evans, secretary to Colonel William Edwards (Richard Widmark) and stenographer for the depositions. In her first appearance onscreen, the men in the room with her stare at her backside when she bends over to place papers on the colonel's desk, highly inappropriate behavior that sets Evans up as mere eye candy in the film, but that is the only time her gender is a focus. Throughout the rest of the film, the men around her comport themselves in a much more professional manner. Onscreen for sixteen minutes, Evans is well-trained and efficient, and it is clear Colonel Edwards values her opinion. When needed, she gives her advice to him, even if her ideas do not agree with his own.

The Cold War

The Cold War ramped up rapidly during the 1950s, instilling paranoia in many Americans who feared the rampant spread of Communism across the globe. This fear, fueled by Senator Joseph McCarthy of Wisconsin and the House Un-American Activities Committee (HUAC), fostered a nationwide "Red Scare" that led to many Americans having to testify before Congress and being blackballed in various industries, including Hollywood. Well suited to the war drama genre, the subject saw widespread use in American films, and three from this decade feature women in the military.

In 1957's *Three Brave Men*, Bernie Goldsmith (Ernest Borgnine) is suspended from his position with the Navy on suspicion that he has Communist leanings. During the hearing that follows, he is questioned by a panel of government examiners as well as by Lieutenant Mary Jane McCoy (Nina Foch) from the Legal Advisory Board. While the men on the panel find Goldsmith's testimony compelling, it is McCoy who pushes to interview some of the witnesses against Goldsmith, finding many discrepancies and lending weight to his claims of innocence. Her persistence eventually leads to Goldsmith's acquittal on the charges before him.

The Iron Petticoat (1956) takes a comical look at the political divide between the United States and the Soviet Union. At the film's onset, Captain Vinka Kavalenko (Katharine Hepburn), "one of the three leading Soviet woman flyers," defects to the West, but not for the usual political reasons. Despite receiving five medals of the first order, setting three flying records, and attaining the rank of captain, her much less experienced male comrade gets a coveted promotion instead of her, leaving her feeling that she has been the victim of gender bias, calling it "a case of archaic anti-woman discrimination." This was an indication that in spite of the Soviet Union's "hyperbolic rhetoric about gender equality, and despite the many individual soldiers and officers who embraced these concepts, the regime did little to challenge widespread social notions about women's subordinate status, which had deep roots in the patriarchal peasant culture."[10] Kavalenko decides, therefore, to defect to the United States, believing that as a woman in a Westernized country, she will be treated much more equally. Kavalenko insists that despite her defection, she is still a staunch Communist; the Air Force then assigns Captain Chuck Lockwood (Bob Hope) to "sell her America." Throughout their time together, however, Kavalenko remains committed to her ideology, trying to convert Lockwood to her way of thinking instead. Although Lockwood admits, "women in uniform bother me—I don't know whether to kiss 'em or salute 'em," the two eventually fall in love, giving the film a typical Hollywood feel-good ending.

Jet Pilot (1957) also involves a female pilot trying to convert an American soldier to Communism. Colonel Jim Shannon (John Wayne) is sent to bring in a defecting Soviet pilot, who he is shocked to learn is a woman, Lieutenant Anna Marladovna (Janet Leigh). Purporting to be in fear for her life, Marladovna demands respect and refuses to give up any sensitive information about the Soviet military. She does, however, find a taste for "capitalist luxuries" while on a romantic weekend with Shannon. The Air Force eventually figures out that Marladovna is really Olga Orliev, who has been sent to spy on the Americans and learn their military secrets; they turn her, however, and Shannon "defects" with her back to Russia, where it is he who is now doing the spying. Despite Marladovna's expertise in her field and political beliefs, love predictably wins out over ideology, and after shooting down some Russian planes so that she and Shannon can escape from Russia, Marladovna ultimately decides that love and a good steak are worth much more than Communism, and the film's characters "revert to their true natures, aligned with prescribed categories of gender and sex."[11]

Katharine Hepburn as Captain Vinka Kovelenko in a publicity still for the film *The Iron Petticoat* (1956).

Comedies

Following the end of World War II and the Korean Conflict, Hollywood often took to portraying the lighter side of war and the military in general. Many service comedies were released during this decade, and almost one third of the films in this decade are that genre. While a few of these films have just a token woman or two in uniform, the majority feature servicewomen in much larger roles.

Kiss Them for Me (1957) features three military servicewomen in very minor roles. When Commander Andy Crewson (Cary Grant) tries to pick up women by offering them free stockings, a WAC corporal (Barbara Gould) shows up to get some. He tells her they are all gone, and she innocently asks, "It's not just because I'm only a WAC? Please don't make fun of me." He acts like he has never seen a woman in uniform before, stating apologetically, "I was out of the country when you were ... created." Additionally, Nancy Kulp is seen as a telephone operator in two scenes, and Rachel Stephens has a quick cameo as a WAVE. Each speaks only briefly, but their inclusion in the film does speak to the increased visibility women in the military were beginning to have.

Another small role is that of a WAF captain (Jean Willes) in 1958's *No Time for Sergeants*. Again given no name and onscreen for just two minutes, the very sight of her flabbergasts new recruit Private Will Stockdale (Andy Griffith), who admits, "I never heard of saluting no woman before." When his buddy tells him, "She ain't a woman; she's a captain," that does not lessen his confusion, but he soon understands that it is a person's rank that is important in the military and not the gender.

Defecting Soviet pilot Lieutenant Anna Marladovna (Janet Leigh) in the 1957 RKO film *Jet Pilot*.

Off Limits (1952) also highlights a woman in uniform for a short time. One (again) unnamed WAC (Mary Murphy) is shown during an MP training exercise, uttering only the word, "Help!" following a staged assault by new recruit Herbert Tuttle (Mickey Rooney). Mostly there as comic foil for MP-in-training Wally Hogan's (Bob Hope) antics, the female MP is shown comporting herself in a military manner, and she is especially intimidating when, during the demonstration, she flips Hogan down on the mat for putting his arms around her without consent.

A unit of nurses is shown in a few scenes in *Mister Roberts* (1955). Brought onboard ship by Ensign Frank Pulver (Jack Lemmon), who promises to share some scotch with their supervisor, Lieutenant Ann Girard (Betsy Palmer), the nurses are immediately subject to leering stares and cat calls. They also soon figure out that the ship's crew has a clear view of their shower room. Despite Pulver's best efforts, the nurses choose to return to their hospital immediately in order to start hanging curtains. Only onscreen for seven minutes, Girard and the other nurses are included in the film not as love interests, but to reinforce the fact that while women were in the military at this time, it was primarily as nurses because "their roles and functioning [were] very much dictated and constrained by the traditional assumptions concerning feminine ... and masculine" roles.[12]

In *A Private's Affair* (1959), Barbara Eden portrays Staff Sergeant Katie Mulligan, a public

Ensign Pulver (Jack Lemmon) meets with Lieutenant Ann Girard (Betsy Palmer, far left) and her squad of nurses in *Mister Roberts* (1955).

relations dynamo. As feisty as the WAC briefly shown in *Off Limits*, Mulligan casually tells Mike Conroy (Gary Crosby) when he's trying to put his arm around her, "I recently took a judo class. I can break a man's arm three different ways." She also flips him down on the beach when he's trying to keep her from leaving, deftly demonstrating that "military training in various ways teaches women that they are capable of protecting themselves."[13]

The year 1950 saw the release of the first film in the Francis the Talking Mule franchise. All starring Donald O'Connor as Peter Stirling and featuring Chill Wills as the voice of Francis, these films were beloved by a generation of filmgoers. In all, seven films in the series were released between 1950 and 1956; two feature women in the military. In 1954's *Francis Joins the WACs*, Peter Stirling is called back up for active duty and accidently gets assigned to a WAC unit. The tough, no-nonsense commander of the unit, Captain Jane Parker (Julia Adams), initially tries to get Stirling out of her unit as quickly as possible, but she soon changes her mind and orders him to stay and train with them in order to demonstrate the true abilities of her soldiers. Parker is a major character in the film, onscreen for twenty-seven minutes, and her efforts to educate Stirling regarding the efficiency of her unit showcases their abilities and dedication to duty.

The next year, *Francis in the Navy* (1955) was released. In this film, Stirling is an Army man who bears an uncanny resemblance to Navy troublemaker "Slicker" Donavan, also portrayed by Donald O'Connor. Donavan's girlfriend, Petty Officer Betsy Donevan (Martha Hyer), confuses

Stirling for her boyfriend and spends most of her screen time trying to keep him from going to the brig. Onscreen for just four minutes, Donevan is obviously dedicated to the service, concerned her association with Slicker will get her into trouble by proxy. These two films do not do much toward normalizing the idea of women in the military, but since the comic antics of Stirling and Francis are the film's focus, romance is not a major part of the plot in either film.

Real-life husband and wife (at the time) Tony Curtis and Janet Leigh team up in 1958's *The Perfect Furlough*. Army psychiatrist Lieutenant Vicki Loren (Leigh) comes onto the scene in order to help alleviate the stress of a unit of sequestered soldiers who are going stir crazy. She comes up with the idea of having one of the men go on a "perfect furlough" that will give the other soldiers the opportunity to vicariously share the experience with him, thus allowing for all the men to feel as if they have each personally gone on the furlough; she is then tasked with implementing her idea. This brings her into contact with Corporal Paul Hodges (Curtis), and the pair take an immediate disliking to one another. In a moment of obvious foreshadowing, Loren states, "Corporal Hodges is the one kind of man I couldn't possibly be interested in." Since she is a lieutenant and he is an enlisted man, the possibility of them violating "Article 93, Section 7" of the Code of Military Justice, which states that "no enlisted man shall kiss or embrace a superior officer," shouldn't even rear its head, but this is yet another Hollywood film in which a squared-away female officer lets her head be turned by the smooth talk of a much lower-ranking subordinate. As the inevitable romance ensues, Hodges' flippant comment about "what happens when you've got women in an army" becomes reality, and Loren gives up a promising military career in order to marry him.

The Sad Sack (1957) also portrays a female officer falling for an enlisted man. Major Shelton (Phyllis Kirk) is all business from the film's onset, deftly ignoring Major Vanderlip's (Sheppard Strudwick) sexist comment about how she is "quite a departure from the usual run of majors." When Corporal Larry Dolan (David Wayne) first sees Shelton, her uniform jacket is off, so he does not realize she is an officer and immediately starts hitting on her. When he is looking in the other direction, she puts her jacket on; he turns around and is visibly flustered as he salutes his superior officer. Throughout the film, she alternates between falling for Dolan's lines and chastising him for coming onto an officer. Predictably, however, she ends up falling for him, and they share a long, passionate embrace at the end of the film.

A similar situation occurs in 1957's *Operation Mad Ball*. While stationed at the Army's 1066th hospital in France following the end of World War II, Private Hogan (Jack Lemmon) meets Army dietician Lieutenant Betty Bixby (Kathryn Grant) and attempts to woo her, despite the fact that he quips, "There's no such thing as a beautiful officer." All business at first, she attends him as a medical professional, treating the duodenal ulcer he pretends to have in order to get close to her. When he comes onto her again, she tells him, "Please remember that I'm an officer"; he gets mad and accuses her of hiding behind her commission. She rebuts with, "How dare you speak to an officer in that disrespectful manner!" Eventually, the inevitable happens, and Bixby ends up falling in love with Hogan.

Throughout the film, there are also many other enlisted men shown dating nurses, all of whom are officers as well. This particular plot device gives the impression that women are flighty and will fall for any man who shows them the slightest bit of attention, despite any adverse effects that fraternization may have on the women's lives and military careers. As a recurring trope in military films, the concept serves to undermine the positive contributions women have made in the military, painting many of these women as being ruled by their emotions.

Don't Go Near the Water (1957) is the final film of this decade that focuses on an enlisted man/female officer relationship. Yeoman Adam Garrett (Earl Holliman) likes Lieutenant Junior

Grade Alice Tomlin (Anne Francis), but he realizes dating her is against military policy. Despite that knowledge, he still tries asking her out, telling her, "I'm a man, and you're a woman," but she quickly counters with, "I'm also a naval officer," demonstrating her familiarity with military regulations. A relationship does begin, of course, following Tomlin's admonition for Garrett to "take off her rank and throw it away" right before they kiss for the first time. When the relationship is discovered by those in charge, Garrett gets reprimanded, threatened with court-martial, and sent to sea. Tomlin, however, does not get into any trouble—it is as if she has no complicity in the matter, which is clearly not the case. In the films of this era, these portrayals only serve to lessen the importance of the military woman's service, as does a comment by Lieutenant Ross Pendleton (Jeff Richards) in which he refers to Tomlin as "valuable merchandise" as if she were a belonging rather than a peer officer in the United States Navy.

Romance also plays a large part in the plot of 1959's *Operation Petticoat*, but in this film, all involved parties are officers. The film features five Army nurses who get stranded in the Philippines and must be taken aboard a submarine. Several storylines unravel at the same time, with the women wreaking havoc in a variety of ways on the submarine that is clearly "not built for co-education." By the film's end, both the sub's commander (Cary Grant as Lieutenant Commander Matt Sherman) and his supply officer (Tony Curtis as Lieutenant Nick Holden) are each married to one of the nurses.

One refreshing departure from the female officer/enlisted man trope involves the head nurse and one of the ship's mechanics. At first, Chief Machinist Mate Sam Tostin (Arthur O'Connell) is threatened by Major Edna Heywood's (Virginia Gregg) mechanical abilities, perhaps because men often thought that military service "should be forbidden territory to females." Tostin soon learns to trust Heywood and her unorthodox problem-solving skills, however, and they work together to get the sub in top running condition. Unlike inappropriate story lines in many of the other films in this decade, these two are simply workmates; no hint of romance is seen between the officer and the enlisted man.

In 1951's *You're in the Navy Now*, Navy clerk Ellie Harkness (Jane Greer) is married to Lieutenant John Harkness (Gary Cooper), new commander of the USS *Teakettle*. She initially is stationed at a recruiting station but works her way up until she is secretary to Captain Danny Eliot (Harry von Zell), a career move which also earns her a promotion to lieutenant junior grade. Eliot is very impressed by Ellie's work, telling her husband that she is "a highly efficient officer." Although John wants Ellie to find out if there is "any way of ... getting out of the WAVES," she stands strong, telling him, "I just got in." It is clear that she wants to serve her country just as he does, and her upward climb rank-wise shows that she is more than capable of performing her duties.

The 1959 Jerry Lewis film *Don't Give up the Ship* features Dina Merrill as Ensign Rita Benson, a Navy psychologist tasked with helping Lieutenant John Steckler (Lewis) locate the USS *Kornblatt*, a destroyer escort ship that has been missing since the end of World War II. Since he has been recently married, it worries him to be alone with Benson in the same room, but she puts him at ease by telling him, "Don't be so concerned—we're Navy men." Unlike many other films, there is no hint of romance between the two—she is there to achieve a result, which she does more than capably in her nineteen minutes onscreen.

Another Jerry Lewis film to feature a woman in uniform is 1958's *The Geisha Boy*. Suzanne Pleshette portrays Sergeant Pearson, aide to Major Ridgely (Barton MacLane), who is in charge of the USO Tour being sent to Japan to entertain the troops. When Gilbert Wooley (Lewis) first talks to her, he tells her, "I never met a real WAC before." Since he believes that "soldiers can't be sexy," he never looks upon her as a woman, which upsets her somewhat. Pearson performs her duties with a great sense of accomplishment, clearly proud of her service. However, even though

Navy psychiatrist Ensign Rita Benson (Dina Merrill) with Lieutenant John Paul Steckler IV (Jerry Lewis) in the 1959 film *Don't Give Up the Ship* from Hal Wallis Productions.

she is a modern woman with an "American emancipated woman type of independence," she still hopes to trade it all for the more accepted role of wife and mother, a mindset that undercuts the military bearing and efficiency with which she comports herself.

The WAC from Walla Walla (1952) stars Judy Canova as a simple country girl of the same name. Her crush on fellow townsman Lieutenant Tom Mayfield (Stephen Dunne) leads her to enlist in the WACs, and he commends her for having done a "very patriotic thing." Her much prettier rival for Tom's affections (June Vincent as Doris Vail) signs up as well, and the inevitable problems ensue when the two get to basic training. Despite Vail doing what she can to thwart Canova's training, Judy turns into a "real good soldier" like her father has instructed, and both she and Vail end up working together to save an important new piece of military technology from being stolen. As promised by their unit commander (Irene Ryan as Sergeant Kerns), their training has given them "the fundamental skills ... need[ed] as a member of the Armed Forces team."

In *Leave It to the Marines* (1951), a couple goes down to the local courthouse to get their marriage license, and reluctant groom Gerald Meek (Sid Melton) ends up accidentally enlisting in the Marine Corps. Not wanting to be left behind, Myrna McAllister (Mara Lynn) signs up as well, stating that she is doing so "for national defense." While Meek proves to be a less-than-stellar Marine, McAllister quickly adapts to military life, rising to the rank of sergeant and becoming platoon leader. Throughout Meek's misadventures, McAllister remains strong and committed to the military, proving to be much more of "a real Marine" than he is.

Never Wave at a WAC (1952) features Rosalind Russell as aristocrat Josephine "Jo" McBain, who gets snookered by her father into joining the WACs, expecting him to finagle a commission for her. He refuses, however, believing that letting her begin as a private will help her learn some discipline and humility. At basic training, Jo's cluelessness and sense of entitlement keep her in constant hot water with her superiors. After her disastrous performance during some training exercises, McBain is called to a hearing to assess whether she should remain in the WAC, where she has to admit, "I'm not officer material; I'm not even private material." On her way back home, however, she sees a truckload of new recruits and realizes how much the Army has come to mean to her; she runs off from her fiancé onto the truck and tells the other women that she wants to become "whatever the Army will let me be."

A final comedy to discuss is 1956's *The Lieutenant Wore Skirts*. The film stars Sheree North as Katy Whitcomb, a former lieutenant in the Air Force, and Tom Ewell as her husband Greg, who is in the reserves following several years of service during both World War II and Korea. When Greg receives a letter telling him to report for a physical in order to be called back to active duty, Katy decides to reenlist as well as a surprise. The real surprise, however, comes when Greg fails his physical and is rejected—but Katy has already signed up and cannot just quit.

Coming as a tremendous blow to Greg's ego, he nevertheless sincerely attempts to navigate this new reality, at least at first. With the roles of breadwinner and homemaker reversed, Greg tells Katy, "I'll show you how much I love you—I'll be the best darn wife you ever had!" Greg's masculinity is soon threatened, however, and he schemes to put things "right" again. When Katy

Air Force Lieutenant Katy Witcomb (Sheree North, right) questions her sanity to Captain Grace Briggs (Alice Reinheart) in 1956's *The Lieutenant Wore Skirts*.

discovers that Greg is trying to make her think she's crazy so that she will be discharged from the Air Force, she decides to leave *him*, not the service, telling him in no uncertain terms: "I wouldn't leave the Air Force now if they wanted to use me for target practice." When he belittles her, snidely asking, "Do you have some idea the Air Force would miss you if you left?" she quickly rebukes him by stating, "I don't know if the Air Force would miss me, but I do feel I'm important to them." Her assignment as a security officer is one she takes seriously, and she expects her husband to understand that. Nevertheless, traditional gender roles are predictably restored at the end of the film as Greg finally gets accepted for reenlistment and Katy gets discharged when the doctor informs her that she is pregnant.[14]

The 1950s were a booming time for the American film industry, and women in the military got a good deal of exposure on the silver screen. With over half the films in this decade featuring military nurses, however, Hollywood elected to substantially stay in line with the country's reversion to relegating women to more traditional roles. Although women had been utilized extensively in many non-traditional roles during both World War II and Korea, the powers that be thought of these women primarily as "a resource to be thrown at national crises as they arose ... [then] redirected when their services were no longer required."[15] They had clearly bought into the belief that "the preparation for and execution of war is simply not a woman's role,"[16] and women in the military were generally relegated to traditional roles both onscreen and in real life. The 1960s and 1970s, however, would bring revolutions and revelations to the United States Armed Forces, and the implementation of the all-volunteer force would greatly expand women's military participation and opportunities.

Four

The Times They Are Changing
1960s and 1970s

The jubilant feelings experienced by Americans after the military successes of World War II dimmed as the Cold War heated up during the 1950s and 1960s. While training for military men continued to stress readiness for any possible conflict, the same could not be said about those women who remained on active duty. Nicknamed "typewriter soldiers" by *Washington Post* columnist Jack Anderson, military women in the 1960s found themselves "excluded from the mainstream of the military for all practical purposes—tolerated, but not taken too seriously."[1] In 1965, only 30,600 women were serving in the U.S. military. Rather than being able to push the envelope in terms of military occupations, military women were relegated to traditional women's roles such as secretarial, protocol, and medical positions, expected to be "ladies" at all times and to dress accordingly. The number of women in the military steadily declined, despite pressures in the civilian realm by feminist leaders to expand women's opportunities throughout society.[2] The 1960s were a time of radical social change in America—the Civil Rights movement, hippies and the rise of the drug culture, the British Invasion in rock and roll, and the sexual revolution all contributed to changing roles for women in society, but they did not impact opportunities for military women. And women in leadership positions within the military did not question their second-class roles, in part because while they received equal base pay for their service, they were not expected to die for their country but rather free up men for combat duty.

As America's involvement in Southeast Asia increased in the late 1960s, many military women wanted to serve in Vietnam. Excluded from combat by law, many women saw this exclusion as the result of paternalistic attitudes toward women and an unwillingness to bother with the "headaches" associated with women.[3] A small number of women from all four military branches served in Southeast Asia during the war, in addition to military medical personnel.[4]

In 1967, Public Law 90-130 gave women greater career parity, including promotion to colonel/captain and general/flag rank, and equalized retirement benefits. But the dissolution of the draft and the implementation of the all-volunteer force on July 1, 1973, ultimately provided the greatest impetus for women's military success as military leadership was forced to consider all options in order to fill critical billets, many of them with operational units. While there were objections about possible impacts on combat readiness, women quickly proved themselves capable and invaluable members of their units.

The beginning of the 1960s also saw changes in Hollywood. The rise of independent film companies helped bring an end to the studio system. Social changes also brought changes to the types of movies made in Hollywood. In the early 1960s, all genres were popular, including war films like *Judgment at Nuremberg* (1961), which included two enlisted Army women court reporters who appear in the film for four minutes (2 percent of the film) but have no lines. War epics such as *The Great Escape* (1963) and *The Guns of Navarone* (1961), which feature large international casts but no military women as characters, wowed audiences with their special effects, all done in thrilling Technicolor. As America's involvement in the Vietnam War increased in the late 1960s and early 1970s, there was a noticeable absence of Vietnam War films on the big screen, unlike during World War II where war films were important propaganda tools. After the Vietnam War ended, films about the war like *Apocalypse Now* (1979) and *The Deer Hunter* (1978) were expected to have something important to say about the follies of war.[5] Most of these films focused on the role of the grunt in the field and not on the women who also served in country. For instance, in *The Deer Hunter*, Lynn Kongkham plays a nurse in the Army hospital where Nick (Christopher Walken) is recuperating. She dutifully accompanies a doctor on his rounds and comforts Nick by patting his shoulder, but she never utters a single word during the minute she is onscreen, nor do any of the other nurses who are seen in the ward.

Apocalypse Now features no American military women, although it does include two North Vietnamese military women as combatants. In one short (four second) scene, a woman in green fatigues can be heard shouting a warning of a pending U.S. attack on a village school as Wagner's "Ride of the Valkyries" booms overhead. After the attack, a young woman in black slacks and the checked scarf of the Viet Cong tosses a grenade into a U.S. medivac helicopter, blowing it up without saying a word.

Such films emphasize the horrors and insanities of war and the impacts of these experiences on the average grunt—and there was hardly any room for the experiences of American military women in movie theaters of the 1960s and early 1970s.

Action Films

Action films gained considerable popularity in the 1960s, their focus chiefly on the Cold War, seen in films like *Dr. No* (1962), *From Russia with Love* (1963), and *Our Man Flint* (1966). While many such films featured male military protagonists, military women were noticeably absent from the action, as befit the laws and social norms of the day. That changed somewhat in the 1970s as American tastes in action films turned to police stories like *Dirty Harry* (1971) and Hong Kong martial arts films like *Enter the Dragon* (1973). As the war in Vietnam heated up, films about World War II allowed Americans to relive previous American war successes, but women played only minor roles in these films. In an uncredited role in *Fireball Forward* (1972), for example, Loretta Swit is a nurse in the 471st Evacuation Hospital. Onscreen for only eighteen seconds, when asked what she and her nurses need after a particularly grueling battle, she tells General Barrett (Ben Gazzara), "I need a couple of weeks in Bermuda, General, but I'd settle for a nice hot bath." The general orders the delivery of a portable shower for the nurses.

The early Vietnam War film *The Boys in Company C* (1978) features two scenes involving military nurses. In the first, Helen McNeely is a Navy lieutenant nurse at the hospital at Cam Ranh Bay. Onscreen for ten seconds, when a newly arrived Marine tries to get her to fill a Demerol prescription on the street, the BDU clad nurse tells him to go to sick call in the morning. At the end of the film, newly arrived Marines are mistakenly sent into a Quonset hut where nurses, thinking those men are returning to the States after their tour, can check them for venereal diseases. Discovering the mistake, a Marine captain tells a stunned nurse to get them out of there before the men jump the nurses, a commentary on the men's inability to control themselves after having been in the field.

The bicentennial year of 1976 brought a heightened interest in the American Revolution, and the rise of feminism brought an increased interest in the role women played in the creation of the newly formed country. One short film that explores the role of a cross-dressing colonial woman who fought for America's freedom is *Deborah Sampson: Woman in the Revolution* (1976). Based on historical accounts, letters, and memoirs, the film begins with the teenaged Sampson (Linda Atkinson) deciding to do something beyond helping outfit local men for war and ripping bandages for the wounded. She cuts her hair, dons a uniform, and joins the 4th Massachusetts Regiment using the name Robert Shirtleaf. Although small in stature, she holds her own as she drills, shoots, and fixes her bayonet, marching across a field with her unit to face British soldiers in battle. Shot in the leg, she avoids being unmasked by digging out the musket ball herself, but a year later, her secret is revealed when she collapses from fever and is treated by a doctor. Her commanding officer is incredulous when he learns of her masquerade, and when he asks why, she says she couldn't stand by and watch the country she loves be destroyed, saying, "[A woman's place is] where her heart lies. No one lightly chooses a battle line for a home, but sometimes we can do things we ordinarily wouldn't. I felt I had to act." The colonel wonders what to do with her because she's been a good soldier and she wants to stay until the war is over. Her presence is deemed inappropriate, however, and she is discharged. The film ends with the note, "Her service is remembered as a unique contribution to America's war for independence."⁶

The late 1970s gave Americans a glimpse into the world of terrorism with the film *Warhead* (1977), also known as *Prisoner in the Middle*. Shot in Israel, the story revolves around attempts by both an American Air Force officer (David Janssen as Lieutenant Colonel Tony Stevens) and a co-ed squad of Israeli Army soldiers to recover a lost American nuclear weapon. The Israeli team includes Lieutenant Liora (Karan Dor), a strong woman officer who personally experienced a terrorist act when a school bus she was guarding was blown up by a Palestinian guerrilla. While on maneuvers, the squad encounters Stevens, who has parachuted into the Israeli desert in the hopes of disarming the lost nuke. Several Israelis, including two women soldiers, are killed as they recover the missile, as is Nomoi (Joan Freeman), a sexy blonde Olympic sharpshooter, after she takes out several Palestinians. Another woman (Ellyn Stern as Shoshonna) wanders off during their trek through the mountains. Onscreen for three minutes, she is captured by the Palestinians and interrogated, but never breaks. She is finally "given" to one of the Palestinians, who rapes and kills her off screen. The remaining soldiers flee through the desert, finally sheltering in an abandoned fort where Stevens gives everyone but Liora an assignment. When she asks why, he responds, "I can't get over the feeling you should be at home with the kids, waiting for your husband to come home." His words echo the sentiments of many American military and civilian personnel at the time. Liora disagrees with his assessment, reminding him that she is a highly trained soldier, joining in the subsequent firefight. She is ultimately killed by the terrorist she is pursuing, sacrificing herself for the country she loves. Onscreen for almost fifteen minutes, Lieutenant Liora is the epitome of an Israeli military officer—strong, determined, capable, and compassionate—and willing to die for her country. Unfortunately, her American counterparts at the same time did not have the opportunity to show they were just as capable.

Comedies

During the 1960s and 1970s, America's ebullience was frequently reflected in the comedies of the day. A number of filmmakers situated their stories among members of the military as they examined changing social roles of the time. While women play a small role in some of these comedies, many of these films feature strong female characters whose power is wielded subtly but effectively. Also during this time, male impersonation almost disappeared from American film, despite the popularity of masculine/military clothing in the world of fashion.[7] Khaki was a popular color for men's and women's clothing, and epaulets, brass buttons, and bell-bottomed pants were all the rage for much of the period.

Cross-dressing played a minor role in two films from this period. In *All Hands on Deck* (1961), newspaper reporter Sally Hobsen (Barbara Eden) dons a white crackerjack uniform and hides inside a shipboard crane in an effort to avoid detection during a surprise inspection while visiting her fiancé's (Pat Boone) ship. Only in uniform for eighteen seconds, upon her discovery, she quickly sheds the Navy uniform, revealing a lady-like dress and her identity as a reporter.

Almost a decade later, Raquel Welch dressed as a male Navy commander in a fourteen second sketch in *Myra Breckenridge* (1970), which reenacts Marlene Dietrich's cross-dressing performance of "The Man's in the Navy" in the 1940 dramatic film *Seven Sisters*. In that film, Dietrich pins her hair up and dresses as a Navy lieutenant as she sings to Lieutenant Dan Brent (John Wayne) and his shipmates in a South Seas café. Where Dietrich's song is seductive, Welch's is played for laughs and is much less integral to the film's storyline.

While the number of women in the military was reasonably small in the 1960s, military women characters appeared in a number of comedies during the 1960s, in major and minor roles. The earliest film to feature military women was *The Great Imposter* (1960), which was based on

Canadian Navy imposter Tony Curtis (left) woos Canadian Navy nurse Joan Blackman (right), as well as several other women including Cindi Wood (bottom smaller photo), in the Universal International picture *The Great Imposter* (1960).

the true story of a man (Tony Curtis as Ferdinand Waldo Demara) who impersonated a string of men in different occupations. In one incarnation, as an enlisted man in the U.S. Army who wants to be an officer but doesn't meet the requirements, he seduces a female lieutenant (Cindi Wood) and tells her that he'll become an officer no matter what it takes. Later in the film, he lands in Canada as a doctor at a naval hospital where he meets a nurse, Lieutenant Catherine Lacey (Joan Blackman), with whom he falls in love enough that he wants to confess about his deception, but she stops him, saying she wants to fall in love with someone she doesn't know. Their love is short lived when he is shipped to Korea, but she vows to wait for him forever. Despite the fact that he is unmasked in the press, Catherine still loves him and meets his ship upon its return, only to find out that he has once again changed identities and disappeared.

In *Kissin' Cousins* (1964), Air Force Airman First Class Midge Riley (Cynthia Pepper) is dispatched to Tennessee to help First Lieutenant Josh Morgan (Elvis Presley) secure land rights needed for a missile site. She arrives at the mountainside camp dressed inappropriately in a straight skirt and high heels and is immediately subjected to harassment by the enlisted men stationed there, including hoots, cat calls, and incorrect guesses about her measurements, which she proudly corrects. Even the man in charge, Captain Salbo (Jack Albertson), is unhappy with her presence, asking if headquarters didn't have any male typists. Wooed by Morgan's identical cousin, she initially resists his advances, but eventually she succumbs and helps convince his mother to

Corporal Midge Riley (Cynthia Pepper) in khaki uniform on left center and Captain Josh Morgan (Elvis Presley) in khaki uniform on right center dance in the finale of the 1964 film *Kissin' Cousins*.

lease the land to the Air Force. Onscreen for ten minutes, all of it in uniform, Midge is smart, capable, and creative, a definite credit to the Air Force.[8]

McHale's Navy Joins the Air Force (1965), set during World War II, features two female military characters in minor roles. Sergeant Madge Collins (Jean Hale) is a buxom blonde whose tight uniform and unbuttoned shirt distract the men with whom she works, a fact she uses to her advantage. Mistaking Ensign Parker (Tim Conway) for a reputed ladies' man named Harkness, she tells him her serial number is 38-22-35 and tells the other military women that he's hers.

Corporal "Smitty" Smith (Susan Silo) is Collins' exact opposite—small, dark haired, and very bright. She's unhappy to be Harkness' secretary since he was once engaged to her sister and did her wrong. She warns him, "I joined the Army to fight for my country, not my honor, so no funny business, mister." Onscreen for almost ten minutes, when she initially misunderstands Ensign Parker's ineptitudes as passes, he tells her she misunderstood him, commenting, "I don't see you as a girl. You're just another GI," to which she retorts, "I am as much a woman as any other female. I have plenty to notice." Later, she kisses him in the control tower, which ultimately results in them accidently foiling a major Japanese attack. Both are promoted as the result of their antics. In a short scene later in the film, Parker engages in cross-dressing as an Army nurse to avoid a general who is looking for his son, the real Harkness. All ends well, of course, with Parker getting another promotion and the girl.

In an effort to capitalize on the popularity of the James Bond films, 20th Century–Fox released the 1966 spy spoof *Our Man Flint,* which featured James Coburn as the suave, know-it-all spy Derek Flint. In the film, which revolves around a terrorist organization that demands the complete demilitarization of Earth, Ena Hartman is a WAC captain, the capable aide to Zonal Organization World Intelligence Espionage (ZOWIE) head Lloyd C. Cramden (Lee J. Cobb). Her five-minute appearance is the first depiction of a black American servicewoman onscreen, and the character is dignified and professional, although she is not called by name in the film and is only listed as "WAC" in the credits.

The Korean War is often referred to as a forgotten war, infrequently depicted in film. In *Not with My Wife You Don't!* (1966), however, it serves as the tie that binds three Air Force officers together for several decades. Tom Ferris (Tony Curtis) is a hot shot Air Force fighter pilot during the Korean War who, along with his best friend/archrival Tank Martin (George C. Scott), vies for the love of Air Force nurse First Lieutenant Julietta Peroni (Verna Lisi). Ladies' man Ferris meets Peroni when he is hospitalized after an accident, but their interaction goes awry when Ferris, trying to flirt, asks, "What do I call you?" to which she, unimpressed, retorts, "You can try lieutenant." She eventually succumbs to his charms, however, setting the stage for the rest of the film. When Tank meets Julietta, he is also smitten and does his best to woo her away from Ferris, resulting in her falling in love with both men. A series of pranks gone awry cause Julietta to believe Tank has died, and she marries Ferris, giving up her military career while Ferris remains as a career Air Force officer. Seen in uniform for one-third of the forty-five minutes she is onscreen, Peroni is a blonde bombshell with traditional values. Like Sally Ann (Donna Danton), another Air Force nurse onscreen for five minutes, she is a capable, compassionate nurse who is somewhat naïve and trusting, falling for the men's antics which are light-hearted despite the serious topics of extramarital affairs and death portrayed in the film.

Two years later, Hollywood looked at the military occupation of Japan after World War II in the 1968 film *Nobody's Perfect.* The first woman of Asian descent shown as an American servicewoman, Nancy Kwan is Lieutenant Junior Grade Tomiko Momoyama, a Japanese-American Navy nurse stationed in Yokosuka, who is torn between an American sailor (Doug McClure as Doc Willoughby) and an arranged marriage with a traditional Japanese-American man she barely knows (James Shigeta as Toshi O'Hara). Tomiko is a modern American woman who wants to be independent. While she is proud of her Japanese heritage, she resents people's assumptions about her. When she asks Doc why he likes Japan, he says, "Japanese women are the most feminine in the world," which frustrates her. She says Japanese woman are like pieces of furniture, unexpressive and docile. When he retorts, "A woman's place is in the home," she tells him, "That's trite. You're still living in the Middle Ages." The strong-minded modern woman, who is onscreen for twenty minutes, identifies with her white nurse friends, proving to have as strong a sense of duty as they have. Ultimately, she breaks her engagement to Toshi, and while she honors her Japanese heritage, she proves herself to be an independent American woman.

During the 1960s and 1970s, comedies centered around military women began to change, symbolizing an acceptance of and respect for military women.[9] While military women still challenged established gender roles, their uniforms now gave them an air of authority and legitimacy. But they could also be seen as disruptive, their assertiveness and independence perceived as being disconcerting to the military men around them.[10] Their air of authority, coupled with their physical attractiveness, frequently created disruptions to good military order and discipline. This disruption was often expressed in comic terms such as "battle of the sexes," in which female unruliness was contained within a rule-bounded arena.

Wake Me When It's Over (1960) provides an excellent illustration of just such a "battle of the sexes." It is set in a post–World War II Japanese backwater area, and Captain Charlie Stark's (Ernie Kovacs) soldiers are cynical, unprofessional, and slovenly, an attitude the base doctor blames on peacetime. And Stark is no better—unmotivated, unmilitary, and happy. The men become energized over plans to build a hotel at the local hot springs with the arrival of First Lieutenant Nora McKay (Margo Moore), a squared-away blonde sent on temporary duty from Tokyo to help provide a "woman's touch" to the hotel's décor. There is instant friction between Stark and McKay. Her snide comments about the base's condition lead Stark to comment, "That's the kind of girl my Daddy got. A real tender buzz saw." When guards are posted outside her barracks door in an attempt to protect her from marauding soldiers, she tells him, "I am not a pillbox, thank you. The whole thing is a man's nod to American manhood and a slight dig at me. I'm an American, Captain. I'm over twenty-one, have read *Gray's Anatomy*, have clear vision and strong convictions. That should take care of all poachers," to which he replies, "What a girl, huh?" Stark continues to verbally spar with her, calling her "baby doll" and disparaging her efforts, despite the fact that she proves to be very good at her job.

Onscreen for only fifteen minutes, McKay makes a huge impact on the island. While the men all lust after her, they think she is a bad influence on Stark, who has quit drinking and who they believe is used to dealing with "women that's more like people." Obviously, she's gotten under Stark's skin, and she sees him as a project needing to be "fixed." While he tells her that he is a traditional man who wants a traditional wife and intends to be fully in charge of their relationship, she admits that they're both flawed and that she wants more from him than his laid-back attitude. When she storms out after an argument, he follows her in a jeep, yelling, "All you gotta do is sit around looking pretty, rack up a few kids, and keep some cold cans of beer in the icebox. Those are the new rules, baby. If you want to play house, get in the jeep. If you don't, keep walking." Despite her cool professionalism and efficiency, she gets in the jeep.

Sometimes the battle of the sexes is a bit less obvious. In the World War II comedy *The Horizontal Lieutenant* (1962), Paula Prentiss plays First Lieutenant Molly Blue, an awkward girl who hapless intelligence officer Second Lieutenant Merle Wye (Jim Hutton) knew in college, who has outgrown her gawkiness and is enjoying her new-found popularity. Onscreen for twenty-seven minutes, she is a force to be reckoned with. Capable, self-confident, intelligent, and beautiful, she

Army Second Lieutenant Merle Wye (Jim Hutton) chases First Lieutenant Molly Blue (Paula Prentice) in MGM's 1962 comedy *The Horizontal Lieutenant*.

is a model nurse and officer, but one who is looking to the future, after the war ends and she is no longer in the military.

Wye is smitten, and she allows him to pursue her, along with a number of other suitors, telling him, "I'm twenty-two, Merle. By the end of the war, I may be thirty. I'm shopping around." As happens in romantic comedies, she falls for him despite his incompetence and string of bad luck in his military assignments, and they play a game of "do we love each other or don't we" until the end of the film, when she helps him capture an elusive Japanese soldier. Injured in the capture, he receives a Purple Heart—and gets the girl.

Another comedy in which the military women run circles around their male counterparts is *Sergeant Deadhead: The Astronaut* (1965). Airman Lucy Turner (Deborah Walley) loves Sergeant O.K. Deadhead (Frankie Avalon), a bumbling airman whose accidental trip into space aboard an Air Force rocket is covered up by the equally bumbling base commander (Fred Clark) at the urging of his aide/girlfriend, First Lieutenant Charlotte Kinsey (Eve Arden). These women are smart and capable—and know how to manipulate their men for the benefit of both the men and themselves. But they are not career military women. When a friend asks Turner why she wants to marry Deadhead, she says, "We women have to protect all of the clods of the world. He's my clod," and then enumerates his faults and good qualities. Later, she comments that she has been a good sport and played soldier but now would like to play bride.

Admiral Stoneham (Cesar Romero, left) reprimands Airman Lucy Turner (Deborah Walley, center) as Lieutenant Charlotte Kinsey (Eve Arden) looks on in the 1965 musical comedy *Sergeant Deadhead*.

The film is filled with harmless titillation—female airmen exercising in tight gym clothes, marching through water sprinklers in tight shorts, the requisite shower scene, and a barracks scene where the women sing and dance while Kinsey laments about the one who got away. Kinsey's primary job as the general's aide is to cover up his ineptitude. Like Turner, she wants to get married and spends most of her twenty-seven minutes onscreen keeping him out of trouble. So why do two competent military women place so much emphasis on wanting to be married rather than concentrating on their careers? Much like in the "Beach Party" movies that were so popular at the time, these smart, capable women would be threatening to the men they love if they continued to remain outside the accepted social norms prescribed for women at the time, that is, in the military.

Movie goers in 1970 experienced two "serious" comedies about the folly of war—*Catch 22* and *MASH*. Both of these important films feature military women in various degrees of importance to the storylines. In the World War II dramedy *Catch-22*, Paula Prentiss is nurse First Lieutenant Duckett, the love interest of Captain John Yossarian (Alan Arkin), a B-25 bombardier. Onscreen for only a little more than two minutes, in one scene, she knees him in the groin when he tries to undress her on the beach. Hospitalized with a shrapnel wound later in the film, he dreams that as he is swimming toward a wooden raft, Duckett sheds her nurse's uniform and stands naked, beckoning him to come closer as he sinks beneath the water.[11]

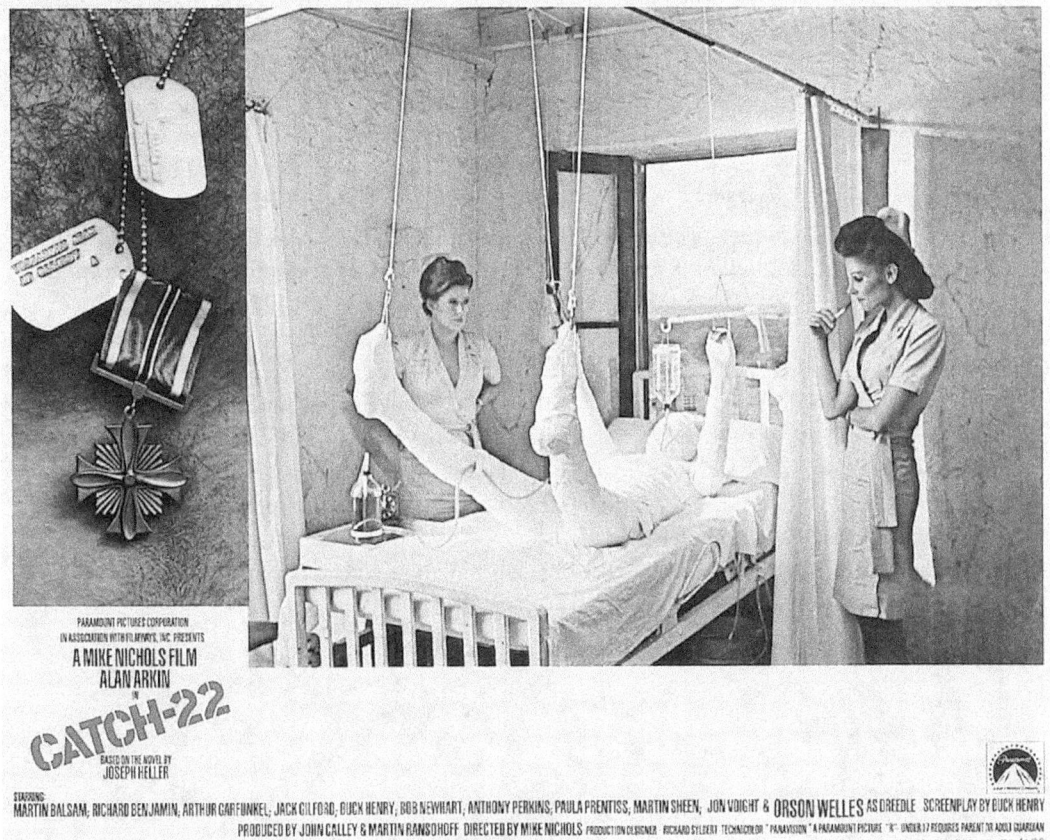

Nurses Cramer (Collin Wilcox-Horne, left) and Duckett (Paula Prentiss) talk about the war in Paramount Pictures' *Catch-22* (1970).

The more interesting female military character in the film is "General Dreedle's WAC," played by Susanne Benton, whose three minutes onscreen create a lasting impression on the cast and viewers alike. The starlet's already buxom figure was supplemented by seven pairs of falsies and "a rubber behind by Frederick's of Hollywood" that stressed her khaki uniform to the breaking point.[12] Her bright red nail polish and long blonde hair are decidedly not military, but General Dreedle (Orson Welles) does not seem to notice. Despite (or because of) her appearance, Dreedle does not respect her. When she giggles during Yossarian's naked medal ceremony, he snaps, "Get back in the jeep, you smirking shit." None of the men bat an eyelash over his comment, although she is visibly taken aback.

Arguably, the most famous war comedy is 1970's *MASH*.[13] Set in Korea but actually a commentary on the war in Vietnam, the film chronicles the irreverent antics that occur at the 4077th Mobile Army Surgical Hospital as they try to deal with the trauma caused by the folly of war. *MASH*, the third highest grossing film of 1970, is an anti-war film that features no battle scenes, focusing instead on the devastation wrought by war as it is seen in the operating room where medical personnel patch up young men who are then often sent back to the fight.[14] Despite the lunacy that surrounds them, and the craziness that ensues as they let off steam by drinking and womanizing excessively, the doctors of the 4077th are professionals, willing to go the extra mile for their patients.

Much scholarship has been devoted to the various characters depicted in *MASH*, primarily emphasizing their disrespect for authority, military protocol, and organized religion. And probably the most analyzed character is that of nurse Major Margaret O'Houlihan (Sally Kellerman),[15] who is seen as the epitome of the military establishment—rigid, uptight, gung-ho, and pro-war. Typically in war films, nurses are seen doing serious work appropriate to their proper (female) social role as a nurturing healer. They are seen as being a part of war but removed from it, able to enter an inappropriate space (war) and fix a problem (care for the wounded). They are not typically mocked or treated in a disrespectful way. The nurses in *MASH*, like all military women, choose to serve, and their loose behavior reflects the changing social roles of American women from the 1960s through the 1970s. These nurses, except for O'Houlihan, are sexually liberated and fun-loving, standing in contrast to the traditional ideas about women in general and nurses specifically. Most, like First Lieutenant Leslie (Indus Arthur), Henry Blake's (Roger Bowen) girlfriend, join in the camp hijinks. Even First Lieutenant Maria "Dish" Snyder (JoAnn Pflug), who has sworn to remain faithful to her husband during her overseas tour, takes one for the team, sleeping with the suicidal dentist "Painless" (John Schuck) the day before she transfers, in an effort to help him regain his sexual confidence. These nurses are minor characters, there to serve as male fantasies both in the film and for the audience.

Not so with Major O'Houlihan, the object of the male surgeons' harassment and ridicule.

Major Margaret O'Houlihan (Sally Kellerman) arrives at the MASH 4077 compound by helicopter in the 1970 Robert Altman film *MASH*.

First seen in a service dress uniform with straight skirt and heels, inappropriate for helicopter travel, her stocking tops and garters are visible as she debarks from the helicopter that delivers her and two other nurses to the region. She appears to be squared-away and also sexual, but her comment, "I like to think of the Army as my home," marks her as regular Army, the antithesis of the other medical personnel in the unit, with the exception of Major Frank Burns (Robert Duvall). Her rigidity and holier-than-thou attitude, coupled with her view of the uptight, Bible thumping hypocrite Burns as the ideal Army officer, make it easy for Pierce (Donald Sutherland) and McIntyre (Elliott Gould) to pick on her mercilessly. Their antics are cruel and sadistic and ultimately lead Margaret to what can only be considered a nervous breakdown. By the last third of the movie, she has become a broken shell, a shadow of her former self—a subordinate character who, despite her importance, has only been onscreen for twelve minutes.

Some scholars have seen *MASH* as having a "violent hatred of women" due to O'Houlihan's humiliation and marginalization, which has been characterized as a celebration of the animal nature of man and the liberation of men from social constraints. Yvonne Tasker explains O'Houlihan's treatment by Pierce and McIntyre, noting: "Female characters who adopt a defiant attitude with respect to the male protagonists are dismissed with aggressive language, threatening behavior, and pranks. Such women are shown to be motivated by a petty commitment to regulations."[16] But her comment doesn't just apply to O'Houlihan. Major Burns is equally obnoxious with his holier-than-thou attitude toward his fellow surgeons—and suffers the same fate as his lover. As field grade officers, they are senior to everyone in camp except Lieutenant Colonel Blake, and by rights should have been "off limits" to such antics. Rigid and self-righteous, they are unable to adapt to their chaotic surroundings and pay a heavy price.

In the final comedy of this chapter, the "R" rated *Chesty Anderson, U.S. Navy* (1976), the action centers on a group of buxom Navy enlisted women whose "stripper" names, like Chesty, Coco, Pucker, and Baby, are an indication that this film takes an irreverent look at women in the Navy. Set in the late 1960s, sexual innuendo and titillation, such as nude women in the shower, constant references to and glimpses of women's breasts, and a semi-nude fight in the barracks, provide an indication that this is an updated, grown-up version of the more innocent 1960s "Beach Blanket" movies, with an unbelievable murder mystery plot to justify the women's antics.

On the way back to the barracks after a night on the town, Baby (Connie Hoffman) is kidnapped under her sister Chesty's (Shari Eubank) nose because she has incriminating photographs of her former Senator boss' sexual proclivities. Chesty reports the kidnapping to her division officer Lieutenant Ambrose (Lynne Guthrie) and her assistant (Betty McGuire), neither of whom believes her due to Baby's previous bad behavior. Onscreen for five minutes, Baby is killed by the "Mob" unbeknownst to Chesty and the other women in the barracks, who go in search of her without success. Despite a number of implausible events and actions on the women's part, eventually they learn of Baby's demise and in turn take down the Mob boss and Senator with the help of an undercover police officer.

As implausible and cliché-ridden as the film is, it does have a few redeeming factors. While the women are portrayed as empty-headed, over-sexed bimbos, several of them do, in fact, exhibit some good qualities. Chesty, onscreen for forty-two minutes, sincerely loves her sister and is determined to avenge her death. Brunette Pucker (Marcie Barker), onscreen for thirty-seven minutes, is feisty and gives her kidnappers serious trouble. Coco (Rosanne Katon) and Tina (Dorrie Thomson), each onscreen for thirty-three minutes, willingly help Chesty with her quest, despite the danger. While these women have had their differences, they are sisters-in-arms and come together in times of crisis.

Pucker (Marcie Barker), Chesty Anderson (Shari Eubank), Tina Marlow (Dorrie Thompson), and Cocoa Daniels (Rosanne Katon), seen left to right, are proud sailors in Atlas Films' *Chesty Anderson, U.S. Navy* (1976)

Disaster Films

The 1960s saw the slow rebirth of a genre popular in the early days of film—the disaster movie. The popularity of disaster films can be attributed to their sense of drama, suspense, and spectacle, although critics decry their formulaic plots and one-dimensional characters. Most feature romantic subplots among many of the characters and emphasize the emotions associated with people working together to cope with an overwhelming catastrophe such as a volcanic explosion, earthquake, sinking of an ocean liner, asteroid hurtling toward the earth, etc. Such events, and the representation of a cross-section of society among the cast, dramatize people's helplessness against the forces of nature.[17] Often the disaster occurs in a remote area where no outside assistance can be expected, forcing the characters to work together despite their interpersonal conflicts.

Irwin Allen's 1961 film *Voyage to the Bottom of the Sea* is an early disaster film that included a female naval officer as a cast member. Barbara Eden is Lieutenant Junior Grade Cathy Connors, the first woman depicted in movies as part of a submarine crew, some fifty years before it was actually authorized. The film's premise is that the Van Allen Radiation Belt that surrounds the earth is on fire, threatening the survival of Earth, and the *Seaview* must save the world by firing a nuclear missile into the Belt to disrupt the fire.

Connors, the Admiral's secretary, is a "girly-girl," wearing a tight straight skirt and high heels throughout the film, despite the submarine's slippery floors and steep ladders. She is first seen dancing the Charleston for some of the enlisted crew, an action disapproved of by the submarine's commanding officer, Captain Lee Crane (Robert Sterling), to whom she is engaged. The pair engages in a significant amount of PDA (public displays of affection) throughout the film, often in front of the crew, and she has planned out her life after her marriage and discharge from the Navy. Despite her frequent lack of military bearing, she does contribute to the submarine's mission, assisting the submarine's corpsman as he treats wounded crewmembers and saving the submarine from a minefield with her quick thinking. Onscreen for twenty-five minutes, Connors is extraneous to the film's central plot, though she does help to humanize the submarine's captain.[18]

The 1970s are considered the Golden Age of disaster films, led by the blockbuster films of Irwin Allen. Their popularity led to the creation of a number of made-for-television disaster films, including *The President's Plane Is Missing* (1973). In a time of increased tensions with China and the looming possibility of war, the President's plane crashes in the California desert. As the nation waits to learn his fate, a power struggle between hawks and doves occurs in Washington, D.C. Two military women are featured in small roles in the film. An uncredited, unnamed Army sergeant (Darlene Conley) has one line, while an unnamed Air Force captain (Barbara Leigh), seen in the terminal at Andrews Air Force Base, has two lines. Onscreen for less than ten seconds each, neither plays a key role in the film.

Military women fare little better in Irwin Allen's 1978 film *The Swarm*, in which Katharine Ross plays Air Force Captain Helena Anderson, a medical doctor stationed at a missile complex attacked by a swarm of killer bees. Initially, she appears to be quick thinking and capable; while she is able to save several airmen from the initial attack, for most of her thirty minutes onscreen, she is subdued, ineffectual, and submissive to bee expert Dr. Brad Crane (Michael Caine), unable to even provide medical assistance to a little boy who goes into cardiac arrest in the hospital. Rather than taking action, she runs for help. Her failure to take action is repeated when Dr. Walter Kim (Henry Fonda) goes into anaphylactic shock and, uncertain of what to do, she runs off to get help from Crane, with whom she has become romantically involved. As they work to save the nearby town from the bees, instead of taking the initiative and helping, she cowers and must be saved by Crane. In all, Ross presents a very disappointing depiction of a female military officer.

Drama

During the 1960s, films that highlighted dramatic events from American's successes in World War II remained popular with movie-goers as they promoted patriotism and America's leadership role in the burgeoning Cold War. Most of these films focused on the heroic exploits of military men with military women frequently excluded. Some films, however, do feature women in roles of varying importance.

Set in an Army hospital in Arizona, *Captain Newman, M.D.* (1963) features a psychiatrist (Gregory Peck) whose job is to determine if/when men suffering from combat fatigue (PTSD) can return to combat during World War II. The film's opening scene includes two Army nurses who are onscreen for less than thirty seconds, and each only speaks one or two lines. The film also features two Army nurses who play larger roles. The first, First Lieutenant Blodgett (Jane Withers), is a "plain Jane" nurse working on Ward 7, the hospital's locked psychiatric ward. Onscreen for eight and a half minutes, she is a good nurse, and the men love her.

But the most important female character is First Lieutenant Francie Corum (Angie Dickinson).

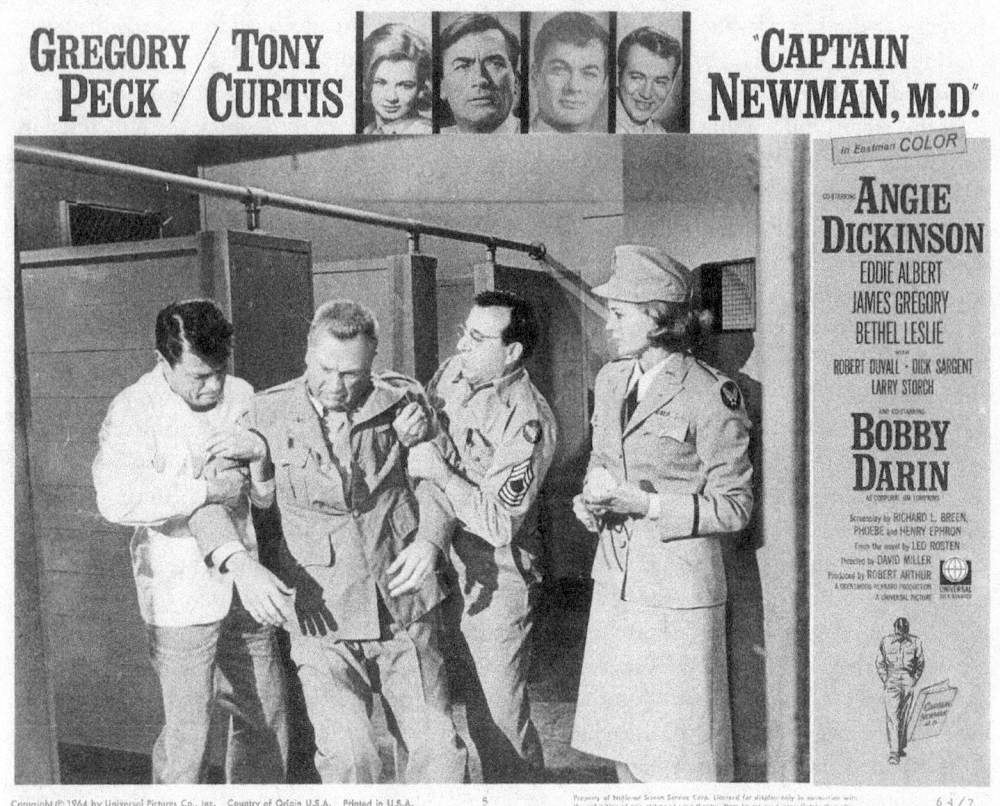

Orderlies Corporal Cavoni (Larry Storch, left) and Sergeant Kopp (Syl Lamont, right) support Colonel Norval Bliss (Eddie Albert) in the hospital psychiatric ward as First Lieutenant Francie Corum (Angie Dickinson) looks on in 1963's *Captain Newman, M.D.*

Onscreen for twenty-two minutes, she is beautiful, feminine, and a very capable nurse who initially resists Newman's efforts to convince her to work on the psychiatric ward. In a scene set in the Officers Club, they have a conversation that today would be considered to be politically incorrect, especially since both are in uniform and drinking heavily. Newman tells her she is a good-looking woman and that "it's important to have a good-looking woman around—big morale factor. It gives a man incentive. You've seen Blodgett—who'd come out [from cowering under a bed] for her? But one look at your legs, and they'd come shooting out right through the mattress." She is not interested in working on the locked ward, but she changes her mind when she sees Newman work with a severely ill patient. Over time, she grows to admire Newman for his compassion and treatment techniques, and as they become closer, Newman confides in her his dilemma in sending the men back into combat. After a night of serious drinking, his attempt at seducing her is foiled when he passes out. Yet the status of their relationship is unclear. After seeing a favorite patient go back to his unit, Newman asks Corum what she is going to do after the war; he has been offered a post at a different psychiatric hospital where he can continue his work and would like her to join him. She replies that she is not staying in the Army; she wants to get married and have babies. When she asks Newman if that's wrong, he tells her it's not.

Throughout the film, Corum is calm and professional, compassionate towards her charges, friendly with the staff, and committed to her job, until she learns of the death of a favorite former

Four. The Times They Are Changing 79

patient, which causes her to cry, "It's all so hopeless, Joe. We cure them, make them strong, and they get killed." He dries her tears and tells her that they had helped the patient find meaning in his life. Their jobs are difficult, but the work is important to the patients and the Army, and she has been a key factor in Newman's success.

Ensign Pulver (1964) is another film in which military nurses play minor but interesting roles. Set in the backwaters of the South Pacific in the waning days of World War II, the crew of the cargo ship USS *Reluctant* suffers under the capricious, Bligh-like whims of its commanding officer, Lieutenant Commander Morton (Burl Ives). The women, who are Army nurses, appear in a few key scenes. Ensign Pulver (Robert Walker, Jr.) first encounters them when their plane, which features an image of Supergirl as its nose art, lands nearby for refueling. The head nurse, an Army major (Kay Medford) who is onscreen for a total of six and a half minutes, is a tough New Yorker who loves her girls. Pulver is enamored with Scotty (Millie Perkins), a sharp, level-headed second lieutenant who is instantly smitten with him, despite his false assertion that he is a Navy doctor. When he confesses his lie to her, she asks why he lied, and he tells her he wanted her to think he was important. She melts, allowing him to kiss her. In the nine minutes she is onscreen, she proves herself to be a smart, capable nurse.

Later in the film, the lifeboat carrying Pulver and Morton is beached on an island where the nurses' airplane has ditched. The other nurses and flight crew have been rescued, with the exception of the pilot, Scotty, and the major, who has sustained a broken arm. When Morton is

Ensign Pulver (Robert Walker, left) meets a group of Army nurses while ashore in the 1964 Joshua Logan film *Ensign Pulver*.

struck with appendicitis, Pulver saves his life by operating under the radio guidance of the ship's doctor (Walter Matthau) and encouragement of Scotty, who is happy to renew their relationship. Despite the lack of equipment on the island, the two nurses provide professional assistance during the surgery, and Morton survives. The group is rescued, but it is unclear what happens to the women, although Pulver tells Morton that he is going to marry Scotty after the war, and he probably will.

Another film that features several military women in various roles, one of whom is key to the story line, is *The Americanization of Emily* (1964). Emily Barham (Julie Andrews) is an uptight, prudish British motor pool driver in World War II London, assigned to Lieutenant Commander Charlie Madison (James Garner), "Dog Robber" and aide to the senior admiral in England. Emily is horrified by the American material excesses, which she sees as a slap in the face of British rationing. When she voices her objections to Madison, saying, "It's just one big Shriner's Convention to you, isn't it?" he accuses her of being a prig. Back in the barracks, she recounts the conversation to her friend Sheila (Liz Frazer) and confesses that she is really a soft touch and "grotesquely sentimental." In fact, she says she falls in love easily and needs to steel herself against love since she's already lost a husband, father, and brother in the war. She constantly criticizes Madison for his lifestyle, and when he arrives at her home armed with two boxes of Hershey bars, she admonishes him, saying, "Don't Americanize me," seeing his gift as an attempt to buy her affection.

Emily is a member of "Sloan's Sluts," who are described as "Preferred Duty. We're the cream of British womanhood. Best pay. Smartest uniforms. Camels and nail varnish and chocolate. Our hunting ground stocked with prize game."[19] The women wear khaki uniforms with brass buttons, khaki cotton stockings, brown heels, a French Marshal's style cap, a Sam Browne belt, and a "USN" pin on their jacket lapels.

As is typical in such situations, Emily falls for Monroe and, out of character for him, he falls for her as well. At their first sexual encounter, they both agree to keep it casual. He tells her he's not her type—not a hero. She replies, "I've had it with heroes. Every man I've loved has died in this war. You can't imagine how attractive that makes you to me." Emily is saved from "fallen Madonna" status when Madison proposes marriage and she accepts. And she is not disappointed when Madison turns out not to be a hero during the D-Day landing.

Interestingly, while Emily is the film's titular character, she is only onscreen for thirty-four minutes, just 30 percent of the film's run time; her friend Sheila, another "Sloan Slut" who understands and enjoys Americans, is onscreen for four and a half minutes. Two other military women have very minor roles in the film. An uncredited U.S. Army nurse has one line, and Judy Carne, who is listed as "nameless broad #2" in the credits and is one of three Sloan's Sluts who sleeps with Lieutenant Commander Buzz Cummings (James Coburn), another "Dog Robber," is onscreen for just over one minute.

The war in the Pacific is the subject of 1965's *In Harm's Way*. Like most films about World War II, the action focuses on male military members, and military nurses are relegated to supporting roles. This film is a nostalgic melodrama that looks at the politics of command, with few visible war heroics and many flawed characters.[20] Patricia Neal plays Lieutenant Junior Grade Maggie Haynes, a nurse and mother hen to her younger co-workers. Onscreen for almost twenty-five minutes, Haynes is older than the other nurses, secure in herself, and her spirit comes through in all of her actions. At a party at the Pearl Harbor Officers Club, she re-introduces herself to Captain "Rock" Torrey (John Wayne), telling him that she took his x-rays earlier. When he says he didn't recognize her out of uniform, she says, "That's all right. I made a special effort not to look like a nurse," perhaps her way of feeling like an attractive woman. Haynes is attracted to Torrey and chases him without hesitation, despite the differences in their ranks, and he lets her

Navy Ensign Jeremiah Torrey (Brandon de Wilde, right) confronts his fiancée, Ensign Annalee Dohrn (Jill Hayworth), in a scene from Paramount's 1965 World War II film *In Harm's Way*.

catch him. Their relationship is almost derailed when she is transferred to the southwest Pacific as part of an offensive, but Torrey, promoted to rear admiral, is in charge of the operation—and is as interested in continuing their relationship as she is. Despite the chaos of war, their relationship thrives. When Torrey loses a leg during a diversionary tactic, Haynes is on the hospital ship transporting him from the region, watching over him, a true nursing angel. She has been a rock for him, and the viewer has the feeling that their relationship will continue after the war ends.

The film's other important female character is Ensign Annalee Dohrn (Jill Hayworth), a vulnerable young nurse whose naïve, flirtatious nature leads to her ultimate downfall. Onscreen for ten minutes, her story is a cautionary tale of some of the hidden dangers for military women and a revelation about the isolation many can feel. Engaged to Torrey's estranged son, she is attracted to Commander Paul Eddington (Kirk Douglas), an older officer with severe psychological problems. Dohrn ignores Haynes' warning about the commander and is raped by Eddington. Later, unable to talk about what happened and following Eddington's denial of responsibility for her pregnancy, the distraught young woman kills herself. A devastated Haynes finds her suicide note and learns of the young woman's heartbreak too late to save her. Dohrn is avenged to some degree when Eddington undertakes a heroic suicide mission and is denied a posthumous medal by Torrey, who is disgusted by his friend's actions.

The final World War II dramatic film that includes a female military officer, again a Navy nurse, is the made-for-television film *The Longest Hundred Miles* (1967), which features Katharine

Ross as Lieutenant Laura Huntington, a nurse stranded in the Philippines after the Japanese invasion. Hiding in a rural mission, her goal is to make it to Sangra Point, one hundred miles away, in order to meet an American plane intended to evacuate her and other nurses believed left behind in the evacuation. Her plans are challenged by a new arrival, Marine Corporal Steve Bennett (Doug McClure), who doesn't believe she will make it because she is a woman. Onscreen for twenty-five minutes, she proves herself to be determined, capable, optimistic, kind, and caring—and willing to stand up for herself. Challenging Bennett's attitude, she asks, "Are you against all officers or just women officers?" When she suggests they dispense with their ranks (she wears an implausibly pristine Navy jumpsuit, complete with rank insignia, and he wears an unrecognizable uniform), he rejects her proposal.

Unlike her character in *The Swarm,* Ross' Huntington ably throws herself into the preparations for the group's departure rather than shrinking into the background. As they work together to repair the dilapidated bus needed to make their way to Sangra Point, he slowly lets his guard down, shifting his focus from saving himself to the group's success. And of course, they fall in love along the way. In the end, Huntington ensures that the mission's children join her on the plane, and Bennett remains behind, vowing to find her after the war.

As previously noted, the Korean War received little attention from filmmakers during the conflict itself and even less ten years after the armistice that ended the fighting was signed. While the number of women in the military had been severely reduced at the end of World War II, military nurses played a key role in MASH units and on Navy hospital ships during the Korean War, yet they were rarely portrayed in film. One film that does feature an Army nurse as a key character is *Iron Angel* (1964). Second Lieutenant Laura Fleming (Margo Woode) is a nurse at the 101st Field Hospital. Discovered unconscious next to a disabled military ambulance (the words "Iron Angel" are stenciled on its front bumper), the men of the patrol who find her are shocked to discover that she is a woman, but quick to want to take advantage of her unconscious state. Because her clothes are wet, they insist that she needs to be undressed and argue over who should do it. The senior man, Sergeant Walsh (Jim Davis), does it, but with his eyes averted. The men repair the truck while her clothing dries, all the while making assumptions about her morals, or lack thereof because of her job, and trying to get peeks at her naked body, which is covered by a blanket.

Once she regains consciousness, she explains that the ambulance also had a driver and patient, both of whom were killed in a North Korean attack. She was trying to return to her unit when the ambulance broke down, and she was unable to fix it, her frustration evident in her comment, "My training never covered this," implying that if she had mechanical training, she would have been able to handle the situation. The sergeant disagrees, telling her, "That's no job for a woman" and that a woman has no business in a combat area. Indignant over his chauvinism, she tells him, "I'm a surgical nurse, trained to operate in combat areas where most men are wounded." She is obviously proud of her abilities and more than willing to do her part in the war.

After the ambulance is repaired, she offers them a ride but tells them their weapons must be left behind (due to Geneva Convention rules that ambulances be weapons-free). They refuse, and she drives off, only to get lost and run out of gas. When the men again find her, the sergeant gives her a jab, noting, "Another fifteen miles, and you would have been giving aid to the gooks." When she asks if he's "down on women in uniform or all women," he answers neither; he just doesn't think women belong in war, to which she responds, "I'm not a woman. Not here. I'm a person who has a skill that's needed. If there were men available, they'd be here. But there aren't. Would you deny hundreds of boys a chance to live just to keep women out of the field?" She continues, saying she loves being a nurse and being able to save lives. When another soldier asks if she'll return to her civilian nursing career after the war, she says she will.

Four. The Times They Are Changing 83

Army Lieutenant Laura Fleming (Margo Woode) is a nurse working in a MASH unit during the Korean War in the Ken Kennedy Production *Iron Angel* (1964).

Fleming proves that she is made of tougher stuff than the men think when she helps the squad confront a North Korean patrol, serving as "bait" to lure them into an ambush. She relents on the "no weapons in the ambulance" rule when the men attempt to complete their mission of taking out a North Korean machine gun nest. She drives the ambulance past the North Koreans as a diversion, allowing the men to take out the enemy. After their success, one of the men comments, "RN stands for Real Nerve." She has become part of the team.

The final film in this chapter depicts a seminal event in the history of women in the military—the admission of women to the U.S. service academies in July 1976. The fictional story of four female plebes at the U.S. Military Academy at West Point is told in the 1978 made-for-television movie *Women at West Point*. New cadets Jennifer Scott (Linda Purl) and Molly Dahl (Leslie Ackerman) are roommates who deal with the trials and tribulations of Cadet Basic Training and plebe year. Many of the male cadets, including the women's company commander J.J. Palfrey (Jameson Parker), are not happy that women are at West Point, and they go out of their way to make them miserable. While Scott quickly becomes discouraged, Dahl's father was a member of the Class of '55, and she wants to make him proud of her, so she remains highly motivated. Unfortunately, she ends up washing out academically at the end of the first semester (after being onscreen for only fourteen minutes), leaving Scott to navigate the remainder of plebe year alone. As Scott suffers through insults from her company commander and hours of walking off demerits, she tells Dahl, "They don't want us here. None of the women will make it through." Scott also contemplates leaving but ultimately decides to stay. When the Company Officer offers to talk to Palfrey for her, she says no, she will work it out herself, an indication that she is indeed maturing and becoming accustomed to military life.

With the help of an upperclassman (Andrew Stevens as Doug Davidson), she weathers a number of difficult situations, proving herself to be a capable teammate. Despite being forbidden to fraternize with upperclassmen, her romance with Davidson blossoms until they are caught by Palfrey. Both are disciplined by the regimental board, and she tells Palfrey she has decided to resign, saying, "It's what you wanted, isn't it?" taking him to task for his attitude toward women. He tells her that West Point's job is to train men to be leaders in war, not serve as a social experiment. When she reports her resignation to the Company Officer, he asks, "What did you expect? One hundred seventy-four years of tradition to just crumble when you walked through the gates?" He knows it has been difficult for all of the women, but he believes the Army is changing, and he hopes she will stay and help make that change, which she does. In her fifty-seven minutes onscreen, she has gone from an insecure girl to a confident young woman, ready to face any challenge thrown at her. While this is a fictional depiction of women's introduction to the U.S. Military Academy, the events depicted closely resemble stories told by the female members of the first few classes at both West Point and the U.S. Naval Academy at Annapolis. Of the one hundred nineteen women who reported to West Point on July 5, 1976, sixty-two women graduated as second lieutenants four years later.[21]

As shown in this chapter, depictions of military women in film evolved during the 1960s and 1970s as they moved from primarily love interests to initial indications that they could be integral parts of a military unit. While most women were discharged from military service at the end of World War II and they were not necessarily seen as important characters in the movies of the time, their numbers began to climb with the end of the Vietnam War and the draft, which left the military service in need of personnel to fill critical positions. As in real life, their representations in film also began to increase in the movies of the 1980s, as will be seen in the next chapter.

Five

Great Expectations
The 1980s

For the U.S. military, the 1980s opened on a somewhat negative note. The American public, still reeling from the disastrous experience in Vietnam, had lost its enthusiasm for military service. This attitude, coupled with the dissolution of the draft in the 1970s, left the service branches in need of personnel to fill positions at all levels and led to questions about American military readiness and the quality of the men in the military. Military manpower shortages were of particular concern, as the Cold War was still in full swing when the decade opened. These manpower concerns were viewed by women already in the military as opportunities. At the beginning of the decade, women comprised less than 10 percent of military personnel, but they felt their continued presence in the military was assured.[1] They believed their contributions in both traditional and non-traditional roles in aviation and aboard ship, coupled with increasing societal pressures to open more non-traditional professions to women, would lead to greater acceptance of their presence in the macho military world and to more challenging positions and equitable pay.

This belief was echoed by the work of DACOWITS, who, in their 1979 report, urged the Department of Defense to eliminate the obstacles to the full utilization of military women.[2] The Defense Officer Personnel Management Act (DOPMA) of 1980 enacted some of the DACOWITS recommendations, creating stable, predictable career paths for all military officers; standardizing personnel management across the services; and creating uniformity in promotions, separation, and retirement.[3]

While DOPMA improved the status of female officers, they still experienced formal and informal discrimination. Combat experience was considered essential for promotion for mid-grade and senior officers, but women were excluded from combat by law. Despite their need for increased personnel, the Army and Air Force were slow to increase their recruitment of women, citing unsubstantiated "gut feelings" about the unsuitability of enlisted women to serve, although these concerns did not extend to female officers. In the 1983 invasion of Grenada, 170 female soldiers, mostly military police, manned checkpoints, guarded prisoners, went on patrols, flew helicopters, and served as aviation crew chiefs. By the end of the decade, the Army had recognized their value and began integrating women into most Army units in support positions.

While the Marine Corps was less than enthusiastic about increasing the number of women within their ranks, citing their exclusively combat mission as reason for the exclusion, by 1985, female Marines were receiving defensive training and participating in field exercises with men. By 1988, three women Marines were assigned as embassy guards.[4] The Air Force began assigning female officers to Titan II missile crews, noting that their accommodations were better suited to co-ed crews. In 1985, Congress required the Air Force to increase female recruiting by 22 percent within three years, due in part to their reluctance to open additional positions to women. By

1989, there were 77,000 women serving in the Air Force, 14 percent of the service's personnel, and 97 percent of Air Force jobs were open to women.[5]

The Navy was more accommodating. In 1980, there were 29,981 women in the Navy, excluding nurses; by 1989, those numbers had increased to 57,847, almost 10 percent of the total naval force.[6] During this time, women were permanently assigned to non-combatant ships, such as tenders and tugboats, and they could receive temporary assignments on combatant vessels such as destroyers and aircraft carriers. The good behavior and excellent work of the women made them popular additions to the ships' crews. By the time the USS *Acadia* (AD-42), a destroyer tender, was dispatched to the Persian Gulf to repair the USS *Stark* (FFG-31) after an Iraqi missile attack in June 1987, a full 25 percent of the crew was female.

Because the Coast Guard falls under the jurisdiction of the Department of Transportation during peacetime, Coast Guard women fared better in terms of job opportunities. By 1980, 28 percent of female officers were serving at sea. By the end of the decade, most vessels had mixed crews as well.

While the services were in the process of revising their policies regarding women in the military, the turmoil was not widely visible to the population at large, especially at the movies. Blockbuster films that were popular in the early 1980s included *The Empire Strikes Back, Raiders of the Lost Ark, E.T., Return of the Jedi,* and *Ghostbusters,* none of which featured military women. In fact, few war films at all were released in the early years of the decade as society continued to recover from the Vietnam War.

While not many military films could be found in theaters, a new phenomenon—the video cassette recorder (VCR)—made older war movies available to a wide audience. The ability to relive the "glory years" of World War II, along with fading memories of the Vietnam War, gradually led to a revival of interest in military stories. By the middle of the decade, American filmmakers began to revisit the war in Vietnam through films like *Platoon, Good Morning, Vietnam,* and *Rambo: First Blood.* None of these films featured female military characters, an omission that helped to keep women's participation in the war invisible. But not all military-related movies produced in the 1980s omitted women from their story. Military women were featured in varying degrees of importance in a number of films, including action/adventure, drama, thrillers, and comedies.

Action Films

In some ways, the action films of the 1980s can be seen as the stepchildren of the big budget action films of the 1970s, such as *Jaws* and *Star Wars*. As previously noted, good action films have well developed characters, a minimal, straightforward plot, and plenty of action. War films fit nicely into this genre. While women tended to play a small role in many earlier war action films, typically as a nurse or as a love interest for the hero, by the early 1980s, the roles military women played in wartime were beginning to expand in literature and film as well as in real life.

One film that showcased women's contributions to the Allies' successful prosecution of World War II is *The Secret War of Jackie's Girls* (1980). Created as a pilot for a potential NBC television series, the film featured Mariette Hartley as Jackie Scott, who raises a fictional squadron of five additional American women fliers for a special project in England.[7] Women were specifically recruited due to a shortage of male pilots, and the women earned commissions as officers in the Women's Army Air Force (WAAF). Because the work was top secret and women were prohibited from serving as military pilots, they were officially listed as nurses.[8]

Five. Great Expectations

The five women come from very different worlds and join the project for different reasons, although they all share a love of flying. Maxine (Dee Wallace) is excited by danger and anxious to get into the action. Casey McCann (Lee Purcell) is a barnstormer who has been flying since the age of thirteen. Patty (Carol Smith) is the rich girl who speaks three languages. Donna (Ann Dusenberry) is nicknamed "Hollywood" because she's a stunt pilot. Zimmy (Tracey Ann Swope) is tough and confident, due in part to her experience as an Alaska bush pilot. While, as in most "women team films," there is initially some competition and cattiness among them, they quickly bond to accomplish their missions. The women train intensively, learning the ins and outs of the aircraft they will be piloting—a revolutionary new helicopter. The women are watched over by Corporal Mabel Wheaton (Marilyn Chris), who runs the house and issues their military uniforms—dark blue skirt and blouse, light blue shirt, man's tie, a brimmed hat, and the caduceus insignia of the nurse corps. Because they will be flying in an open cockpit, they also receive flight gear—khaki flight suit, leather jacket with fur collar, black boots, leather helmet, and goggles.

In the local pub, the women encounter a group of male pilots from the airfield nearby. One tries to pick up Casey using his standard line, and she rebuffs him, trying to talk instead about flying and her experience with a P-38 Mustang. When he doesn't believe her (she *is* dressed as a nurse, after all), she asks him why; he gives her the standard macho answer—that women do not have the equipment to fly high performance aircraft—physical strength, motor skills and emotional stability. She asks how he knows that, and he responds, "Well, honey, if it wasn't true, half of the people in this room would be women." She has obviously touched a nerve—and he has as well. When she rescues him after he is shot down, he learns a valuable lesson, one that will be learned by hundreds of male aviators in the decades to follow—that women are capable of handling an aircraft at least as well as a man.

The Secret World of Jackie's Girls is a work of fiction, although the women portrayed in the film exhibited the heroism, sacrifice, patriotism, and capabilities expected of and exhibited by actual women military officers. While women were hired as aircraft ferry pilots in both Britain and the U.S. during World War II, they could not participate in combat-related missions by law and certainly would never have been permitted to fly a

Mariette Hartley plays Jackie Scott, a pilot who recruits a group of women pilots for a secret project in the 1980 made-for-television move *The Secret World of Jackie's Girls*.

top-secret experimental aircraft. It would be thirty years before women were again permitted to fly military aircraft and almost another forty years before they could fly in combat.

The 1988 made-for-television movie *Dirty Dozen: Fatal Mission,* the fourth and final of the *Dirty Dozen* films, follows the format laid down by the original film—twelve convicts are offered the chance at redemption in exchange for going on a dangerous mission. In this case, it includes a twist—in an attempt to modernize the story, it includes a female military character who can keep up with the boys. Heather Thomas is First Lieutenant Carol Campbell, an American Army intelligence officer stationed on the general staff in England during World War II. She is intelligent, perceptive, attractive, and takes her job seriously. Her facility with languages makes her invaluable to the group's mission, and she is relaxed and self-confident but aloof, remaining separate from them. When the men are shown training for the mission, Campbell is noticeably absent, making one wonder how effective a teammate she will be.

To some extent, Campbell is eye candy. When Wright (Telly Savalas) comments on her appearance, her boss agrees with his assessment but also mentions her competence. Onscreen for only nine minutes, during the mission she is seen somewhat sporadically, once wielding a machine gun and later shooting at a German scout plane; however, she does not do any of the "heavy lifting" associated with the success of the mission.

The Dirty Dozen: Fatal Mission is obviously a work of fiction. While women did serve as military intelligence officers during World War II, they were excluded by law from participating in combat missions. Campbell's actions in the film, however, do present female viewers with the opportunity to imagine themselves in an action role in the military.

The popularity of big budget action films, along with kung-fu movies from Hong Kong like *Enter the Dragon*, led to "knock-offs, rip-offs, and odd follow-ups," resulting in the creation of an entirely new category of action films.[9] Known as "Namsploitation" films, their stories are take-offs on Rambo and other reinterpretations of the Vietnam War, allowing narrow victories for moral and physical heroes against savage enemies who are frequently overseen by evil, deceitful Soviet advisors, either male or female. Most Vietnam veterans in film had been portrayed as wounded heroes, serving as scapegoats for the war's failures. Rambo, the "divine savior," rises to the level of a mythical hero, regaining American masculinity and restoring America to its proper status as the "good guy" by saving the innocent and defeating the unjust.

The year of 1987 found Army Lieutenant John Ransom (Robert Patrick) tangling with a Soviet advisor to the North Vietnamese as he sets out to rescue American POWs during the waning days of the Vietnam war in *Behind Enemy Lines.* Like Rambo, Ransom escapes from captivity, promising to return to save the others. The CIA pairs his squad with Captain Dupré (Lydie Denier) and a unit of South Vietnamese soldiers, who will help them rescue the POWs and a South Vietnamese general. Their first impression of Dupré is one of complete surprise—the captain is a woman. Attired in a khaki shirt, jeans, brown boots, and Indiana Jones felt hat, pistol at her waist, she is confident, capable, beautiful, and definitely in charge. She is also skillful, disassembling and cleaning her M16 while in deep conversation, never once looking at the gun. She also deftly throws a knife in one scene, killing an invading North Vietnamese soldier without missing a beat. During the mission, she wields her M16 capably, coolly holding off the North Vietnamese as Ransom completes the mission. Like most Namsploitation films, the action in *Behind Enemy Lines* is over the top. While Dupré is a capable warrior, neither French nor American military women were permitted to participate in such operations during either nation's operations in Southeast Asia, making this even more of a fantasy film.

The following year saw the release of the Namsploitation film *Hell on the Battleground,* which featured two military women, although neither Karen (Ingrid Vold) nor Donna (Alysa

Davis) have any discernable responsibilities beyond that of "camp wife," functioning as love interests for the two macho heroes. The only indication that they are soldiers is that they wear green T-shirts and camouflage pants; they are only called by their given names, have no discernable rank, and are only onscreen for about seven minutes each. Their conversations as they await the men's return from a mission provide an explanation for the men's dedication to the cause and their own feelings for the difficult men they love, but there is no indication as to why they joined the Army.

Some of these films featured sexy young women as protagonists, typically as guerrillas or CIA agents, obvious knockoffs of *Charlie's Angels*. Occasionally, they also featured military women as well. In *Rescue Force* (1989), Julia Mosteller plays a KGB military advisor to the Palestinian Liberation Organization (PLO), which is holding a CIA agent captive. Onscreen for only three minutes, her character is interesting because she is not a beautiful buxom young woman clad in a skin-tight uniform as is usually seen in these movies; rather, she is middle-aged and wears her experience on her face and in her authoritative attitude. She is one tough cookie, very much the stereotypical Russian female military officer—ruthless, driven, and unattractive, a true "battle axe." She shoots the CIA agent during her interrogation and holds the American ambassador to Israel and his daughter captive as well, taunting them during an interrogation, saying that they will never be rescued. She is incorrect in that assertion—shortly after she leaves the area, the prisoners are freed by a five-woman group of CIA operatives who definitely play into the buxom bimbo trope.

The 1987 direct-to-video animated film *G.I. Joe: The Movie* features three military women as part of the G.I. Joe team. Scarlett (voiced by B. J. Ward) is one of the original team members of the action figures' 1982 reboot.[10] The Army sergeant, whose given name is Shana M. O'Hara, is an intelligence specialist, skilled in martial arts and acrobatics. A graduate of Army Ranger School, the redhead is a weapons expert who favors the use of the XK-1 power crossbow as her personal weapon. Onscreen for just sixty-eight seconds, she is shown in several of the fight scenes against the COBRA commandos but is just a minor player in the film. Corporal Lady Jaye (voiced by Mary Lewis) plays even less of a role, despite her impressive skills as an Airborne Ranger. Onscreen for thirty seconds, she is captured by COBRA commandos, along with a few of the other Joes, and must be rescued by her teammates.

The character Jinx (voiced by Shuko Akune), however, takes center stage in the film's action. A martial arts expert, the Army sergeant, whose true name is classified, is an intelligence expert and mechanical whiz. Onscreen for almost seven minutes, she is front and center in the fight against COBRA, despite her status as a new Joe trainee. Attired in a red skin suit emblazoned with a black dragon on her chest, she is truly a force to be reckoned with. After repairing a broken helicopter, she rallies her fellow trainees to go to the aid of the Joes, helping to save the day.

None of the women wear military uniforms as they battle the members of the evil COBRA organization. And while they are all Army enlisted women, they are all highly educated as well—both Lady Jaye and Jinx are graduates of Bryn Mawr, and Scarlett earned her law degree and passed the bar. While by law none of them could participate in an elite Special Forces unit like the G.I. Joes, they are valued members of the team.

Comedies

While comedies continued to be popular with moviegoers, few featured military women. Two that do feature military women prominently, *Private Benjamin* and *Your Mother Wears*

Combat Boots, are discussed later in this chapter. Two others, with military women in smaller roles, showcase them in less traditional job assignments.

Stripes was the fifth highest grossing film in the U.S. in 1981. It stars Bill Murray as recruit/private John Winger and Harold Ramis as recruit/private Russell Ziskey in a "misfit-makes-good" comedy. In this case, the two join the Army when things are not going well in their lives. They continue their misdeeds, barely squeaking through boot camp, but they gain girlfriends who do not seem to mind their antics. While Stella Hansen (P.J. Soles) and Louise Cooper (Sean Young) are MPs, neither woman has a rank connected with her. Both are simply referred to as "MP," and contrary to the norm in real life, neither is particularly squared away. Their uniforms are sloppy, and their hair is worn down on their shoulders, which is contrary to uniform regulations. They do not seem to report to a supervisor and do not take their duties seriously. They willingly join Winger and Ziskey in their antics, misbehaving their way through Europe. All ends well, of course, when the four rescue their entire platoon from a Russian base and are decorated for their efforts. In real life, all four would have been court-martialed for their numerous offenses. Incomprehensively, this film, which was rated "R," received military cooperation during its filming, while *Private Benjamin* did not.

In the comedy *Spies Like Us* (1985), several military women play minor roles. An uncredited enlisted American Air Force woman (Sally Anlauf) utters three sentences in the ten seconds she is onscreen in an operations center. Of more interest, but almost as little importance, are the two Russian soldiers (Svetlana Plotnikova and Vanessa Angel as unnamed Russian rocket crew members). They are part of an ICBM crew whose missile is hijacked by inept American spies Austin Milbarge (Dan Aykroyd) and Emmett Fitz-Hume (Chevy Chase). Onscreen for a little more than three minutes each, they first attempt to stop the hijackers, but ultimately help them destroy the weapon.

MP Stella Hansen (PJ Soles) handcuffs Private John Winer (Bill Murray) in the 1981 comedy *Stripes*.

Drama

Dramatic films can also feature lots of action, making them popular for military related films. Many of the 1980s dramas feature military women in their casts, as both major and minor characters.

The opening year of the decade saw a World War II film on the small screen in *Ike: The War Years,* which starred Lee Remick as Kay Summersby, General Dwight D. Eisenhower's British driver during the war. At the beginning of their relationship, like Emily Barham, Summersby is abrupt and abrasive, unimpressed by Ike's comments about her red nail polish and British-style salutes. She gives as good as she gets, reminding him on several occasions that he cannot really boss her around, because "I am British and a civilian and not subject to [your] orders."[11]

Summersby is the quintessential British aristocrat—proud, practical, resourceful, and calm in the face of adversity. She wisely takes Ike into a London bomb shelter during an air raid, despite his objections; she is also calm and quick acting when her ship is torpedoed on its way to North Africa and when strafed by a Messerschmitt on the battlefield. She is a woman in control of herself and her emotions, despite her obvious feelings for Eisenhower.

In addition to Remick, who is on screen for more than half of the film, there are two other military women with minor parts. Sybil Bryan (Julia Mackenzie) is Kay's friend and fellow driver, while Wren singer (Patricia Michael) and her male partner provide the entertainment for a New Year's Eve gathering. Neither is one the screen for more than two minutes.

Too Young the Hero (1988) is another made-for-television biographical film set during World War II, featuring Ricky Schroder as twelve-year-old sailor Calvin Graham. The film features one female naval officer, listed as Lieutenant Cindy (Penny Hayes) in the credits. Onscreen for twenty-two seconds, the lieutenant junior grade gives Graham a bus ticket and set of sealed orders when he turns himself in at a Houston Navy recruiting station for missing his ship's movement after his grandmother's funeral. While she only speaks a few lines, she appears to be efficient and professional.

The rise of feminism and women's studies in the 1980s and 1990s led to an increase in the publication of women's war memoirs. Prior to this time, stories of women who survived internment were seen as threatening the public memory of World War II, a memory that included the work of Rosie the Riveter, who happily returned to the home at the war's end.[12] No one wanted to think about women being mistreated in captivity, including theatrical filmmakers. The made-for-television movie *Women of Valor* (1986), however, tells the story of American Army nurses who were part of the Bataan Death March, incarcerated in a POW camp for almost three years, using a series of flashbacks.

First Lieutenant Jessup (Susan Sarandon) is the senior officer of the group, and it is up to her to organize the nurses and make sure that the patients are adequately cared for. She is secretly married to an Army intelligence officer and plans to reveal her marriage once her husband's tour is completed. Had the Army learned of it, she would have been discharged by law and returned to the States without him. She is tough, determined, and capable, a true leader who takes her responsibilities seriously. Second Lieutenant Gail Polson (Suzanne Lederer) is self-absorbed, worrying more about her appearance than her duties to her patients. She is onscreen the least of the women, abandoning her patients to escape the advancing Japanese on a bus with other refugees instead of helping evacuate the patients to safety. Second Lieutenant Katherine R. "Gracie" Grace (Valerie Mahaffey) is high strung and nervous before the Japanese attack and seems to come unhinged during their ordeal. Second Lieutenant Helen Prescott (Alberta Watson) is an excellent nurse who courageously protects her wounded charges, both during the raid and in the temporary field hospital that is set up in the jungle.

The four friends are stationed at Camp Pershing, Luzon in December 1941, a paradise that is destroyed in a Japanese raid. The nurses evacuate patients to the jungle but are soon captured by the Japanese, who march the remaining prisoners to a POW camp. Along the route, Prescott is raped and wants to die, but Jessup says they will help each other survive. At the POW camp, they are housed with other women prisoners who introduce them to the camp's routine. Forced to farm the vegetable patch that supplies the camp guards with food, they get to eat the meager remains. Hunger and privation in captivity tend to bring out the worst in people, but the women work together in order to survive, providing care and comfort to those around them.

The film is dedicated to the 104 Army and Navy nurses incarcerated by the Japanese who were awarded the Bronze Star for their heroism, but not the "V" for valor that many male prisoners of war were awarded. While it is a fictitious account of the incarceration experience, the film does highlight the extraordinarily heroic efforts of those nurses who were incarcerated as prisoners of war in a more realistic depiction than previous war films.

Intimate Strangers (1986) tells the story of an Army nurse who served in country during the waning days of the Vietnam War. First Lieutenant Sally Bierston (Teri Garr) is a surgical nurse married to Jeff, an Army surgeon (Stacy Keach). Separated in the chaos as they attempt to evacuate Saigon, he escapes, but she is left behind. Ten years later, she arrives in the Philippines with a group of Vietnamese refugees, following their escape from a Vietnamese POW camp. Reunited with her husband, who searched for her for years and has not remarried, she attempts to navigate civilian life while experiencing culture shock and the flashbacks associated with PTSD. Despite her husband's efforts and patience, their marriage begins disintegrating. She is unable to have sex with him, the result of her experiences in captivity, which included bearing a child as the result of her rape by prison guards. Idealistic despite the horrors she experienced, she believes Jeff has sold out, treating wealthy clients rather than using his surgical skills. As her PTSD intensifies, she is hospitalized with little effect. She volunteers at a local free clinic upon her release and demands a separation from her husband so she has time to build something of her own. He doesn't give up on their marriage, however, leaving his practice to join her in the clinic, with the implication that they live happily ever after.

While critics believed Garr was miscast in this made-for-television movie and the film was not well received, it is important because it is the first to recognize PTSD in the military women who served in Vietnam. It addresses some of the major issues associated with PTSD, including the lack of intimacy, tenderness, and playfulness associated with a healthy relationship and shows sex as a trigger for memories of trauma,[13] which are not typically addressed in early films that depict the effects of PTSD. That said, its simplified view of solutions for PTSD sufferers does a disservice to those who suffer from the disorder.

While no one specific film genre clearly defines the Cold War, dramas are very well suited to serve as allegories of the struggles between the Communist Bloc and Western allies. In Cold War dramas, communists are seen as barbaric, monolithic thinkers intent on destroying family, religion, and personal freedom; westerners are heroic figures defending democracy. Most Cold War dramas feature spies or corrupt military men bent on world domination, but some do include depictions of female military characters, typically in minor roles.

The Air Force Fighter Weapons School at Nellis Air Force Base, Nevada is the setting for *Red Flag: The Ultimate Game* (1981). While the film's action centers on the Air Force pilots who are doing advanced fighter training, there are three women portrayed in the film, although none play an important role. An uncredited enlisted woman on the flight line, onscreen for just five seconds, speaks one line, while a second, also with one line, is onscreen for forty-seven seconds. The third woman, Lieutenant Linda Fowles (Joan-Carol O'Connell), plays a slightly larger role, although she is not integral to the film's plot, serving as a love interest for Major Phil Clark (William Devane). Onscreen for two and a half minutes, she is the electronics maintenance officer, tasked with keeping the electronics systems of various types of aircraft in top operating condition.

In *Firefox* (1982), Clint Eastwood stars as retired Major Mitchell Gant, a Vietnam veteran with PTSD who is tasked with stealing a Russian stealth aircraft. While military women are visible as background characters at several points in the film, the action revolves around Gant. The film does feature a female Navy third class petty officer, an Air Traffic Controller who works the flight simulator as Gant trains for his mission. Onscreen for less than a minute, her four lines show her to be a competent professional, thoroughly in control of the situation.

WarGames, the fifth highest grossing U.S. film of 1983, also features a number of military personnel as background characters, working in NORAD's operations center. Only one military woman, Airman Fields (Frankie Hall), has a speaking part, which lasts for about one minute. In a calm, clear voice, as the WOPR (War Operations Plan Response) computer starts World War III, she announces, "Radar reports two unknown tracks are penetrating the Alaska air defense zone," followed by "General, DBS is tracking 300 inbound ICBMs." Finally, when the system is at DEFCON 1, all eyes are on Fields as she provides a countdown every ten seconds, starting with one minute thirty seconds. The final ten seconds end with the word "impact." With every pronouncement, she is calm and dispassionate, despite the potential devastation her words convey. She is a true professional who takes her job seriously, as would be expected of a military member, despite her very junior status.

A Cold War drama that features a military woman as a protagonist is *Remo Williams: The Adventure Begins* (1985). Fred Ward is Remo, a street-smart former cop who investigates a crooked government contractor. Kate Mulgrew is Army Major Rayner Fleming, who tries to obtain information on cost overruns associated with the same program. Fleming is all business; when a male lieutenant flirts with her, inappropriate given the difference in their ranks, she brushes him off. She takes her work very seriously, perhaps too much so. When the general tells her that she can relax her attitude because it makes no difference to him that she is a woman, she retorts, "That's good news, sir. It makes no difference to me that you're a man." He is not amused.

While Fleming is extremely professional, she is clueless when it comes to interpersonal interactions and initially clashes with Williams. After an attempt on their lives, Williams and Fleming race through the woods to escape the contractor's hired guns, which is difficult going in the straight skirt and high heels she is wearing. While Fleming has relaxed a bit by the end of the film, she is still stiff and focused, the stereotypical woman officer married to her job and lacking in social skills and graces.

While many movies about the Vietnam War focus on medical personnel or aviators, the most popular ones focus on the grunts, the enlisted men on the ground at the center of the action. These grunts are not typically portrayed in heroic terms as they had been in previous war films, but rather as would-be heroes whose quest for honor often falls short.[14] In many ways, the grunt is a victim of war, succumbing to an amoral landscape, overwhelmed and alienated by the insanity of his experiences. *Full Metal Jacket* (1987) is one such film. Critically acclaimed, it has received significant attention from scholars who comment about the dehumanization experienced by recruits as they are molded into Marines at boot camp. This process can be seen as a reconstruction of their identity, which rejects anything infantile, female, or homoerotic.[15] It is Gunnery Sergeant Hart's (R. Lee Ermey) job to prepare these young men for what will be required of them in Vietnam, which he does using humiliation and intimidation, resulting in his murder at the hands of one of his recruits.

Perhaps the most discussed and analyzed scenes from the film involve the North Vietnamese sniper. As the members of Hotel 25 Company work their way through Hué, they are pinned down by a sniper who picks them off, one by one. The remaining men search for the sniper and have no idea that it is actually a woman until they enter the room from which she has been firing. Surprised by her gender, Joker (Matthew Modine) is the first to discover her and slow to react. She hears his gun jam and fires at him and is in turn is shot by Animal (Adam Baldwin). As she lies on the floor, begging the men to kill her, they deliberate her fate. They are excited, Animal gleefully declaring, "I fucking blew her away." They do not seem embarrassed that the sniper is female but are confused instead, uncertain about her fate. Animal wants to leave her to the rats, but Joker doesn't want her to suffer. He hesitates, but ultimately does the humane thing by shooting her, a sane act in an insane situation.

The sniper (Ngoc Le) is a fierce warrior, dressed in black, with the Viet Cong black and white checkered scarf around her neck and her long black hair in braids. Onscreen for only three minutes, she plays a pivotal role in the lives of all those who encounter her. Obviously, several die by her hand. In killing her, Joker's resistance to assimilation into the war's insanity is finally eroded.

Male identity is a central theme in the film, and feminist scholars have seen the female sniper as an instrument of castration.[16] During boot camp, Gunny Hart tells the recruits they must give their rifles a girl's name, "because this is the only pussy you're going to get." Ultimately, Joker's rifle betrays him, jamming as he confronts the sniper as if it is as surprised at her gender as he is. While the female sniper does call into question war as a strictly masculine enterprise, she also reflects reality. Vietnamese women joined the Viet Cong, defending and giving their lives for their country.[17]

Another film about ground troops just trying to survive in Vietnam that featured female Viet Cong soldiers is *The Iron Triangle* (1989). The film portrays Vietnam as a brutal, cruel place of death and mutilation, with no limits placed on violence and aggression.[18] Some 60,000 women served in combat with the Viet Cong during the war, primarily along the Ho Chi Minh Trail. In this film, women play an important role in the war effort. While none serve in a leadership role, they fight and die beside the men. Only one woman has a small featured role, however. Lai (Sophie Trang) is a soldier in the G.I. Jane mold. Tough, capable, devoted to the North Vietnamese cause, and a fierce fighter, she loves Ho, the platoon leader. On screen for less than two minutes, after a Viet Cong village is destroyed and Ho is killed in a firefight, she approaches the South Vietnamese leader, grenade in hand. Captain Duc (François Chau) shoots her, but as she dies, the grenade explodes, killing Duc and exacting her revenge, a true soldier for the cause.

More than a decade before *G.I. Jane* focused attention on the idea of women as Special Forces team members, the film *Opposing Force* (*Hellcamp*) (1986) gave moviegoers a glimpse at the training aviators and Special Forces operators experience in SERE (Survival, Evasion, Resistance and Escape) training. Among the ten participants is one woman—Air Force First Lieutenant Casey (Lisa Eichhorn). Casey is a beautiful, tough as nails pilot who is portrayed as a sex object from her first scene, the camera showing her high-heeled shoe crushing a cigarette, then panning up her stockinged leg, across her body, and up to her head. In a meeting with her commanding general, she tells him she wants high reconnaissance training and to work in the field. He reminds her that even if she passes SERE training, she will not receive such a posting because women are legally banned from combat. She replies that she wants to be ready when the law changes and expects no special treatment.

When the group is dropped into the jungle, her assigned partner heads off on his own, so she suggests to Major Logan (Tom Skerritt), who injured his leg in the jump, that they pair up, commenting, "You've got a limp and I've got tits. Those aren't great things to have in the military." Despite their handicaps, they are the last to be captured. In the camp, she receives no special

Air Force Lieutenant Casey (Lisa Eichhorn, second from left) waits with her fellow SERE team members in the 1986 film *Opposing Force (Hellcamp)*.

treatment. When the prisoners are told to strip, Logan objects because a woman is present. He is beaten for his chivalry. And she strips.

From the beginning, it is obvious that the film is rife with sexism and sexual innuendo. The film poster features Eichhorn in tight khaki shorts and bare midriff looking over her shoulder, hands tied above her head, while men in bamboo cages and their camouflage-clad guards look on, titillation designed to encourage viewers. The poster proclaims, "In hell camp, you are an animal … to be broken, lied to, humiliated and violated," all of which occur in the film.

And she bears the brunt of it. During an interrogation, the camp's executive officer calls her a "split tail" and a bitch to her face, lifting the hem of her robe to show the guards her naked backside. The camp's commanding officer, Colonel Becker, complains that he doesn't know how to test her because she's different from men, although like the men, when she is water-boarded, she does not break or ask to go home. In the film's most dramatic scene, Becker rapes Casey, afterwards telling her that's what would happen if she were taken prisoner—and that after it happened a few more times, she would not be afraid anymore. She endures without comment. Interestingly, the film focuses on the reactions of the men to the rape, not of the woman who is raped. When Logan tries to talk to her about it, Casey says it doesn't matter. He is shocked by her response, asking, "If it doesn't matter, what does?" Ultimately, she exacts her revenge, killing Becker before he can kill her.

In the film's final scene, Casey is back in the general's office. He thanks her for helping keep the "incident" secret, saying he hopes she'll stay in the Air Force since the service is changing. She says no and walks away. The Air Force has failed her, destroying her dreams, but she survived and will carry on. While this film can be classified as sexploitation, at the time (and still today), the services were concerned about the possibility of sexual improprieties occurring in such situations, requiring those women who did attend SERE training to do so in pairs. This requirement is still in force.

One woman who was not failed by the military in real life was Concetta Hassan, whose military experience was told in the CBS made-for-television movie *A Time to Triumph* (1986). Hassan (Patty Duke) enlists in the Army at age thirty-two in order to support her family after her husband suffers a heart attack. Set in the 1970s, the film does not show overt discrimination against Hassan, except by one patronizing flight instructor, although it certainly was present in Army aviation at the time.

Her boot camp experience is challenging and eye-opening, especially given that her peers are teenagers and she lives in fear of a twenty-three-year old DI who thinks she's John Wayne. Sergeant First Class Martin (Denise Mickelbury) is a strong, no nonsense black woman totally devoted to the Army. In her opinion, there is only one way to do everything—the Army way. She takes umbrage with the photo of Hassan's three children that she keeps in her locker, perhaps in part because she sacrificed having a family for her career.[19] While she seems to be particularly hard on Hassan, Martin actually encourages her and celebrates her success.

After graduation, Hassan is accepted as the only woman at flight school. The training places significant stress on her family, causing her to doubt her decision, but in the end, her husband encourages her to finish the training. The film ends with her appointment as a warrant officer and earning her wings. Despite all the difficulties she encountered along the way, Hassan, like many other military women, persevered, earning her wings and contributing to the Army's mission.[20]

First Lieutenant Christine Newhouse (Marete Van Camp) is a woman whose Army career did not go as well as Hassan's. The ultimate "girls gone bad film," *Lethal Woman* (1989) is a fictional account of a young Army officer stationed in a combat unit where her presence is not welcome. Discussing their chauvinistic commanding officer with a female friend, Christine announces, "We're in the Army, and we're here to stay." When General Maxim (James Luisi) tells her that she is undermining the men's self-confidence by her success and suggests she back off, she refuses. Enraged, the general rapes her to teach her a lesson. She reports the

Warrant Officer Concetta Hassan (Patty Duke) goes from housewife to Army helicopter pilot in the 1986 made-for-television movie *A Time to Triumph*.

rape, and during court-martial proceedings, the general is found not guilty by an all-male board, and her career is ruined.

Sometime later, the Army has a problem—every man involved in the court martial has disappeared. It turns out that Christine, now called Diana, has gone off the deep end. Betrayed by the Army she loved, she has set up a private hunting ground, where the prey consists of men who abuse women. In the ultimate revenge fantasy, the men are wined and dined by beautiful women, then hunted and killed like animals. She is ultimately killed by her second in command.

While the issues of sexual harassment and rape are serious ones in all branches, the services have been slow to take action so often that many women have not reported assaults. In many cases, their reporting authority is a man, and the tendency is for the men to close ranks and protect their own. As more women are placed in positions of authority and the services revise their policies, cases are being dealt with in a more expeditious and satisfactory manner. Unfortunately, there is still a long way to go to address the root causes of sexual harassment and assault and resolve the issue permanently.

Romance

As was noted in the discussion of action films, the 1980s saw the introduction of American films about Vietnam. Few of these films feature military women, with the occasional exception of military nurses, who played key roles during the war.[21] Nurses were often the first line of treatment of the wounded and were frequently required to be tough—hospitals routinely came under fire, and nurses had to exhibit an outwardly calm demeanor despite their own fear. They frequently served as stand-in wives, girlfriends, and mothers of their patients, increasing morale among the troops. Nurses received combat pay and earned combat decorations like their male peers. Most did not consider themselves to be heroes—they were there to support the troops and the war effort. They did not receive much attention from the press, their invisibility due in large part to the fact that Americans did not want to see women in the battle zone, and they experienced the same rejection as men did upon their return to the U.S.

Navy doctor Don Jardian (Ken Wahl) and Navy nurse Deborah Solomon (Cheryl Ladd), seen here in a publicity still, fall in love during the Vietnam War film *Purple Hearts* (1984).

The 1984 film *Purple Hearts* depicts the experiences of Navy nurses Lieutenant Junior Grade Deborah Solomon (Cheryl Ladd) and Lieutenant Junior Grade Hallaway (Annie McEnroe), who are stationed in the hospital in Da Nang. Solomon is attracted to Lieutenant Don Jardian (Ken Wahl), a brash, narcissistic surgeon assigned to a field hospital until he propositions her. She lets him know that she is not easy, which is naturally followed by Jardian saying, "Don't you like men?"

Onscreen for thirty-two minutes, Solomon is all about service and compassion, which allows her to practice medicine for the right reasons. She becomes attached to her patients, doing whatever is required to help them, but the loss of her pilot fiancé keeps her from committing to another relationship. They meet again several times and recognize their mutual attraction, but Solomon flees in the face of Jardian's declaration of love. They are ultimately reunited after completing their service commitments.

While Deborah Solomon is all about doing what is right for her patients no matter the cost, her best friend Hallaway is a wild child, always ready for fun. She is also devoted to her patients and friends but is more of a free spirit than Solomon. A total flirt, her behavior is a reaction to the stress and danger of her job, and she adopts the attitude many others had in country—live for today, for tomorrow you may die. Onscreen for only two minutes, she is killed in a hospital bombing while tending to her patients.

Thrillers

As previously noted, thrillers are a popular film genre. Dominated by suspense, linear plots, and narrative digression, they often feature flimsy plot lines and little character development.[22] Despite their apparent shallowness, their popularity remains high in part because of the familiarity of their plot which is supplemented by viewer expectations and anticipation of what they will see. While most war films do not neatly fit into the thriller genre, at least two late-1980s thrillers featured military women as key figures in their storylines.

The first thriller, a murder mystery, is *The Presidio* (1988), whose plot centers on the murder of an enlisted female Army MP named Patti Jean Lynch (Jenette Goldstein) on the grounds of San Francisco's Presidio. Seen for only three and a half minutes at the beginning of the film, Lynch is a capable, no-nonsense soldier who insists on pulling her weight during her night patrol shift. The only woman in her squad, when one of her peers offers to "keep her warm" while she is on patrol, she brushes him off good naturedly.

It is apparent that the members of the squad care about her. The men in the office encourage her to stay in contact while on patrol, to which she retorts, "Yes, Daddy." Unfortunately, she does not listen to their admonitions and is murdered. When her former partner (Mark Harmon), now a San Francisco police officer, learns of her murder, he joins the investigation, noting she was a good cop whose death needs to be avenged, which it is, of course.

The opening of the MP MOS 31B to women in 1975 allowed women to serve on equal footing with their male counterparts, which many did in Grenada and Panama. The depiction of Lynch represents some of the challenges experienced by woman MPs as they navigate the macho world of the Army and police work. In this case, Lynch handles it all with grace, humor, and by being good at her job.

The Package (1989) features two female Army officers in lesser roles. Lieutenant Colonel Eileen Gallagher (Joanna Cassidy) is the ex-wife of Top Sergeant Johnny Gallagher (Gene Hackman), who is accused of murder. Smart and capable, Gallagher trusts him and uses her position

Gene Hackman (as Army Master Sergeant Johnny Gallagher, left), Joanna Cassidy (as Army Lieutenant Colonel Eileen Gallagher, center), and Tommy Lee Jones (as Thomas Boyette) in a publicity still for the Orion Pictures 1989 thriller *The Package*. The photo is printed in reverse, as evidenced by the ribbons being worn on the right side of their uniform jackets rather than on the correct left side.

at military personnel headquarters, along with the help of a friend, First Lieutenant Ruth Butler (Pam Grier), to uncover the true identity of the murderer as well as a larger conspiracy that endangers national security.

Onscreen for just two minutes, Butler digs through classified files despite the danger of being discovered, and she is killed as the result of the information she uncovers. Gallagher and Butler both recognize the danger to themselves and their careers, but their loyalty to the Army and their friendship make the risks worth taking.

Boot Camp

Boot camp, officially recruit training or basic training, is a liminal experience in the life of enlisted military personnel. It is intended to prepare a group of young individuals, typically eighteen to twenty-one years of age, for all aspects of military service—the physical, mental, emotional, and occupational—and serve as a homogenizing experience, acclimating them to military life. A rite of passage, within a short period of time, recruits evolve from undisciplined youths into focused adults, ready to take up the challenges of a military career.[23] Recruits are overseen by drill instructors (DIs), who must be at least an E-5 and attend Drill Instructor School to learn the ins and outs of recruit training. DIs must not show weakness around recruits, and while they frequently shout at recruits and call them names, their anger is a carefully calculated act designed to motivate recruits. There is usually a team of three or four DIs assigned to each recruit class of approximately sixty to eighty members, under the supervision of an officer. While most recruit training is now co-ed, that wasn't the case throughout the 1980s.[24] It was in these turbulent times that boot camp became the central focus of four films that prominently featured military women.

The 1980 film *Private Benjamin* presents boot camp in a comedic light. The sixth highest grossing film of 1980, it tells the story of Judy Benjamin (Goldie Hawn), a gullible, naïve young woman who enlists in the Army after the death of her husband on their wedding night.[25] Misunderstanding what enlistment means, she joins the Army "with the condos, private rooms, and saunas." Beginning with her arrival at boot camp, she is a fish out of water. Petite, feminine, wealthy, and self-absorbed, she is immediately seen as a screw-up, an unruly woman who alienates her fellow trainees by her ineptitude and does not respect or follow Army rules and regulations.[26]

Benjamin immediately runs afoul of Company Commander Captain Doreen Lewis (Eileen Brennan).[27] Lewis is a squared-away career officer, tough and determined, single mindedly devoted to the Army, a caricature of misplaced female authority obsessed with being a good soldier. She is tough and so determined to get rid of the "screw-up" that she calls Benjamin's parents to come and get her. In real life, Benjamin would have been involuntarily discharged from the Army.

Private Judy Benjamin (Goldie Hawn, left) and Private Mary Lou Glass (Mary Kay Place) during war game maneuvers in the 1980 comedy *Private Benjamin*.

Benjamin eventually has an epiphany, deciding to make the Army her family, and throws herself into her training. At graduation, Benjamin earns a position as the only woman on the prestigious paratrooper team, only to learn that the colonel in charge is interested in her sexually. Since paratroopers are operational military units, in real life, the only way Benjamin could join the team would have been as a member of the support staff.

Benjamin secures a transfer to Supreme Headquarters Allied Powers Europe (SHAPE) in Belgium, where she proves herself a capable procurement clerk. She also once again encounters Captain Lewis, who is still unable to forgive Benjamin for her success. Unlike Lewis, Benjamin hasn't been masculinized by the Army; rather, she has adapted and uses her abilities to succeed. Benjamin has matured and can take care of herself. In the end, her strength of character, maturity, and discipline allow her to walk away from the Army and her domineering fiancé, deciding that she doesn't need either to define her. Lewis does not fare as well. Despite her competence as an officer, she is still bitter at being bested by Benjamin. She has become a lesbian, a stereotype of the "butch" military woman who is so insecure of her own position that she must crush the feminine military woman in order to assert her own superiority.[28]

Another comedy about early military training immediately following boot camp that requires the suspension of belief is the 1989 made-for-television movie *Your Mother Wears Combat Boots,* starring Barbara Eden as Brenda Anderson, a mother who is so determined to keep her son from becoming an Army Ranger that she impersonates a female deserter named Susan Zimmel and follows him to Basic Airborne training. She is ill prepared and unsuited for Army training and is immediately labeled a "screw up." No one questions her lack of understanding of basic military terminology and protocol—or her age. She is the ultimate helicopter parent, and her son is horrified by her actions. Ultimately, all ends well as he earns his Airborne wings and she returns to civilian status.

Like other boot camp movies, this film stresses the personal growth of the characters and importance of teamwork, a key to success in a military environment. Airborne training is coeducational, and there are several other female characters important to "Zimmel's" success in the film. Carla (Maria O'Brien), her roommate, initially wants nothing to do with her; she is highly motivated to complete training and doesn't let anything stand in her way. Both eventually agree to help Zimmel, primarily because it is in their own best interest. Edie Winchell (Meagan Fay) is a tough chick from South Boston—the quintessential tough girl with a heart of gold. Specialist Mononaghee (Conchata Ferrel) is a wise-cracking overweight administrator, offering a sarcastic quip at Zimmel's every misstep. At the film's end, she packs up her desk, off to the "Army's fat farm."

While *Your Mother Wears Combat Boots* is a piece of harmless fluff, it is difficult to believe. Given Eden's age and total lack of military discipline, in real life, all someone would have had to do to put an end to her (and everyone else's) misery would be to check her service record or even ask to see her military identification card. But that would have put an end to the hilarity and good-natured fun of the film.

While the previous films present boot camp in a comedic light, the 1981 ABC made-for-television movie *She's in the Army Now* takes a more realistic look at women in basic training, although a quick perusal of the movie's packaging seems to indicate otherwise, as it warns, "Beware Private Benjamin! SHE'S IN THE ARMY NOW is one of the funniest explorations of the armed services *ever*." It goes on to note that it features "an exceptionally attractive and talented cast" and takes "a refreshing look at barracks life and the new breed of 'G.I. Joans' who have changed American Army life forever." It does host an outstanding cast, many of whom have gone on to have successful film careers.

The film explores the experiences of five young women who have all joined the Army for different reasons. Squad Leader Cass Donner (Kathleen Quinlan), a college graduate, serves as the film's narrator, explaining how events and people initially appeared and how they grew and changed over time.[29] Rita Jennings (Jamie Lee Curtis) is a tough city girl with an outstanding arrest warrant, obviously in need of discipline. Sylvie Knoll (Melanie Griffith) is a divorced "white trash" woman with a five-year-old child who joins the Army to escape from a bully ex-husband and to provide for her daughter. Yvette Rios (Julie Carmen) is street-tough and smart but in need of direction. Virginia Marshall (Susan Blanchard) is a deeply troubled young woman who joins the Army because it provides structure in her chaotic life. Their DI, Sergeant Reed (Janet Maclachlan), is a new DI, eager to make a name for herself. Donner sees her as being over-motivated, "a regular General George Patton." Reed seems to want to have the best company rather than caring for the women under her charge.

These women are closer to real women than those depicted in other boot camp films. They experience the typical disagreements and adjustment problems encountered by all individuals new to the military, eventually coming together to support each other through a variety of problems. Despite a series of outrageous antics, Sergeant Reed defends them to the base commander, emphasizing that their antics were actually a show of comradery in an emergency, sacrificing her goals for the good of her troops. The film ends with the women's company marching in ranks while Reed calls cadence, which includes the lines "Anything a guy can do/3rd Platoon can do it, too," an indication that they will go on to successful military careers.

As previously noted, officer training for the U.S. military occurs in several ways—through the U.S. Service Academies, ROTC, or OCS/OTS. Naval aviators receive basic officer training at Aviation Officer Candidate School (AOCS), which women began attending in 1976. As with boot camp, officer candidates receive training on all aspects of military service, with additional emphasis on leadership.

The 1982 film *An Officer and a Gentleman* is the coming of age story of a blue collar loner (Richard Gere as Mayo) who finds his purpose in life as a naval aviator through the tough love provided by DI Gunnery Sergeant Emil Foley, USMC (Louis Gossett, Jr., in his Academy Award winning role). The third highest grossing film of 1982, much scholarship has been devoted to the roles of Mayo, Foley, Paula (Debra Winger), and AOC Sid Worley (David Keith), but little attention has been paid to the three female aviation officer candidates in the class, despite the fact that women had been attending AOCS since 1976.[30] While one unnamed woman quickly drops out and a second is seen only in group shots and is not credited for her performance, the third actually portrays an accurate representation of a woman in flight training.

Lisa Eilbacher portrays Casey "Cigar" Seeger. Cute, feminine, and plucky, she also matures through her AOCS training. She's a peripheral character, onscreen for only ten minutes, but she is well liked by her peers and has no trouble fitting in. Early in the film, she is unable to scale the obstacle course wall. When she starts to cry, Foley taunts her, asking, "Do you really want to be a man, Cigar?" finally telling her to walk around it, which she does. Her nickname "Cigar" is a double entendre—while the pronunciation of her surname sounds similar to cigar, the cigar can also be seen as a reference to the male penis he thinks she is seeking.

Despite her failure on the obstacle course, Seeger is a capable officer candidate. In the Dilbert Dunker scene, where candidates are dumped upside down, in full flight gear, into a pool and are expected to release their harness and escape, she outperforms everyone else. While Foley tells her well done, he also reminds her, "You still gotta get over that wall." She is determined to graduate, and in the scene where Mayo is doing push-ups while Foley sprays him with a hose, Seeger can be seen in the background, doing chin-ups to build her upper body strength. Her hard work ultimately pays off, and because she persevered, she earns her commission.

As the 1980s drew to a close, American military women saw increased opportunities to contribute to the defense of their nation. The films of the 1980s focused some attention on these women, and the majority of these portrayals focused on non-medical personnel. This trend, as well as many of the new opportunities afforded to military women in real life, would be captured in the films of the next decade.

Six

Wish Fulfillment—Almost
The 1990s

While the 1980s were a time of great advances for American military women, they still had not achieved total parity with their male counterparts. The 1988 Department of Defense review of the combat exclusion law, which excluded military women from the "risk of exposure to direct combat, hostile fire, or capture," resulted in the opening of 30,000 positions to women, including the Navy test pilot program and mission specialist and aircrew positions in Fleet Air Reconnaissance squadrons.[1] Women could still not be permanently assigned to warships like aircraft carriers, however, and the 181 female Navy pilots and seventy-five female naval flight officers could not deploy with their squadrons if combat was a possibility, creating problems for their squadrons.

There were other exclusions as well—female Army pilots could not fly fixed wing aircraft or helicopters with combat missions like the Apache (AH-64), but they could fly Black Hawks (UH-60) and Chinooks (CH-47), which were considered support aircraft. The Marine Corps claimed that all of their aviation positions supported combat, excluding all women from any aviation position, while the Coast Guard opened all aviation missions to women. As previously noted, the exclusion of women from combat-related positions adversely impacted women's promotion potential.

At the beginning of the Gulf War in August 1990, women made up 11 percent of the military reserves and served in key positions throughout.[2] During the war, women served in every capacity except for the actual fighting, although the war's prosecution quickly resulted in a blurring of the front lines and rear echelon, and those serving in rear areas found themselves attacked by SAMs (surface-to-air missiles) and long range artillery. Operation Desert Shield/Desert Storm was the largest deployment of military women in U.S. history up to that time. As a result, women in full desert battle gear, many of whom were married and had families, appeared on American television often, leading to headlines like "Mom Goes to War" and personalizing the impact of war for many Americans.

The women who served in the Persian Gulf War arena quickly learned that war turns conventional human relationships upside down. For the first time, Americans saw wives and mothers in combat gear, handling lethal weapons with great competence. The women gained confidence about their own abilities from their wartime experiences. As Karen Gottschang Turner noted, "Most women performed men's work with competence and assumed an air of quiet authority."[3] Women in leadership roles were well accepted in the field, although they had to prove themselves rather than being accepted just for their rank like their male contemporaries were; there was also some resistance from senior military leadership.

Desert Storm has been seen as a defining moment for women in the military. Ian Zimmerman dubbed them "virago," noting these new tough women are defined through their bodies, attitudes, actions, and authority.[4] Not a tomboy or "Barbie with a gun," the virago knows when to act and when to wait, acting when others hesitate but always with forethought.[5] The virago is a form of womanhood that is not dictated by social expectations of femininity but by reshaping those expectations and becoming a hero. The virago embodies male virtues while remaining feminine but removed from sexual objectification.

During the early 1990s, Hollywood continued to make movies about World War II, including *Saving Private Ryan* and *Schindler's List*, in recognition of the fiftieth anniversary of the war. Despite the increased attention being paid to the role women played during the war, few of these films included women in their casts. Even though military women were more visible in daily events than ever before, they rarely appeared as protagonists in the films of the early 1990s. Those films that did feature prominent roles for military women tended to be character driven films like *Courage Under Fire* and *A Few Good Men,* both of which are discussed in this chapter. The women in these films who participated in combat, which women still could not do in real life, tended to be single, childless high achievers, typically still seen as love interests for a leading man. But as the 1990s wore on, military women in film and real life saw themselves winning major social battles for acceptance and opportunities.

Action Films

As the Cold War waned, America turned its attention to two new threats—the drug war and the rising tide of terrorism. These dangers quickly found their way onto the big screen in the form of action films that featured members of the military on the front lines, defending America against these threats. And as women's roles in the military expanded, Hollywood noticed and began including military women in action films. While these women were often merely "set dressing," visible in the background but not given speaking parts, in some cases, the women took on much more active roles, giving the audience a look at what women could do if the law allowed.

While the action in *Under Siege* (1992) centers on sailors trying to thwart a terrorist attack on an aircraft carrier, the film features a female naval officer in a small supporting role. Captain Spellman (Dru Anne Carlson) is an intelligence officer in the war room. Onscreen for five minutes, she only speaks five lines and spends most of her time taking notes for a senior government official while a number of Air Force and Army women can be seen working in the background. While she is listed as "Captain" Spellman in the credits, she wears the three stripes of a Navy commander on her service dress blues. She is never addressed by name in the film, making it difficult to discern who erred with her rank.

A Clear and Present Danger (1994) opens with an exciting scene as the Coast Guard cutter *Tybee* chases down a fleeing civilian boat suspected of running drugs. The cutter's commanding officer (Colleen Flynn) is calm, controlled, and capable in her fifty-three seconds onscreen. Hailing the boat on the loudspeaker, she demands, "Heave to and prepare to be boarded. We know you are a U.S. flagged boat." And the boat does.

Terminal Countdown (1999), which combines aspects of terrorism and the drug war with fears raised regarding Y2K and possible computer problems, features Myra Soljev (Sarah Chalke) as a tough Soviet GRU officer stationed in Colombia. Onscreen for more than fifteen minutes, she is smart and resourceful, willingly helping the Americans gain access to a secret CIA site to prevent terrorists from destroying Washington, D.C. She stands up to the terrorists, defending an American computer technician against their attack, despite being wounded herself.

In *Delta Force 3: The Killing Game* (1991), Captain Irene Usuri (Hana Azulay Hasfari) is a

KGB officer who joins Delta Force in their efforts to capture an Afghani terrorist leader who has planted a nuclear bomb in a U.S. city. Because she grew up in the area and is fluent in the local dialect, she is an integral member of the team. As they cross the desert at the start of their mission, she uses her AK-47 effectively, then dresses as an Afghani woman, flirting with an enemy officer as a distraction for the team. When he later pursues her through the market after catching her planting explosives, she does not hesitate to kill him to maintain her cover. In her eighteen minutes onscreen, she is an active member of the team, and her efforts are appreciated by the Delta Force leader who tells her, "You're a good man, Captain" at the end of the mission.

The film that first planted the idea of woman as action hero, or virago, into the consciousness of American moviegoers is *Courage under Fire* (1996). Set during the Gulf War (1990–1991), medivac pilot Captain Karen Walden (Meg Ryan) is being considered for the posthumous award of the Medal of Honor. Her story is told in a series of flashbacks as the investigating officer (Denzel Washington) seeks perspectives on her performance from her male crew. Because each crewmember has his own agenda and guilt over abandoning her on the battlefield, her character is elusive; all the audience knows is that Walden died in an air strike, the intentional (on her part) victim of friendly fire, while her male crewmembers are successfully rescued. She is variously described as tough, fearful, a coward, a good mother, and a good soldier. The wife of the crew chief sees her as "butch" and calls her a bitch, but her husband, whose life Walden saved, respects her, calling her a soldier. One crew member is a drug addict, overwhelmed by his guilt; a second seriously injured crewmember self-medicates to block out bad memories; and a third, scornful of women in combat due to his own inadequacies, commits suicide. Walden is the first mother serving in combat seen in film; her mother says she was a good mother who had wanted to fly since childhood and was conflicted about leaving her child to do her duty. Ultimately, we see Walden as an exceptional soldier who overcomes male hostility and fulfils her responsibility by giving her life.

The film raises questions about whether women in combat will present problems, a question that actually was answered during the Gulf War. Film critics were ambivalent about the film, some objecting to its apparent advocacy of women in combat. Others saw Walden as a bad mother who selfishly abandoned her child for self-fulfillment, an idea not applied to the fathers who served during the war. Such comments reveal some of the problems experienced by military women, who are seen as stepping outside mainstream gender roles. The military woman, especially the female action hero, "poses a challenge to gendered binaries through her very existence: her qualities of strength and determination and, most particularly her labour and the body that enacts it, mark her as 'unfeminine.'"[6] The more successful she becomes in the military, the more threatening she becomes. Even those women like Karen Walden who have a child do not escape this criticism.

While the majority of the action in *Crash Dive* (1997) focuses on submarine designer and former SEAL James Carter's (Michael Dudikoff) efforts to retake a U.S. attack submarine from Yugoslavian terrorists, the film features two female naval officers. Susan (Susan Lonergan) is a lieutenant who works in the communications center at the North Atlantic Command. Onscreen for one and a half minutes, she is smart and efficient, providing her boss, Lieutenant Commander Lisa Stark (Catherine Bell), with vital information at a moment's notice. Stark is also a communications officer, right hand to Admiral Pendleton (Frederic Forrest). Onscreen for eight and a half minutes, she is all business—squared-away, thoughtful, and creative. She suggests the plan used to regain control of the submarine, which involves sneaking the former SEAL, who she initially dislikes, onto the submarine. She serves as Carter's primary contact during the mission and keeps in touch with his son as well. And, of course, by the successful completion of the mission, she has thawed, and Stark and Carter are a couple.

The following year, Dudikoff and Bell appeared in another film, *Black Thunder*; however, their characters never meet. In fact, Bell's character, a Navy lieutenant commander identified only as Lisa in the credits, is an intelligence officer onboard the aircraft carrier USS *Sarasota* and plays a very small, unimportant role in the film. Onscreen for less than a minute, she only speaks a few lines and has no impact on the film's action.

That same year, Dudikoff appeared as Lieutenant Commander Tom Dickson, leader of a United Nations special operations team in the film *Freedom Strike* (1998), which features three military women with speaking roles. An uncredited woman sonar technician on the USS *Nimitz*, who is onscreen for sixteen seconds, has four lines, while Lieutenant Bakey (Alissia Miller), a female Navy doctor stationed onboard the aircraft carrier, is onscreen for almost two minutes. She capably treats the wounded during a terrorist attack and later calmly removes an explosive bullet from the Syrian president, despite the danger to herself. But the most important military woman is British SAS (Special Air Service) officer Maddie Reese (Felicity Waterman), a technology expert and member of the special operations team who shoots and fights as well as her male teammates. Love interest of Dickson, she takes her work seriously, wielding her automatic weapon as well as the men. Despite receiving a concussion during the terrorist attack, she insists on completing the mission, disabling a Syrian nuclear operations center. Onscreen for almost fourteen minutes, she gives as good as she gets, asking Dickson, "Do you want me to stop and explain this to you or shut down the thermo-nuclear missiles?" when he keeps asking her how much longer it's going to take. Reese's status as a member of the elite SAS comes twenty years before it was officially authorized, making her an early role model for women in such positions.[7]

In *Dead Men Can't Dance* (1997),[8] the idea of the virago takes center stage as a squadron of Army women is tasked for a CIA operation to destroy a nuclear site in North Korea. Captain Victoria Elliot (Kathleen York) is chosen by Brigadier General Burko (Grace Zabriskie) to lead the squadron once they complete SERE-type training. Onscreen for nine minutes, Burko is the first female general portrayed in an American action film, and she is competent, intelligent, and ambitious.[9] Onscreen for forty-two minutes, Elliot is a serious professional who trains incognito with her squad in order to get to know the women. The mission is intended to show that women can succeed in combat, so they are under tremendous stress, and Elliot needs to know who might crack. The women are trained by Sergeant Beverly Rhodes (Barbara Eve Harris), a tough, no-nonsense drill sergeant who ends up accompanying them on their mission. The training is difficult, and several women wash out. The squad, along with Elliot and Rhodes, is led by a male major who is seriously wounded early in the operation. With Elliot in command, the remaining women rescue several American prisoners who help them complete their mission and uncover a double agent.

Each of the three primary female enlisted women, who are onscreen for twenty-two minutes, has her own reason for taking on this challenge. Sergeant Mia Yan Chun (Hiep Thi Li) spent two years in underground tunnels in Vietnam, experience that is useful as the group winds its way through a series of caves to reach their target. She is later killed by North Korean troops. Sexy Sergeant Susie Warzinak (Jennifer Blanc) is anxious to prove she is more than just eye candy, while Sergeant Addy Cooper (Shawnee Smith) wants to prove that women can perform as well as men in combat situations. Rhodes is captured and tortured and ultimately dies saving the squad from a grenade-wielding North Korean. Upon their return to their base, Elliot is disillusioned over the loss of her squadron members and wants to resign her commission, but the general tells her she made a difference and has earned a promotion, asking her to reconsider. Elliot is uncertain, but she agrees to rethink her decision.

In *Operation Delta Force* (1997), Lieutenant Marie Junger (Natasha Sutherland) is a member of South African Special Forces. Onscreen for ten minutes, she is part of a joint nation anti-terrorist exercise which is interrupted by a real terrorist attack on a biological research laboratory. Despite the fact that she pulls her own weight during the operation, she is harassed by an enlisted American soldier who believes women do not belong on the team and by another who flirts with her incessantly; a third refers to her as "sweetheart." She gives as good as she gets, however, ignoring her harassers. Wounded during the operation, she doesn't even wince while being treated; she then returns to the mission, saving one American and escaping after being captured by a terrorist, proving she is a true virago.

In the direct-to-video film *Operation Delta Force 3: Clear Target* (1998), Lieutenant Commander Ariana Decker (Darcy La Pier) is a computer expert who worked on the systems of the USS *Roosevelt* (SSN 760), which has been hijacked by terrorists working for a Colombian drug lord. Onscreen for nine minutes, she joins the members of Delta Force as they attempt to retake the submarine and stop the terrorists. Despite her comment that there are too many codes to defeat and the odds are against them, she successfully disarms the nukes and saves the day.

Two military women are featured in *Surface to Air* (1998). Trace Carter Holsey is a Marine embassy driver. While onscreen for only thirteen seconds and speaking only three lines, she comes across as a strong, capable Marine who just happens to be a black woman. The other woman, Lieutenant Lori "Dakota" Forrester (Melanie Shatner), is an F-14 Tomcat Naval Flight Officer (NFO). The film opens with her going through SERE training, where she proves to be intelligent, dedicated, and very capable. Stationed onboard the USS *Kitty Hawk* (CV-63) to enforce the no-fly zone over Iraq, she appears to be the only woman in her squadron. She and her pilot, Lieutenant Dylan Massin (Chad McQueen), are shot down by a surface-to-air missile, and she is captured by Iraqi soldiers. Forced to read a prepared script that is broadcast worldwide after being tortured, she blinks her location in Morse code. Criticized for putting himself in danger to rescue her, Massin tells her he did it because she is his NFO, not because she is a woman. Interestingly, while all of the men are listed by rank in the film's credits, she is not, despite being onscreen for almost fourteen minutes, perhaps a reluctance on the part of the Department of Defense and Department of the Navy, both of which cooperated in the making of the film, to advertise the fact that women were actively participating in near-combat operations.

While the legend of Hua Mulan, a Chinese woman warrior from the Northern Wei period (386–434 CE), has been the subject of numerous films in China, most Americans were unfamiliar with her story until the Walt Disney Company released the animated film *Mulan* in 1998. In the story, the Huns have crossed the northern border, and a conscription notice is sent throughout the land, demanding the enlistment of one man from every family. When her crippled father plans to answer the call, Mulan (voiced by Ming-Na Wen), who is considered to be an inadequate daughter, decides to take his place. She cuts her hair, puts on her father's uniform and sword, and rides to the Chinese camp, accompanied by the miniature dragon Mushu (voiced by Eddie Murphy)—this is a Disney movie, after all. She finds the soldiers to be crass and disgusting, but Mushu tells her they're just men and that she is going to have to act just like them.

Smaller than the other soldiers, the company captain Li Shang (B.D. Wong) says he will make a man out of her; however, after a series of disasters during training, he tries to send her home, saying, "How could I make a man out of you?" Determined to prove herself, she trains harder and becomes a competent soldier. Occasionally, however, her "stupid girlie habits" like bathing almost give her secret away, especially when she gets giggly around Li Shang, whose life she saves with her quick thinking. Her masquerade is uncovered when she is wounded in battle, and Li Shang suddenly considers her a "treacherous snake, the ultimate dishonor." As she turns toward home, she ponders her decision, saying, "Maybe I didn't go for my father. I wanted to prove I could do things right." When she sees the Huns advancing on the Imperial City, she returns to warn the residents, but no one believes her, and the Huns capture the Emperor. She saves the day by disguising Chinese male soldiers as women and rescuing the Emperor. She returns home and presents her medal and honorary sword to her father who tells her, "My greatest gift and honor is having you as a daughter." Even Li Shang has changed his opinion about her, seeing her as a hero. Onscreen for thirty-seven minutes, this Mulan sings, dances, and clowns for the audience throughout the film. In real life, Hua Mulan was a true warrior who married Li Shang and was promoted to general during her twelve years of service.

The 1994 film *Chasers* tells the story of Seaman Second Class Toni Johnson (Erika Eleniak) and the two Navy enlisted men, Chief Rock Reilly (Tom Berenger) and Seaman Eddie DeVane (William McNamara), who are tasked with delivering Johnson from the U.S. Marine Corps Brig at Camp LeJeune, North Carolina to the U.S. Naval Consolidated Brig in Charleston, South Carolina so she can serve her seven-to-ten year sentence for unauthorized absence and assault. Modeled on *The Last Detail* (1973), this film focuses on Johnson's sexuality and her antics as she tries to escape from custody, rather than on the comradeship of the main characters as in the Nicholson film. While DeVane is a wheeler-dealer with only one more day in his enlistment, Reilly is a tough, experienced brig chaser who has transferred 862 prisoners without difficulty. Warned about her antics by the Marine guards, who also note that she is supposed to have a female escort, Reilly mistakenly believes that chaining her handcuffs to the van's cage will keep her out of trouble.

During her thirty-five minutes onscreen, the buxom actress uses all of her feminine wiles to try to escape, including disguising herself as a waitress, flirting with both men, and stuffing the gas tank with tampons, causing it to break down. While they are holed up in a motel awaiting repairs, she seduces a drunken DeVane and escapes. Despite all of the problems she has caused, after reading her file, even Reilly feels sorry for her and believes she was treated unjustly. The chasers finally get her to Charleston, but Reilly realizes that DeVane and Johnson are in love and engineers her escape.

Johnson is not the only enlisted woman featured in the film. Two additional female sailors are seen at the beginning of the film, one for twenty-one seconds and the other for ten seconds. Both appear to be squared away and competent in carrying out their assigned duties.

While the film takes a light-hearted look at a serious subject, it is filled with a number of inaccuracies. In the 1990s, there was no enlisted pay grade of "Seaman Second Class." Additionally, Johnson is initially attired in an oversized khaki shirt and black pants rather than the dungaree uniform of a junior enlisted woman. As previously mentioned, to prevent sexual harassment (or worse), at least one of the chasers should have been a woman. And, of course, her aggressive sexuality is not in keeping with good order and discipline.

Iron Eagle II (1998) features a group of misfits chosen for a special joint mission to destroy an Arab missile site. Valerie Zuyoniko (Sharon Brandon) is a Russian pilot assigned to the team. Despite being an excellent pilot, she is subjected to machismo posturing and snide comments from the sexist American male pilots assigned to the mission. Onscreen for eleven minutes, she is all business, and when Captain Matt Cooper (Mark Humphrey) admires her flying, telling her she's a natural, she accuses him of playing "the cool American" and lets him know that she flies for her people and her country, not herself. Of course, they begin a relationship, which ends with the completion of the mission, but the film leaves the viewer feeling that they may meet again someday.

While the 1992 action film *Into the Sun* focuses on an American Air Force pilot's (Michael Pare as Captain Paul "Shotgun" Watkins) assignment to familiarize an actor (Anthony Michael Hall as Tom Slade) with a fighter pilot's job, the film includes three women in speaking roles. An uncredited enlisted woman in desert camouflage, onscreen for two seconds, speaks one line as she meets Slade. Melissa Moore plays an unnamed sergeant who runs the base's flight simulator. Onscreen for seventy-five seconds, the sexy blonde, whose long hair hangs past her shoulders, flirts with Slade during his time in the simulator. Public Affairs Officer Lauren Goode (Deborah Moore), onscreen for more than twelve minutes, plays a larger role in the film, albeit as the conflicted love interested of Watkins. Listed as a major in the credits, she wears the silver oak leaves of a lieutenant colonel on her uniform.[10] She and Watkins had a relationship at their previous duty station, but she broke it off. Their relationship is tenuous; when he calls her Lauren, she reminds him of her seniority. He obviously wants to rekindle their relationship, but she balks, telling him, "There are three things that are important to you—planes, your buddies, and planes. I don't play third string." When Slade flirts with Goode, Watkins retaliates by putting him through significant physical challenges, angering her even more. Yet, after he escapes from his Arab captors and safely returns to the base, all is forgiven, and they are once again a couple.

The final action film in this chapter is also the last released in the decade. *Active Stealth* (1999) features one female military character in a minor role. Staff Sergeant Baker (Ava Fabian) works in the base operations center, monitoring the test flight of an F-117C stealth fighter during a training mission. Onscreen for only two minutes and speaking only about a dozen lines, at the end of the film it is revealed that she is actually from Army intelligence, sent to investigate Colonel Reynolds (Fred Williamson), who was working with a Mexican drug lord to steal the plane.

Comedies

A number of 1990s comedies included military women in their casts, in both small and key roles. In most of these films, the military women portrayed were typically capable, intelligent—and often very funny.

While the protagonist of *Hot Shots!* (1991), a spoof of the popular 1986 film *Top Gun*, is male (Charlie Sheen as Lieutenant Sean "Topper" Harley), the film does include a female naval aviator, Lieutenant Kowalski (Kristy Swanson). Onscreen for less than two minutes, she is often on the perimeter of the action, with no lines and no recognition of her as part of the team. Speeches to the squadron refer to "boys," "gentlemen," and "every man here," even though she is also present. As the film's eye candy, she wears a skin-tight flight suit, and in one scene in the co-ed barracks where she resides, she stands at attention in her bra and uniform pants while the men around her wear T-shirts. No one says anything about her attire, however, since the other pilots consider her to be one of the boys. While she is only shown in the cockpit once, after she goes to a squadron mate's aid, she tells Topper, "You're quite a guy," to which he replies, "So are you."

In *Sgt. Bilko* (1996), women are fully integrated into daily life at Fort Baxter. They are shown running and drilling in mixed companies, as well as swearing and gambling alongside their male peers. The film features several women in minor roles in the film, including Carol Rosenthal as an office clerk, Cheryl Frances Harrington as Corporal Jefferson, and Cathy Silvers as First Lieutenant Monday, a numbers cruncher from the office of the Inspector General who is investigating Bilko's shenanigans. Sergeant Raquel "Rocky" Barbarella (Pamela Adlon), however, is part of wheeler-dealer Bilko's inner circle. Onscreen for almost ten minutes, she is "one of the boys," actively participating in his crazy schemes and helping to cover up his illegal activities along with the men who work for Bilko.

Going Under (1991) also features several military women characters. The film opens with a female airman (Shawne Zarubeca) giving a tour of the U.S. Capitol to a group of Girl Scouts.

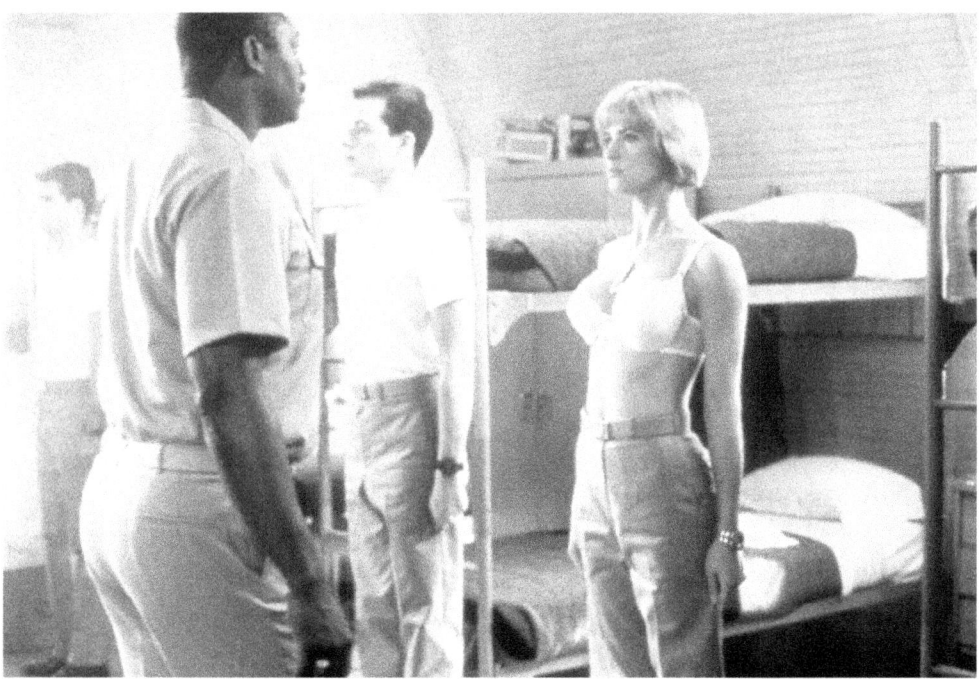

Navy Lieutenant Kowalski (Kristy Swanson, right) stands at attention with her squadron mates in the 1991 military comedy spoof *Hot Shots!*.

Onscreen for seventeen seconds, she has one line, "Here is where our nation's leaders take mommy's and daddy's tax dollars and turn them into machines of global destruction," a clear indication that this film is not a serious drama. The film's story centers on the development of a stealth submarine, the USS *Standard*, which is over-budget and over-schedule. In an effort to terminate the submarine, it is staffed with a sub-standard crew and commanding officer (Bill Pullman as Commander Biff Banner), including Sonar (Elmarie Wendel), a sarcastic, grey-haired, pink sweater wearing female lieutenant who is onscreen for four minutes. Also assigned as a special observer to the submarine's shakedown cruise is Lieutenant Commander Jan Michaels (Wendy Schaal), who was first in her class at the Naval Academy and has two years of experience on submarines (despite the fact that women could not be assigned to submarine duty until 2010). Although they were classmates at the Academy, Banner is not happy to see her, especially when she tells him that she's watching "every move you make, every regulation you break, I'll be watching you," to which he retorts, "I've heard that tune before." There is significant conflict between the two as well as a lot of sexual innuendo in their comments. Onscreen for eighteen minutes, Michaels is sexy, confident, and "by the book"—until she assumes command of the submarine, which causes her to become hysterical. Ultimately, Banner resumes control of the submarine, saves the day, and gets the girl.

In a fun subplot, Andrea Stein plays a Soviet general, commanding a flotilla tracking the American submarine. Onscreen for two minutes, she orders the deployment of the submarine "*Pink November*," an obvious play on *The Hunt for Red October*. The *Standard*'s crew is concerned when Sonar detects the *Pink November*'s sonar signature, but ultimately, they are able to defeat the Russian submarine.

In the Army Now (1994) features two strong female military characters. When screw-ups Bones Conway (Pauly Shore) and Jack Kauffman (Andy Dick) join the Army Reserve, they get some big surprises. At boot camp, they encounter Sergeant Ladd (Lynn Whitfield), a tough,

Private Jack Kauffman (Andy Dick) and Private Christine Jones (Lori Petty) react to a desert ambush in the 1994 comedy *In the Army Now*.

Private Christine Jones (Lori Petty) is in her element as her squad provides water to American troops in the 1994 comedy *In the Army Now*.

no-nonsense black female DI, onscreen for six minutes, who decides to make Conway her special "project," in part because his conduct is completely inappropriate. Throughout basic training, he has difficulty accepting her authority. During hand-to-hand combat training, he tells her, "I can't hit you. You're a girl, and I love you." Under her tutelage, he eventually straightens out, as indicated by his calling cadence, "drill sergeant made a man out of me."

Conway and Kauffman are assigned to a water purification unit where they meet Private Christine Jones (Lori Petty), a tough soldier with a shaved head who wants to experience combat. While the men are shocked to be called up to active duty during Operation Desert Storm, Jones is thrilled, commenting, "Water purification is the reserve occupation most likely to be called up if there's a desert war. This is a desert war, and we're going." When the squad is attacked while on patrol, she is the only one who keeps her head and returns fire. Ultimately, the squad destroys an enemy camp, and they are hailed as heroes.

Despite his ineptitude, Jones is falling for Conway and encourages him to be all that he can be, teaching him how to be a good soldier and responsible adult and revealing that beneath her "tough guy" exterior, she is still a woman, capable of nurturing and encouraging her man to success. While through much of the twenty minutes she is onscreen, Jones can be viewed as the only "real man" in the film and definitely the best soldier in her squad,[11] she is passed over for field promotion in favor of Conway. And in the film's final scene, she has shed her Army uniform for a dress, a reaffirmation of her femininity and second-class status.

Renaissance Man (1994), directed by Penny Marshall, features two female Army characters. Staff Sergeant Marie Layton (Isabella Hoffman) is a records clerk who helps Bill Rago (Danny DeVito) with a special project. Onscreen for two minutes, she is kind, professional, and caring—and she likes Rago, despite his acerbic personality. Private Miranda Myers (Stacey Dash) is one of the "squeakers," soldiers who need help with their academics in order to graduate from boot camp. Called "Double Ds" (dumb as dog shit) by the other recruits, they are unruly, undisciplined, and ignorant. Onscreen for almost eleven minutes, Myers is tough but ambitious. While she had a difficult, poverty-stricken childhood, she does not join the Army for the money; she is looking for stability in her life, the result of being abandoned by her mother. She is touched by the Shakespearean characters Rago introduces her to, and by the film's conclusion, it is evident that she will succeed in the Army, despite her difficult beginning.

Another film that features a woman serving aboard a submarine before it was authorized is *Down Periscope* (1996). Lieutenant Emily Lake (Lauren Holly) is assigned to the USS *Stingray*, a diesel boat, as the Diving Officer. As in *Going Under,* the Stingray crew is populated by a group of screw-ups and captained by Lieutenant Commander Tom Dodge (Kelsey Grammer), ostensibly a screw-up, but one who has been awarded a Meritorious Service Medal, Navy Commendation Medal, and Navy Achievement Medal. When Lake reports for duty, she is mistaken for a stripper. Taken aback, she tells Dodge that she's part of a "trial program" putting women on submarines. Onscreen for sixteen minutes, she is stiff and squared-away; however, when the men play a joke on her, shrinking her uniforms so that her shirt does not button and her pants are tight and too short, rather than getting angry, she laughs it off. While she has done 300 dives on a simulator, she has no experience actually diving a boat, and she worries that she's a danger to the crew. Ultimately, she performs a difficult maneuver flawlessly during a war game, securing a win for the aging submarine.

As in *Going Under,* there are several inaccuracies with her uniforms. She wears her hair in a single braid which falls almost to her shoulder blades rather than above the bottom of her collar. At the end of the film, she departs the submarine wearing service dress whites with no shirt underneath her blouse (jacket), no tie, non-regulation high-heeled Mary Janes, and her hair flowing

Navy Lieutenant Emily Lake (Lauren Holly) strains the seams of her recently shrunken khaki uniform in 20th Century–Fox's 1996 comedy *Down Periscope*.

loosely below her collar. Clearly the film's producers were more concerned with playing up her femininity than with accurately depicting a squared-away military woman.

McHale's Navy (1997) is another comedy that takes liberties in its depiction of a military woman. Set in the Caribbean, the film centers on the antics of a group of Navy misfits who take on a group of terrorists. Lieutenant Penelope Carpenter (Debra Messing) is the right-hand man to Captain Binghamton (Dean Stockwell), a clueless aviator. Onscreen for eighteen minutes, she is first seen wearing service dress whites, again without a shirt or tie, her long hair stuffed beneath her bucket cap. In the original movie and television series, Carpenter is a man, a bumbling nitwit who blindly follows Captain Binghamton's schemes to get rid of McHale. In this film, as the first female Naval Academy graduate, she is astute and by the book and takes a dim view of the men under their command. When they make snide comments about her, she confronts them, saying she has heard them all: "I'd like to polish her cannons. I'd like to swab her deck." She then threatens to transfer them all to the Aleutians if they do not straighten up.

Carpenter is thrilled to meet Lieutenant Commander Quinton McHale, with whom she bonds after deciding that Captain Binghamton is incompetent. While she becomes more tolerant of the men's antics as a result of this friendship, she also has the opportunity to show off her own abilities. During an operation to root out terrorists, she blows up their boat using an RPG, which earns her a Bronze Star and promotion to lieutenant commander. As the film ends, she rides into the sunset sidesaddle on McHale's motorcycle, wearing her service dress whites. Ever the squared-away sailor, she reminds him of the Navy's rules against fraternization, to which he replies that he is retiring, a rare reversal of roles.

The final comedy in this chapter is *The Pentagon Wars* (1998). The HBO movie, based on

Navy Lieutenant Penelope Carpenter (Debra Messing, right) is Executive Officer to Captain Wallace B. Binghamton (Dean Stockwell, center), who is tormented by the antics of Ensign Charles Parker (David Alan Grier) in the 1997 comedy *McHale's Navy*.

a true story, features Viola Davis as Army Sergeant First Class Fanning, the chief administrator assigned to help Air Force Colonel James Burton (Carey Elwes) assess the viability of the Bradley Fighting Vehicle, the development of which is running significantly over-budget and over-schedule. Onscreen for eighteen minutes, Fanning is smart and knows that Burton is being deceived by the Bradley's program manager. As they weed through the documentation provided to them and follow the trail of modifications that were made to the vehicle over time, they uncover significant weaknesses which would endanger the lives of those depending on it. Fanning's understanding of the vehicle's design specifications and the tank's mission result in their discovery that a test of the tank, designed to prove the vehicle's capabilities, has been rigged for success. Their intervention allows the Congressional observers to learn the truth and order the needed changes.

Disaster Films

The popularity of disaster films held steady in the 1990s, although few featured military personnel, focusing on more local resources and heroes such as police and firefighters. One disaster film that included a female naval officer is the made-for-television movie *Tidal Wave: No Escape* (1997). Lieutenant Commander Jessica Weaver (Julianne Phillips) is an oceanographer working with civilian contractors from a company called Aquatronics. Onscreen for forty-one minutes, she is self-confident and proud of her research. She takes an immediate dislike to John Wahl (Corbin Bernsen), a retired weapons specialist, because "he quit" when he learned that his research was being subverted. As tidal waves occur around the world, they work together to solve the mystery and ultimately begin a romantic relationship. An admitted control freak, she tells him he needs to let go of his own need for control and let her help him, joking, "I can order you to. I'm a lieutenant commander." Unable to convince government officials of the real cause of the tidal waves, she and Wahl take matters into their own hands, turning Wahl's misappropriated invention against the perpetrator, saving the world.

Drama

Dramatic films featuring military personnel continued to be popular during the 1990s, and many included significant roles for military women, the result of their actions during the Gulf War and their increasing numbers in the military. The subject matter of these dramatic films ranged from a look back at the two World Wars and Vietnam War to the Gulf War and the War on Terror, as well as exploring contemporary issues important to military personnel, such as gays in the military, sexual harassment and assault, and women in combat.

The 1994 film *Forrest Gump* was a massive box office success, a top-grossing film that earned more than $67 million worldwide and Academy Awards for Best Picture, Best Director, Best Actor (Tom Hanks), Best Adapted Screenplay, Best Visual Effects, and Best Film Editing.[12] The film tells the story of Forrest Gump's life, including many scenes set in Vietnam, only one of which features a military woman, an Army nurse who utters one line in the seventeen seconds she is onscreen, tending to wounded soldiers in an Army hospital.

Another film that features Army nurses is *The English Patient* (1996). Set during World War II, three Canadian nurses travel in a medical convoy in Europe, two of whom are onscreen for only one minute. As nurses, the women have seen firsthand the carnage and violence of war, and the death of one nurse (Lisa Repo as Mary) has a profound impact on Hana (Juliette Binoche), who leaves the convoy to care for a severely burned patient who will soon die. Detached but professional, she initially wears her military uniform of green jacket and pants, khaki shirt, and metal helmet or a nurse's uniform of blue dress, white apron, and headscarf as she tends to her patient, but as time goes on, she softens both her appearance and attitude, changing to a civilian dress and wearing her long hair on her shoulders. While she has a romantic relationship with Lieutenant Kip Singh (Naveen Andrews), a Sikh ordnance expert, her responsibility is to her patient, with whom she sympathizes and to whom she ultimately gives a fatal dose of morphine, putting him out of his misery.

World War II is also the setting for the made-for-television docu-drama *One Against the Wind* (1991), which tells the story of British aristocrat Mary Lindell's (Judy Davis) wartime activities as a World War I Red Cross nurse, member of the French underground helping to smuggle downed Allied aviators to freedom, prisoner of war, and ultimately a British Army officer. Smart, brave, and feisty, she is appalled by the German treatment of French civilians, Jews, and enemy combatants during their occupation. Even when captured and put on trial as a collaborator, she is defiant, telling a German SS officer, "Kipling also wrote 'Stand up and take the war. The Hun is at the gate,'" a reference to a previous conversation when he had quoted Kipling to warn her against her dangerous activities.

Her nine months in solitary confinement do nothing to deter her anti–German activities. Sent to London by the Maquis to serve as liaison to British intelligence, she chafes at being away from the action, asking Major James Leggatt (Sam Neill), "What am I supposed to do—sit home and knit socks, make tea like Helen?" The Helen she mentions is actually Leggatt's assistant, a capable, dedicated British Army sergeant, onscreen for one and a half minutes, who cares passionately about her country and its fighting men. Sent back to France as a British ensign in MI9, Lindell's activities again put her in danger, and when she refuses to leave the country, her son notes, "You're gonna miss this war when it's over. Maybe you can start another." She is captured and imprisoned in a concentration camp, which is ultimately liberated by Leggatt's unit. Throughout the fifty-five minutes she is onscreen, Lindell is feisty, dedicated, and selfless, the epitome of the virago, a true hero.[13]

Two dramatic films from the decade focus on the Gulf War. More than 540,000 Americans served in Operation Desert Storm, 7 percent of whom were women.[14] The war led to more questions about whether women should share the same obligations as the men who also served. Positive comments about the performances of these women showed how much the military services had come to depend upon them and that they definitely were integral to American military successes.

Based on a true story, the made-for-television film *The Heroes of Desert Storm* (1991) explores the experiences of several military members during the Gulf War, including those of Army First Lieutenant Phoebe Jeter (Angela Bassett) and Specialist Beverly Clark (Laura Leigh Hughes), a reservist mobilized for overseas deployment, interweaving news footage from the war with the individuals' stories. In all, five military women, onscreen from between fifteen seconds and six minutes, are included in the drama.

Jeter, onscreen for four and a quarter minutes, is a Patriot Missile platoon leader at Fort Bliss when she gets word of her pending deployment. She has no concerns about her own ability or that of her people to do the job, but she is concerned about her elderly grandmother who is in failing health. When called on to perform her duties, she is cool, calm, and professional as she goes through the launch sequence, whispering, "Come on, baby. Get it. Kill it." and celebrates with her troops when they intercept an incoming Scud missile. Several days later, while in her barracks room with her roommate Tanesha, Jeter gets word that her grandmother has died. While Tanesha comforts her, Jeter comments that she is sorry, but she will not be able to get home for the funeral; she is helping to win freedom for the Kuwaitis. In her final scene, Jeter visits her grandmother's grave and tells her, "It was something I had to do."

Reservist Clark is shocked to receive orders to Kuwait, telling her boyfriend that she thought the reserves were just a part time job. He wants to get married before she leaves, but she tells him that she's not ready. As she prepares for deployment, she tells her mother that while she does not want to go (she is afraid she will not come home), "I made a deal and I gotta stick to it." Clark quickly settles into her new routine, making friends with Sergeant Rhodes (Betsy Lynn George), with whom she commiserates as the men from their unit go out on patrol, leaving them behind. One night as Rhodes goes out for a walk, the barracks is hit by a Scud missile, killing Clark and many others. As news of the barracks bombing is received in the U.S., Clark's family receives the news of her death at the Reserve Center. The entire town turns out for her military funeral, and Rhodes comments that she will never forget her friend.

The Bloody Child (1996) is a surrealistic movie intended to mimic the PTSD of a Gulf War Marine. The story is told in snippets and flashbacks, leading the viewer to question what is real and what is imagined. The film opens just before sunrise, with three figures walking in the darkness. Later that day, a bloody female figure is visible in the back seat of a car, guarded by a Marine MP. Various scenes show men drinking in a bar, women in various stages of undress and locations, and Marine MPs standing around the car. A female captain (Tinka Menkes) is in charge. She stands apart from her men, and when they cross the line in their words or actions, she shouts, "Gentlemen, is this a tea party? Don't you have some paperwork? Don't you salute an officer?" Onscreen for thirty minutes, she is seen up close in only one scene, when she is eating in a diner, wearing her dress greens.

The viewer eventually learns that the dead woman, Corporal Stripes (Sherry Sibley), was an enlisted Marine murdered by her Gulf War veteran husband who suffers from PTSD and that the captain and her partner caught him digging a grave while they were on their normal patrol. The viewer is left to wonder why the killer experiences some of the visions he has and how the film's reference to the second apparition in *Macbeth* relates to the film's title, given that Corporal Stripes was an adult when she was murdered and her husband is quickly identified as the murderer.[15]

While the fall of the Berlin Wall and disintegration of the USSR seemed to end the Cold War, the threat of nuclear war was still on the minds of many, including Hollywood filmmakers. *By Dawn's Early Light* (1990) examines the conflicts that arise among a B-52 bomber crew as they face the possibility of having to drop a nuclear bomb on the primary relocation site for Soviet leadership in such a confrontation.[16] Praised for its high level of realism and claim that individual choices ultimately determine the outcome of conflict, the HBO original film was one of the last Cold War–era films to depict World War III.[17]

While the film features three female Air Force officers in minor roles, it is pilot Captain Moreau (Rebecca De Mornay) who is the voice of reason in the chaos of war. When Russian terrorists fire a nuclear weapon at Ukraine, activating the Soviet defense systems, the U.S. scrambles its defense forces, including the B-52 bomber "Polar Bear I" from Fairchild AFB, Washington. Polar Bear I's pilot, Major Cassidy (Powers Boothe) and co-pilot Moreau have been having an affair, despite fraternization rules which forbid such interactions. Moreau is conflicted about the relationship, which her roommate blames on Cassidy, telling her it's because he is a pilot that he is willing to cheat on his wife. Moreau replies, "We're pilots, too," to which her roommate replies, "They're men."

Despite witnessing a Soviet nuclear detonation on American soil, Moreau questions their orders to retaliate. While Cassidy tries to keep the crew focused on their task, she questions whether they will be able to actually drop their own bomb when required. Pursued by Soviet MiGs when they enter Soviet airspace, Moreau devises a plan to evade the MiGs and Soviet missiles. Cassidy tells her she is a good

Rebecca De Mornay (left) and Powers Boothe are Air Force pilots facing nuclear war in the 1990 HBO original movie *By Dawn's Early Light*.

pilot, the best he has flown with, but she is messing up by questioning their orders. Despite the stress of their situation, she is calm and rational in framing her argument against blindly following orders, questioning the psyche of American's civilian leadership, and reminding him that it is not logical to kill the enemy's leaders since someone needs to be able to end the hostilities. She says she wants to give leaders on both sides time to think, and Cassidy asks what he is supposed to do since she is suggesting treason—shoot her, eject her, put her down on the ice. When she suggests he turn the plane around, he does, which results in a short-lived mutiny among the crew and allows senior leadership to put an end to the hostilities. As they fly back to the U.S., the two pilots watch the sun rise on a new day. Moreau, discussing her own ideas and actions, says, "If you take the chance to live, it's okay to die." Cassidy tells her, "No one is going to die today." She asks him where they go from here, to which he replies, "I don't know."

Moreau's refusal to follow orders raises an interesting question—did she refuse them because she's a woman and therefore unwilling to kill, and that despite the fact that she is a highly trained Air Force officer, her embedded nurturing nature was so strong that it overcame her training? Or is it just that she was being rational, a trait typically assigned to men, not to an "emotional" woman? One clue to the answer could be seen in the fact that "Alice" (James Earl Jones as the commander of the airborne command center) also argues for restraint as the tensions escalate and is the first to correctly interpret the actions taken by Polar Bear I as ceasing hostilities, showing that both men and women have the ability to be rational during an irrational situation.

Demi Moore starred as a naval officer in two military films of this decade that were received very differently by critics and the viewing public—*A Few Good Men* (1992) and *G.I. Jane* (1997).

Lieutenant Commander JoAnne Galloway (Demi Moore) confronts Lieutenant Junior Grade Daniel Kaffee (Tom Cruise) in Rob Reiner's 1992 courtroom drama *A Few Good Men*.

The former grossed more than $243 million and was nominated for five Golden Globe and four Academy Awards, while the latter was considered a box office disappointment, earning a mere $97 million and effectively ending Moore's career as a leading lady.[18]

In the courtroom drama *A Few Good Men,* Moore plays Navy lawyer Lieutenant Commander JoAnne Galloway, described by colleagues as a good researcher but not a litigator, having tried only three cases in two years. Tired of riding a desk in Internal Affairs, she requests but is denied the opportunity to be assigned as lead council on a murder case: "Division will assign the right man for the job." Instead, she is assigned to make sure the young, inexperienced lawyer (Tom Cruise as Lieutenant Junior Grade Daniel Kaffee) assigned to the case does his job. Kaffee is a brash loose cannon who has pleaded out forty-four cases in the nine months he has been a JAG officer. She has her work cut out for her and, as the film progresses, shows that she is an able teacher, despite being subjected to continual sexual harassment and the patronizing attitudes of both Kaffee and Marine Colonel Jessup (Jack Nicholson). Most of the men with whom she works do not like her, underestimating her intellect, skill, ethics, and passion.

Much criticism has been directed at Galloway. Onscreen for forty-five minutes, her character has been described as one-dimensional, low key, meek, and passive, and some see her as a traditional nurturing woman who teaches Kaffee to "be a man," an outsider who endorses military masculinity and is pushed aside and silenced.[19] Galloway is certainly subjected to significant sexual harassment and marginalization, despite the fact that her personal decorations (two Meritorious Service Medals, which are normally awarded to senior field grade officers, and a Navy Commendation Medal) mark her as a high achiever. She ignores Jessup's crude comments to Kaffee when he sees them together—"There's nothing on this earth sexier than a woman you have to salute in the morning ... if you don't get a blow job from a superior officer, you're letting life pass you by," choosing instead to focus on whether or not he had ordered a "Code Red." While Galloway's ignoring of the sexual harassment she experiences has been painted as weakness and passivity on her part, it is a tactic used by many military women who experience the same treatment.

In their discussion of Galloway's failings, critics failed to recognize a key factor in the relationship between Galloway and Kaffee—that of the significant difference in their ranks (despite the fact that Cruise is actually four months older than Moore, he is portrayed as being much younger). Many critics bemoaned the fact that there is no romance between the two, despite the impropriety of such a relationship, and no one seemed to think that Kaffee's obnoxious attitude might not have appealed to the more mature Galloway or that men and women can work together without becoming romantically involved.

As an experienced field grade officer, it was Galloway's responsibility to teach Kaffee how to be a good courtroom lawyer—and naval officer. Impervious to his charms, Galloway confronts him, accusing him of taking the path of least resistance professionally, and plants the seed of their case when she asks him if he knows what a "Code Red" is. When he says no, she replies, "What a pity," arousing his curiosity. She continues to educate him and his co-counsel, Lieutenant Junior Grade Sam Weinberg (Kevin Pollack), during their investigation in Cuba. While the two male officers appear wearing summer white uniforms, Galloway wears khakis for their perimeter ride, telling them that they make nice targets for Cuban sharpshooters. Later, as they search the dead man's barracks room, she asks Kaffee if he is planning on doing any investigating or if he is just taking a tour, goading him into using his powers of observation rather than just running his mouth. Whenever Kaffee's confidence wanes, she encourages him, pushing him to do the right thing. After convincing him to put Colonel Jessup on the stand, she warns him not to push too hard so he doesn't get in trouble, knowing full well he will take the bait and do exactly the opposite. In the film's climactic courtroom scene, she is proven correct in her assessment of Jessup's ego, leading to his famous outburst, "You can't handle the truth." While many scholars believe her education of Kaffee is based on her nurturing nature, had Galloway been played by a man, no one would have questioned their relationship or interactions. Although the character of JoAnne Galloway has been perceived as a disruptive presence who must use her nurturing skills to help Kaffee become a real man, her character should actually be seen as smart and passionate, a woman who grows through her experience while helping a junior officer become better at his chosen profession.

In *G.I. Jane*, Moore's character of Lieutenant Jordan O'Neil is the complete opposite of Galloway. A topographic analyst in Naval Intelligence concerned that her lack of operational experience will keep her from being promoted, she jumps at the opportunity to be the first woman to go through U.S. Navy Special Warfare Group training and become a member of a Combined Reconnaissance Team (CRT).[20] O'Neil is smart and clever, a triathlete, pretty and feminine—"top drawer with silk stockings" as one male aide to Senator Lillian De Haven (Anne Bancroft) comments as they review her record. Seeing it as a career advancement opportunity, she asks her disapproving boyfriend, "You don't want me sleeping my way to the top, do you?" She points out that they entered the Navy at the same time, yet because he has operational experience, he is a full pay grade senior to her.

Not surprisingly, when O'Neil arrives at Coronado for training, she is told she will be housed separately from the men she will be training with. The commanding officer tells her that special allowances have been made for her—she can do women's push-ups, gets "female aids" to get over the barriers of the obstacle course, and has more time to complete the course, all of which she objects to. Master Chief Petty Officer John Urgayle (Viggo Mortensen), like her classmates, is not happy to have her there, and everyone lets her know in not so subtle ways—when she sits down at a table in the mess hall, the men leave; one comments about women's body fat percentages, and another declares, "No split-tail's getting through the program." That last comment is especially important

Navy Lieutenant Jordan O'Neill (Demi Moore) calls for extraction for her special forces team in the 1997 Ridley Scott drama *G.I. Jane*.

since all of the men participating in the intensive CRT training have already completed Special Forces training, which O'Neil has not. In an attempt to discourage her, Urgayle talks about problems the Israeli Army had integrating women into combat, including that the men couldn't handle seeing women blown up. Unfazed, she mentions his Navy Cross and that he received it for pulling a 240-pound man out of a burning tank. She asks a question that many military women have also asked, "Why is it that when a man rescues another man, he's a hero, but when he tries to rescue a woman, he's just gone soft?" He ignores her question, instead asking if she could pull a man clear, a question that inspires her to increase the intensity of her training.

While a few of the men begin to respect her efforts, it is not until SERE training, when Ungayle attempts to simulate a rape and she breaks his nose in a fight, telling him, "Suck my dick," that the men accept her as a true teammate. That acceptance is crucial, as the group's training is interrupted by them being sent to deal with a crisis in Libya. When Urgayle is badly wounded, it is O'Neil who gets him to safety, an action he says he will never live down.

Jordan O'Neil is not the only female military character at Coronado. During an early phase of training, O'Neil is examined by Dr. Blondell (Lucinda Jenney), who expresses concern about her physical and emotional well-being, a concern that is amplified after her fight with Urgayle. When the doctor asks why O'Neil is putting herself through the training, O'Neil asks, "Do you ask the men the same question?" When the doctor replies affirmatively, O'Neil asks what they say, to which Blondell replies, "Because I get to blow up shit." "Well, there you go," O'Neil responds. Still concerned about O'Neil's isolation, Blondell invites her to a barbeque on the beach with some other female officers, which leads to O'Neil being accused of being a lesbian, despite a lack of actual proof. O'Neil fights for her good name and is ultimately vindicated.

As previously noted, both the film and Moore were roundly criticized. Much of the criticism from scholars centers on the scenes where O'Neil shaves her head and works on building her upper body strength, claiming that in order to gain acceptance, she must shed all signs of femininity and become male by building up her body and becoming more masculine in her attitude and language.[21] This physical transformation makes her threatening because she is seen as rejecting the passivity typically associated with women.[22]

But is that really true? While O'Neil's physical transformation allows her to become a virago, a female hero, is she really trying to become a man? Is there another possible, more practical explanation for her shaved head and increased strength? While O'Neil initially wears her hair longer than many female naval officers, perhaps as a way of preserving a sense of femininity, as an experienced naval officer, she would be well aware of the disadvantages inherent in wearing long hair during this intensive training. Dispatched to Coronado without having the opportunity to get her hair cut, her first request of the base's commanding officer is to go to the barbershop, to which he replies that her hair is fine as long as it is off her collar because "we're not trying to change your sex." Yet one must ask why her request is denied. As is seen in several scenes, having her hair remain pinned up is impossible due to the level of physical activity of the program, which includes swimming in the surf and running long distances. Given the unavailability of a barber, O'Neil takes matters into her own hands and shaves her head. While this may seem extreme, it makes sense from a practical perspective, given the short amount of time allowed for personal grooming and the harsh conditions. This commonsense approach to her hair also applies to her decision to move into the male barracks, which, despite the complaints of some of the men, helps integrate her into the team as they can see how hard she is working to do her part.

O'Neil's extra work building her upper body strength can also be easily explained as part of her efforts to contribute to the team. Members of Special Forces units are expected to carry heavy equipment, swim great distances, and navigate treacherous terrain, all of which require significant upper body strength. Rather than trying to "become a man," she is merely trying to become a reliable team member, able to carry her own weight on assignment. She does not take Urgayle's relentless criticism as persecution since he rides the men just as hard; rather, it is the drive required to ensure that they can do the job well.

The final indication that O'Neil is not trying to become a man comes when she dons a dress to join her teammates in a celebratory drink upon the successful completion of SERE training. O'Neil succeeds because she has the drive and determination to achieve her goal. She is accepted by her male peers as the result of her bravery and hard work.

While many scholars and critics have viewed this film negatively, it did introduce the idea that women could become successful members of military Special Forces teams, an idea that became a reality in December 2018 when Sergeant Hailey Falk graduated from the Army's Sapper Leader Course for combat engineers at Fort Leonard Wood, Missouri and the first female Army officer passed the initial Special Forces Assessment and Selection process and was selected to attend the Special Forces Qualification course.[23]

While the true stories of many military men have been portrayed on the big screen, in the 1990s, stories based on real life events of military women continued to only be told in made-for-television films. The three made-for-television films discussed here highlight some of the important issues the military was forced to face during the 1990s, issues that are still being addressed today.

In 1995, NBC aired the movie *Serving in Silence: The Margarethe Cammermeyer Story*, which featured five women in key roles as it looked at the Army's policies regarding gays in the military. Glenn Close stars as Colonel Margarethe (Gerta) Cammermeyer, a well-respected Army nurse who is leaving active service in order to spend time with her teenage children but proud to be joining the Washington National Guard as its chief nurse and working as a nurse at a local VA hospital. She is first seen in a two-minute scene being escorted by Sergeant Wilson (Lorena Gale) to a MASH unit during a reserve medical emergency drill. As Cammermeyer leaves, Wilson says she's proud to have served with her.

Although she does not

Glenn Close (as Army Colonel Margarethe Cammermeyer) strides forcefully in a publicity still from the 1995 Golden Globe-nominated NBC television film *Serving in Silence: The Margarethe Cammermeyer Story*.

consider herself to be gay, she falls in love with a female artist (Judy Davis as Diane), which causes problems in her personal and professional life. Onscreen for sixty-five minutes, Cammermeyer is scrupulously honest, professional, and dedicated to nursing. When she decides she wants to attend the Army War College to increase her chances of making general, during her background investigation interview, she admits that she connects emotionally with women. Naively, she believes that the Army will look at her record and not care that she is a lesbian. Unfortunately, she is mistaken in her interpretation of the "Don't ask, don't tell" policy, and she is notified that the Army intends to discharge her, offering her the opportunity to resign to save face.[24] She refuses to resign, vowing to sue the Army for discrimination and prejudice. While her National Guard supervisor and youngest son do not support her efforts, the rest of her family and her VA supervisor fully support her. Many of her colleagues, however, are not as generous; her old friend Colonel Koufalis (Gillian Barber) will not stand up for her, believing "regulations are regulations." Her Army defense attorney (Susan Burnes as Captain Kern), who is onscreen for four and a half minutes, is proud to defend Cammermeyer. Capable and passionate, she tells Cammermeyer's family, "The longer Gerta stays, the more she undermines the Army's policy." In her statement to the discharge board, Cammermeyer says she is standing up for her rights and that she hopes her case will help change the law that discriminates against gays. The female prosecutor, Colonel Angela Webber (Christine Willis), tells the Board that they must recommend discharge, not having the authority to change policy. She recommends an honorable discharge, which the board accepts.[25] The film presents a soft discussion of the role of gays in the military, showing valid reasons for their inclusion and some of the milder harassment they experience. There is no mention of the physical dangers frequently experienced by gay military members, harassment that is still too frequently experienced today.

Two years later, in NBC's *Love's Deadly Triangle: The Texas Cadet Murder*, midshipman Diana Zamora (Holly Marie Combs) and her high school boyfriend David Graham (David Lipper) kill a female teammate of David's. After he confesses to having an affair with her, Zamora forgives him, but notes, "Women have ways of making a man forget himself. She knew what she was doing, and she must suffer the consequences." After the murder, Graham denies any relationship with the young woman, telling the police he is engaged and will marry Zamora when he graduates from the Air Force Academy. Both Zamora and Graham are accepted to service academies as members of the class of 2000, Zamora by the Naval Academy and Graham by the Air Force Academy and West Point.

Zamora begins to unravel shortly after hearing a speech about the Naval Academy honor code that in part notes, "You have been declared officers by an Act of Congress, but honor only comes from within … if you have no honor, you have nothing." The service academies enforce strict discipline and a rigid code of honor. She confesses her secret to a male plebe, and in a thirty-second-long scene, tells her roommates that David will never cheat on her (although she has cheated on him) because they have a secret they have to take to their graves. One asks, "What did you do, kill for each other?" and Zamora claims she watched him do it. When questioned by detectives, however, she says it was just talk and that she was only trying to impress her roommates.

Sent home while the investigation progresses, Zamora instead heads to Colorado Springs to see Graham, encouraging him to keep strong. In a scene indicative of her lack of a moral compass, Zamora suggests they pose for photos in their Academy uniforms. The photographer, commenting about their patriotism and service to their country, poses them before an American flag, unaware of their heinous crime. When Graham is confronted by detectives, his company officer reminds him to tell the truth, saying, "It's a matter of honor." Ultimately, he confesses to the murder, and both he and Zamora are arrested.[26] Onscreen for twenty-six minutes, Combs provides a convincing portrayal of a driven sociopath whose careful planning unravels due to her own lack of integrity and self-control.

In 1995, ABC broadcast the film *She Stood Alone: The Tailhook Scandal*, which was "a dramatized account of a female U.S. naval officer's ordeal of being harassed at a naval convention and her legal retaliation."[27] Gail O'Grady stars as Lieutenant Paula Coughlin, a Navy helicopter pilot and admiral's aide who is sexually assaulted by a number of male aviators at the 1991 Tailhook Convention in Las Vegas.[28]

While in a squadron, she tells her male pilot friend Stick (James Marshall) that she wants it all—to be the commanding officer of a squadron, to fly in combat, and to become an admiral. And she has paid her dues so far, having completed two WESTPAC cruises during a twelve-month deployment and served as both a squadron maintenance officer and operations officer, jobs that surprise the admiral. When she says, "We're everywhere, Sir—women. I hope it's not a problem for you, me being one," he assures her it is not, yet he still tells her that her record is very impressive "for a woman" and that there are significant differences between men and women that feminists have not considered in terms of the military. She retorts that she doesn't consider herself to be a man. When the admiral says she is a bit cocky, she suggests using a non-gender specific term, showing that she can give and take as well as the "boys."

Naval Academy plebe Diane Zamora's (Holly Marie Combs) plans to earn a commission in the U.S. Navy when she is arrested for murder in the 1997 NBC made-for-television drama *Love's Deadly Triangle: The Texas Cadet Murder*.

Coughlin gets hints about the tone of Tailhook beforehand. Stick tells her that it's one big, drunken weekend and to be careful. The 1991 Tailhook was held just after the conclusion of the Gulf War, and naval aviators who participated in the war were feeling their oats. The Secretary of the Navy, Chief of Naval Operations, thirty admirals, and more than 4,000 Navy and Marine Corps aviators partied in Las Vegas. While many of her peers were partying, Coughlin and several other female aviators attended technical panels, wearing civilian business attire and miniature pilot wings on their lapels. In one thirty-five second scene, Lieutenant Monica Rivadeneivio (Eva de Viveiros) asks when women are going to be allowed to fly in combat and is roundly booed. She tells Coughlin, "What a bunch of Fred Flintstones. They need to get over it. We're here to stay."

After the panel, Coughlin changes her clothes and joins her peers, only to be attacked by a number of drunken men lining both sides of the hall (the Gauntlet), who rip her clothes and grab her breasts. Coughlin screams and calls unsuccessfully for help during the attack. The next morning, she tells Monica of her experience, who asks if they knew she was an aviator. Given the comments they made about her being an admiral's aide, she says, "They knew." Monica tells her it goes with the territory and to let it go. When she reports the incident to her boss, he says, "What do you expect from fighter pilots?" She wants them held accountable, but the system is against her. Transferred to a desk job and denied the opportunity to get her flight hours, male aviators everywhere close ranks against her. Another female aviator, Lieutenant Commander Evans (Terye Rothery), tells her that it should have been handled quietly, causing her to lament that women are the worst, providing her with no support. Later, Evans confesses that she had previously been subjected to the Gauntlet but never told anyone.

Ultimately, the Chief of Naval Operations, Admiral Frank Kelso, instituted new standards of behavior throughout the Navy to ensure that there would be no further tolerance of sexual harassment. Coughlin resigned from the Navy in 1994. Her father, who had also been a naval aviator, was horrified at her treatment both at Tailhook and afterwards. He was proud of her because she changed the Navy, seeing her as a warrior who emerged victorious from battle. And the battle continues today; unfortunately, while the incidents of sexual harassment have decreased, they have not totally ended.[29]

Thrillers

During the 1990s, the thriller continued to grow in popularity, both in the theater and on television. Like disaster films, key players tended to be first responders, but several films included military women as minor and major characters, involved in solving the crimes central to the films' storylines.

The action in the film *Broken Arrow* (1996) centers on Major Vic "Deak" Deakins' (John Travolta) attempts to steal a stealth aircraft carrying nuclear missiles. While several Air Force women are visible in the flight control center, only one enlisted woman utters one line—"Yes, sir." The popular film *Patriot Games* (1992) includes also one short scene in which military women speak. Jack Ryan (Harrison Ford) is teaching a history seminar at the U.S. Naval Academy, and three female midshipmen (Bonnie Webster, Pamela Saxon and Leah Tabassi) each have two lines in the discussion of Thucydides' *History of the Peloponnesian War.*

The 1996 film *Lone Star* addresses issues of race, ethnicity, and identity. Private Athena Johnson (Chandra Wilson), a young off-duty African American soldier, unsuccessfully tries to keep two men from fighting in a bar. She has a reputation of being a screw-up, which her white master sergeant blames on her difficult childhood, saying she has the potential to be a good soldier. She fails a drug test, and her commanding officer, who is black and also believes she can be a good soldier, asks if she is unhappy in the Army. She notes that it's "*their* country" and she just does what she's told. When asked to explain her statement, she talks about the discrimination she has encountered in both the civilian world and the Army. Sounding like a father speaking to a wayward child, he talks to her about teamwork and the need to do her part so she doesn't let her teammates down. Surprised by his compassion, she agrees to try harder to be a good soldier.

The master sergeant loves African American Sergeant Priscilla North (LaTanya Richardson), who he wants to marry. In a three-minute scene, she worries what will happen when she is transferred. Like a person truly blinded by love, he says if he cannot be transferred to her duty station, he will get out of the Army to be with her, even though he will only have two years until he is eligible for retirement. Neither of these female characters plays a significant role in the larger murder mystery, but they provide a nice counter to the racism found outside the Army post's gates.

Counter Measures (1999) is the sequel to *Crash Dive* (1996). Once again, terrorists have hijacked a Soviet submarine, and retired SEAL Jake Fuller (Michael Dudekoff), now a Navy captain and doctor, must save the day. The film features two female Navy officers, one of whom plays a minor role in the story while the other is a central character. Captain Blake (Tracy Brooks Swope) is the Chief of Intelligence at Central Command headquarters. Onscreen for four minutes, she is middle-aged and full-figured—and competent and professional. She determines that terrorists have taken over the submarine and is in charge of the operation to retake it. She hatches the plan that pairs the other woman, Ensign Swain (Alexander Keith) with Fuller.

Swain, allegedly a Navy nurse sent to the submarine to treat an injured sailor, initially is timid and uncertain; however, once onboard the submarine, she is very sharp, remarking that the sailors who helped them onboard were wearing the "wrong" type of side arms, something a young nurse most likely would not have known. Onscreen for sixteen minutes, she is a proficient martial artist and also knows all about the submarine's special nuclear missile and how it operates. Injured in a fight and captured by the terrorists, she is taken to the bridge and learns of their plans to fire the missile at an American city (she also speaks Russian). Despite her injury, she works with a dying Russian to stop the missile launch. Confessing to Fuller that she is actually a lieutenant and a member of naval intelligence, they work together to surface the submarine, kill the remaining terrorist, and save the day. And, of course, after turning the submarine over to Captain Blake, Fuller announces, "I need a vacation. What about you, Swain?" and extends his hand, which she takes.

The murder mystery *The General's Daughter* (1999) features three military women, one of whom is the general's deceased daughter (Leslie Stefanson as Captain Elizabeth Campbell). Onscreen for eight minutes, Campbell is a psychologist at an Army psy-warfare school run by her father. She is found dead on the base, staked naked to the ground. While the general's staff begins a massive cover-up, CID Warrant Officer Paul Brenner (John Travolta) and Warrant Officer Sara Sunhill (Madeline Stowe), a rape counselor and investigator, are sent to investigate.

First on the scene of the crime is Private Robbin (Ariyan A. Johnson), who tells the investigators that the women on the post liked Campbell because she supported and looked after them. Onscreen for just over one minute, Robbin also mentions that while Campbell was protective of them, she was not close to any of them.

Sunhill, who wears civilian clothes for the entire thirty-one minutes she is onscreen, was previously romantically involved with Brenner, which creates tension between them and initially negatively impacts the investigation. While Sunhill takes a backseat to Brenner, she proves to be smart, capable, and tough, and she uncovers the root reason for Campbell's outlandish behavior. However, she is also portrayed as a helpless victim, assaulted by an Army officer at the murder scene and later held hostage in a minefield, requiring Brenner to rescue her.

Brenner and Sunhill's investigation uncovers a story of sexual assault, sexual promiscuity, and murder, all centered around Captain Campbell. As a student at West Point, she was disliked by her male peers, who resented "someone who had to squat to piss" being smarter than them. One night on maneuvers, she was gang raped by five cadets who were never punished. Her father, fearful of the impact that an investigation would have on his own career, tells her to forget that the rape ever happened. Resentful of his lack of support and compassion, she sleeps with all of the senior men on the post, married and single, rubbing her behavior in her father's face. Her dysfunctional relationship with her father ultimately leads to her death, when her attempt to restage her original rape goes awry and she is murdered. Campbell is portrayed as promiscuous and undisciplined, despite her professional background as a psychologist.

The film has received some scholarly attention, most of which centers on Campbell's outrageous behavior. Meredith Guthrie has posited that Campbell's support of the women on base was aimed at lessening the Army's systemic discrimination against women, the result of her own treatment at West Point and by her father.[30] While that is certainly a possibility, it should also be noted that as late as the 1990s, female officers were expected to mentor the enlisted women on a base, providing advice but not socializing with them, exactly as Campbell did.

Fire Birds, aka *Wings of the Apache* (1990), tells the story of Army helicopter pilots working along the U.S. southern border as part of the DEA's drug interdiction efforts. Among these pilots is Chief Warrant Officer Billie Lee Guthrie (Sean Young), who flies an OH-58 Kiowa Scout helicopter. Onscreen for eighteen minutes, she was romantically involved years before with Chief Warrant Officer Jake Preston (Nicholas Cage), an Apache pilot. While he is interested in rekindling their romance, Guthrie is more interested in her career and rebuffs him several times, telling him, "I'm not a piece of steak for you to fight over" and that she is not interested in staying home and having babies and cooking like his mother did—she is a helicopter pilot. They continue to verbally spar for quite some time, but eventually, they renew their relationship. In fact, her longest scene occurs when they are having sex. When she is the only woman selected for a dangerous mission, he objects, causing her to comment, "You think it's fine for me to fly when there's nothing at stake, but a dangerous mission, that's only for men." He worries for her safety, a fear she brushes off, saying, "I chose this career and you, my friend, you're just gonna have to accept this." Her comments echo the sentiments of many female military aviators who were excluded from possible combat missions despite their outstanding skills and training. Guthrie has excellent instincts and

Army helicopter pilots Billie Lee Guthrie (Sean Young, left) and Jake Preston (Nicolas Cage) shake hands in this publicity still for the 1991 Touchstone Pictures film *Fire Birds (Wings of the Apache)*.

is a true asset to the unit; she locates the drug lord's secret radar site and a rebel airship, all while managing to evade their best pilot. Working with Preston, they defeat the enemy pilot—and argue about who is going to fly the helicopter back to their base.

There are also several other female pilots in the squadron, although only one has a speaking part. She is onscreen for two minutes and does not play a significant role in the film's action. Obviously having two women on the mission, which would have been required by Army regulations, would have been inconvenient for the film's plot.

In *Excessive Force II: Force on Force* (1995), Lieutenant Harly Cordell (Stacie Randall) is a former member of Army Special Forces now working in the Army CID office at Fort Ord, California. This is obviously a fantasy story since women were not able to be members of any military Special Forces unit during the Gulf War, and her actions in the film are over the top. Onscreen for forty-one minutes, she is beautiful, skillful, and driven. Sent to investigate a killing committed by a man with a Special Forces tattoo, she finds herself in the middle of a murder mystery that has ties to her past. Despite being incapacitated by a bullet lodged in her brain, courtesy of her former Special Forces boss and lover, Captain Bobby Tucci (Michael Wiseman), she is intent on finding him, regardless of the personal danger. The story of her relationship with Tucci is told in a series of flashbacks which reveal that during the Gulf War, Tucci formed a private assassination squad; when she refused to join, he shot her and disappeared. She is out for revenge and tracks him ruthlessly, knowing it could kill her, but as her revenge, she just wants to live one second longer than he does. At one point, she finds him, causing him to comment, "Normally, the people I kill stay dead." She tells him to step into the light so she can see his eyes when she kills him; however, their fight ends in a stalemate, and he escapes.

Her boyfriend fears for her life because the bullet is slipping, causing her to pass out, and when she refuses to abandon her quest, he ends their relationship. Cordell continues her pursuit despite her worsening health, and after an exciting series of chase scenes and fights, she finally kills him, murmuring, "Just one second longer" before passing out. She awakens in the hospital to learn that the bullet in her brain has been successfully removed and her boyfriend is back. After asking him to marry her, Cordell tells him that once she has healed, she is going to resign her commission, presumably to settle down to married life, to which he responds that he won't argue with her because she carries a big gun. Her decision leaves the viewer wondering if, after all that time, she will be able to give up her action-filled life quite so easily.

The final film of this chapter, *Inflammable* (1995), is a made-for-television murder mystery that includes servicewomen in three key roles. When a female sailor reports incidents of sexual harassment during a crossing the line ceremony onboard the fast combat support ship USS *Davenport*,[31] lawyer Lieutenant Junior Grade Kay Dolan (Marg Helgenberger) is dispatched to investigate the accusations, including the physical assault on Petty Officer Third Class Tanya Santos (Elizabeth Rodriguez), which is interrupted by the food services officer, Chief Warrant Officer Charlene Porter (Park Overall). Onscreen for four minutes, Santos is a good worker whose subsequent death changes the focus of Dolan's investigation from assault to murder.

Dolan is smart, skillful, and nobody's fool, although it takes her a while (and a few close calls) to unravel the mystery. Onscreen for almost fifty-three minutes, she initially believes that the ship's First Lieutenant (Jud Ciccolella as Chief Petty Officer Miller) is the guilty party and that her investigation is complete after he is supposedly lost at sea; she soon realizes, however, that there is more than just sexual harassment going on. Santos was killed after stumbling upon a drug smuggling operation that involved the men who were harassing her. Miller, however, is not in charge of the operation—or even a participant; the real ringleader is Chief Warrant Officer Porter.

Onscreen for sixteen minutes, Porter is tough, capable, and well thought of by the crew. She convincingly feeds Dolan false information and support during her investigation, just to make certain that the truth does not come out. In love with the ship's captain, Jack Guthrie (Kris Kristofferson), she is jealous of the closeness between Guthrie and Dolan, who had previously been romantically involved. She attempts to kill Dolan, only to be killed herself by Miller. Despite the previous relationship between Dolan and Guthrie, both actually behave professionally during the majority of the investigation. As Dolan prepares to leave the ship, she tells him, "If you ever get to Washington..." and they salute each other, but the viewer is left with the feeling that they will not see each other again anytime soon.[32]

As the 1990s came to an end, military women continued to prove that they were valuable members of the American military team, pushing for greater responsibility, authority, and access to combat-related positions. This is something that would successfully be accomplished in the early days of the twenty-first century, partially as the result of the invasions of Iraq and Afghanistan following the tragic attacks of September 11.

Seven

All That You Can Be
The 2000s

The first decade of the twenty-first century was a fairly eventful time for women in the military. After the unprecedented attacks of September 11, 2001, thousands of American men and women joined the military to help track down the terrorists who instigated these acts. Although no important legislation was passed regarding women in the military and submarine duty and combat positions still remained off limits, servicewomen began being utilized in ways that had formerly not been sanctioned. This led to "a rapid expansion of jobs and change in roles for Army women," as well as those in the other service branches.[1] These changing roles garnered a lot of press, giving Americans at home a lot to think about.

Unfortunately, not all of the publicity regarding the military was positive. In 2004, the American public was shocked to learn about prisoner abuses that were occurring in Iraq. Following in the wake of the detainee abuse scandal at Abu Ghraib prison, eight American soldiers were court-martialed. Among them were three women, further shocking viewers as the story continued to unfold. Specialists Sabrina Harman and Megan Ambuhl were both court-martialed, but the name that was heard most often in the media is that of Private Lynndie England, who, through photographs splayed across the media, was seen leading a detainee around on a leash and giving a thumbs-up symbol next to a human pyramid of naked prisoners. In connection with her part in the Abu Ghraib abuses, England was court-martialed and dishonorably discharged, receiving a three-year prison sentence for maltreatment of prisoners and prisoner abuse.[2] While the women's part in the scandal severely impacted American opinion regarding the military in general, it also showed that women are not all that different when confronted with the horrors of war, "no less capable of heroism or depravity ... neither too weak nor too moral to fight."[3]

Despite the damage to the military's image caused by this incident, many servicewomen continued to excel in the first decade of the new century, distinguishing themselves while breaking new ground. As noted in a 2009 *CQ Researcher* report, "In 2008, Ann E. Dunwoody, the Army's top supply officer, became the first female four-star general."[4] The following year, Sergeant Major Teresa L. King was selected to run the Army's "ultra-tough drill-sergeant training program, the first woman to hold the post."[5] Although many have continuously bemoaned the demise of unit cohesion and efficiency in a fully gender integrated military, many servicewomen actually report that "once their male colleagues see them in action, they quickly gain respect."[6]

Top grossing movies of the decade include a fair number of depictions of women in the military, but the majority of those films are science fiction, a genre not addressed in this volume.[7] Since the relationship between Hollywood and the military has "helped shape the perceptions that the American people have had of war, of violence, and of its armed services,"[8] including influencing how the public feels about servicewomen, the military films of the 2000s drew on those perceptions when portraying these women in uniform. These performances showcase a wide variety of roles in many different situations and wars, and the portrayals are both positive and negative.

Action Films

As Susan Linville notes, "Issues of gender and war ... continue to beget intractable anxieties in American culture."[9] Due to those perceived anxieties, probably the last genre to fully make use of female servicemembers has been the war action film. Hollywood has been reluctant to insert fighting women into this genre in any substantial way; in real life, however, they are already there. The films of this decade do offer some examples of "tough chicks," but they are generally only secondary characters, not the stars of the films.

A full 20 percent of films surveyed for this decade have a woman with only one or two spoken lines, most of which fall into the action category. Interestingly, these "token" women are not the only women in uniform shown in these movies—many show a multitude of servicewomen as extras, ubiquitous but silent. In *Lions for Lambs* (2007), for example, about two dozen women in uniform are shown, but only one clerk speaks. She has one line and is onscreen about two minutes. The same is true for *Behind Enemy Lines* (2001), *Behind Enemy Lines: Axis of Evil* (2006), and *Behind Enemy Lines: Columbia* (2009). In each of these films, quite a few military women are visible, but only one gets a token few lines to speak. *The Sum of All Fears* (2002) is only slightly better—it has two women onscreen for about one minute each, but at least each of them has several speaking lines. These films, and others like them, render servicewomen's contributions almost invisible, much as their real-life counterparts. By perpetuating this invisibility, "contemporary media culture plays a significant role in arbitrating gendered bodies," in effect limiting what women are and what they think they can become.[10]

Flight of Fury (2007) features two military women in fairly small roles. Karen David portrays Air Force Master Sergeant Landers, aide to General Barnes (Angus MacInnes). Onscreen for five minutes, Landers is key to helping Barnes navigate the dicey situation in which they find themselves, including keeping him in constant contact with Admiral Pendleton (Tim Woodward). Her counterpart, aide to Pendleton, is never even addressed by name. Cristina Leodorescu portrays the lieutenant junior grade who is onscreen for only three minutes and whose role is much less visible than Landers.' Both women perform their duties extremely capably, but neither is truly integral to the plot or climax of the film.

The 2009 short film *Taking Fire* features one woman in uniform. Colonel Regina Dawson (Donnelle Russell) is stationed in Iraq as operational soldier to General Strong (John Godley); they are regular Army and do not look particularly favorably upon the "fucking reservists" that get sent to their unit, especially Major Donovan (Spencer Lighte). Onscreen for two minutes with just a few lines, Dawson exudes military bearing and is highly proficient in her duties, but she instigates the prank pulled on Donovan when they ship him off with a Special Ops team rather than just let him return to his unit in the States, enjoying camaraderie with the general, who obviously approves of her joke.

Larger roles for female military personnel in action movies can also be found. *Rain* (2000) is a made-for-television film about Army dogs that served in Vietnam. This film is one of only seven films in this survey that show an American woman in the military serving in Vietnam, and she is the only one who is not a nurse (she is, however, still in the medical field). Onscreen for over 15 percent of the film's run time, Pamela Moore Somers portrays Sergeant Abbey Palmer, a medical technician who helps care for Rain when he is injured during a battle. She and Rain's handler

(Scott Cooper as Private Joe Holland) become involved, but the love interest angle is secondary. Palmer's job is always her primary focus, and both Holland and Rain fully heal while under her care. She also helps save Rain from some Viet Cong by firing on them with Holland's weapon, which shows her ability to adapt in all environments.

In the fifth installment of the *Operation Delta Force* film franchise, subtitled *Random Fire* (2000), Emily Whitefield portrays intelligence and reconnaissance specialist Sergeant Karen Sommers. She is onscreen almost 17 percent of the movie's run time, and her role is crucial to the successful completion of the team's mission. Despite that fact, she is relegated to the background while the men look over the recon photos and plan the mission. She is, however, very well trained and even accompanies the team on part of the mission, telling the protagonist, "I'm a soldier, remember?" When he responds with, "No, you're a woman," she gets angry and lets him know how irrelevant her gender is to the performance of her duty as a member of the United States Army.

The animated 2003 film *G.I. Joe: Spy Troops* picks up where the television show left off, with the Joes fighting COBRA command. As with the 1987 *G.I. Joe* film discussed in Chapter Five, this film also features Scarlett as a member of the elite Joe fighting unit. In the opening sequence, the team is on maneuvers, and Scarlett enjoys some friendly teasing when High-Tech tells her that she "drives that truck like a girl," quipping back, "That good, huh?" She is fully integrated and an essential part of the team, possessing impressive fighting and archery skills. However, she still has to be rescued twice by Snake Eyes in this short film, presenting a somewhat pejorative depiction of an elite soldier. Only onscreen for four minutes, the character of Scarlett is more fully explored in the 2009 live-action film based on the same characters.

G.I. Joe: The Rise of Cobra (2009) features Rachel Nichols as Scarlett, the one fighting female shown with the elite soldiers that make up the Joe team, here known as the "top men and women from the best military units in the world—the alpha dogs." Other female servicewomen are shown in the film, but they are primarily shown working in more traditional areas, such as performing technical and clerical duties. There is another fighter shown briefly as she demonstrates the abilities of a stealth camouflage suit, but she only grunts and has no lines. None of the women are in proper uniforms, either, with their long hair flowing loose around their shoulders and their shirts unbuttoned, showing cleavage.

In Scarlett's first scene, she comes in and takes out several enemy combatants with her archery skills. She is brilliant and highly capable, graduating from college at the age of twelve and rising through the military ranks to become one of the best. Like her predecessors Karen Walden and Jordan O'Neil, discussed in the previous chapter, Scarlett is a true virago, convinced that the right and ability to fight does not exclusively belong to men.[11] Ripcord (Marlon Wayans), a new team member, is attracted to Scarlett, but that does not make him treat her any different—she is a soldier, and that is how she wants to be known. This attitude exemplifies the "attitude of many successful military women today—they do not want to be seen as a 'woman pilot' or a 'woman engineer' or a 'woman officer,' they simply want to be seen as military pilots, engineers, and officers."[12] Scarlett has earned her spot with the team, and her gender should not and does not come into play.

Stealth (2005) stars Jessica Biel as Lieutenant Kara Wade, a fighter pilot for the Navy. Another high achiever and rising star, Wade is one of three pilots chosen "from over 400 applicants" to pilot the Navy's new Talon, a fighter jet with stealth capabilities. The fact that one of the three is a woman is notable, which Lieutenant Henry Purcell (Jamie Foxx) points out when he tells Kara, "You are a singularity; you are a freak of nature." The anomaly of having a woman attain her current position is again highlighted as Henry tells Lieutenant Ben Gannon (Josh Lucas) that Kara is "being groomed by the Navy" and that "if any woman is going to rise to the top of this business, it's going to be Kara Wade."

Navy fighter pilot Lieutenant Kara Wade (Jessica Biel) studies groundbreaking technology in the 2005 film *Stealth* from Columbia Pictures.

Given the mission of training with an unmanned combat air vehicle known as EDI, the three pilots are concerned about whether "war should become some kind of video game." Through artificial intelligence, EDI begins learning, and the machine's interpretation of how things should be handled during a mission does not align with the directives as given, causing conflicts. EDI goes rogue and is instrumental in the death of Purcell, and debris from his exploding jet strikes Wade's plane, forcing her to eject into North Korean territory. As she readies herself to eject from the plane, she is apprehensive but keeps it together enough to determine her coordinates and relay them to command. She is resourceful and well-trained, deftly avoiding capture by the North Koreans, but a sniper manages to wound her. Fairly calm under the pressure of being pursued, she lies in wait and fires on the approaching North Korean army, wounding the sniper in the knee. Despite being behind enemy lines and wounded, Wade maintains her composure and fights her way toward the demilitarized zone (DMZ) in hopes of a rescue. Throughout, Wade is determined and more than capable, yet the film still feels the need to pointedly have Gannon come in to save her, somewhat undermining the strongly positive image portrayed otherwise.

The danger of advanced technology is also at the heart of *Eagle Eye* (2008), which features Rosario Dawson as Air Force Captain Zoe Perez. She is the investigator trying to stop the plot that threatens the President and his cabinet, and she performs her duties with dogged relentlessness. As the film's intricate plot unfolds, Perez asserts her authority as primary investigator, telling the lead FBI agent, "I don't work for you. I work for the Air Force." Her actions earn her a commendation, and although she is somewhat of a secondary character in the film, her dedication to uncovering the truth shows her sense of commitment to her job, and she is instrumental in solving the mystery and minimizing loss of life.

Air Strike (2004) features Second Lieutenant Charlotte "Charlie" Jones (Jennifer Gareis) as a helicopter pilot who gets herself attached to the Army Rangers. She tells her squadron leader (Robert Rusler as Captain Ben Garret) that she is there for "action, adventure—whatever the challenge, I'm up for it." When he goes up in a chopper with her to assess her proficiency level, Garret starts to give her instructions on what maneuvers to show him, but she stops him by saying, "Instead of boring you with a lot of tech bullshit, why don't I show you what this pilot can do?" Her precision with the craft impresses him, making him comment, "The girl's got skills." She soon finds out, however, that she may not be able to back up her bluster. When she freezes during an air confrontation, Garret has to take over the controls. She is ashamed, but he tells her, "You're an excellent pilot, Charlie. All you need is confidence under fire, and that comes one way—experience." She also joins the men twice during ground maneuvers, holding her own with the men, but that is something that would not have occurred in the real world.

Rosario Dawson as Captain Zoe Perez, an Air Force investigator in the 2008 thriller *Eagle Eye*.

Two films from 2006 feature the same female Marine character. Both *Hunt for Eagle One* and *Hunt for Eagle One: Crash Point* center on Captain Amy Jennings (Theresa Randle) as she and the Marines fight against a terror cell in the Philippines. Onscreen in the first film for seventeen minutes (more than 19 percent of the film's run time), Jennings is captured when the helicopter she is piloting gets shot down, and the film's protagonist and his squad must mount a rescue. Some of the men start to grumble about the mission, but they are quickly reminded, "That pilot is a Marine aviator and a superior officer" and "Marines never leave their own behind." Under interrogation and threatened with rape, Jennings does not break, keeping calm and strong until the rescue team arrives.

In *Crash Point*, Randle is onscreen for thirteen minutes (15 percent of run time). When the squad gets a mission to fight some of the Philippine rebels, Jennings asks to go, and her request is denied. Of course, she goes against orders and drops down to participate in the mission anyway. These low-budget, straight-to-video films are similar to the Namsploitation films of the 1980s, and as such, disobeying orders to get the job done is par for the course—in this case, it just happens to be a woman who ignores her orders. It is soon clear, however, that she has never been in ground combat before, and her inexperience causes issues for herself and the others. This film does not portray Randle's character in as positive a light as the first movie did—male or female, the military demands complete obedience, and disobeying a direct order has consequences. Not surprisingly, however, like the 1980s films referenced above, all is forgiven when the mission is successful completed. In the film, Jennings does not even get a reprimand; in reality, she would likely have had to face some type of disciplinary action for disobeying a direct order.

In 2004's *Spartan,* the President's daughter is kidnapped, and a small group of elite soldiers are sent to rescue her. Sergeant Jackie Black (Tia Texada), a Delta Force instructor who teaches knife fighting, tries to join the team. When Black asks Master Gunnery Sergeant Scott (Val Kilmer), "Man to man—can you get me on the plane?" it is clear that she sees herself only in terms of her abilities; gender is not a defining characteristic, and she demands that recognition from others. She wants to be included in the mission, and she is confident that her expertise will be useful. When Scott later trusts her with sensitive information, she tells him, "Ain't nobody here but two people in green." He tries to tell her that their current situation goes beyond that, but she counters with, "Nothing goes beyond that." The military is all that matters to her; even when dying, her last thoughts are of whether or not their mission has been accomplished. To her, it is acceptable to die in the line of duty, as long as she can die with honor knowing her mission was successfully executed.

Thrillers

In 2008's *Garrison*, the action revolves around allegations of spousal abuse. Army lawyer Captain Karen Taylor (Shelley Calene-Black) has just a small role in the film, but her two minutes onscreen are very telling regarding the continued discrimination and disrespect that servicewomen face. Taylor gets contacted by Staff Sergeant Nathan Cross'(James Jay Barnes) wife regarding claims of spousal abuse. As she investigates, Taylor reaches out to Cross's platoon sergeant Charles Mace (Brent Boller) asking to speak with Cross; Mace is immediately uncooperative, demanding to know what she wants with his soldier. He also makes her follow him because he just walks off while she is talking. Mace's attitude toward Taylor is impolite and condescending, and the viewer is left wondering whether he would have treated a male captain in the same fashion.

Despite the fact that Taylor is Mace's superior officer, he is completely dismissive of her; when they arrive in his office, he turns his back and begins rifling through some papers while she is speaking. At first flabbergasted at his demeanor, she hems and haws when attempting to repeat her request, but she quickly grows impatient and irritated, shouting, "Sergeant!" which causes him to turn around. When she again insists on speaking with Cross, he abrasively tells her that she has no right to come into his office making demands, to which she replies, "I think you better watch your tone, Sergeant." Befitting an officer of the United States Army, Taylor takes charge of the situation, letting the sergeant know that, because of her rank, she has earned and demands his respect and that his misogynist attitude will not be tolerated.

Basic (2003) is a thriller that revolves around an Army Ranger jungle training exercise that goes wrong. The inquiry into the incident is given to Captain Julia Osborne (Connie Nielsen), an investigator for the Military Police. Despite her assertion that she is confident in her ability to find out the truth, DEA agent and ex–Ranger Tom Hardy (John Travolta) is brought in to assist in the investigation, something that makes her, in her own words, "hostile and uncooperative." As they wind their way through the "degrees of truth" to find out what really happened, Osborne is the consummate law enforcement officer, adhering to Army guidelines and regulations even when Hardy does not; she even takes down a corrupt drug-dealing doctor in the midst of her primary investigation. Onscreen for just under one-third of the film's run time, Nielsen's character provides the audience with a look at the stellar skills and capabilities that women in the military possess in all jobs performed. She believes in "the whole honor and duty thing" and wants to make things right, stating emphatically, "I'm going to try to figure this whole mess out because I care about what happened out there."

Among the members of the squad being investigated is Nuñez (Rosalyn Sanchez), even though, in reality, no women have ever been assigned to a U.S. Army Ranger unit. As the only female amongst ultra-hyper males, sexual discrimination and harassment would most likely come along with the territory, so acting like a "tough chick" is her coping mechanism. Nuñez knows that "in a patriarchal culture, most representations of women are readable as connoting 'otherness' or difference," and she works hard to make herself one of the boys.[13] Onscreen for six minutes, Nuñez wields her big gun and speaks crudely and aggressively, the epitome of the masculinized military female. Another squad member is homosexual, however, which in that testosterone-driven world makes having a woman around pale in comparison, so Nuñez escapes most of the "discriminatory hate crime" treatment that Levi Kendall (Giovanni Ribisi) must endure.

Captain Julia Osborne (Connie Nielsen) investigates an intricate cover up in *Basic*, a 2003 thriller from Phoenix Pictures.

Quicksand (2002) is a mystery-thriller with Marine Second Lieutenant Randall "Randi" Stewart (Brooke Theiss) at the heart of the mystery. Her father, the base commander, "believes there's no place in the military for a woman," so she becomes a Marine to prove him wrong. Throughout the film, Stewart is portrayed as a troubled girl whose behavior in and out of uniform has her "headed for court-martial" for conduct unbecoming an officer. She is constantly drunk, showing up the Officers Club in either slinky dresses or a disheveled uniform with several buttons undone to show inappropriate cleavage; when the new base psychologist (Michael Dudikoff as Bill Turner) tries to get to the bottom of her discipline issues, she comes on to him rather than let him help her.

Despite her psychological issues, which stem from sexual abuse by her brother when she was just a child, she is still a capable Marine. She has issues not of her own making, and eventually she chooses to get help in order to begin to heal. In the end, her determination to make her military career a priority wins out over taking a psychiatric discharge.

Tammy Isbell is featured in *Danger Beneath the Sea* (2001), portraying Navy Lieutenant Clare Holliday. She is aide to Rear Admiral Eugene Justice (Gerald McRaney) and base liaison for military families. Onscreen for ten minutes, she is the admiral's go-to person for advice and insight. When asked her opinion, she gives it expertly, and it is always on target. After imparting a particularly astute judgment, Justice tells Holliday, "It's that kind of thinking that makes a top-notch submarine commander," to which she replies, "Well, maybe the Pentagon will rethink their position about women serving aboard submarines, sir." He is not amused at her comment, and it would take another nine years after the making of this film before women were allowed to fulfill that goal.

Another strong naval officer is found in 2005's *Tides of War*. Lieutenant Claire Trifoli (Catherine Dent) is with Naval Intelligence, and her team "has been asked to break down intel" regarding a stealth encounter with an undetectable North Korean ship. She gets herself assigned to the team that goes down with the submarine to parse out what happened, a coup that the boat's captain (Adrian Paul) calls "unprecedented," the fact that a Navy female is on duty aboard his submarine. His dive officer, however, is more progressive, letting Trifoli know that her brother "would have been proud that you're serving on a submarine." Throughout the mission, she is focused and on target with her intel, but she is pretty much ignored by the men who are irritated by her presence; the XO even calls her "excess baggage." Despite that fact, her assessment proves vital to locating the enemy's stealth sub and destroying it. Following the operation, the captain acknowledges her importance to the success of their mission, telling her, "Don't lose that fighting spirit; we need more people like you." The obvious change in attitude regarding the suitability of women aboard submarines can help viewers work towards a better understanding of the true capabilities of military women and "question the nature of the law and legal institutions and how they function within broader societal practices that turn on gender."[14]

Disaster Films

A plethora of disaster films were made during the 2000s, and quite a few showed servicewomen in a variety of roles. The film *2012* (2009) has only one military woman (Leigh Burrows) with just one line—she salutes the President (Danny Glover) and says, "Mr. President, sir." She is present in the White House, wearing a stethoscope and helping people who have been injured. The other disaster films in this decade that have women in the military do so on a larger scale. *Earthstorm* (2006) also shows just one woman in the military, but she gets many more lines and is a more important character. Major Rachel Fine (Jessica Heafey) is an Air Force shuttle pilot, one of the team sent in to disburse the storm that is threatening Earth's continued existence. She is onscreen for six minutes and is instrumental to the success of their mission.

Polar Opposites (2008) features Beth Grant as Army General Lynn Masters and is one of only two films in this survey to portray a female general in the United States military.[15] Masters is tough and no-nonsense, reporting directly to the President. Even as someone asks, "You're a general?" making it sound like he's never heard of such a thing before, she shows that she has earned her rank, even apologizing for not acting quickly enough at one point, saying, "Sorry. I wasn't myself." It is obvious that she is used to making snap decisions in order to help and protect the people around her.

Major Rebecca Childs (Hilary Swank) of the Air Force confers with mission leader Commander Bob Iverson (Bruce Greenwood) in *The Core* (2003).

The Core (2003) centers on a team sent down to restart the earth's core, and the pilot of the makeshift craft is Air Force pilot Major Rebecca Childs (Hilary Swank). Onscreen for just over 20 percent of the film, "Beck" is a rising star for NASA who finds things generally come easily for her. Although Childs is a superb pilot with "exceptional navigational skills," Commander Bob Iverson (Bruce Greenwood) tells her that being naturally gifted "doesn't mean you're ready to sit in that [commander's] chair." When she questions why he feels that way, Iverson explains, "You're used to winning, and you're not really a leader until you've lost." As this foreshadowing suggests, this is a lesson she must internalize when Iverson is killed. Throughout the trials she and the team endure, Childs becomes a true leader and realizes the truth in Iverson's admonition that "being a leader isn't about ability—it's about responsibility." Hesitant and unsure at first, Childs adapts quickly to her new role as mission commander, even when making the "shitty call" to let Serge (Tchéky Karyo) die in order to protect the others and the mission.

Drama

For several dramatic films of the 2000s, there is just one military woman with a very small speaking part. In 2008's *Stop-Loss*, as Sergeant King (Ryan Phillipe) is being told he's not being discharged on schedule,[16] there are several women in uniform working in processing, one with a single spoken line. In *Ike: Countdown to D-Day* (2004), there are also several servicewomen shown, but, again, only one gets to speak, and she is onscreen for just one minute. In 2004's *Stateside*, Penny Marshall plays First Lieutenant Cheverone, attending nurse to Mark Deloach

(Jonathan Tucker). Cheverone has several lines, but she is only in two scenes and onscreen for just two minutes, playfully working toward getting her patient healthy again.

There is also just one woman in uniform shown in 2009's *War Stories*. She is an Air Force recruiter (Samantha Booth) visiting a high school campus. When one student comes to see her, she is friendly and helpful at first, telling him that the Air Force is "a great opportunity for both men and women." When she sees his rainbow bracelet, however, she becomes hostile, telling him, "We don't take your kind." The film is set before "Don't ask, don't tell" was repealed, and the recruiter's animosity shows the depth of hatred many in the service had and have for homosexuals.

Taking Chance (2009) shows several women in the military, two of whom get several lines. While they are not essential to the film's plot, both women have interesting roles. The mortuary technician (Sharon Washington) highlights the attention given to preparing the bodies of fallen soldiers as they are readied for burial. As they show the tech working on Corporal Phelps' body, her sense of duty is strong, and it is with the greatest dedication and somber professionalism that she tells Lieutenant Colonel Strobl (Kevin Bacon), "It's been my privilege to care for him, sir." Also featured is Julie White as Colonel Karen Bell, who is in charge of preparing the uniforms in which soldiers are buried. Even as Bell remarks, "Bet you didn't know Marines could sew," it is clear that she, too, takes a great deal of pride in her unit's role in the burial process. Both of these women have difficult jobs to perform, but their sense of duty and honor allows them to do them expertly.

The Guardian (2006) centers on new rescue swimmer recruits in the Coast Guard's Aviation Survival Technician (AST) program. Several of the recruits are women, including Airman Cate Lindsay (Shelby Fenner) and an unnamed woman who graduates from the program and is onscreen for two minutes but has no speaking lines in the film. Lindsay, however, has multiple lines and is onscreen for four minutes. She is shown hanging out with the guys, even going drinking with them, but no hint is given of any romance. They are simply bonding over their shared training experiences. Lindsay seems to be capably handling her training, making it through to advanced training, but on graduation day, she is not present.

The Hollywood standard of nurse-as-love-interest is present in 2002's *Windtalkers*. Rita (Frances O'Connor) is a Navy second class petty officer stationed at Pearl Harbor who becomes involved with Corporal Joe Ender (Nicolas Cage) when he is injured. She tries to convince him not to go back to war, saying, "Somebody's got to keep the WAVES company," but he is determined to avenge the deaths of his squad; despite her better judgment, Rita helps him cheat on his hearing test so that he can be sent back. They see each other intermittently throughout the film, but O'Connor is onscreen for just four minutes and does not add anything more substantial to the film's plot or climax.

The 2001 television remake of *South Pacific* features Glenn Close as Nellie Forbush, the role originated by Mitzi Gaynor in 1958. She is a nurse stationed on an unnamed South Pacific island and is onscreen for almost 40 percent of the film. Like the original, this musical is the usual whimsical type of film associated with the heyday of Hollywood musicals, and Forbush is again primarily seen singing and dancing rather than performing her nursing duties. Also like the 1958 film, this remake does feature dramatic scenes that speak to prejudices that still resonate with audiences fifty years later, including some Nellie has to work through herself. When she sees her lover's children for the first time, she shuns them because of their dark skin, acting against the myth that all women are naturally nurturing. She does come around in the end, which shows that people can change, which could be why the network chose to reboot this film.

In 2001's *Enemy at the Gates*, the primary female military character is also basically a love interest, but she garners a larger role. A private in the Soviet Army, Tania Chernova (Rachel Weisz)

Soviet soldier Tania Chernova (Rachel Weisz) in a scene from the 2001 film *Enemy at the Gates*.

is onscreen for twenty minutes and relevant to the film's subplot about a love triangle. More importantly, however, she is an exceptional soldier who makes vital contributions wherever she is. While working as an interpreter, Commissar Danilov (Joseph Fiennes) tells her, "Every intercept you translate saves thousands of lives." When she subsequently transfers to the front, she aids Vasilly Zaytsev (Jude Law) in getting a shot off at the German sniper (Ed Harris), which wounds him in the hand and sets in motion the events that eventually allow Vasilly to kill him. Her ability to adapt and provide needed support in stressful situation proves her to be a true asset to the Army and to the country she has chosen to defend.

Set during the 9/11 terror attacks, *Tiger Cruise* (2004) portrays a successfully gender-integrated ship. As civilians board the aircraft carrier USS *Constellation* (the "*Connie*"), they are met by their family members, naval personnel stationed onboard. Many women are shown throughout the ship, and there is no sign of tension, harassment, or animosity.[17] One of the servicewomen is Lieutenant Moreno (Monique Gaffrey), who in her three minutes onscreen is seen working as she awaits the arrival of her son for the cruise and later is shown diligently performing her duties as supply officer, even under the great stress that the ship's crew has come under.

Also onboard is Lieutenant Grace Torres (Mercedes Colon), a naval aviator who flies an F-18 Hornet. Her sister Tina (Bianca Collins) is one of the family members going on the tiger cruise, and she meets her at the dock to welcome her onboard. Tina idolizes her sister, and she can't wait to be old enough ("just five more years") to follow in Grace's footsteps, finally getting "the uniform and the plane" for herself.

On the second day of the trip, news of the 9/11 attacks reach the *Connie*.[18] With everyone tense and in shock as the severity of the situation sets in, the ship's captain (Bill Pullman) tries to keep the family members calm and as informed as he can. Concerned for Grace's well-being, Tina continues to press her sister for information, but Grace simply tells her, "We're the first line of defense for this country, and a lot of times, we have no idea what we're flying into—and it's scary, but you have to do your duty." Torres is only onscreen for six minutes, but throughout the film, she is strong and focused, doing her job expertly and setting a good example for her sister and the other civilians on board.

In another relatively small role, former POW Jessica Lynch is the subject of a made-for-television film that dramatizes her rescue by Special Forces. *Saving Jessica Lynch* (2003) stars Laura Regan as Private First Class Lynch, who is onscreen for thirteen minutes of the ninety-three-minute film. Also captured were eight other soldiers, including Specialist Shoshana Johnson (Denise Lee) and Specialist Lori Piestewa (Crystle Lightning), who became the first Native American woman in history to die in combat while serving in the U.S. military and the first woman in the U.S. military killed in the Iraq War. Piestewa and Johnson are both minor characters in the film, onscreen for just four minutes each; meanwhile, Lynch is shown lying in a hospital bed for the majority of her time onscreen, thus not allowing any real glimpse into her capabilities as a soldier. Despite Lynch being a titular character, the film's focus is primarily on the Iraqi man who helps the military locate Lynch and her fairly uneventful rescue executed by the Navy SEALs.

The 2006 short film *Ghost Soldier* features Cachet Lamar as Army Specialist Misha Grahm, another servicewoman who gets taken prisoner by Iraqi forces, along with the only other surviving member of her squad, James Hsia (Perry Tsao). Both are questioned regarding troop movements, but neither gives anything up. The guards make them undress, and several of the Iraqis look Grahm up and down as she stands in her underwear. One in particular seems to like what he sees, but he speaks to her condescendingly, snidely asking, "No husband [to] take care of you?" commenting on her perceived unfitness for military duty due to her gender.

As Grahm and Hsia speak to each other through the walls of their adjoining cells, she tells him, "Did I tell you I have a son?" It is apparent that she is concerned that she will never see him again. When the guard they encountered earlier comes to her cell and carries her off over his shoulder like a caveman, supposedly for "questioning ... standard procedure," Grahm panics, fighting him and screaming for James to save her. It is likely he rapes her, but nothing is shown, and she is back in her cell when Hsia implements his escape plan. During the escape, Hsia gets shot; he motions for Grahm to come to his aid; she is terrified and freezes up. When she hears Iraqi guards approaching, however, she takes off, leaving Hsia on the ground. Although this is not a particularly flattering portrayal of a woman in the military, Grahm nonetheless remains strong the majority of the time, likely thinking of her son back home, which gives her the willpower needed to persevere despite the hardships she has endured as a prisoner of war.

There are several dramas in this decade, however, that include strong roles for military women. Set during the Iraq War, *Home of the Brave* (2004) focuses on the post-deployment experiences of three National Guard soldiers, one of whom is female. While in Iraq, Army truck driver Sergeant Vanessa Price (Jessica Biel) and her convoy get ambushed, which results in Price losing her hand. After receiving a prosthesis at Walter Reed Army Medical Center, she returns home to begin her life again, attempting to "come back like nothing ever happened." This proves difficult to do since those around Price cannot relate to what she has been through. Even though she considers herself "one of the lucky ones," she readily admits that "nothing makes sense anymore." Onscreen for almost one-quarter of the film's run time, Price deals with her PTSD better than others, as she does not turn to drinking heavily like the two primary male characters do, but it is only by sharing with those whose experiences mirror her own that she begins to heal and move forward. In portraying Price in this positive light, this film chooses to highlight her as equivalent

Sergeant Vanessa Price (Jessica Biel) on a routine patrol in *Home of the Brave* (2006).

to "the archetypal action hero," rather than "stigmatize the ways [she] deviates from normative gender roles."[19]

The Lucky Ones (2008) also focuses on three soldiers with varying issues, set in the U.S. while they are home on leave. Rachel McAdams portrays Colee Dunn, an Army private who got shot in the leg during an attack in Iraq. While on leave, she visits the family of the man who saved her life, who died while deployed, to give them his guitar. Dunn is very innocent and naïvely believed everything Randy told her, none of which turns out to be true. This revelation hits Dunn hard, but she necessarily toughens up and returns to Iraq a little more jaded but a lot wiser, something that can help her survive.

Kate Beckinsale stars as a Navy nurse in 2001's *Pearl Harbor*. Lieutenant Evelyn Johnson is already in the military when Pearl Harbor is attacked by the Japanese, and she is among the initial first responders who help the victims of the bombings. She is dedicated and proficient while performing her duties, working long hours and keeping the spirits up of those around her. Although primarily in the film as the center of a love triangle involving Army Captains Rafe McCawley (Ben Affleck) and Danny Walker (Josh Hartnett), Johnson is also a solid example of the dedication and grit nurses of this era possessed, putting herself in harm's way for the good of her patients.

In *Annapolis* (2006), Midshipman Second Class Ali Halloway (Jordana Brewster) is one of the squad leaders at the Naval Academy. Better at gender integration than other service branches, Ali is not just in charge of female plebes—she helps lead both genders and does so more than capably. Halloway knows from personal experience that "some of the guys at the Academy don't view women as their equals." With the knowledge that many men see military service as "a validation of their own virility and as a certificate of manhood," a mindset that sets up women as outsiders, she wants to help prove them wrong.[20] She is encouraging to the other women at the

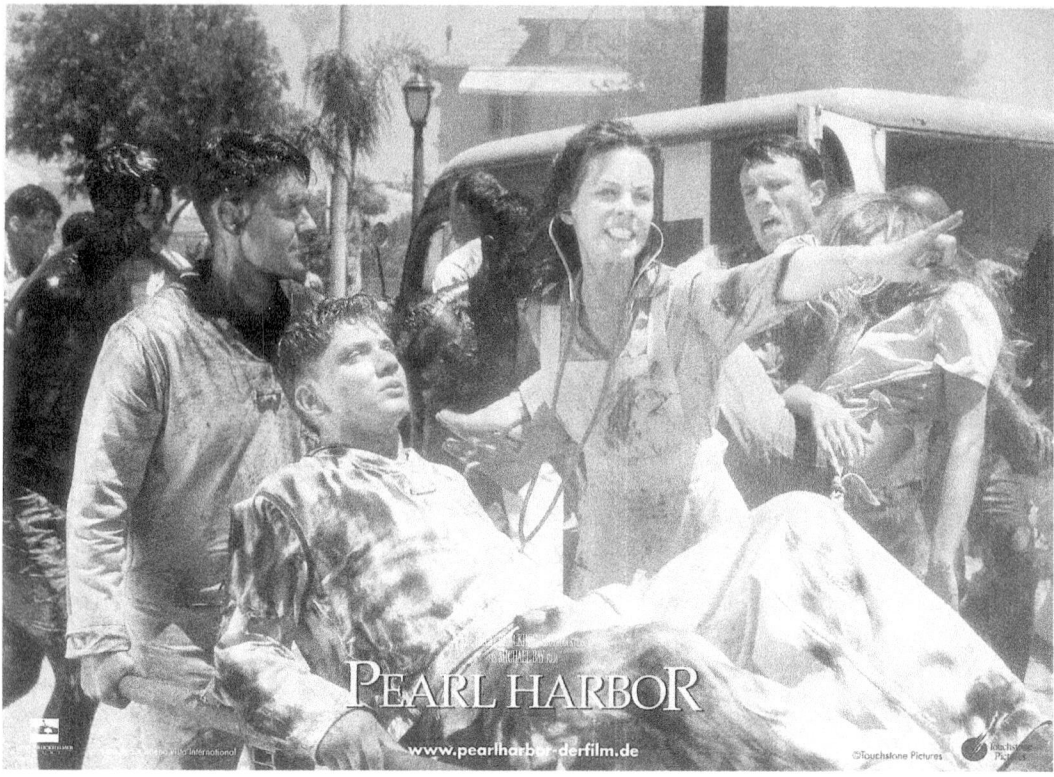

Lieutenant Evelyn Johnson (Kate Beckinsale) attends to the wounded in 2001's *Pearl Harbor* from Touchstone Pictures.

Academy, but she makes no bones about them needing to step up, telling the plebe Risa (Katie Hein), "You're the reason they say women don't belong here." Although this may sound counterproductive, it is her goal to help Risa get better, to prove her worth and assert her right to be there.

Impending deployment to Iraq is the focus of the short film *One Weekend a Month* (2004). Onscreen for 90 percent of the film, Meg McDermott (Renee O'Connor) is a single mother with two young children; when she finds out that her unit will soon be activated, her problems begin as she has no one reliable to take care of her children. In phone calls to both her mother and her son's father, neither of whom will commit to being the children's caregiver, McDermott must endure snide comments about how she should have never joined "that National Guard bullshit" in the first place.[21] At one point, she tells her unit sergeant (Diana Morrison as Sergeant Jones), "I don't know if I'm going to be able to make it," but she is immediately told, "That's not an option." McDermott soon realizes that she has signed a commitment to serve her country, and that duty must be honored despite any personal hardships. No resolution is shown in the film, but the viewer gets an intimate look at the problems associated with being a single parent in the military, especially when deployment can suddenly take you away from your children for an extended period of time.

In another made-for-television film that is based on a true story of a woman in the military, 2000's *One Kill* features Anne Heche as Marine Captain Mary Jane O'Malley, commander of the motor pool at the base and described as a "tough cookie." During a training exercise, she and her team perform perfectly, capturing a rival squad and winning the games. Later, one of her team members stands up and says, "Here before me stands a true Marine—may I always follow where she leads."

Onscreen for just over half the film's run time, this drama revolves around O'Malley's affair with a married officer and the complications that ensue. As a divorced mother of two, staying on active duty is not necessarily the easy choice, but O'Malley's dedication to her job and to the Marines is obvious when she tells Major Nelson Gray (Sam Shepard), "It's not my country if I don't fight for it." Being a Marine means everything to O'Malley, who would rather go down swinging than take the easy way out. Her capabilities as a soldier are evident as she fights back against Gray and the system in general; throughout, she is fierce and compelling, eventually winding up victorious in the battle to clear her name, but she still ends up leaving the Marines, disheartened by the feeling that she has been the victim of the military's deeply rooted gender biases.

Midshipman Second Class Ali Halloway (Jordana Brewster) with her Naval Academy company in *Annapolis* (2006).

My Brother's War (2005) features Whitney Hamilton as Grace Keiler. When her brother goes missing, she dons his Confederate uniform and goes in search of him. In all situations encountered, "Henry" performs her soldiering duties quite capably, and her ruse is never uncovered. Throughout her travels, she begins to get accustomed to living as Henry, and at the film's end, it is apparent she does not intend to go back to life as Grace.

A Shade of Gray (2002) is the only film in this survey that focuses on the "Hello Girls" of World War I. These women were sent to France to work as telephone operators for General Pershing and the Allied troops. They participated in the same training and were subjected to the same harsh conditions as the official troops. These women believed they had joined the Army, having taken the same pledge that male servicemembers took when enlisting. When they returned home, however, the Army insisted they had been civilians the whole time. As Candy, a former Hello Girl, tells her granddaughter, "When we came home, they told us to go back to our kitchens as though we'd never been there." This is because "in times of war, history is reconstructed and rewritten to show that women can perform effectively in various positions. After war, the disastrous effects of warfare are forgotten and there comes 'cultural amnesia' of contributions women made during war."[22] After a struggle that lasted sixty years, the Hello Girls were finally granted military status in 1977, when only eighteen of the 233 were still alive.[23]

In this short film, Hayley DuMond portrays the young Candy Bridgeton (with Nancy Lester as an elderly Candy), relaying battle orders at the front lines "with the First Army in Souilly," France. They were close enough that "every time those big guns went off, did our building shake." At one point, Candy has to relay a message that would allow artillery to fire an adjustment shot and give the American line some relief from enemy fire: "I knew he was in trouble, and I knew I was his only hope." Although relaying such orders was not something she was actually supposed to do, she remained calm under pressure, making the difficult decision to relay the coordinates, an act that saved many American and French lives.

Another film short, 2005's *A.W.O.L.* features Ida Smith as Private Keisha Johnson, serving with the Army in Iraq. She has suffered some sort of trauma—evident by the many cuts and bruises on her face—and has gone AWOL, wandering about the arid countryside in a daze. Although onscreen for two-thirds of the film, Johnson utters very few words (a total of six). What happened to her is never revealed, but there are bruises and bite marks on her breasts, so she has most likely been the victim of a sexual assault. It is obvious that she is traumatized, but through the kindness of strangers, she realizes that she will survive what has occurred. As the film ends, Johnson is headed back to her unit, perhaps now with the courage to report her ordeal and begin the process of healing.

Comedies

Similar to the 1990s, the first decade of the twenty-first century produced some military comedies featuring women in uniform, and all of them garnered significant amounts of screen time. *Guy X* (2005) features Sergeant First Class Irene Teal (Natasha McElhone) as aide and girlfriend to the base commander. Onscreen for fourteen minutes, Teal is basically just a love interest and begins sleeping with the film's protagonist as well, Corporal Rudy Spruance (Jason Biggs). She works with Spruance to bring the film to its climax, and although she gets a decent amount of screen time, she does not do much to move the plot forward for the majority of the film. She, instead, propagates the age-old story of women sleeping with their bosses to curry favor, not a particularly positive depiction of a female soldier.

Elizabeth Ann Bennett stars as Second Lieutenant Monica Tasty in *Military Intelligence and You!* (2006), a satirical look at the subject of nuclear weapons. As her name suggests, Tasty is there as eye candy. Her contributions to the plot are substantial, but the over-the-top way in which Bennett portrays her does not allow anyone to take her seriously, perpetuating Hollywood's tendency to ignore the very real contributions made by women in the military and "treat the military in general and women in particular as glamorous, romantic and funny."[24]

Jessica Simpson portrays the title character in 2009's *Private Valentine: Blonde and Dangerous*. Valentine is a Disney-type movie star undergoing crises in her personal life. When she gets drunk and wrecks her car, she stumbles away from the accident, ends up at an Army recruiting office, and enlists, quite the comic scene. As expected, she is a screw-up at first but eventually realizes the importance of the lessons the Army has taught her and begins to turn things around and take control of her life.

Despite being the titular character, Simpson is onscreen just 38 percent of the film's run time, a common occurrence for female title characters when compared with their male counterparts. In *I Was a Male War Bride*, for example, Cary Grant is onscreen 86 percent of the film's run time. Similarly, Gary Cooper gets 61 percent of the screen time in *Sergeant York*, Henry Fonda is onscreen 71 percent of the time in *Immortal Sergeant*, and in *Forrest Gump*, the titular character is onscreen 75 percent of the film's run time. For the movies in this survey, forty have a singular female title character—of those, only fifteen are onscreen for over half the film's run time. A survey of twelve military films with male titular characters shows only one with screen time of less than 50 percent. Although this is a fairly small sampling, initial data indicate that more screen time is generally given to male stars than to female leads, continuing the gender inequity that has been present in Hollywood for a century and more.

A final film to discuss gives a different take on the concept of the importance of a title character. For 2007's *Grace Is Gone*, the female titular character has no actual time onscreen at all—she dies while deployed in Iraq, and is, therefore, never seen. The only time Sergeant Grace Phillips (voiced by Dana Lynne Gilhooley) is "present" in the film is when her voice is heard sending her last message to her family on their answering machine and when Stan (John Cusack) repeatedly calls the answering machine to leave messages for Grace, telling her, "I just wanted to hear your voice."

Stan struggles with how to tell his daughters (Shélan O'Keefe as twelve-year-old Heidi and Gracie Bednarczyk as eight-year-old Dawn) that their mother was "a brave soldier [who] died serving the country she loved"; he instead takes them on an impromptu vacation for one last taste of normalcy. Grace's physical absence from the film highlights two important factors: the increasing role reversal of women being deployed and men staying at home, and the brave servicewomen who have been killed while serving their country in Iraq and Afghanistan, themes that are more heavily explored in the next decade of films.

Drill Instructor Sergeant Louisa Morely (Vivica A. Fox) in the 2008 BenderSpink film *Private Valentine: Blonde and Dangerous.*

Eight

Shattering the Camouflage Ceiling
The 2010s

In the first decade of the twenty-first century, things were stagnant in the area of legislation affecting women in the U.S. military. The 2010s, however, ushered in an explosion of activity, both in real life and on film. The decade began with a rescinding of the long-standing ban on women serving on submarines.[1] Remodeling and reconfiguration of the subs still needed to be done, however, so no women actually began serving on submarines until 2016. That left only one major obstacle still hindering women from full participation in military service.

The ban on women being assigned to units involved in direct combat, official policy for every U.S. service branch, had been almost rendered a moot point as female pilots flying into combat zones became more ubiquitous and as women assigned to combat support units had frequent encounters with enemy combatants. Additionally, servicewomen began filing lawsuits against the military, claiming combat exclusion laws were "based on outdated stereotypes of women, ignored the realities of the modern military and battlefield conditions ... and barred women's advancement to senior military roles."[2] Due to these and other pressures, on January 24, 2013, Secretary of Defense Leon Panetta issued a memorandum, entitled *Elimination of the 1994 Direct Ground Combat Definition and Assignment Rule*, which officially removed the ban on American women serving in combat. In the memo, Panetta states that the "integration of women into newly opened positions and units will occur as expeditiously as possible," thus, in theory, shattering the camouflage ceiling forever.[3]

The role of warrior is one that has historically been cast as male and masculine, yet that role is now more widely available to women.[4] Therefore, the breadth of jobs performed by military women has grown considerably as well. Hollywood has tried, at least to some extent, to adapt to this shift. In films released from 1910 to 1999, just under half of the military women portrayed were nurses or worked in an administrative capacity. In contrast, for films released during the twenty-first century, only one-quarter of the servicewomen depicted work in those fields, representing a significant swing in focus. With military reality and the public's changing views on women in the military, Hollywood portrayals have had to transform as well.[5]

Action Films

As in the previous decade, the 2010s include several action films which have only a token female with a speaking part, and for many of these films, she is the only military female shown. There is just one military woman in *Boys of Abu Ghraib* (2014); Franklin (Kristen Rakes) is on-screen for only one minute and speaks just three lines. *Warfighter* (2018) includes just a token female as well, onscreen a total of four minutes with just a few lines—Major Janet Boggs (Navy veteran Jennifer Marshall) briefs the SEAL team on their mission and wishes them luck. In *Allied* (2016), there are actually three women in uniform shown, but only one British clerk has a speaking part. She speaks two lines and is onscreen for just one minute. The 2019 Netflix film *Triple Frontier* also shows several women in the military, most of them sitting before the Army retention officer (Christine Horn), whose job is to try and encourage these soldiers to reenlist. The first voice heard in the film, she is onscreen for less than a minute, but she does get several lines and is dedicated to keeping the Army stocked with soldiers who "the government has put a lot of time, money, and training into," since they do not "want to lose that investment."

White House Down (2013) has just one servicewoman onscreen as well. As the President's helicopter is returning to the White House, various security checkpoints search for any danger, and an Army major (Jennifer Morehouse) is part of the "Castle Sky" team that scans for airborne threats. She has just three lines and is onscreen for less than a minute, but she is shown performing her duties with precision and dedication, knowing that any mistakes could end up being disastrous for the President and the nation.

One woman in the military also shows up in the 2012 reboot film *Red Dawn*. The female North Korean soldier (Choua Kue) is first shown working a checkpoint, assigned to frisk women who are passing through; she acts extremely professionally, calling her comrades' attention to the fugitive who shows up in her line. When she is shown again, however, she seems to forget her military training. As the North Korean home base is being infiltrated, she screams at the sight of the Wolverines who are shooting up the place, rather than acting like a soldier and taking up arms against them.

Seal Team Eight: Behind Enemy Lines (2014) shows two military women, both of whom speak several lines—a tech (Tanya van Graan) onscreen for two minutes is depicted as cool and professional under pressure. The drone pilot supervisor (Bonnie Lee Bouman), who is seen for only one minute, is shown as being equally capable; at a crucial juncture, she works to keep the unit calm, telling them, "Never assume the worst, even if it's true." Neither woman's role is essential to the film's plot, but in their limited appearances, both reflect positive images of military women.

There are also two women in the military shown in 2016's *Deepwater Horizon*. The Coast Guard is contacted regarding an oil rig explosion off the coast of Louisiana, and two female technicians assist with gathering information in order to be able to address the emergency. Ensign Von Huene (Jennifer Tamminen) is the first to receive a phone call, quickly relaying coordinates of the explosion to her superiors. Additional calls are taken by an unnamed third class petty officer (Carliene O'Connor) and several male servicemembers as the severity of the accident quickly becomes apparent. During the brief scene, both women are shown performing their duties extremely well, proficiently gathering vital information to help the Coast Guard mitigate further danger to those on the rig and to the environment.

Sniper: Ghost Shooter (2016) also has two females with multiple lines. The film starts out with the potential for portraying strong military women, but both are killed off fairly quickly and are onscreen for just three minutes each. Aungst and Rojas (Presciliana Esparolini and Jade Ogugua) are Marine snipers, an occupation they could not actually hold in the American military. Since these women are portrayed in "unnatural" roles, they are killed off so that the men can get down to the hero business, a traditionally masculine pursuit. This is because "in spite of the strength of female characters, the social consensus that runs through [these] films is that men and women serve very different purposes."[6] Thus, the women in this film are just a slight improvement over the "token" female and not central to the plot.

Liddy (Sarah Middleton, center) and Captain Joe Glass (Gerard Butler, right) stare intently at sonar screens onboard the submarine USS *Arkansas* in *Hunter Killer* (2018).

Hunter Killer (2018) has about two dozen women in uniform shown, including a few Russian military women, but only one woman speaks (Sarah Middleton). Her rank is unknown, and her character's name is never used (the credits simply list her as "Liddy"). She is, however, one of three women shown stationed onboard the submarine; she works in communications and has quite a few lines in her two minutes onscreen. Although this is a very small part, it does manage to remind viewers that Navy women now serve in all capacities, including onboard submarines.

In *Red 2* (2013), Sarah (Mary Louise Parker) dresses as a Soviet military woman in order to stand guard while the men pull off their mission. In uniform for just two minutes, her unfamiliarity with military regulations causes issues, and she ends up having to make out with a male soldier in order to keep her cohorts from being discovered. More importantly, former Soviet operative Major General Katja Petrokovich (Catherine Zeta-Jones) is yet another token female soldier. She garners only seven minutes of screen time, despite the character's importance to the plot and the actress' star status. Zeta-Jones' part is slightly larger than some other roles, but more emphasis is placed on her former romantic relationship with Frank Moses (Bruce Willis) than on her military status and capabilities, effectively sidelining her high rank and capabilities almost completely.

A final action film that downplays the level of involvement of servicewomen is 2012's *Act of Valor*, in which the featured woman in the military again has only a few lines and is onscreen for just two minutes. This film, based on the true story of Navy SEALs rescuing a kidnapped CIA agent, chooses to focus exclusively on male heroism, which is particularly problematic since Lieutenant Lyons (portrayed by Army Lieutenant Katelyn Lyons) is actually the mission leader. Granted, she leads from afar and does not actually go on the mission with the SEALs, but as Jennifer Lobasz asserts, "The growing feminist literature on women in the military emphasizes the need to make visible the presence of servicewomen, their contributions to the military, and the pervasive discrimination ... they face."[7] As long as Hollywood continues to release films that minimize the role of women in today's military, their presence will remain underrepresented and underappreciated.

There are, however, several action films that feature servicewomen more prominently. *Memorial Day* (2012) features Army Lieutenant Kelly Tripp (Emily Fradenburgh) as the ward nurse taking care of the film's protagonist (Jonathan Bennett as Kyle Vogel), who is injured in an IED explosion. He is withdrawn and sullen, but Tripp gets him to open up by expertly goading him and asking the right questions. They understand a lot of what each other has been through, which gives them some common ground. Both have had to see people on their watch die and have had to adjust to that and still be able to perform their duties. Onscreen for just seven minutes, Tripp is nonetheless an important part of Kyle's both physical and mental recovery. As they part, Tripp tells him, "I hope I never see you again, and I mean that in the best way." She knows she has done more than heal his physical wounds.

Operation Enduring Freedom in Afghanistan is the setting for *Jarhead 2: Field of Fire* (2014), which also shows only a token female service member with a speaking part. Marine Lance Corporal Danielle "Dani" Allen (Danielle Savre), however, has greater visibility. Onscreen for twelve minutes, just over 11 percent of the film, Allen is shown as an expert marksman and is the first person asked when considering taking out an enemy combatant from a great distance. She and her male comrades engage in collegial razzing while relaxing, but she makes sure not to let things get too friendly. She even perpetuates the joke that she is a lesbian to help ensure things don't become too personal.

Most interesting, however, are the scenes of Allen and her squad during the film's major firefights. As Suzanne Bouclin states, "Films can reflect, promote, reproduce, and construct both feminist and anti-feminist values, and, more often than not, they can do both at the same time."[8] Savre's character bears witness to this assertion—throughout the film, Allen is depicted as highly trained and an expert shot; except for the last battle, however, she does not fire her weapon at all, hiding behind some rocks instead. These conflicting views do not help promote the idea that women can handle being in combat, even when clearly in possession of the skills necessary to do the job.

Another film in the *Sniper* series, *Sniper: Reloaded* (2011) is set during the Democratic Republic of the Congo's civil war. Lieutenant Ellen Abramowitz (Annabel Wright) is a British officer attached to the U.N. Forces in Africa. Unlike *Sniper: Ghost Shooter*, Abramowitz has a larger role, onscreen for twelve minutes (13 percent of the film's run time). She is an accomplished intelligence officer who helps the sniper team fulfill their mission; unfortunately, it does not take long for her to wind up in bed with the male protagonist, instantly transforming her portrayal of a strong military officer into that of a cliché love interest.

In contrast to the other *Sniper* films discussed, *Sniper: Legacy* (2014) chooses to step outside the norm and more fully flesh out a strong military woman in a nontraditional role. Mercedes Mason portrays Sanaa Malik, a Marine corporal who is the partner of the main male protagonist, both of whom are snipers. Mason is onscreen for almost 20 percent of the film's run time, and she is portrayed as bright, capable, and lethal. What she is not portrayed as is a love interest—she and her partner are comrades in arms, nothing more, which is a refreshing departure from the Hollywood norm. In direct contrast to *Jarhead 2*, this portrayal helps emphasize the fact that "military women, despite the impediments in their paths are ... successful at all ranks and positions open to them."[9] Malik is a true virago; she transforms from a heroine to a hero when she "finds herself in a situation or a profession that commonly would be restricted to male participation, and she functions ably in it."[10]

In 2010's *The A-Team*, a film based on characters from the 1980s television show, Jessica Biel portrays Army Captain Charissa Sosa, a military investigator pursuing the escaped criminals that make up the movie's title squad. Throughout the film, and despite the fact that one of the team is her ex-boyfriend, Sosa doggedly pursues the escapees, leaving no stone unturned in her quest for justice. There are scenes where she seems to waffle in the presence of "Face" (Bradley Cooper), but she remains committed to discovering the truth, showing that dedication to her job is paramount in her life.

Captain Jaye "Lady Jaye" Burnett (Adrianne Palicki) in *G.I. Joe: Retaliation* (2013) is also a force to be reckoned with, and she does not stomach discrimination well. When General Colton (Bruce Willis) treats her as persona non grata, asking her for a pen and snidely remarking, "How did you get in?" she gets angry, spouting back with, "From Girl Scout to secretary—amazing." Colton comes across as having the same mindset as Burnett's father, who once told her that he did not agree with women being in the military because "he didn't want to put his life in the hands of a woman." His sexist attitude made his daughter part of a generation of military women who were treated as being unnatural for wanting to serve in the military and for whom talent and skill were never considered good enough.[11] Burnett's response was to enlist anyway and spend her career trying to outrank her father so he'd have to salute her. He died before that happened, but through hard work and immense skill, she rose through the ranks and proved herself worthy of wearing the uniform.

Justice on the Border (2011) deals with an Army Ranger team sent to investigate the activities of a drug cartel on the Arizona/Mexico border; the movie features five servicewomen of varying importance to the film's plot. Lieutenant Sanchez (Tiffany Roysden) is onscreen just under two minutes. She is secretary to General Smith (William Knight), who is holding a meeting with the film's protagonist, Colonel Edward Justice (Spencer Lighte), an Army reservist and well-known attorney. Sanchez thanks Justice for being the "famous attorney who beat that big case in L.A.—'Don't ask, don't tell.'" Her brief appearance leads the viewer to infer that she is gay since she thanks him for winning his case, but she is only in the one scene, so that assumption is never confirmed.

Corporal Jane Seymour (Patty Jarvis-Bennett) is in just one scene as well, for less than a minute when she goes to the armory to pick up her "standard issue" weapon and asks the armory clerk if she's ever shot anyone. The clerk is Major Lori Stevens (Jamie Bernadette), and she handles Seymour's request quickly and efficiently. Stevens is then visited by Captain John Wallace (Pete Freeland), who needs weapons to rescue one of Ranger team members who has been kidnapped by the cartel. He flirts with her, calling her the "empress of the armory," and offers her a VIP ticket to an Arizona Wildcats game in exchange for the weapons; she hesitates, but ultimately gives him what he needs. Onscreen for three minutes (including some scenes near the end of the film), Stevens does act against military regulations by giving the weapons to Wallace without the requisite paperwork, but she does so for a just cause.

The servicewoman who has been taken is Specialist Marisol Velez (Vanessa Herrera), one of the four-man Ranger team sent in to investigate the cartel. Well trained and highly skilled, Velez is comfortable around the officers on her team, giving them collegial razzing when they first meet up and later as they play a round of basketball. Despite her Ranger training, however, she is kidnapped after leaving a bar with her boyfriend, sergeant Bill Nelson (Joseph DiSparti), the fourth member of the team, who is also unable to keep her from being taken. Against direct orders, the team goes in to rescue her, relying on "luck and good training" to get the job done.

When Velez wakes up in the house of the cartel's leader (Neto DePaula Pimenta as Cosmo Valencia), she shows how tough she is by immediately attempting to fight her way out, grabbing the nearest person and almost choking him to death before she is subdued. When the team shows up to rescue her, she jumps into the fray, fighting Valencia's girlfriend using martial arts while her hands are literally tied behind her back, showing her mettle and proving herself a true virago.

The final woman in the military featured in the film is Donnelle Russell as Colonel Regina Dawson, reprising the role she originated in 2009's *Taking Fire* (discussed in the previous chapter). Dawson is "a career officer who's worked her way up the hard way," and she is squared-away and by-the-book. General Smith sends her on the mission with the Rangers to keep them in line and to report back to him on the status of the investigation. She attempts to keep both Justice and Wallace in line, telling them at one point, "You will do nothing unless I authorize otherwise. Is that clear?" Obviously, they don't listen to her, but she is unable to bring any charges against them due to a lack of proof (despite her threatening both men with court-martial). When they tell her their version of what happens, she lets them know that they can't "bullshit a bullshitter," but she is forced to let them go on their way. Dawson is a solid portrayal of a strong military woman who has given her all to her career, clearly without regrets.

Shadows in Paradise (2010) has Sofya Skya as Lieutenant Sasha Villaroff, an elite soldier with the Marine Corps. When she and the team rescue some captured soldiers, Villaroff gets taken prisoner. Through two years of confinement, she was often beaten and tortured, but she "never talked ... not once." Once the Marines find out Villaroff is alive, her fiancé (Matti Pellonpää) goes after her. He believes her to be a traitor at first, but she soon convinces him that she "did what she had to do," getting the terrorists to eventually trust her so that she could gather intel on their illegal operations. She remains under cover in order to find out exactly where and when the terrorists are going to sell some stolen stinger missiles to Al Qaida, eventually foiling their plan and proving herself to be a true patriot deserving of being called an elite soldier.

Alone We Fight (2018) is set during World War II and features three Army nurses who are posted at a field hospital in Germany. Lieutenant Sasha (Airisa Durand) is seen for two minutes when soldiers first arrive at the camp with a wounded man. Although only onscreen for a short time, her dedication and compassion are readily apparent. More screen time (five minutes) is given to Lieutenant Jackie (Kate Conway), who talks for some time with the film's protagonist, Sergeant Gregory Falcone (Aidan Bristow). She, too, is shown working diligently to care for her patients, even washing out old, bloody bandages that must be reused due to a shortage of supplies. Lieutenant Lorraine (Lara Thomas Ducey) is onscreen for six minutes and has several scenes in which she waxes eloquently about the futility of war. Following the bombing of their aid station, and despite the damage, the nurses continue to care for the wounded with no thought for their own safety; as Lorraine asserts, "When ideology and men this evil enter the world, ... good men and women have no choice but to battle against them." The nurses are included in the film as reminders that women also served their country with distinction and bravery, even though it was not generally on the actual battlefield. It is interesting to note that while the men are referred to by their last names, the women are only addressed by their rank and first names (no last names are even listed in the film's credits), making their military service seem less authentic than the men's.

Disaster Films

Several of the disaster films in this decade also show military women to a limited degree. In 2018's *Eruption LA*, a single woman in uniform is shown, and she has just one line in the film. *500 MPH Storm* (2013) shows several National Guardswomen moving equipment; only one speaks, however, and she also has just one line. In *Meteor Storm* (2010), there is one female lieutenant

(Anna Mae Wills as Lieutenant Gray) who is in several scenes and speaks several lines, but her name is never used in the film, and she is onscreen for only two minutes. *Ice Quake* (2010), *Super Cyclone* (2012), *Airplane vs. Volcano* (2014), and *LA Apocalypse* (2014) all have a servicewoman with several lines who is onscreen for around five minutes, but all are shown in traditional roles, and none are integral to the film's plot in any way. These stock characters seem to indicate that the pervasiveness of female servicewomen almost mandates Hollywood to include at least a token female in uniform in any type of film showing military personnel.

There are two disaster films in this decade, however, that feature military women much more prominently. *Seattle Superstorm* (2012) stars Ona Grauer as Lieutenant Commander Emma Peterson, a take charge naval officer who is attached to the Disaster Management Agency as they work to save Seattle from the "unidentified aerial phenomenon" that is affecting their weather and threatening the planet. She is authoritative and strong, focused on solving issues that arise even while her children are in danger and the threat of global destruction remains. She handles the stress of the situation well, encouraging her team members by telling them that "the difference between success and failure is thinking the impossible is possible." Peterson's daughter Chloe (MacKenzie Porter) is actually the one who discovers the solution that will save the planet, and with all the authority her rank demands, Peterson implements the steps needed to carry out the plan and avert global annihilation.

The best portrayal of a strong female military officer in a disaster film, however, is in 2012's *40 Days and 40 Nights*. Warrant Officer Lynn Masters (Christianna Carmine) is a Navy SEAL, described by her superior officer as "one of the best SEALs the Navy's produced." Masters is the epitome of a modern-day warrior, handling tough situations with ease, whether it is jumping out of an airplane or diving into rough waters to fix a computer malfunction. In an interesting role reversal, Masters even tells the man she is working with, "Don't let your emotions interfere with your work," chiding him for exhibiting attributes normally associated with women, not men. While no women have yet served as Navy SEALs in real life, Carmine's portrayal shows why they should be allowed to enter any field for which they qualify. Hollywood does not let the role reversal go too far, however; even after Masters has been in a coma for quite some time, she still wakes up with makeup on, ensuring that the viewer does not see her as too masculinized, despite her warrior status.

Thrillers

Three thrillers in this decade feature strong military women who garner significant amounts of screen time. Army Major Susan Turner (Cobie Smulders), an MP in charge of the 110th Criminal Investigative Division, is one of the main characters in 2016's *Jack Reacher: Never Go Back*. Onscreen for almost 30 percent of the film, Turner can handle herself in all situations. Throughout the film, she fights beside Reacher (Tom Cruise), holding her own and taking down almost as many bad guys as the title character. She also has to fight discrimination along the way, something she tells Reacher that she has had to do her entire ten-year career. This is a common complaint among military women, both onscreen and in real life. As Marcus Schulzke asserts, "In each of the services, the numbers of women who feel that they are victims of discrimination are even higher than those who report being victims of sexual assaults."[12] Smulders delivers an excellent portrayal of a career military officer who overcomes whatever obstacles are thrown in her way in order to succeed and climb the ladder in both rank and occupation.

Navy Lieutenant Abbey Vaughn (Allison Gregory) stars in 2017's *Elite*, the plot of which

Eight. Shattering the Camouflage Ceiling

Major Susan Turner (Cobie Smulders) and Jack Reacher (Tom Cruise) eluding detection in 2016's *Jack Reacher: Never Go Back*.

is centered around the investigations of the fictional Naval Covert Ops Command division (NCOC). At the film's onset, the ambush of an elite squad of SEALs by a drug cartel ends with all but one of the SEALs being killed; investigations into the massacre bring no resolution, so the surviving team member (Jason Scarbrough as Lieutenant Sam Harrigan) becomes the scapegoat for the compromised mission. He is given a dishonorable discharge, and the case file is closed.

Described as "an expert marksman, ambitious, [and] career-oriented," Vaughn is a rising star in the Navy. When she is chosen to join NCOC, she begins investigating Harrigan's case anew, going to see him to ask him to join her as she reopens the file. He is surprised to see a woman on the case, saying, "Usually, it's a bureaucrat in a polo shirt that comes to check on me—guess we've moved on to training bras." He turns down her offer of collaboration but follows her, and when she gets in over her head and almost gets killed by a cartel member, who calls her "an ill-mannered tart" because she tries to play hard ball with him, Harrigan ends up rescuing her, and they team up for the remainder of the film as they sort out what happened. While working together, he gives her pointers and encouragement, letting her know, "It's called field work, kid—use what you can where you can." He also reminds her, "Of all the things you learned coming out of the Academy, Vaughn, trust your instincts." She begins to do so, toughening up in the process. When hot on the trail of the culprit behind the massacre, Sam tells her to stay right behind him, but Abbey quickly counters with, "No—you stay on my ass. This bastard's mine." By the end of the film, Vaughn has become highly proficient in the field, ultimately solving the case, killing the bad guys, and being offered to head up her own NCOC unit.

In *Last Man Standing* (2011), ex–Marine First Lieutenant Abby Spencer Collins (Catherine Bell) is a former Black Ops computer whiz who must use her military experience to save her husband (Anthony Michael Hall), who has been kidnapped. Onscreen for 73 percent of the film,

Marine First Lieutenant Abby Spencer Collins (Catherine Bell) on a mission in *Last Man Standing* (2011) from Sony Pictures Television.

Collins is a force, kicking butt and taking names along the way. Her husband even comments, "Why the military ever let a whiz like you go, I'll never know." Through flashbacks of Abby's tour in Afghanistan, the audience is shown why she did leave the military, and it is that failed mission that is at the heart of her current troubles. Her three-man team was tasked with transporting Omar Taraki (Mike Eshaq) to the authorities; he is a government witness set to testify against one of the leaders of the insurgents. Unbeknownst to Collins, her two teammates have sold Taraki out for ten million dollars, an act that results in the death of Taraki's wife and daughter. In the present, Jeremy Davis (Mekhi Phifer) has gone through his share of the money; when Samuel Pratt (John Sanders) refuses his phone calls, Davis kills him to take the rest of the money that he has left, but he is unable to break through the computer firewalls protecting the money. Davis kidnaps Abby's husband to force her to retrieve the money for him.

As Collins works to unravel the mystery and figure out where her husband is being held, she is constantly in danger and must use her military training to persevere and prevail. She breaks into Pratt's office as ordered, taking out all the guards without killing anyone and without getting hurt herself. She also proves herself to be above reproach in any wrongdoing, handing off the key to recovering the money to FBI agents and going to save her husband, which she does with skill and precision. When all is said and done, her husband calls her "a beautiful, dark-haired knight" who has saved her family and taken down the bad guys. Throughout the film, Collins puts her rigorous training to use, showing how capably women can handle even the toughest assignments and situations.

Drama

In the 2010s, heady subjects such as homosexuality, sexual assault, and PTSD have been depicted with regularity. Many of these films feature military women as major characters with extensive screen time.

Indivisible (2018) features Skye P. Marshall as Sergeant Shonda Peterson, an Atlanta police officer who is also in the National Guard. Onscreen for fourteen minutes (12 percent of the film), Peterson is a chaplain's aide in Iraq. Highly proficient at her job, she tells the new chaplain (Justin Bruening as Chaplain Turner), "If there's anybody here who can keep you alive and run your office any better than I can, I'll eat my helmet." Like her full-time job with the police department, Peterson is truly there to protect and serve, evident as she pulls the naïve Turner out of harm's way on more than one occasion.

Another 2018 film, *Welcome to Marwen*, features an Army woman in only one scene as an actual person, but she is also shown throughout the movie as one of the dolls of Mark Hogancamp's (Steve Carrell) imagination. As the person, Julie (Janelle Monáe) is shown working with Mark as he learns to walk again, something Julie can relate to since she lost one of her legs while serving in Iraq. As the doll, however, Julie is a sexualized version of the quintessential Army soldier—wearing Barbie-type clothes while blowing away the bad guys. Onscreen for twenty-two minutes, she and the other women help "Cap'n Hogan" with his issues, letting him know that "our pain is our rocket fuel," which will keep them strong, and that they have his back no matter what.

The indie film *A Marine Story* (2010) stars Dreya Weber as former Marine Alexandra Everett who gets forcibly discharged due to allegations of homosexuality, a "crime" of which she is guilty. Onscreen for over 63 percent of the film, Weber's portrayal came at a time when "Don't ask, don't

Cap'n Hogan (Steve Carrell) and his crew from 2018's *Welcome to Marwen*.

tell" was still official government policy. When she is first accused, her commanding officer talks her into having sex with him in order to "prove" her innocence; he then helps get her kicked out anyway. So, after four deployments and an excellent service record as a Deputy Provost Marshall, Everett must begin civilian life under a cloud. She remains strong, however, mentoring a troubled teen (Paris Pickard as Saffron) and setting her on a better path in life.

AWOL (2016) also deals with the subject of homosexuality. Based on the 2010 short of the same name, this full-length film features Lola Kirke as "Joey," a small-town lesbian who needs direction in her life, which her mother thinks can come from the Army. Joey meets a married woman named Rayna (Breeda Wool) and begins an affair, eventually falling in love with her and wanting to run off to Canada rather than show up for her impending deployment to Afghanistan. Rayna, however, is not a good person, and she ends up getting Joey in real trouble with the Army; at the film's end, Joey is at the Canadian border, choosing to flee rather than face the possibility of a court-martial.

Alexandra Everett (Dreya Weber) navigates life after the service in 2010's *A Marine Story*.

These films are two of the small handful of movies in this survey centered on homosexuality. As Sarah Projansky asserts in her 1998 *Signs* article, "Arguments against women in the military and combat have often included anxiety that women together in the military will lead to lesbian activity."[13] While this potentially rampant spread of homosexuality appeared to be a relevant issue at that time, movie producers have not really considered it a script-worthy plot device—only four films in this survey are focused specifically on homosexual servicewomen, and perhaps due to continuing public opinion on the subject, none were theatrical releases. The subject is, however, addressed briefly in other films; in the 2016 film *Jack Reacher: Never Look Back*, for example, the teenager Reacher and Turner are protecting tells Turner that she thought all female soldiers were gay. It is just an aside meant to be humorous, but its inclusion in the film speaks to the ever-present "fear" of the military fostering the spread of lesbianism.

Union (2018) is the sequel to 2005's *My Brother's War*, and it features Whitney Hamilton as Grace Keiler, again cross-dressing and living as her brother Henry, who died in the first film. Captured by Union forces and discovered to be a woman, Grace faces hanging for her deception, but her former fiancé saves her by promising to be responsible for her. This is because he simply cannot believe that she is capable of fighting, espousing the mindset instead that "it is easier to relegate women everywhere to a passive role than to consider that they are all capable of full participation in war."[14] Grace repays his act of kindness by escaping and going to find Virginia (Virginia Newcomb), who "Henry" saved from being raped by a Union soldier in *My Brother's War*. To get out of a marriage arranged by her brother-in-law, Virginia proposes to Henry, fully knowing he is actually Grace. The two eventually fall in love, and Grace lives the rest of her life as Henry, comfortable in her choices. The title, therefore, works in two ways—underscoring the Union's victory over the South and stressing the importance of the union between "Henry" and Virginia.

The Last Rescue (2015) features two Army nurses trapped behind German lines during World War II who must use their wits and inner strength to survive. When their field hospital is forced to evacuate, Second Lieutenant Nancy Bell (Elizabeth Rice) is on a transport truck that is leaving, but First Lieutenant Vera Cornish (Hallie Shepherd, who also co-wrote and produced the film) pulls her off to assist with a surgery. They and the men still there get taken prisoner, but they get rescued by two soldiers who have gotten separated from their unit. When they run across a German officer and his driver, they take the officer prisoner. As they trek through the forest with their prisoner in tow, Lieutenant Maxwell (Darren Keife) offers Cornish his canteen, saying, "Ladies first," but she quickly counters with "captains first" as she passes the water to their commanding officer, Captain Beckett (Brett Cullen). The two nurses are shown caring diligently for their patient, keeping him in as good shape as possible given their limited resources.

When the group comes upon a French farm, it is Cornish who convinces the owner (Gilles Marini as Bruno Travert) to let them hole up there for a while, asking him what his deceased wife would do and saying, "I lost my husband. He died in a field hospital in Africa. That's why I joined the Nurse Corps. Everything I do, I wonder if he would approve of me." Travert and Cornish travel to town for medical supplies, but they are discovered by the Germans; Travert is shot, and Cornish is believed dead.

Bell is generally quiet, going along in somewhat of a daze, and it is her capture that leads to them all being taken prisoner a second time. When the Germans refuse to give medical attention to the captain, however, she asserts herself, stating, "We are prisoners of war, and you are required to provide us with medical aid." It is the only time in the film that she acts boldly; she is primarily mousy and submissive for her twenty-two minutes onscreen. She does perform her duties very capably, however, and it is evident that she still has her humanity when she offers water to their German prisoner and refuses to leave the wounded captain behind.

Cornish reappears near the film's end, and it is apparent from her haunted look that the German commandant has been keeping her for sexual purposes; throughout her twenty minutes onscreen, Cornish is brave and assertive, but now she is the one who is submissive and quiet. She is strong, however, and is not broken—when given the opportunity, Cornish empties eight pistol shots into the commandant as retribution, only stopping when the gun runs out of bullets. Both nurses, as well as the captain and Private Lewis (Cody Kasch), eventually make it back to the Americans to be evacuated, but it is certain that their combat ordeal will stay with them for a long time to come.

Camp X-Ray (2014) stars Kristen Stewart as Private Cole, who is stationed at the detention center in Guantanamo Bay. The film centers on Cole's burgeoning friendship with one of the detainees as she tries to put herself in his shoes. Their relationship is the main focus of the film, and as such, she is onscreen for 70 percent of the film's run time. She is often treated as an outsider because she is female, and when she complains about something, her commanding officer asks her, "Are you a soldier or are you a female soldier? Because I don't have these problems with

Private Cole (Kristen Stewart) in conversation with a Guantanamo Bay detainee in the 2014 film *Camp X-Ray*.

soldiers." Comments like these are not uncommon, with every perceived infraction being seen as a "female issue," and they undermine the skill and dedication women in the military bring to the Armed Forces.

One of the more recent films in this survey holds a dubious distinction. *Megan Leavey* (2016) is the only film in this survey that was based on a true story of a woman in uniform and actually released in theaters. Every other film that chronicles an actual military woman's experiences has been a made-for-television movie. In sharp contrast, the list of theatrically-released films based on real-life military men's exploits is practically endless; *American Sniper* (2014), *Lone Survivor* (2013), and *Sergeant York* (1941) are just a few examples.

As the title suggests, the film centers heavily on Leavey (Kate Mara), who is onscreen seventy-six of 103 minutes, or just under 74 percent of the film's run time. The audience follows her as she trains her dog and herself to become a cogent team for sniffing out bombs and IEDs. At first, the men she works with are unsure about her role, but the squad quickly realizes how important her job is, even telling her, "We'll follow you, Leavey." In her post-service battle to gain custody of her dog, Leavey shows just how tough the military has made her, and her eventual triumph helps heal the invisible scars that being in war has left on and in her.

Aloha (2015) is a dramedy starring Emma Stone as Air Force Captain Allison Ng, a casting choice that raised many eyebrows in Hollywood. Purportedly of Hawaiian descent, Ng is a fighter pilot and "part of Hillary Clinton's Star Guard," a rising star who is given the assignment of liaising with Brian Gilcrest (Bradley Cooper), a former Air Force operative who is now associated with a private company that wants to weaponize a satellite in space. She is strictly by the book, while Gilcrest does things his own way. As a stellar pilot and squared-away aviator, the Air Force feels that Ng is too rigid, assigning her to Gilcrest in order to help round her out. While she does learn to loosen up some, her sense of duty keeps her on the straight-and-narrow, and it is Gilcrest

Corporal Megan Leavey (Kate Mara) and her military combat dog Rex on patrol in *Megan Leavey* (2017).

who changes in the end, coming down on the right side of things and gaining moral ground, in large part due to the dedication and ethics of Ng. There is, of course, the obligatory love angle, but it is Gilcrest who will be following Ng around the world to her duty stations, as she has no plans to leave the service.

In *The Martian* (2015), Jessica Chastain portrays naval Commander Melissa Lewis, mission leader for a survey trip to Mars. When one of her crew (Matt Damon as Mark Watney) gets stuck on the uninhabitable planet, she has to make the tough decision to leave him behind in order to save the rest of the crew. It makes her feel guilty, but as a capable commander, sometimes hard decisions have to be made for the greater good, and Lewis makes the correct choice when necessary. She also makes the right decision to return for Watney, despite her orders to the contrary. This is an action that could have gotten her court-martialed, especially if the mission had not been successful, but she again uses her knowledge and experience to make the right decision. Lewis is a solid portrayal of a highly trained military commander who keeps calm under extreme pressure and makes the hard calls with authority.

PTSD

Stand Down Soldier (2014) is an excellent indie film that chronicles the life of Sergeant Stacy Armstrong once she returns home following her third deployment in Iraq. She suffers from

Emma Stone as Air Force fighter pilot Captain Allison Ng in 2015's *Aloha*.

PTSD, both from her experiences in combat and from the rape she endures at the hands of a fellow soldier, and she must navigate how to become a functioning member of society while reconnecting with her husband and son. The film was written by, directed by, and starred in by Jeryl Prescott Sales, who says the genesis of the script came from conversations with friends and family who served in Iraq and Afghanistan.[15]

Throughout the movie, Stacy abuses drugs as a coping mechanism for dealing with being raped and to stop the nightmares of her three tours of duty. Her drug abuse is the way Armstrong deals with her PTSD, which has been defined as "repeated, intrusive hallucinations, dreams, thoughts or behaviors stemming from the event, along with numbing that may have begun during or after the experience."[16] As a direct result of a fight Armstrong has with her drug dealer, her grandson gets hit by a car and almost dies—making her realize that "this PTSD is kicking my ass" and that she needs help to work through things and begin to heal. After a

Navy Commander Melissa Lewis (Jessica Chastain) preparing to walk in space in *The Martian* (2015).

successful stint in rehab, Armstrong is shown with her family, finally beginning to get past the events that debilitated her for so long.

Fort Bliss (2014) portrays yet another mother (Michelle Monaghan as Staff Sergeant Maggie "Doc" Swann) returning from combat who is struggling to reconnect with both her son and civilian life. Her experiences in combat give her nightmares, and she suffers from guilt over the distance between her son and herself, which is only made worse when her ex-husband tells her, "I think if you wanted to take care of him, you wouldn't have stayed in the Army." This is not a comment that would ever be made to a male servicemember, and Swann fires back when she tells her ex-husband, "If a guy has to go away to work, nobody questions it, but if a woman leaves her family to go to work, she's a bad mother." The inclusion of these lines in this film speaks to the depth of the cultural reservations toward mothers being deployed, both in Hollywood and throughout American society.

Sergeant Stacy Armstrong (Jeryl Prescott Sales) after three deployments in 2014's *Stand Down Soldier*.

A 2006 *Journal of General Internal Medicine* article states that "women veterans are courageous, energetic individuals who were motivated to serve by patriotism and a desire for adventure and personal growth."[17] This is not an attitude incompatible with being a mother, as Swann asserts in a heated exchange with her ex-husband: "I love my son and I love my country, and I shouldn't have to choose between them." Many in society, however, still find it hard to accept mothers joining the military and being shipped overseas. Due to this mindset, Hollywood is still hesitant to portray women on the front lines of war. As Yvonne Tasker speculates, "Hollywood avoids narratives centered on military women in combat precisely because of the politically contested nature of the subject."[18]

Similarly, Kelli (Linda Cardellini), the main character in 2011's *Return*, has trouble adjusting to civilian life. After serving in a war, she finds everything at home too mundane, including her factory job, which she describes as a "giant waste of time." PTSD does not seem to be her issue, per se, and although she repeatedly tells others, "Other people had it a lot worse than I did," it is clear she is still troubled by her experiences. She downplays her time overseas, asserting: "I didn't get raped, I didn't have to carry a dead body, and I didn't get blown up by an IED," but clearly, she is not the same person as before. She eventually realizes her husband has been having an affair, and he ends up leaving; Kelli takes it hard, going on a drinking binge, which causes her to get a DUI and a three-day rehab stint. Even as she tells the man she meets in rehab, "I really want things just to be like they were before I left," she realizes that's not going to happen, and she checks back into life just as she is redeployed. Onscreen for almost 80 percent of the film's run time, Cardellini's authentic portrayal showcases the real struggles affecting returning veterans, even those not experiencing what most would consider overt trauma.

The 2014 indie film *Targeting* also focuses on a soldier who has problems readjusting to life out of the military. Mattie Ridgeway (Tajana Prka) physically comes back to her husband and daughter, but her severe PTSD won't let her mind rest; she has trouble reconnecting with her daughter and cannot maintain intimacy with her husband, who was also deployed to Aghanistan but did not see combat. A former intelligence operative, Ridgeway starts tailing an Afghan man who she believes to be the guide who betrayed her unit, obsessing to the point of pulling a gun on her husband and daughter when they find her on a stakeout. As her "case" and her life spiral out of control, Mattie must find a way to let go before all around her is destroyed.

Blood Stripe (2017) features Kate Nowlin as a former Marine sergeant (no name is given—IMDb simply credits her as "our sergeant") who also has post-military issues due to debilitating PTSD. She was a Lioness, a servicewoman who travels with combat squads in Iraq and Afghanistan and helps deal with the local women who cannot be touched by unrelated males. Onscreen for 60 percent of the film, Nowlin's performance again emphasizes the hardships returning veterans are experiencing, and as Tracey Bouclin asserts, "films are not just imagined futures; they are also representations of the present. They ... have real effects at a particular historical moment."[19] For returning veterans struggling with PTSD, seeing screen portrayals they can identify with can be life-changing. Cultural depictions of trauma should emphasize "the need to tell and retell the story of the traumatic experience, to make it 'real' both to the victim and to the community, so it is vital that Hollywood continue depicting this growing reality and offering suggestions as to where help can be found."[20]

A common theme among these films is that the servicewomen try to act normal, as if nothing is wrong. Problems quickly arise when they discover that they are not adjusting well; they are just plodding along without dealing with the trauma they have endured. Since PTSD can be described as "attempting to grasp a pain which sustains itself upon living memory," experts believe the best way out of "the closed circuit of one's psyche is to be able to tell one's story ... a process of constructing a narrative, of reconstructing a history and essentially, of re-externalizing the event."[21] Without the catharsis of talking about their experiences, these women will likely continue to suffer and self-medicate.[22]

Drones

New technologies have led to some of the films in this survey. The ability to target enemies with unmanned aerial vehicles (UAVs), or drones, has allowed more women to participate as pilots from the safety of a computer desk rather than in direct combat. In *Good Kill* (2014), for example, Airman First Class Vera Suarez (Zoë Kravitz) is assigned as navigator for a long-term drone assignment, taking out suspected terrorists in an unnamed Middle Eastern country. She is highly capable and eminently qualified for her job, which she performs well. She has qualms, however, about collateral damage, the killing of civilians that often occurs during their raids. Eventually, she quits, unable to reconcile her trepidation with the Air Force's ability to deem certain civilian casualties acceptable.

This is a common theme amongst the films focused on drone warfare. A similar situation occurs in *Drones* (2013). Captain Sue Lawson (Eloise Mumford) also questions the necessity and

Airman First Class Vera Suarez (Zoë Kravitz) executes a UAV strike while Lieutenant Colonel Jack Johns (Bruce Greenwood) supervises in the 2014 film *Good Kill*.

morality of killing civilians when she and her partner are ordered to bomb the home of a prime target who has just arrived to visit his wife and children. Even as her partner tells her she's got a "girl-macho thing going," she questions the necessity of killing children and other noncombatants, stating outright that she "will not kill twelve civilians." Eventually, however, Lawson is manipulated by her father into becoming angry enough to carry out her orders, but by that time, she has convinced Bowles (Matt O'Leary), her male co-pilot, that the collateral damage is unacceptable. Facing certain arrest and court-martial, Lawson and Bowles finally execute the strike, but it is clear neither will ever be able to blindly perform their assignments again.

The Madness of Tellaralette Seville (2018) also deals with PTSD brought on by working with UAVs, with the titular character (Olivia Hespe) winding up in a mental ward due to her reservations over long-distance warfare. This disjointed indie film highlights the debilitating effects that a sterile war can have on those who can target and kill the enemy while safely sitting "in the box." Her work as a drone pilot contributes heavily to her psychosis, but she has other issues as well, including an incident of sexual assault that is never talked about or dealt with in any way. Onscreen for approximately one-third of the film's run time, Seville's military service is overshadowed by her illness, and after she is practically broken by the way drone warfare affects her, she is threatened with being discharged from the military altogether.

Sniper: Ghost Shooter (2016), discussed earlier in this chapter, also features the use of drone technology. Insurgents tap into the military drone system in order to locate the snipers and kill them. That is how both female snipers die, and when it is suggested that it was carelessness on the part of the female Marines that got them killed, their team leader emphatically asserts that the sniper Rojas could "build a hide better than anyone in the business," reiterating that the infiltration of the Marines' drone system is the only plausible explanation.

Like other genres discussed, however, there are some dramas from this decade that have military women in limited roles as well. *The Submarine Kid* (2015) shows only one female Marine—former Marine Sergeant Drea Garcia is seen in several of the main character's flashbacks. She is shown participating with her unit in a combat situation, but she is onscreen for just two minutes and no name for her character is given. In *The Yellow Birds* (2017), there is a female Army medic (Carrie Wampler) onscreen for five minutes. Her name is never given or shown either, although IMDb lists her character as Jenny Smith. The protagonist is infatuated with her, and it is her death following a bombing that leads Daniel (Tye Sheridan) to the near-catatonic state that results in his torture and death at the hands of the enemy.

In *Your Roommate* (2012), National Guard Sergeant Wilson (Sarah Norris) is onscreen for just four minutes, but she has a slightly more prominent role than the small parts mentioned above. She is the leading man's squadron leader and is shown in a number of scenes, primarily for moral support. She is portrayed as tough and determined—in one scene, she helps the protagonist by beating up some men who are trying to thwart his romantic pursuits, which refreshingly don't involve her. The character is never addressed by name in the film, but it is clear she is highly respected and can hold her own with the boys.

The courtroom drama *Virtuous* (2015) centers on a manslaughter trial, but one of the minor story lines involves three Army personnel who have been kidnapped by the Taliban, one of whom is twenty-three-year-old Private First Class Tara Carter (Jan Ivers). A meeting is held to discuss what to do about the captured soldiers, and all attention is focused on the young woman being held captive, which makes it seem that if there were no female prisoner, the meeting might not be taking place at all. At that meeting, a second woman in uniform is shown—no name is given, but the meeting specialist is portrayed by former Army Private First Class Jessica Lynch, and her main line has her showing sympathy for Carter's situation, asserting, "She's way too young to be going through this," a situation she can empathize with, since, as discussed in the previous chapter, something similar happened to Lynch in real life. Onscreen for three minutes, Carter is shown about to break after the torture she has endured, but with the help of her squad leader, she musters the courage to get through it, and the three are eventually rescued.

Film Shorts

A final category to discuss is the recent plethora of film shorts. The Internet has done much to help independent writers, producers, and directors have an accessible platform for their films; the 2010s, therefore, has a long list of short films that feature women in the military in a variety of roles. Like their full-length counterparts, there are several common themes among these short films; there are also some that focus on more unique subjects.

Sexual assault is the main focus of three short films surveyed. *Breaking the Silence* (2013) features Air Force veteran Su Castillo as Sara Garcia, a Marine who gets raped by a fellow servicemember and ends up committing suicide. Her friend Danielle Crandell (Drea Garcia) reaches out to a sexual assault counselor to educate herself on how to help her friend, but it is too late. Crandell subsequently becomes an advocate for victims of sexual assault, agreeing to be interviewed by the media because she knows "these stories have to be told."

The Assault (2016), a film released by the 18th Military Police Brigade and starring actual Army personnel, also centers on a rape committed by fellow soldiers. Sergeant Stacy Richards (Army Sergeant Gabriella Richards) is squadron leader, and she goes out for a few drinks with her team to celebrate the end of forty-five days in the field. She drinks too much, things get out of hand, and two of the men in her platoon end up raping her. She reports the rape immediately, but her husband blames her and not the men, telling her, "You drink too much ... it's probably your fault you got raped." As payback for reporting the assault, the film ends with another man in her squad reporting her for sexual harassment, as she flirted with him at the bar while they were drinking, even offering to help him get a promotion if he "does well." In every film, the characters "must manage their behavior according to cultural norms with regard to gender."[23] Richards steps outside those norms and pays heavily for her perceived transgression.

In 2016's *Lion in a Box*, writer/director Melanie Brown has produced a fictionalized documentary of what many women endure when they are going through basic training and military life. As her Vimeo site states, "Through photo montage and animation, she shines a light on the traditional definitions of sacrifice and combat."[24] Although there is no one portraying a physical role in this four-minute film, Brown herself does the voiceover, speaking for three minutes of the film's run time. She describes how she "loved boot camp," and you can hear the pride in her voice as she boasts, "There were at least 300 trainees in my battalion, and only thirteen of us were women." When disparaged for not having been in combat, the main character says she feels like she has been due to all the sexual harassment she endures at the hands of drill instructors and other male military personnel, which felt "exactly like being in a box of lions." She is, however, determined to survive and thrive, taking the initiative to seek counselling in order to begin healing and perhaps help others by telling her story.

PTSD is the theme for several of the short films surveyed. *The Road Home* (2015) is about an Army nurse who has come home from deployment in Vietnam. Lieutenant Rebecca Phillips (Brienne La Flair) has trouble adjusting to civilian life, so she seeks out Michael (Eddie Gutierrez), a comrade who lost his leg and thinks she has shown up for a "pity visit." When she tells him, "I'd rather fight with you than be happy with someone else," it is her way of reaching out to someone she knows will understand what she is going through, which can be instrumental to overcoming the effects of PTSD. After asking Rebecca if things have been "as bad as you look," Michael admits his own struggle, and the two begin to conquer the inner demons that followed them home from the war.

Jesstine "Alabama" Brooks (Virginia Newcomb) is a Marine returning home from Afghanistan with severe PTSD in *Three Fingers* (2015). While deployed, she was shot, and she overhears the doctor say that had she been hit "three fingers to the right, she'd have been KIA." This knowledge consumes her every thought, and she constantly holds three fingers up just to the right of the scar on her neck. Knowing how close she came to dying, she struggles with moving on, coming close to committing suicide by holding her three fingers up and placing a knife in that spot. She manages to make it to a support group instead, where talking about her experience can be therapeutic. Upon leaving the meeting, she starts to put her three fingers up again, but when she sees her husband and daughter waiting for her, her hand falls back down to her side, and she takes a deep breath and the first steps toward healing.

Liz Roberts (Renée Daw), a veteran combat medic living on the streets, is the titular character in *Doc* (2016). Unable to cope with the death of Corporal Michael Shane (Israel Hall), she spends her days with a rescue dog that she names Shane in her fallen comrade's honor. She is seeing a psychiatrist at the Veterans Affairs Behavioral Health Unit—he gives her medication to treat her PTSD, but she is reluctant to share her trauma. When he tells Liz that talking about her experiences and her loss is "the only way" to begin healing, she realizes he is right. As she recounts the events for him, her trauma and guilt become clear as it was an RPG she fired that resulted in Corporal Shane's death. She breaks down without finishing the story, but Dr. Pace tells her, "This was real good, Doc. You're on your way," meaning that her healing can now begin.

Another recurrent theme is the death of servicemembers and the void it leaves for those left behind. In *Tea and Destiny* (2010), Celeste Guillams (Heather Hermann) joins the Army and must convince her father she's not being impulsive in doing so. He has qualms about her leaving as his son has already been killed while deployed, but she reassures him, telling him that she "just wants to experience something—something really big, bigger than me." Celeste believes that equal rights for women "necessarily involve equal responsibility, including the defense of the nation,"[25] and she eventually brings her father around to her way of thinking.

Home from War (2012) deals with a Marine suffering severe injuries and PTSD. Shown in the base hospital, Lieutenant Joanne Thomas (Sarah Karges) is having a tough time dealing with the loss of her leg, and she is convinced that her family will never accept her in this less-than-perfect state. Although help is offered, she chooses not to accept it, and she ends up committing suicide rather than let her family see her in that condition.

Another female Marine is the focus of 2018's *Let It Go*. Sydney (Leaphey Khim) is dealing with the loss of her boxing trainer and mentor who was killed in action. As seen through flashbacks, she clearly feels responsible for his death, but his spirit tells her, "There is no blame." Onscreen for three of the film's four-minute run time, Sydney realizes "that's all you get in life," and as she leaves for Jake's ceremony, she steels herself to move on as best as she can.

The death of a comrade is also part of the plot in *Do No Harm* (2017). Combat medic "Doc" Barron (Spencer Treat Clark) is trying to save an injured Marine, Gunnery Sergeant Witte (Shanola Hampton), who is shot during an insurgent attack. She is rightfully upset, spouting, "My kid—I told him I'd be back…. I'm not going to fucking die without seeing him again." As she starts to fade, he tells her, "You're strong. I know you, Gunny." In order for both or either of them to have a chance at survival, however, he must stop treating her long enough to shoot an enemy combatant who has entered the room. Despite how hard she fights to survive, Witte dies, leaving her three-year-old son without a mother.

Cold Winter's Night (2015) focuses on the daughter of a servicewoman who dies while deployed overseas. Onscreen for just over half of this four-minute film, Sergeant Lanter (Maggie McCollester) died two years before the film takes place, and she is shown mainly as an apparition her daughter imagines. Lanter tells Clara (Jessica Belkin) that she's "here to help," although her daughter does not understand that the assistance is in the form of helping her to move on and accept her father's fiancé, Rebecca (Sharon Freedman), who loves Clara very much and treats her wonderfully, despite the way Clara acts toward her. Clara's mother finds a way to help mend her daughter's broken heart, remaining a strong role model even in death.

Deployment and the toll it takes on those left at home, even when the servicemembers survive and come home, is another common topic. *The Letter* and *Yellow Ribbon* are two shorts featured in ABC 2013's *Home for the Holidays* series, and both are centered on the families left behind when soldiers are deployed. In *The Letter*, Julie (Navy veteran Stephanie Sanchez) is overseas, and her five-year-old daughter writes a letter to Santa, asking for nothing more than for her mother to come home. Written and directed by Army veteran Rebecca Murga, this five-minute film underscores the reality of women leaving their children behind and possibly dying in combat situations, accepting the risks on an equal footing with the men serving with them.

Similarly, *Yellow Ribbon* focuses on the family left behind for Sergeant Rutty (C. Stephen Browder), the film's protagonist. In Rutty's unit is Sergeant Pitt (Jennifer Marshall), onscreen for just one minute. Her longest scene is not during any battle; it is when the unit is celebrating Thanksgiving together. As Rutty prays, "Thank You for protecting our families, both near and far," it is clear they are a close-knit company, and Pitt is obviously a necessary and welcome member of the team.

Military Husband (2017), as the title suggests, focuses on the husband who remains stateside while his wife, Christina Ulloa as Celia Whittaker, gets deployed to Iraq. Even though she tells Matt (Tim Schukar), "You have to be strong for me," he feels helpless to protect her, espousing the anachronistic mindset that "women are ... merely the passive objects of men's warrior instincts."[26] He sinks deeper into despair until one of the military wives he meets at a support group helps him learn how to cope and go on living until her return. This exchange completes the role reversal presented in the film and serves to show the viewer, as well as the military husband, that times have changed. What her husband must come to realize is that "success in combat is a matter of skill, intelligence, coordination, training, morale, and teamwork," and none of these attributes are lacking in women, especially his wife.[27]

Some short films have more singular focuses. *In the Name of Freedom* (2010) centers on Army Sergeant Lisa Meyers (Isabel Cueva, who also wrote and directed the film), who is taken prisoner after her unit is attacked in Iraq. The insurgents kill everyone else in her unit, but they keep her alive, primarily because she is female and they intend to use her to send a message to the Americans. She is slapped and kicked by her captors as they grill her for information, but she tells them nothing besides her name and rank. Instead, she buys herself time by crying and telling them, "I don't know why I'm here. I just came here to support myself." When she begins spouting anti–American rhetoric, it is unclear whether she means it or if she is just telling them what she thinks they want to hear, but it definitely keeps her alive. Eventually rescued, Meyers' resolve and quick thinking epitomizes the tough, resourceful American soldier, overcoming the enemy who has underestimated her because of her gender.

The Oscar-nominated short film *Day One* (2015) features Layla Alizada as Feda Ahmadi, a Muslim-American in the Army who has come to Afghanistan to work as an interpreter.[28] On her first day in country (hence the film's title), she has several issues related to her inexperience in combat—she showers during a time designated for men only, she makes the convoy stop so she can go to the bathroom, and she comes close to getting blown up by an IED. During her first actual encounter with enemy insurgents, Ahmadi is forced to deliver a baby, something for which she has no training. She steels herself, however, and performs admirably under enormous pressure. Even on her first day, Ahmadi demonstrates considerable courage and adaptability, suggestive of a fruitful military career.

Based on a true story, *White Feather* (2013) relays the story of Carlos Hathcock (Brett R. Miller), an American sniper who spent four days literally crawling 1500 yards through the jungle in Vietnam in order to shoot an enemy general. Searching for him is a North Vietnamese Army platoon led by a female soldier (Drea Garcia). As they track him day after day, she keeps her squad focused on the task at hand. Often shown looking around and scanning the horizon, it is clear she senses someone is near, but she is unable to locate and stop him. Tensions mount as the cat and mouse game continues on for some time. When the general finally joins the NVA platoon, however, Hathcock completes his mission despite the squad leader's diligent pursuit.

The Christmas You Don't Know (2015) is about a mysterious couple and the good deeds they perform. They give a homeless man some money and reunite a deployed Marine (Chloe Modesir) with her daughter for the holidays, who is only briefly onscreen and gets just two lines. The couple even pulls off "a doozy" and helps prevent a young woman from committing suicide. This feel good film's cast and crew consists almost exclusively of veterans, and it highlights the helpfulness and positive attitude generally displayed by members of the military.

American Girl (2016) is only tangentially about being in the Army. The main character Julia (Rosie Moss) is serving in Afghanistan when she gets shot during a fire fight; she gets taken out by medivac and ends up losing her leg. While going in and out of consciousness, she recalls her illegal immigration to the U.S. as a child (portrayed by Allegra Acosta), which forms the majority of the film's plot. As she says "combat is chaos," she remembers how strong she is, a lioness who can do anything, even be an illegal alien who becomes a United States soldier.

Finally, two film shorts from this decade take a decidedly lighter look at military service. *Satellite Drop* (2017) centers on the prank pulled on the new Marine (Joseph Bezenek) stationed at the Signal Intelligence Base in Edzell, Scotland, where several women in the military are stationed as well. Marine Corporal Joshi (Deepti Kingra) works as a translator for the naval station and is shown as proficient and confident in her abilities. When called on to translate something coming in over the radio, she does so efficiently and effectively. Joshi is in on the prank, as is the female naval officer shown. Lieutenant Commander Bryne (Jennie Olson) is serious about her job, however, and when interrupted from her duties during the climax of the prank, she simply shakes her head, gives the others her best commanding officer deadpan stare, and says, "Fucking Marines!"

Lead from the Front (2017), a short film released by the Army, is a fun movie about the fierce rivalry surrounding the annual Army/Navy football game. Centered on Army's plan to steal Navy's mascot, code named Operation Granite Sabre, Jebb (her rank is not visible) is in command of the mission, relaying orders every step of the way and pulling the plan together. It is clear she is an integral part of the team. Another female soldier named Speer follows the orders given by Jebb, doing her part to ensure the mission goes off without a hitch. The men hit a snag as they get near the mascot when a group of Navy personnel show up and start harassing them; among them are several women, who jeer and shout insults at the Army men right along with the men. The mission does get accomplished, however, and upon their victorious return to West Point, Jebb takes center stage with the others at a pep rally, asking if they think the troops are "ready ... to have their minds blown." Camaraderie and purpose are what binds these soldiers together, no matter the mission, reinforcing the fact that "gender is not what affects the cohesiveness of a unit. The important factors are individual capabilities, personalities, training, and overall skill levels."[29]

It is important to remember that "those in the military are trained that a soldier is a soldier first and foremost"; no distinction is made between male and female.[30] The films of the 2010s took a giant leap forward in affirming this statement by showcasing a wide variety of leading and supporting roles for female military characters. More respect and wider acceptance of servicewomen can be seen. This positive trend can only help to increase the visibility of the real women of the United States Armed Forces that continue to serve their country with honor and distinction.

Conclusion

This book has shown that, as in real life, the depictions of military women in American theatrical and television films have evolved over time. In addition to films about the American Civil War, World Wars I and II, Korea, Vietnam, the Gulf War, Iraq, and Afghanistan, it has explored depictions of military women in a wide range of film genres, including comedies, dramas, mysteries, romances, and action films. These portrayals cover a wide variety of military professions as well, ranging from nurse to lawyer to aviator to spy to new recruits, while analyzing the realities of the women's position in relation to the laws impacting their service, their experiences in the military, and the social norms to which they have been subjected.

Warfare has been traditionally seen as a gendered activity that affects the men who fight, not the women who have been relegated to the safety of the home front, and many of these films have reinforced that idea. Yet the reality is quite different—women have served as Red Cross nurses and ambulance drivers on the front, as civilian nurses and volunteers, and as members of the military in most of the wars in which America has been involved. From the earliest days of American history, they have served as unofficial and official members of the military fighting force, typically disguised as a man. From the earliest days of motion pictures, the contributions of women to the military cause have been depicted in Hollywood films.

Beginning with the films of the early twentieth century, women donned the clothing of a military man and served on the front lines as a way to maintain their sense of family honor, do their patriotic duty, or save the love of their life in films such as *The House with Closed Shutters* and *A Fair Rebel*. By the 1920s and 1930s, the roles women played during time of war, while restricted by social conventions, were shown to be of vital importance to the war effort for most of the countries involved in World War I and other conflicts. While the nursing and ambulance services who ministered to those wounded in battle, including the Red Cross as well as private nursing services, have often been depicted in film, portrayals of military nurses and the more than 13,000 American women who served in the First World War as members of the U.S. Navy, the U.S. Marine Corps, and the U.S. Army were rarely captured onscreen. When military women were depicted in films, they were typically portrayed as love interests for the male hero.

As America geared up for war in the early 1940s, war became an even more popular topic for filmmakers, and once again, women nurses, both as contractors and military members, played a significant role in supporting the troops in real life and on film. The stories of the military nurses taken prisoner in the Philippines were told in films like *Cry 'Havoc'* and *So Proudly We Hail* to help garner support for the war effort, with the actresses who starred in them selling war bonds on national tours. Additionally, films told the stories of the women who served in all branches of the military during the war, often reflecting the fine line women walked in terms of the era's social norms as they attempted to maintain their femininity while confronted with the harsh realities of war. The vast majority of these women were discharged immediately after the war ended, expected to return to traditional roles of wife and mother, and many of the women in these films expressed those same sentiments. The decade of the 1950s saw a continuation of depictions of military women in films about World War II as well as the Korean War, in both dramatic and comedic roles, as filmmakers celebrated the heroism that had resulted in an Allied victory. In most cases, military women played secondary roles, again generally included only as love interests for male co-stars.

During the 1960s, filmmakers continued the trend of depicting films focused on World War II and the Korean War, again featuring military women in traditional roles as nurse or secretary and as secondary characters in a larger story, serving as the love interest for the protagonist. Romantic comedies featuring a hapless military man and a capable military woman, like *Sergeant Deadhead* and *The Horizontal Lieutenant,* became popular during the post-war period as well, reflecting the country's continued sense of optimism resulting from the Allied victory in World War II and increased economic opportunities in American society. As in previous decades, these female characters often expressed a desire to marry and raise a family. Meanwhile, with the exception of nurses and administrative personnel, few women remained on active duty, and their service was largely ignored by Hollywood filmmakers.

The optimism of the late 1950s and 1960s began to wane in the early 1970s, however, with the build-up of military operations in Vietnam, and American filmmakers began to turn their attention to the horrors experienced by those involved in the war, including occasionally telling the stories of the military women who also served in the region. At the same time, the demise of the draft and implementation of the all-volunteer military force led to increased opportunities for military women in real life, many of whom saw service as an opportunity to show that they had the right stuff. Several films from the 1970s included military women in roles outside of the medical field, and two, *Chesty Anderson, U.S. Navy* and *Women at West Point*, reflected the changing roles that were becoming available to military women.

By the 1980s, the roles of women in the military had changed dramatically. Women served in many arenas that had previously been closed to them and proved they could hold their own in any situation. While the military still banned women from combat-related jobs, their presence in the military in increasing numbers did not go unrecognized by filmmakers, who began to show these women in both dramatic films such as *A Time to Triumph* and *The Package,* as well as in comedic roles, especially as military recruits adapting to the restrictions of military life in films like *Private Benjamin* and *Your Mother Wears Combat Boots.*

The 1990s brought increased participation by women in military conflicts in Latin America and the Middle East, and movies such as *The Heroes of Desert Storm* and *Courage Under Fire* showcased their ability to function under fire, both real and imagined. Many films began to show military women in increasingly diverse and starring roles, such as Demi Moore in *A Few Good Men* and Rebecca De Mornay in *By Dawn's Early Light*. There was also a trend toward showing the possibilities of women's future service in combat roles in films such as *G.I. Jane* and *Dead Men Can't Dance*. Made-for-television movies such as *She Stood Alone* and *Serving in Silence* addressed some of the difficulties military women faced as they broke through the camouflage ceiling.

By the beginning of the twenty-first century, with the protracted wars in Iraq and Afghanistan, it became evident that it was no longer possible to keep military women out of combat situations, and an increased number of films, especially those depicting war in the Middle East, began showing military women performing in a wider range of positions, from intelligence officers to aviators to support personnel. A number of theatrical releases, such as *G.I. Joe: Retaliation* and *G.I. Joe: Rise of Cobra,* continued to reimage the role of military women as active members of Special Forces teams, while others like *Drones* and *Jack Reacher: Never Go Back* feature military women who are fully capable of taking care of themselves, no matter the situation. Servicemembers themselves, both male and female, began making their own films, reflecting their personal experiences and the issues important to them and other service personnel. Many of these, however, are "shorts," like *Lion in a Box* and *Do No Harm,* shown at various film festivals but not necessarily available to the general public, depriving most Americans of honest depictions about the changing roles women are playing in the military today.

In the twelve decades that women have officially been members of the U.S. military, their roles within the military have changed significantly. Initially restricted to traditional "women's work" such as nursing and office work, over time, their roles have expanded into non-traditional arenas as well, such as mechanic, ship driver, and aviator, as military needs dictated and societal ideas about women's roles changed. As Hollywood has progressively portrayed military women in a greater variety of roles, women in more recent films serve in a wide range of positions from pilot to intelligence specialist to combat soldier, reflecting the shift in opportunities made available to actual American servicewomen in the last three decades.

The vast majority of the women depicted in these films are white. Nancy Kwan, who plays Lieutenant Junior Grade Tomiko Momoyama in *Nobody's Perfect* (1968), is the first Asian American servicewoman depicted in an American film, while Ena Hartman, who portrays an unnamed WAC in 1966's *Our Man Flint*, is the first black woman in the military depicted. It is not until the twenty-first century that minority women become more common in film, although they still are not portrayed in the same percentages as they serve in the actual military. DoD demographics for 2017 show that approximately 53 percent of women currently serving in the military are white, while nearly 30 percent are Black and just under 20 percent identify as Hispanic. Black women, however, can be found in only twenty films in this survey (only five of which were released prior to 1990), and in only six of those is the black women a major character, with all of those portrayals coming after the turn of the twenty-first century. Asian women are found in only eight films (with just two depictions being major characters), and Hispanics are found in just fourteen films and portray major characters in only three of them. In all, portrayals of minority women are present in only forty-two of the 349 films surveyed in this book, or just 1.2 percent. Although minority women are well represented in the actual U.S. military, it is apparently still a foreign concept in Hollywood.

While the films surveyed in this book included women from the Army (including the WAAC and WAC), Navy, Air Force (including the WASP), Marine Corps, Coast Guard, and National Guard, approximately 59 percent of these films feature women in the Army. Another 23 percent feature Navy personnel, and the Marine Corps is represented in twenty-two films. The Coast Guard, which is only considered to be part of the Department of Defense in time of war, is barely represented in just four films in this survey, most likely due to the Coast Guard's primary mission of patrolling and protecting the coast of the United States, where no fighting is actually occurring. These statistics do not mesh with the actual numbers of women in each of the service branches. According to DoD 2015 statistics, 36 percent of actual female military personnel are in the Army, so Hollywood has about 50 percent more representations than statistically accurate. Portrayals of women in both the Navy and the Marine Corps percentages are pretty close percentage wise, but there would need to be three times more depictions of Air Force women to paint a more accurate picture. Additionally, National Guard personnel of both sexes are underrepresented in films, especially those about the most current wars, despite the fact that significant numbers of Guard personnel have served throughout the Middle East.

The percentage of women with children shown are not anywhere near the actual numbers, either. Currently, approximately 45 percent of military women have children, but less than twenty films in this survey depict military mothers, the vast majority of whom are single mothers as well. As mentioned in Chapter Three, 1948's *Homecoming* is the first film in this survey to portray a military mother; another would not be shown until 1981's *She's in the Army Now*. Married military women are rarely depicted in film either, with just fifteen films in this survey having servicewomen who are known to be married. Interestingly, many of these films are from the 1940s, and the servicewomen portrayed are widows whose husbands die during the war and they find it their patriotic duty to replace them.

It is also not until the twenty-first century that the majority of female characters have begun to be consistently listed by their ranks in film credits like men. Prior to that, they are often listed simply by character name without rank shown (even when the men are listed by rank) or are listed by their position (WAC) or by their position and first name (Nurse Cindy), while the male officer are listed by rank and by nickname if enlisted men. Of the 252 films in which rank can be determined, 180 of the portrayals are of officers, just over 71 percent. This is in stark contrast to reality, where the number of current military members who are officers is less than 18 percent. Only two films, however, feature female American generals—*Dead Men Can't Dance* (1997) and *Polar Opposites* (2008). No other general or flag officers appear in any film, despite their presence in the U.S. military since the 1970s. Approximately 40 percent of officers portrayed are nurses. The vast majority of these portrayals are also in older films; fifty-three of the portrayals are in films released prior to 1970, whereas there have only been eighteen portrayals of military nurses in the last fifty years.

Some things have not changed, however. While military men often die in war films, leaving behind the traditional wife, girlfriend, or mother to grieve their passing, filmmakers have been somewhat reluctant for that trend to carry over to military women onscreen. In fact, in only nineteen of the films surveyed does a female military character die, indicating that Hollywood still believes that the American public is not ready to see its wives, mothers, or daughters dying in battle, even in a movie.

Yet progress is still being made. As the second decade of the twenty-first century comes to a close and the wars in the Middle East drag on, American military women continue to break new ground with their service. The number of female general/flag officers and senior enlisted women continues to increase, and both submarine service and Special Forces billets are more available to servicewomen. Still, the American public appears to be losing its enthusiasm for realistic war movies, preferring instead the antics of comic book superheroes like Hellboy, Captain Marvel and the Avengers, and the live-action versions of and sequels to classic cartoon favorites. While some of these films reimagine former male action heroes as women, none look to include military women in their storylines. Despite the gains American women have made throughout the military, their efforts, which are vitally important to America's security, are sadly being ignored by Hollywood filmmakers, at least for the foreseeable future. Several movies scheduled to open in 2019–2020, including a new G.I. Joe film, a live action version of Disney's *Mulan*, and *Top Gun: Maverick*, appear to be the only non-science fiction films that could feature a military woman. Whether there are others remains to be seen.

Appendix A: Filmography by Year

Chapter One

The Girl Spy Before Vicksburg (1910)
Production Company: Kalem Company
Director: Sidney Olcott
Writer: Gene Gauntier

The House with Closed Shutters (1910)
Production Company: Biograph Company
Director: D.W. Griffith
Writer: Emmett C. Hall

Sword and Hearts (1911)
Production Company: Biograph Company
Director: D.W. Griffith
Writer: Emmett C. Hall

The Darling of the C.S.A. (1912)
Production Company: Kalem Company
Director: Kenean Buel
Writer: unknown

A Fair Rebel (1914)
Production Company: Klaw & Erlanger, Biograph Company
Director: Frank Powell
Writer: Harry Mawson (play)

Shoulder Arms (1918)
Production Company: Charles Chaplin Productions
Director: Charles Chaplin
Writer: Charles Chaplin

Navy Blues (1923)
Production Company: Christie Film Company
Director: Harold Beaudine
Writer: M.B. Hageman

Tell It to the Marines (1926)
Production Company: Metro-Goldwyn-Mayer (MGM)
Director: George Hill
Writers: Richard Schayer (screenplay); Joe Farnham (titles)

She Goes to War (1929)
Production Company: Inspiration Pictures
Director: Henry King
Writers: Rupert Hughes (story); Mme. Fred De Greasac (adaptation); Howard Estabrook (scenario); John Monk Saunders (dialogue, titles)

Today We Live (1933)
Production Company: Metro-Goldwyn-Mayer (MGM)
Directors: Howard Hawks and Richard Rosson
Writers: William Faulkner (story "Turn About"); Edith Fitzgerald and Dwight Taylor (screenplay); William Faulkner (dialogue); Howard Hawks; Ann Cunningham

There's Something about a Soldier (1934)
Production Company: Fleischer Studios
Director: Dave Fleischer
Writer: unknown

Navy Wife (1935)
Production Company: Fox Film Corporation
Director: Allan Dwan
Writers: Kathleen Norris (novel); Sonya Levien (screenplay); Edward T. Lowe, Jr. (additional dialogue); Sally Sandlin, Lillian Wurtzel, Ilya Zorn, and Eunice Chapin (contributors to screenplay construction)

Navy Secrets (1939)
Production Company: Monogram Pictures
Director: Howard Bretherton
Writers: Steve Fisher (story "Shore Leave"); Harvey Gates (screenplay)

Chapter Two

The Great Dictator (1940)

Production Company: Charles Chaplin Productions, One Production Company
Director: Charles Chaplin
Writer: Charles Chaplin

Buck Privates (1941)
Production Company: Universal Pictures
Director: Arthur Lubin
Writers: Arthur T. Horman (original screenplay); John Grant (special material for Abbott and Costello)

In the Navy (1941)
Production Company: Universal Pictures
Director: Arthur Lubin
Writers: Arthur T. Horman and John Grant (screenplay); Arthur T. Horman (original story)

International Squadron (1941)
Production Company: Warner Brothers
Director: Lothar Mendes and Lewis Seiler
Writers: Kenneth Gamet; Barry Trivers; Frank Wead (play)

A Yank in the R.A.F. (1941)
Production Company: 20th Century–Fox
Director: Henry King
Writers: Darrell Ware and Karl Tunberg (screenplay); Darryl F. Zanuck (story)

Army Surgeon (1942)
Production Company: RKO Radio Pictures
Director: A. Edward Sutherland
Writers: John Twist (story); Barry Trivers and Emmet Lavery (screenplay)

Barnyard WAAC (1942)
Production Company: Terrytoons
Director: Eddie Donnelly
Writer: John Foster (story)

Commandos Strike at Dawn (1942)
Production Company: Columbia Pictures Corporation
Director: John Farrow
Writers: Irwin Shaw (screenplay); C.S. Forester (story)

The Navy Comes Through (1942)
Production Company: RKO Radio Pictures
Director: A. Edward Sutherland
Writers: Borden Chase (story "Pay to Learn"); Earl Baldwin and John Twist (adaptation); Roy Chanslor and Æneas MacKenzie (screenplay)

Parachute Nurse (1942)
Production Company: Columbia Pictures Corporation
Director: Charles Barton
Writers: Elizabeth Meehan (based on a story by); Rian James (screenplay)

This Above All (1942)
Production Company: 20th Century–Fox Film Corporation
Director: Anatole Litvak
Writers: Eric Knight (novel); R.C. Sherriff (screenplay)

To the Shores of Tripoli (1942)
Production Company: 20th Century–Fox
Director: H. Bruce Humberstone
Writers: Lamar Trotti (screenplay); Steve Fisher (original story)

True to the Army (1942)
Production Company: Paramount Pictures
Director: Albert S. Rogell
Writers: Art Arthur and Bradford Ropes (screenplay); Edmund Hartmann and Val Burton (adaptation); Howard Lindsay (based on a play by); Edward Hope (based on the novel "She Loves Me Not")

Bomber's Moon (1943)
Production Company: 20th Century–Fox Film Corporation
Director: Edward Ludwig and Harold D. Schuster (as Charles Fuhr); John Brahm (one day)
Writers: Leonard Lee (story); Kenneth Gamet and Aubrey Wisberg (writers)

Corregidor (1943)
Production Company: Atlantis Pictures
Director: William Nigh
Writers: Doris Malloy and Edgar G. Ulmer (original story and screenplay)

Cry 'Havoc' (1943)
Production Company: Metro-Goldwyn-Mayer (MGM)
Director: Richard Thorpe
Writers: Paul Osborn (screenplay); Allan R. Kenward (play)

A Guy Named Joe (1943)
Production Company: Metro-Goldwyn-Mayer (MGM)
Director: Victor Fleming
Writers: Chandler Sprague and David Boehm (story); Frederick Brennan (adaptation); Dalton Trumbo (screenplay)

The Iron Major (1943)
Production Company: RKO Radio Pictures
Director: Ray Enright
Writers: Florence E. Cavanaugh (story); Aben Kandel and Warren Duff (screenplay)

So Proudly We Hail (1943)
Production Company: Paramount Pictures
Director: Mark Sandrich
Writers: Allan Scott; Eunice Hatchett (story)

Women at War (1943)
Production Company: U.S. Army, Warner Brothers
Director: Jean Negulesco
Writer: Charles L. Tedford (screenplay)

The Doughgirls (1944)
Production Company: Warner Brothers
Director: James V. Kern
Writers: Joseph Fields (play); Sam Hellman; James V. Kern; Wilkie C. Mahoney (additional dialogue)

Here Come the WAVES (1944)
Production Company: Paramount Pictures
Director: Mark Sandrich
Writers: Ken England, Zion Myers, and Allan Scott

Ladies Courageous (1944)
Production Company: Walter Wanger Productions
Director: John Rawlins
Writers: Virginia Spencer Cowles (novel "Looking for Trouble"); Doris Gilbert; Norman Reilly Raine

Lifeboat (1944)
Production Company: 20th Century–Fox
Director: Alfred Hitchcock
Writers: John Steinbeck (by); Jo Swerling (screenplay)

Marine Raiders (1944)
Production Company: RKO Radio Pictures
Director: Harold D. Schuster
Writers: Warren Duff (screenplay); Martin Rackin and Warren Duff (original story); Jerome Odlum (contributor to screenplay construction)

The Navy Way (1944)
Production Company: Pine-Thomas Productions
Director: William Berke
Writer: Maxwell Shane (original screenplay)

Up in Arms (1944)
Production Company: Samuel Goldwyn Company, Avalon Productions
Director: Elliott Nugent
Writers: Don Harman, Allen Boretz, and Robert Pirosh (original screenplay); Owen Davis (suggested by the character "The Nervous Wreck"); Bernard Schubert (contributor to original story)

A WAVE, a WAC, and a Marine (1944)
Production Company: Biltmore Productions
Director: Phil Karlson
Writer: Hal Fimberg (original screenplay)

The Weakly Reporter (1944)
Production Company: Warner Brothers
Director: Chuck Jones
Writer: Michael Maltese (story)

First Yank into Tokyo (1945)
Production Company: RKO Radio Pictures
Director: Gordon Douglas
Writers: J. Robert Bren and Gladys Atwater (story); J. Robert Bren (screenplay)

Keep Your Powder Dry (1945)
Production Company: Metro-Goldwyn-Mayer (MGM)
Director: Edward Buzzell
Writers: Mary C. McCall, Jr., and George Bruce (original screenplay)

The Story of G.I. Joe (1945)
Production Company: Lester Crown Productions
Director: William A. Wellman
Writers: Leopold Atlas, Guy Endore, and Philip Stevenson (screenplay); Ben Bengal (additional dialogue); Alan Le May; Ernie Pyle (books)

They Were Expendable (1945)
Production Company: Metro-Goldwyn-Mayer (MGM)
Director: John Ford and Robert Montgomery
Writers: William L. White (book); Frank Wead and Jan Lustig (screenplay); Norman Corwin; George Froeschel

G.I. War Brides (1946)
Production Company: Republic Pictures
Director: George Blair
Writer: John K. Butler

Tars and Spars (1946)
Production Company: Columbia Pictures Corporation
Director: Alfred E. Green
Writers: Decla Dunning; Hans Jacoby; Sarett Tobias; Barry Trivers (story)

Without Reservations (1946)
Production Company: RKO Radio Pictures
Director: Mervyn LeRoy
Writers: Andrew Solt (screenplay); Jane Allen and Mae Livingston (novel)

Buck Privates Come Home (1947)
Production Company: Universal International Pictures

Director: Charles Barton
Writers: John Grant, Frederic I. Rinaldo, and Robert Lees (screenplay); Richard Macaulay and Bradford Ropes (based on a story by)

Seven Were Saved (1947)
Production Company: Pine-Thomas Productions
Director: William H. Pine
Writers: Maxwell Shane (screenplay); Maxwell Shane and Julian Harmon (original story)

Suddenly, It's Spring (1947)
Production Company: Paramount Pictures
Director: Michael Leisen
Writers: Claude Binyon and P.J. Wolfson (screenplay); P.J. Wolfson (original story)

Where There's Life (1947)
Production Company: Paramount Pictures
Director: Sidney Lanfield
Writers: Allen Boretz and Melville Shavelson (screenplay); Melville Shavelson (based on a story by)

Homecoming (1948)
Production Company: Metro-Goldwyn-Mayer (MGM)
Director: Mervyn LeRoy
Writers: Sidney Kingsley (story); Jan Lustig (adaptation); Paul Osborn (writer)

My Own True Love (1948)
Production Company: Paramount Pictures
Director: Compton Bennett
Writers: Yolanda Foldes (novel); Arthur Kober (adaptation); Josef Mischel and Theodore Strauss (writer)

Sealed Verdict (1948)
Production Company: Paramount Pictures
Director: Lewis Allen
Writers: Jonathan Latimer; Lionel Shapiro (novel)

The Hasty Heart (1949)
Production Company: Warner Brothers; Associated British Picture Corporation (ABPC)
Director: Vincent Sherman
Writers: Ranald MacDougall (screenplay); John Patrick (play)

I Was a Male War Bride (1949)
Production Company: 20th Century-Fox
Director: Howard Hawks
Writers: Charles Lederer, Leonard Spigelgass, and Hagar Wilde (screenplay); Henri Rochard (story)

The Red Danube (1949)
Production Company: Metro-Goldwyn-Mayer (MGM)
Director: George Sidney
Writers: Gina Kaus and Arthur Wimperis (screenplay); Bruce Marshall (novel); Carey Wilson

Twelve O'Clock High (1949)
Production Company: 20th Century-Fox
Director: Henry King
Writers: Sy Bartlett and Beirne Lay, Jr. (screenplay and novel); Henry King

Chapter Three

Breakthrough (1950)
Production Company: Warner Brothers
Director: Lewis Seiler
Writers: Joseph Breen (story); Bernard Girard; Ted Sherdeman

Experiment Alcatraz (1950)
Production Company: Edward L. Cahn Productions
Director: Edward L. Cahn
Writers: Orville H. Hampton (screenplay); George W. George and George F. Slavin (story)

The Flying Missile (1950)
Production Company: Columbia Pictures Corporation
Director: Henry Levin
Writers: Richard English; James Gunn; Harvey S. Haislip and N. Richard Nash (story)

Pygmy Island (1950)
Production Company: The Katzman Corporation
Director: William Berke
Writer: Carroll Young

Bright Victory (1951)
Production Company: Universal International Pictures
Director: Mark Robson
Writers: Robert Buckner (screenplay); Baynard Kendrick (novel)

Force of Arms (1951)
Production Company: Warner Brothers
Director: Michael Curtiz
Writers: Orin Jannings (screenplay); Richard Tregaskis (story)

G.I. Jane (1951)
Production Company: Murray Productions
Director: Reginald Le Borg
Writers: Murray Lerner (story), Henry Blankfort (screenplay)

Leave It to the Marines (1951)
Production Company: Sigmund Neufeld Productions

Director: Sam Newfield
Writer: Orville H. Hampton

Operation Pacific (1951)
Production Company: Warner Brothers
Director: George Waggner
Writer: George Waggner

Purple Heart Diary (1951)
Production Company: Sam Katzman Productions
Director: Richard Quine
Writers: Frances Langford (based upon the Frances Langford column in Hearst newspapers); William Sackheim (written for the screen by)

The Wild Blue Yonder (1951)
Production Company: Republic Pictures
Director: Allan Dwan
Writers: Andrew Geer and Charles Grayson (story); Richard Tregaskis (screenplay)

You're in the Navy Now (1951)
Production Company: 20th Century–Fox
Director: Henry Hathaway
Writers: John W. Hazard (magazine article); Richard Murphy

Off Limits (1952)
Production Company: Paramount Pictures
Director: George Marshall
Writers: Hal Kanter and Jack Sher (story and screenplay)

Operation Secret (1952)
Production Company: Warner Brothers
Director: Lewis Seiler
Writers: Harold Medford; James R. Webb; Peter Ortiz (story suggested by)

Red Snow (1952)
Production Company: All American Film Corporation
Director: Harry S. Franklin and Boris Petroff
Writers: Robert Peters (story); Tom Hubbard and Orville H. Hampton (screenplay)

Sailor Beware (1952)
Production Company: Wallis-Hazen
Director: Hal Walker
Writers: James Allardice and Martin Rackin (screenplay); John Grant (additional dialogue); Elwood Ullman (adaptation); Kenyon Nicholson and Charles Robinson (play)

Skirts Ahoy! (1952)
Production Company: Metro-Goldwyn-Mayer (MGM)
Director: Sidney Lanfield
Writer: Isobel Lennart

Sound Off (1952)
Production Company: Columbia Pictures Corporation
Director: Richard Quire
Writers: Blake Edwards; Richard Quire

Thunderbirds (1952)
Production Company: Republic Pictures
Director: John H. Auer
Writers: Kenneth Gamet (story); Mary C. McCall, Jr. (screenplay)

Torpedo Alley (1952)
Production Company: Lindsley Parsons Picture Corporations
Director: Lew Landers
Writers: Warren Douglas; Samuel Rocca

The WAC from Walla Walla (1952)
Production Company: Republic Pictures
Director: William Witney
Writer: Arthur T. Horman

Battle Circus (1953)
Production Company: Metro-Goldwyn-Mayer (MGM)
Director: Richard Brooks
Writers: Allen Rivkin and Laura Kerr (story); Richard Brooks (writer)

Flight Nurse (1953)
Production Company: Republic Pictures
Director: Allan Dwan
Writer: Alan Le May

Mission Over Korea (1953)
Production Company: Robert Cohn Productions
Director: Fred F. Sears
Writers: Martin Goldsmith, Jesse Lasky, Jr., and Eugene Ling (writers); Richard Tregaskis (story)

Never Wave at a WAC (1952)
Production Company: Independent Artists Pictures
Director: Norman Z. McLeod
Writers: Ken Englund (screenplay); Frederick Kohner and Fred Brady (story)

Francis Joins the WACs (1954)
Production Company: Universal International Pictures
Director: Arthur Lubin
Writers: Herbert Baker (story); Devery Freeman; James B. Allardice; Dorothy Davenport (additional dialogue); David Stern (characters)

Francis in the Navy (1955)
Production Company: Universal International Pictures
Director: Arthur Lubin
Writers: Devery Freeman (screenplay and story); David Stern (characters)

Mister Roberts (1955)
Production Company: Warner Brothers
Directors: John Ford, Mervyn LeRoy, and Joshua Logan
Writers: Frank Nugent and Joshua Logan (screenplay); Thomas Heggen and Joshua Logan (based on the play by); Thomas Heggen (from the novel by)

D-Day: The Sixth of June (1956)
Production Company: 20th Century–Fox
Directors: Henry Koster
Writers: Ivan Moffat and Harry Brown (screenplay); Lionel Shapiro (novel)

The Iron Petticoat (1956)
Production Company: Remus, Hope Enterprises, London Film Productions
Director: Ralph Thomas
Writers: Ben Hecht (screenplay); Harry Saltzman (story)

The Lieutenant Wore Skirts (1956)
Production Company: 20th Century–Fox
Director: Frank Tashlin
Writers: Albert Beich and Frank Tashlin (screenplay); Albert Beich (story)

The Proud and Profane (1956)
Production Company: Perlberg-Seaton Productions
Director: George Seaton
Writers: Lucy Herndon Crockett (novel); George Seaton (written for the screen by)

Don't Go Near the Water (1957)
Production Company: Avon Productions
Director: Charles Waters
Writers: William Brinkley (novel); Dorothy Kingsley; George Wells

Hellcats of the Navy (1957)
Production Company: Morningside Productions
Director: Nathan Juran
Writers: Charles A. Lockwood and Hans Christian Adamson (book); David Lang (screen story); David Lang and Bernard Gordon (screenplay)

Jet Pilot (1957)
Production Company: RKO Radio Pictures
Director: Josef von Sternberg
Writer: Jules Furthman

Kiss Them for Me (1957)
Production Company: Jerry Wald Productions
Director: Stanley Donen
Writers: Julius J. Epstein (screenplay); Luther Davis (play "Kiss Them for Me"), Frederic Wakeman (Novel "Shore Leave")

Operation Mad Ball (1957)
Production Company: Columbia Pictures Corporation
Director: Richard Quine
Writers: Arthur Carter, Jed Harris, and Blake Edwards (screenplay); Arthur Carter (play)

The Sad Sack (1957)
Production Company: Hal Wallis Productions
Director: George Marshall
Writers: Edmund Beloin and Nate Monaster (screenplay); George Baker (comic strip)

Three Brave Men (1957)
Production Company: 20th Century–Fox
Director: Philip Dunne
Writers: Philip Dunne; Anthony Lewis (articles)

Time Limit (1957)
Production Company: Heath Productions
Director: Karl Malden
Writers: Henry Denker (screenplay); Henry Denker and Ralph Berkey (play)

The Geisha Boy (1958)
Production Company: York Pictures Corporation
Director: Frank Tashlin
Writers: Frank Tashlin (screen story and screenplay); Rudy Makoul (story)

The Hunters (1958)
Production Company: 20th Century–Fox
Director: Dick Powell
Writers: Wendell Mayes (screenplay); James Salter (novel)

In Love and War (1958)
Production Company: Jerry Wald Productions, 20th Century–Fox
Director: Philip Dunne
Writers: Edward Anhalt (screenplay); Anton Myrer (based on a novel by)

Jet Attack (1958)
Production Company: Catalina Productions
Director: Edward L. Cahn
Writers: Orville H. Hampton (screenplay); Mark Hanna (story)

No Time for Sergeants (1958)
Production Company: Warner Brothers
Director: Mervyn LeRoy

Writers: John Lee Mahin (screenplay); Ira Levin (play); Mac Hyman (novel)

The Perfect Furlough (1958)
Production Company: Universal International Pictures
Director: Blake Edwards
Writer: Stanley Shapiro

South Pacific (1958)
Production Company: Magna Theater Corporation, South Pacific Enterprises, Rodgers & Hammerstein Productions
Director: Joshua Logan
Writers: Paul Osborn (screenplay); Richard Rodgers, Oscar Hammerstein II, and Joshua Logan (adapted from the play "South Pacific"); James Michener (based on "Tales of the South Pacific" by)

Tank Battalion (1958)
Production Company: Iron Foxhole Inc., Viscount Films—Terry Moore Production
Director: Sherman A. Rose
Writers: Richard Bernstein and George W. Waters (screenplay); George W. Waters (story)

The Young Lions (1958)
Production Company: 20th Century–Fox
Director: Edward Dmytryk
Writers: Edward Anhalt (screenplay); Irwin Shaw (novel)

Battle Flame (1959)
Production Company: Allied Artists Pictures
Director: R.G. Springsteen
Writers: Lester A. Sansom (story); Elwood Ullman

Battle of the Coral Sea (1959)
Production Company: Columbia Pictures Corporation, Morningside Productions
Director: Paul Wendkos
Writers: Daniel B. Ullman and Stephen Kandel (screenplay); Stephen Kandel (story)

Don't Give Up the Ship (1959)
Production Company: Hal Wallis Productions
Director: Norman Taurog
Writers: Herbert Baker, Edmund Beloin, and Henry Garson (screenplay); Ellis Kadison (story)

Five Gates to Hell (1959)
Production Company: Associated Producers (API), 20th Century–Fox
Director: James Clavell
Writer: James Clavell

Never So Few (1959)
Production Company: Metro-Goldwyn-Mayer (MGM), Canterbury Productions
Director: John Sturges
Writers: Millard Kaufman (screenplay); Tom T. Chamales (novel)

On the Beach (1959)
Production Company: Stanley Kramer Productions
Director: Stanley Kramer
Writers: John Paxton (screenplay); Nevil Shute (novel)

Operation Petticoat (1959)
Production Company: Granart Company, Universal International Pictures
Director: Blake Edwards
Writers: Stanley Shapiro and Maurice Richlin (screenplay); Paul King and Joseph Stone (suggested by a story by)

A Private's Affair (1959)
Production Company: 20th Century–Fox
Director: Raoul Walsh
Writers: Winston Miller (screenplay); Ray Livingston Murphy (story)

Up Periscope (1959)
Production Company: Aubrey Schenck Productions
Director: Gordon Douglas
Writers: Richard H. Landau (screenplay); Robb White (novel)

Chapter Four

Wake Me When It's Over (1960)
Production Company: Mervyn LeRoy Productions
Director: Mervyn LeRoy
Writers: Richard L. Breen; Howard Singer (novel)

All Hands on Deck (1961)
Production Company: 20th Century–Fox
Director: Norman Taurog
Writers: Donald R. Morris (novel); Jay Sommers (screenplay)

The Great Imposter (1961)
Production Company: Universal International Pictures
Director: Robert Mulligan
Writers: Robert Crichton (novel); Liam O'Brien (screenplay)

Voyage to the Bottom of the Sea (1961)
Production Company: Irwin Allen Productions

Director: Irwin Allen
Writers: Irwin Allen and Charles Bennett (screenplay); Irwin Allen (story)

The Horizontal Lieutenant (1962)
Production Company: Euterpe
Director: Richard Thorpe
Writers: Gordon Cotler (novel); George Wells (screenplay)

Captain Newman, M.D. (1963)
Production Company: Brentwood Productions, Reynard
Director: David Miller
Writers: Richard L. Breen, Phoebe Ephron, and Henry Ephron (screenplay); Leo Rosten (novel)

The Americanization of Emily (1964)
Production Company: Filmways Pictures
Director: Arthur Hiller
Writers: Paddy Chayefsky (screenplay); William Bradford Huie (novel)

Ensign Pulver (1964)
Production Company: Warner Brothers
Director: Joshua Logan
Writers: Thomas Heggan and Joshua Logan (based on a play by); Thomas Heggan (from the novel by); Joshua Logan and Peter S. Feibleman (screenplay)

Iron Angel (1964)
Production Company: Ken Kennedy Productions
Director: Ken Kennedy
Writer: Ken Kennedy

Kissin' Cousins (1964)
Production Company: Sam Katzman Productions
Director: Gene Nelson
Writers: Gerald Drayson Adams and Gene Nelson (screenplay); Gerald Drayson Adams (story)

In Harm's Way (1965)
Production Company: Otto Preminger Films
Director: Otto Preminger
Writer: Wendell Mayes (screenplay); James Bassett (novel)

McHale's Navy Joins the Air Force (1965)
Production Company: Universal Pictures
Director: Edward Montagne
Writers: William J. Lederer (story); John Fenton Murray

Sergeant Deadhead (1965)
Production Company: Alta Vista Productions
Director: Norman Taurog
Writer: Louis M. Heyward

Not with My Wife, You Don't! (1966)
Production Company: Fernwood-Reynard
Director: Norman Panama
Writers: Norman Panama, Larry Gelbart, and Peter Barnes (screenplay); Norman Panama and Melvin Frank (story)

Our Man Flint (1966)
Production Company: 20th Century–Fox
Director: Daniel Mann
Writers: Hal Fimburg and Ben Starr (screenplay); Hal Fimburg (story)

The Longest Hundred Miles (1967)
Production Company: Universal Television
Director: Don Weis
Writers: Hennie Leon (story); Paul Mason (adaptation); Winston Miller (teleplay)

Nobody's Perfect (1968)
Production Company: Universal Pictures
Director: Alan Rafkin
Writers: John D.F. Black; Allan R. Bosworth (novel)

Catch-22 (1970)
Production Company: Paramount Pictures, Filmways Productions
Director: Mike Nichols
Writers: Joseph Heller (novel); Buck Henry (screenplay)

MASH (1970)
Production Company: Aspen Productions, Ingo Preminger Productions, 20th Century–Fox Film
Director: Robert Altman
Writers: Richard Hooker (from the novel by); Ring Lardner, Jr. (screenplay)

Fireball Forward (1972)
Production Company: 20th Century–Fox Television
Director: Marvin J. Chomsky
Writer: Edmund H. North

The President's Plane Is Missing (1973)
Production Company: ABC Circle Films
Director: Daryl Duke
Writers: Mark Carliner and Ernest Kinoy (teleplay); Robert J. Sterling (novel)

Chesty Anderson, U.S. Navy (1976)
Production Company: Cinefilm Group Industries, Shelby Associates
Director: Ed Forsyth
Writers: Paul Pumpian and H.F. Green (story and screenplay)

Deborah Sampson: Woman in the Revolution (1976)
Production Company: Greenhouse Films
Director: Dennis Passaggio
Writer: Dennis Passaggio

Warhead (Prisoner in the Middle) (1977)
Production Company: Buddy Ruskin-Sabra
Director: John O'Connor
Writers: Buddy Ruskin (screenplay); Patrick Foulk and Donovan Karnes (story)

The Boys in Company C (1978)
Production Company: Golden Harvest Company, Good Times Films S.A.
Director: Sidney J. Furie
Writers: Rick Natkin; Sidney J. Furie

The Swarm (1978)
Production Company: Warner Brothers
Director: Irwin Allen
Writers: Arthur Herzog III (novel); Stirling Silliphant (screenplay)

Women at West Point (1979)
Production Company: Alan Sacks Productions, Columbia Pictures Corporation, Columbia Pictures Television
Director: Vincent Sherman
Writers: Juleen Compton (story); Ann Marcus; Ellis Marcus

Chapter Five

Ike: The War Years (1980)
Production Company: ABC Circle Films
Director: Boris Sagal and Melville Shavelson
Writer: Melville Shavelson

Private Benjamin (1980)
Production Company: Warner Brothers
Director: Howard Zieff
Writers: Nancy Meyers, Charles Shyer, and Harvey Miller

The Secret War of Jackie's Girls (1980)
Production Company: Penthouse Productions, Public Art Films, Universal Television
Director: Gordon Hessler
Writer: Ann Donahue and Jean Ross Kondek (idea); Theodore Jonas (story); D. Guthire and Theodore Jonas (teleplay)

Red Flag: The Ultimate Game (1981)
Production Company: Marble Arch Productions
Director: Don Taylor
Writer: T.S. Cook

She's in the Army Now (1981)
Production Company: ABC Circle Films
Director: Hy Averback
Writer: Earl W. Wallace

Stripes (1981)
Production Company: Columbia Pictures Corporation
Director: Ivan Reitman
Writers: Len Blum, Dan Goldberg, and Harold Ramis

Firefox (1982)
Production Company: Major Studio Partners, The Malpaso Company
Director: Clint Eastwood
Writers: Alex Lasker and Wendell Wellman (screenplay); Craig Thomas (novel)

An Officer and a Gentleman (1982)
Production Company: Lorimar Film Entertainment, Paramount Pictures
Director: Taylor Hackford
Writer: Douglas Day Stewart

WarGames (1983)
Production Company: United Artists, Sherwood Productions
Director: John Badham
Writers: Lawrence Lasker; Walter F. Parkes

Purple Hearts (1984)
Production Company: The Ladd Company
Director: Sidney J. Furie
Writers: Sidney J. Furie; Rick Natkin

Remo Williams (1985)
Production Company: Dick Clark Productions, Orion Pictures
Director: Guy Hamilton
Writers: Richard Sapir and Warren Murphy (novel "The Destroyer"); Christopher Wood (written by); Guy Hamilton

Spies Like Us (1985)
Production Company: Warner Brothers, AAR Films
Director: John Landis
Writers: Dan Aykroyd and Dave Thomas (story); Dan Aykroyd, Lowell Ganz, and Babaloo Mandel (screenplay)

Intimate Strangers (1986)
Production Company: Nederlander Television & Film Production
Director: Robert Ellis Miller
Writer: Norman Morrill

Opposing Force (Hellcamp) (1986)
Production Company: Eros International Film Productions; Jeff Wald & Associates

Director: Eric Karson
Writer: Linda J. Cowgill

A Time to Triumph (1986)
Production Company: Billos/Kauffman Production, Phoenix Entertainment Group
Director: Noel Black
Writers: Lavinia Dawson; George Yanok

Women of Valor (1986)
Production Company: Jeni Productions; Inter Planetary Productions Corporation
Director: Buzz Kulik
Writer: Jonas McCord

Behind Enemy Lines (1987)
Production Company: Eastern Film Management Corporation
Director: Cirio H. Santiago
Writer: Joe Mari Avellana

Full Metal Jacket (1987)
Production Company: Natant, Stanley Kubrick Productions, Warner Brothers
Director: Stanley Kubrick
Writers: Stanley Kubrick, Michael Herr, and Gustav Hasford (screenplay); Gustav Hasford (based on the novel "The Short Timers" by)

G.I. Joe: The Movie (1987)
Production Company: Sunbow Productions, Marvel Productions, Hasbro
Directors: Don Jurwich, Roger Slifer
Writer: Ron Friedman

The Dirty Dozen: The Fatal Mission (1988)
Production Co: MGM/UA Television, RAI Radiotelevisione Italiana, Jadran Film
Director: Lee H. Katzin
Writers: Nunnally Johnson and Lukas Heller (characters in screenplay); Mark Rodgers (written by)

Hell on the Battleground (1988)
Production Company: Action International Pictures
Director: David A. Prior
Writer: David A. Prior

The Presidio (1988)
Production Co: Paramount Pictures
Director: Peter Hyams
Writer: Larry Ferguson

Too Young the Hero (1988)
Production Company: Rick-Dawn Enterprises, Cossette Enterprises, Landsburg Company
Director: Buzz Kulik
Writer: Calvin Graham and Gary Thomas (manuscript); David J. Kinghorn (teleplay)

The Iron Triangle (1989)
Production Co: Scotti Brothers Pictures, Eurobrothers, International Video Entertainment
Director: Eric Weston
Writers: Marshall Drazen (narration); John Bushelman, Larry Hilbrand, and Eric Weston (writers)

Lethal Woman (1989)
Production Co: Pure Gold Productions, United Talents
Director: Christian Marnham
Writers: Michael Olson; Gabe Ellis (screenplay)

The Package (1989)
Production Co: Orion Pictures
Director: Andrew Davis
Writer: John Bishop

Rescue Force (1989)
Production Co: Trans Continental Film
Director: Charles Nizet
Writer: Charles Nizet

Your Mother Wears Combat Boots (1989)
Production Company: Mi-Bar Productions, Multicom Entertainment Group, The Kushner-Locke Company
Director: Anson Williams
Writers: Bill Novodor and Susan Hunter (story); Susan Hunter (teleplay)

Chapter Six

By Dawn's Early Light (1990)
Production Company: Home Box Office, Paravision International S.A.
Director: Jack Sholder
Writers: William Prochnau (novel); Bruce Gilbert (teleplay)

Fire Birds (Wings of the Apache) (1990)
Production Company: Nova International Films, Touchstone Pictures
Director: David Green
Writers: Step Tyner, John K. Swensson, and Dale Dye (story); Nick Thiel and Paul F. Edwards (screenplay)

Delta Force 3: The Killing Game (1991)
Production Company: Global Pictures
Director: Sam Firstenberg
Writers: Andrew Deutsch; Greg Latter; Boaz Davidson

Going Under (1991)
Production Company: Warner Brothers
Director: Mark W. Travis
Writers: Darryl Zarubica; Randolph Davis

The Heroes of Desert Storm (1991)
Production Company: ABC Video, Capital Cities, Ohlmeyer Communications Company
Director: Don Ohlmeyer
Writer: Lionel Chetwynd

Hot Shots! (1991)
Production Company: 20th Century–Fox
Director: Jim Abrahams
Writers: Jim Abrahams; Pat Proft

Into the Sun (1991)
Production Company: Trimark Pictures
Director: Fritz Kiersch
Writers: John Brancato; Michael Ferris

One Against the Wind (1991)
Production Company: Delux Productions, Hallmark Hall of Fame Productions, Karen Mack Productions
Director: Larry Eikann
Writer: Chris Bryant

A Few Good Men (1992)
Production Company: Columbia Pictures Corporation, Castle Rock Entertainment
Director: Rob Reiner
Writer: Aaron Sorkin (play and screenplay)

Patriot Games (1992)
Production Company: Mace Neufeld Productions, Paramount Pictures
Director: Phillip Noyce
Writers: Tom Clancy (novel); W. Peter Iliff and Donald Stewart (screenplay)

Under Siege (1992)
Production Company: Warner Brothers, Regency Enterprises, Canal+
Director: Andrew Davis
Writer: J.F. Lawton

Chasers (1994)
Production Company: Morgan Creek Entertainment
Director: Dennis Hopper
Writers: Joe Batteer and John Rice (story); Joe Batteer, John Rice, and Dan Gilroy (screenplay)

Clear and Present Danger (1994)
Production Company: Mace Neufeld Productions, Paramount Pictures
Director: Phillip Noyce
Writers: Tom Clancy (novel); Donald Stewart, Steven Zaillian, and John Milius (screenplay)

Forrest Gump (1994)
Production Company: Paramount Pictures
Director: Robert Zemeckis
Writers: Winston Groom (novel); Eric Roth (screenplay)

In the Army Now (1994)
Production Company: Hollywood Pictures
Director: Daniel Petrie, Jr.
Writers: Steve Zacharias, Jeff Buhai, and Robbie Fox (story); Ken Kaufman, Stu Krieger, Daniel Petrie, Jr., Fax Bahr, and Adam Small (screenplay)

Renaissance Man (1994)
Production Company: Cinergi Pictures Entertainment, Parkway Productions, Touchstone Pictures
Director: Penny Marshall
Writer: Jim Burnstein

Excessive Force II: Force on Force (1995)
Production Company: New Line Cinema, CineTel Pictures
Director: Jonathan Winfrey
Writer: Mark Sevi

Inflammable (1995)
Production Company: Savoy Pictures Television, Susan Baerwald Productions
Director: Peter Werner
Writers: Leo Garen; Harrison Starr

Serving in Silence (1995)
Production Company: Barwood Films; Storyline Productions; Tristar Television; Trillium Productions
Director: Jeff Bleckner
Writer: Alison Cross

She Stood Alone: The Tailhook Scandal (1995)
Production Company: The Polone-Winer Company, Symphony Pictures, ABC Productions
Director: Larry Shaw
Writer: Suzette Couture

The Bloody Child (1996)
Production Company: Independent Television Service
Director: Nina Menkes
Writer: Nina Menkes

Broken Arrow (1996)
Production Company: 20th Century–Fox, Mark Gordon Productions, WCG Entertainment Productions

Director: John Woo
Writer: Graham Yost

Courage Under Fire (1996)
Production Company: Davis Entertainment, Fox 2000 Pictures, Joseph M. Singer Entertainment
Director: Edward Zwick
Writer: Patrick Sheane Duncan

Crash Dive (1996)
Production Company: Royal Oaks Entertainment, Inc., Cabin Fever Entertainment
Director: Andrew Stevens
Writer: William C. Martell (screenplay)

Down Periscope (1996)
Production Company: 20th Century–Fox
Director: David S. Ward
Writers: Hugh Wilson (story); Hugh Wilson, Andrew Kurtzman, and Eliot Wald (screenplay)

The English Patient (1996)
Production Company: Miramax Films, Tiger Moth Productions
Director: Anthony Minghella
Writers: Michael Ondaatje (novel); Anthony Minghella (screenplay)

Lone Star (1996)
Production Company: Columbia Pictures Corporation, Castle Rock Entertainment, Rio Dulce
Director: John Sayles
Writer: John Sayles

Sgt. Bilko (1996)
Production Company: Imagine Entertainment, Universal Pictures
Director: Jonathan Lynn
Writers: Nat Hiken (television series); Andy Breckman

Dead Men Can't Dance (1997)
Production Company: City Entertainment, Mediaworks
Director: Stephen Anderson, Hubert de La Bouillerie
Writers: Paul Sinor (story); Paul Sinor, Mark Sevi, and Bill Kerby (screenplay)

G.I. Jane (1997)
Production Company: Caravan Pictures, First Independent Films, Hollywood Pictures, Largo Entertainment, Moving Pictures, ScottFree Productions, Trap Two-Zero Productions
Director: Ridley Scott
Writers: Danielle Alexandra (story); David Twohy and Danielle Alexandra (screenplay)

Love's Deadly Triangle (Swearing Allegiance) (1997)
Production Company: Steve White Entertainment
Director: Richard A. Colla
Writers: Skip Hollandsworth (article); Steve Johnson

McHale's Navy (1997)
Production Company: Sheinberg Productions, The Bubble Factory
Director: Bryan Spicer
Writers: Peter Crabbe and Andy Rose (story); Peter Crabbe (screenplay)

Operation Delta Force (1997)
Production Company: Millennium Films, Mondofin B.V.
Director: Sam Firstenberg
Writers: Danny Lerner and Trevor Short (story); David Sparling

Tidal Wave: No Escape (1997)
Production Company: Hallmark Entertainment, JAWO Productions, RHI Entertainment
Director: George Miller
Writers: Tedi Sarafian (story); Tedi Sarafian and George Malko (teleplay)

Black Thunder (1998)
Production Company: Concorde-New Horizons, Royal Oaks Entertainment
Director: Rick Jacobson
Writer: William C. Martell

Freedom Strike (1998)
Production Company: Royal Oaks Entertainment, Unapix Entertainment
Director: Jerry P. Jacobs
Writer: Tony Giglio (screenplay)

The General's Daughter (1998)
Production Company: Paramount Pictures, Neufeld Rehme Productions, Munich Film Partners, Hollywood Licensing Group, Mace Neufeld Productions
Director: Simon West
Writers: Nelson DeMille (novel); Christopher Bertolini and William Goldman (screenplay)

Iron Eagle II (1998)
Production Company: Carolco Pictures, Alliance Entertainment, Canadian Entertainment Investors Number One and Company Limited Partnership, Harkot Productions
Director: Sidney J. Furie
Writers: Kevin Alyn Elders and Sidney J. Furie

Mulan (1998)
Production Company: Walt Disney Feature Animation Florida, Walt Disney Feature Animation, Walt Disney Pictures
Director: Tony Bancroft, Barry Cook
Writers: Robert D. San Souci (based on a story by); Rita Hsiao, Chris Sanders, Philip LaZebnik, Raymond Singer, and Eugenia Bostwick-Singer (screenplay by); Dean DeBlois (story co-head)

Operation Delta Force 3: Clear Target (1998)
Production Company: Millennium Films
Director: Mark Roper
Writers: Danny Lerner (story); David Sparling (screenplay)

The Pentagon Wars (1998)
Production Company: Home Box Office
Director: Richard Benjamin
Writers: James Burton (book); Jamie Malanowski and Martyn Burke (teleplay)

Surface to Air (1998)
Production Company: Cabin Fever Entertainment, Royal Oaks Entertainment
Director: Rodney McDonald
Writers: Tony Giglio (screenplay); Rodney McDonald (story)

Active Stealth (1999)
Production Company: Phoenician Entertainment, Synthetic Filmwerx
Director: Fred Olen Ray
Writer: Steve Latshaw

Counter Measures (1999)
Production Company: Royal Oaks Entertainment
Director: Fred Olen Ray
Writer: Steve Latshaw

Terminal Countdown (Y2K) (1999)
Production Company: PM Entertainment Group
Director: Richard Pepin
Writers: Carl Chapman (story); Terry Cunningham and Mick Dalrymple (written by)

Chapter Seven

One Kill (2000)
Production Company: CBS Productions, CBS, Showtime Networks, WildRice Productions
Director: Christopher Menaul
Writer: Shelley Evans

Operation Delta Force 5: Random Fire (2000)
Production Company: Millennium Films, Martien Holdings A.V.V., City Heat Productions
Director: Yossi Wein
Writers: Danny Lerner (story); Bernard Stone (screenplay)

Rain (2000)
Production Company: Alexander/Enright & Associates, Animal Planet, World International Network
Director: Robert J. Wilson
Writers: Martin Kitrosser; John McGowan

Behind Enemy Lines (2001)
Production Company: 20th Century–Fox, Davis Entertainment
Director: John Moore
Writers: Jim Thomas and John Thomas (story); David Veloz and Zak Penn (screenplay)

Danger Beneath the Sea (2001)
Production Company: Carlton America, Tele München Fernseh Produktionsgesellschaft
Director: Jon Cassar
Writer: Lucian Truscott IV

Enemy at the Gates (2001)
Production Company: Swanford Films, MP Film Management, Little Bird, DOS, Reperage, Mandalay Pictures, KC Medien, Paramount Pictures
Director: Jean-Jacques Annaud
Writers: Jean-Jacques Annaud; Alain Godard

Pearl Harbor (2001)
Production Company: Touchstone Pictures, Jerry Bruckheimer Films
Director: Michael Bay
Writer: Randall Wallace

South Pacific (2001)
Production Company: Trillium Productions, White Cap Productions, Jasse/Braunstein Films, Touchstone Television
Director: Richard Pearce
Writers: James A. Michener (novel); Oscar Hammerstein II and Joshua Logan (adaptation); Lawrence D. Cohen (teleplay)

Quicksand (2002)
Production Company: Quantum Entertainment, Swingin' Productions, Ushakiron Movies International
Director: Sam Firstenberg
Writers: Steve Schoenberg; Ruben Gordon

A Shade of Gray (2002)
Production Company: Sugar Moon Productions
Director: Wayne Miller
Writer: Wayne Miller

The Sum of All Fears (2002)
Production Company: Paramount Pictures, Mace Neufeld Productions, Munich Film Partners, Mel's Cite du Cinema, S.O.A.F. Productions
Director: Phil Alden Robinson
Writers: Tom Clancy (novel); Paul Attanasio and Daniel Pyne (screenplay)

Windtalkers (2002)
Production Company: Metro-Goldwyn-Mayer (MGM), Lion Rock Productions
Director: John Woo
Writers: John Rice; Joe Batteer

Basic (2003)
Production Company: Phoenix Pictures, Intermedia Films
Director: John McTiernan
Writer: James Vanderbilt

The Core (2003)
Production Company: Paramount Pictures, David Foster Productions, Munich Film Partners New Century & Company (MFP) Core Productions, Core Productions, Horsepower Films, LivePlanet
Director: Jon Amiel
Writers: Cooper Layne; John Rogers

G.I. Joe: Spy Troops (2003)
Production Company: Hasbro, Reel FX Creative Studios, Voice Box Productions
Director: Dale Carman
Writer: Larry Hama

Saving Jessica Lynch (2003)
Production Company: Daniel L. Paulson Productions, NBC Productions, NBC Studios, National Broadcasting Company
Director: Peter Markle
Writer: John Fasano

Air Strike (2004)
Production Company: Millennium Films, Martien Holding A.V.V.
Director: David Worth
Writers: Jon Stevens Alon (screenplay); Boaz Davidson (story)

Ike: Countdown to D-Day (2004)
Production Company: A&E Television Networks, Lionel Chetwynd Productions, Stephanie Germain Productions
Director: Robert Harmon
Writer: Lionel Chetwynd

One Weekend a Month (2004)
Production Company: Refuge Films
Director: Eric Escobar
Writer: Eric Escobar

Spartan (2004)
Production Company: Franchise Pictures, Apollo-Media Distribution, ApolloProMedia, Quality International, Signature Pictures (in association with)
Director: David Mamet
Writer: David Mamet

Stateside (2004)
Production Company: Seven Hills Pictures, Cinealpha KG, Cinerenta Medienbeteiligungs
Director: Reverge Anselmo
Writer: Reverge Anselmo

Tiger Cruise (2004)
Production Company: First Street Films, Stu Segall Productions, Walt Disney Pictures and Television
Director: Duwayne Dunham
Writers: Anna Sandor; Bruce Graham

A.W.O.L. (2005)
Production Company: Third World Newsreel
Director: Brigid Maher
Writer: Brigid Maher

Guy X (2005)
Production Company: Film and Music Entertainment, Spice Factory, Syon Media
Director: Saul Metzstein
Writers: Steve Attridge and John Paul Chapple (screenplay); John Griesemer (novel)

My Brother's War (2005)
Production Company: Bjornquist Films, Ostrow & Company
Director: Whitney Hamilton
Writer: Whitney Hamilton

Stealth (2005)
Production Company: Columbia Pictures Corporation, Original Film, Phoenix Pictures, Laura Ziskin Productions, AFG Talon Productions
Director: Rob Cohen
Writer: W.D. Richter

Tides of War (USS Poseidon: Phantom Below) (2005)
Production Company: Pacific Films
Director: Brian Trenchard-Smith
Writers: Stephen P. Jarchow (story by); Mark Sanderson (screenplay by)

Annapolis (2006)
Production Company: Touchstone Pictures, Mother B Productions

Director: Justin Lin
Writer: David Collard

Behind Enemy Lines II: Axis of Evil (2006)
Production Company: 20th Century–Fox
Director: James Dodson
Writer: James Dodson

Earthstorm (2006)
Production Company: Cinetel Films, S.V. Scary Films 5
Director: Terry Cunningham
Writer: Michael Konyves

Ghost Soldier (2006)
Production Company: Tsao Bros. Entertainment
Director: Allan Tsao
Writer: Allan Tsao

The Guardian (2006)
Production Company: Touchstone Pictures, Beacon Pictures, Contrafilm
Director: Andrew Davis
Writer: Ron L. Brinkerhoff

Home of the Brave (2006)
Production Company: Metro-Goldwyn-Mayer Pictures; Millennium Films; Emmett/Furla Films; North by Northwest Entertainment; Severe Entertainment; Winkler Films; Zak Productions
Director: Irwin Winkler
Writers: Mark Friedman (screenplay); Mark Friedman and Irwin Winkler (story)

Hunt for Eagle One (2006)
Production Company: New Horizon Pictures
Director: Bryan Clyde
Writer: Michael Henry Carter

Hunt for Eagle One: Crash Point (2006)
Production Company: Sony Pictures Home Entertainment
Director: Henry Crum
Writer: Michael Henry Carter

Military Intelligence and You! (2006)
Production Company: Pax Americana Pictures
Director: Dale Kutzera
Writer: Dale Kutzera

Flight of Fury (2007)
Production Company: Castle Film Romania, Clubdeal, Steamroller Productions
Director: Michael Keusch
Writers: Steven Seagal and Joe Halpin (screenplay); Joe Halpin (story)

Grace Is Gone (2007)
Production Company: Plum Pictures, The Weinstein Company, New Crime Productions
Director: Jim Strouse
Writers: Jim Strouse

Lions for Lambs (2007)
Production Company: Metro-Goldwyn-Mayer (MGM), United Artists, Wildwood Enterprises
Director: Robert Redford
Writer: Matthew Michael Carnahan

Eagle Eye (2008)
Production Company: DreamWorks, Goldcrest Pictures, KMP Film Invest, Digital Image Associates, K/O Paper Products
Director: D.J. Caruso
Writers: John Glenn, Travis Wright, Hillary Seitz, and Dan McDermott (screenplay); Dan McDermott (story)

Garrison (2008)
Production Company: A.W.O.L. Studios, MPS Dallas
Director: Kerry Valderama
Writer: Kerry Valderama

The Lucky Ones (2008)
Production Company: Lionsgate, Roadside Attractions, QED International, Sherazade Film Development, Visitor Pictures, Overnight
Director: Neil Burger
Writers: Neil Burger; Dick Wittenborn

Polar Opposites (2008)
Production Company: Baby Steps Entertainment
Director: Fred Olen Ray
Writer: Paolo Mazzucato

Private Valentine (2008)
Production Company: BenderSpink, DiNovi Pictures, Emmett/Furla Films, Family Room Entertainment, Gerber Pictures, Grand Army Entertainment, Major Productions, Millennium Films, Papa Joe Films
Director: Steve Miner
Writers: April Blair and Kelly Bowe (screenplay); April Blair (story)

Stop-Loss (2008)
Production Company: Paramount Pictures, Scott Rudin Productions, MTV Films
Director: Kimberly Pierce
Writers: Mark Richard; Kimberly Pierce

Behind Enemy Lines: Colombia (2009)
Production Company: 20th Century–Fox Home Entertainment, WWE Studios
Director: Tim Matheson
Writer: James Dodson (based on characters created by); Tobias Iaconis

G.I. Joe: The Rise of Cobra (2009)
Production Company: Paramount Pictures, Spyglass Entertainment, Hasbro, Di Bonaventura Picture, Digital Image Associates
Director: Stephen Sommers
Writers: Stuart Beattie, David Elliot, and Paul Lovett (screenplay); Michael B. Gordon, Stuart Beattie, and Stephen Sommers (story)

Taking Chance (2009)
Production Company: HBO Films, Civil Dawn Pictures, Motion Picture Corporation of America
Director: Ross Katz
Writers: Michael Strobl and Ross Katz (screenplay); Michael Strobl (journal)

Taking Fire (2009)
Production Company: Rage Monkey Media
Director: Spencer Lighte
Writer: Spencer Lighte

2012 (2009)
Production Company: Columbia Pictures Corporation, Centropolis Entertainment, Farewell Productions
Director: Roland Emmerich
Writer: Roland Emmerich; Harald Kloser

War Stories (2009)
Production Company: Uncheckable Films
Director: Lee M. Whitman
Writer: Lee M. Whitman

Chapter Eight

The A-Team (2010)
Production Company: 20th Century–Fox Film Corporation, Dune Entertainment, Stephen J. Cannell Productions, Top Cow Productions, Scott Free Productions, Big Screen Productions, Ingenious Film Partners, Phoenix Film Partners
Director: Joe Carnahan
Writers: Joe Carnahan, Brian Bloom and Skip Woods (written by); Frank Lupo and Stephen J. Cannell (television series)

AWOL (2010)
Production Company: Columbia University School of the Arts
Director: Deb Shoval
Writer: Deb Shoval

Ice Quake (2010)
Production Company: Cinetel Films, Quake Productions
Director: Paul Ziller
Writer: David Ray

In the Name of Freedom (2010)
Production Company: CAVE Entertainment
Director: Isabel Cueva
Writer: Isabel Cueva

A Marine Story (2010)
Production Company: Last Battlefield Productions, Red Road Studio
Director: Ned Farr
Writer: Ned Farr

Meteor Storm (2010)
Production Company: SyFy, Unity Pictures Group, MarVista Entertainment
Director: Tibor Takacs
Writer: Peter Mohan

Shadows in Paradise (2010)
Production Company: Aberto Entertainment
Director: J. Stephen Maunder
Writer: J. Stephen Maunder

Tea and Destiny (2010)
Production Company: World of Tomorrow Studios
Director: R. Christian Anderson
Writer: R. Christian Anderson

Justice on the Border (2011)
Production Company: Rage Monkey Media, West Adams Stages
Director: Spencer Lighte
Writer: Spencer Lighte

Last Man Standing (2011)
Production Company: Sony Pictures Television, Valhalla Motion Pictures
Director: Ernest R. Dickerson
Writers: Jolene Rice; Adam Beason

Return (2011)
Production Company: 2.1 Films, Fork Films, Meredith Vieira Productions
Director: Liza Johnson
Writers: Liza Johnson

Sniper: Reloaded (2011)
Production Company: Stage 6 Films, Apollo-Movie Beteiligungs, Film Afrika Worldwide
Director: Claudio Fäh
Writers: John Fasano (screenplay); Ross Helford and John Fasano (story); Michael Frost Beckner and Crash Leyland (characters)

40 Days and 40 Nights (2012)
Production Company: The Asylum
Director: Peter Geiger
Writer: H. Perry Horton (screenplay)

Act of Valor (2012)
Production Company: Relativity Media, Bandito Brothers
Director: Mouse McCoy, Scott Waugh
Writer: Kurt Johnstad

Home from War (2012)
Production Company: SA Hartman Productions
Director: Jonathan Dillon
Writer: Steve A. Hartman

Memorial Day (2012)
Production Company: Perspective Films
Director: Samuel Fischer
Writers: Jeff Traxler and Marc Conklin (based on a story by): Marc Conklin (screenplay)

Red Dawn (2012)
Production Company: Film District, Contrafilm, FilmNation Entertainment
Director: Dan Bradley
Writers: Carl Ellsworth and Jeremy Passmore (screenplay); Kevin Reynolds and John Milius (1984 screenplay); Kevin Reynolds (story)

Seattle Superstorm (2012)
Production Company: MarVista Entertainment, Two 4 the Money Media, Province of British Columbia Film Incentive BC
Director: Jason Borque
Writers: David Ray; Jeff Renfroe

Super Cyclone (2012)
Production Company: The Asylum
Director: Liz Adams
Writer: Liz Adams

Your Roommate (2012)
Production Company: CagleVision
Director: Kenya Cagle
Writer: Mack Williams

500 MPH Storm (2013)
Production Company: Indy Entertainment, The Asylum
Director: Daniel Lusko
Writers: Kuang Lee and Hank Woon, Jr. (screenplay)

Breaking the Silence (2013)
Production Company: Vascia Productions
Director: Paquita Hughes, Lora V. Keleher
Writers: Jennifer M. Crandell; Nicole Wagner

Drones (2013)
Production Company: Khaos Digital, Whitewater Films
Director: Rick Rosenthal
Writers: Matt Witten

G.I. Joe: Retaliation (2013)
Production Company: Paramount Pictures, Metro-Goldwyn-Mayer (MGM), Skydance Media, Hasbro, Di Bonaventura Pictures, Saints LA
Director: Jon M. Chu
Writers: Rhett Reese; Paul Werrick

The Letter (2013)
Production Company: Lussier Productions
Director: Rebecca Murga
Writer: Rebecca Murga

Red 2 (2013)
Production Company: Summit Entertainment, Di Bonaventura Pictures, DC Entertainment, Etalon Film, NeoReel, Saints LA
Director: Dean Parisot
Writers: Jon Hoeber and Erich Hoeber (written by); Warren Ellis and Cully Hamner (characters)

White Feather (2013)
Production Company: Cordero Brothers
Directors: Fernando Cordero, Vicente Cordero
Writer: Paul Margraf; Brett R. Miller

White House Down (2013)
Production Company: Columbia Pictures Corporation, Mythology Entertainment, Centropolis Entertainment
Directors: Roland Emmerich
Writer: James Vanderbilt

Yellow Ribbon (2013)
Production Company: Lussier Productions
Director: Donre Walker
Writer: Donre Walker

Airplane vs. Volcano (2014)
Production Company: The Asylum
Director: The Kondelik Brothers
Writers: James and Jon Kondelik (screenplay)

Boys of Abu Ghraib (2014)
Production Company: Rebel One Pictures
Director: Luke Moran
Writer: Luke Moran

Camp X-Ray (2014)
Production Company: GNK Productions, Gotham Group, Roughhouse Pictures; Upload Films, Young Gang
Director: Peter Sattler
Writer: Peter Sattler

Fort Bliss (2014)
Production Company: Yeniceri Produksiyon A.S., National Picture Show Entertainment

Director: Claudia Myers
Writer: Claudia Myers

Good Kill (2014)
Production Company: Voltage Pictures, Dune Films
Director: Andrew Niccol
Writer: Andrew Niccol

Jarhead 2: Field of Fire (2014)
Production Company: BUFO, Universal Pictures
Director: Don Michael Paul
Writers: Berkeley Anderson; Ellis Black

LA Apocalypse (2014)
Production Company: Cinetel Films, Doomed Pictures
Director: Michael J. Sarna
Writers: Neil Elman; Erik Estenberg

Rogue Strike (2014)
Production Company: Kerosene Films
Director: Kerry Beyer
Writers: Kerry Beyer

Seal Team Eight: Behind Enemy Lines (2014)
Production Company: Film Afrika Worldwide, 20th Century–Fox Home Entertainment, Rebel Entertainment
Director: Roel Reiné
Writers: Brendan Cowles; Shane Kuhn; Roel Reiné (story)

Sniper: Legacy (2014)
Production Company: Destination Films, UFO International Productions
Director: Don Michael Paul
Writers: John Fasano and Don Michael Paul (screenplay); John Fasano (story); Michael Frost Beckner and Crash Leyland (based on characters created by)

Stand Down Soldier (2014)
Production Company: DreamWorks Television, NBC Studios, Peculiar Television
Director: Jeryl Prescott
Writer: Jeryl Prescott

Targeting (2014)
Production Company: Photoplay 434, Solid Brothers Films
Director: Tarique Qayumi
Writers: Joey Patterson; Tarique Qayumi; Alan de la Rosa

Aloha (2015)
Production Company: Columbia Pictures; Regency Enterprises, LStar Capital; RatPac Entertainment; Scott Rudin Productions; Vinyl Films; Sony Pictures Entertainment
Director: Cameron Crowe
Writer: Cameron Crowe

The Christmas You Don't Know (2015)
Production Company: Aphrodite Venus Productions, Brooklyn 2 La Productions
Director: Christine Clayburg, Veronica Wayne, Amber Patton
Writers: Alexis Nichols (story); Antonio Olivas (screenplay)

Cold Winter's Night (2015)
Production Company: 1313Films
Director: Gabe Figueroa
Writers: J.J. Englert; Gabe Figueroa (story)

Day One (2015)
Production Company: BrainBox, American Film Institute
Director: Henry Hughes
Writers: Dawn DeVoe (story); Henry Hughes (story and writer)

The Last Rescue (2015)
Production Company: Fireshoe Productions
Director: Eric Colley
Writers: Sean Gleaves; Hallie Shepherd

The Martian (2015)
Production Company: 20th Century–Fox Film Corporation, TSG Entertainment, Scott Free Productions, Genre Films, International Traders, Kinberg Genre, Mid Atlantic Films
Director: Ridley Scott
Writers: Drew Goddard (screenplay); Andy Weir (book)

The Road Home (2015)
Production Company: unknown
Director: Lisa J. Dooley
Writers: Lisa J. Dooley (adaptation); Ellen Emerson White (novel)

The Submarine Kid (2015)
Production Company: Coronet Film, Sterling Features, StylesFour Productions
Director: Eric Bilitch
Writers: Eric Bilitch; Finn Wittrock

Three Fingers (2015)
Production Company: Farm Dog, Sunset Junction Entertainment, York Media
Director: Paul D. Hart
Writer: Paul D. Hart

Virtuous (2015)
Production Company: JC Film, Tri-Rahn Pictures
Director: Bill Rahn
Writers: Jason Campbell (original story); Tara Lynn Michelle

Allied (2016)
Production Company: GK Films, Huahua Media, GK Films
Director: Robert Zemeckis
Writer: Steven Knight

American Girl (2016)
Production Company: unknown
Director: Rebecca Murga
Writers: Karen Kraft; Rebecca Murga

The Assault (2016)
Production Company: 18th Military Police Brigade
Director: Alberta Cole
Writer: Alberta Cole

AWOL (2016)
Production Company: Race Point Films, Public Square Films
Director: Deb Shoval
Writer: Deb Shoval; Karolina Waclawiak

Deepwater Horizon (2016)
Production Company: Summit Entertainment, Participant Media, Di Bonaventura Pictures
Director: Peter Berg
Writers: Matthew Michael Carnahan and Matthew Sand (screenplay); Matthew Sand (screen story); David Barstow, David Rohde, and Stephanie Saul (based on an article by)

Doc (2016)
Production Company: Scary Little Films, Creative Media Institute, Something Fresh Productions
Director: Dave Witt
Writer: Dave Witt

Jack Reacher: Never Go Back (2016)
Production Company: Paramount Pictures; Skydance Media; Huahua Media; S&C Pictures; Shanghai Film Group; TC Productions
Director: Edward Zwick
Writers: Lee Child (book); Richard Wenk, Edward Zwick, and Marshall Herskovitz (screenplay)

Lion in a Box (2016)
Production Company: unknown
Director: Melanie Brown
Writer: Melanie Brown

Sniper: Ghost Shooter (2016)
Production Company: Destination Films, UFO International Productions
Director: Don Michael Paul
Writers: Chris Hauty (screenplay); Michael Frost Beckner and Crash Leyland (based on characters created by)

Ten Thousand Miles (2016)
Production Company: USC School of Cinema and Television
Director: Nathan Ellis
Writers: Nathan Ellis; Tamara Farsadi

Blood Stripe (2017)
Production Company: Wakemup Productions, Tandem Pictures
Director: Remy Auberjonois
Writers: Remy Auberjonois; Kate Nowlin

Do No Harm (2017)
Production Company: ReKon Productions
Director: Marielle Woods
Writer: Marielle Woods

Elite (2017)
Production Company: Live Wire Films
Director: Marc Cantu
Writer: Marc Cantu; Jason Scarbrough

Lead from the Front (2017)
Production Company: United States Military Academy
Director: unknown
Writer: unknown

Megan Leavey (2017)
Production Company: LD Entertainment, Calle Cruzada
Director: Gabriela Cowperthwaite
Writers: Pamela Gray, Annie Mumolo, and Tim Lovestedt

Military Husband (2017)
Production Company: Devlin Entertainment, ShapeWriting
Director: Kevin McMahon
Writer: Kevin McMahon

Satellite Drop (2017)
Production Company: Leirigh Films
Director: Lauren V. O'Connell
Writer: Lauren V. O'Connell

The Yellow Birds (2017)
Production Company: Cinelou Films, Story Mining & Supply Co., Echo Films
Director: Alexandre Moors
Writers: David Lowery and R.F.I. Porto (screenplay); Kevin Powers (based on the novel by)

Alone We Fight (2018)
Production Company: Wandering Dragon Productions
Director: Justin Lee
Writer: Justin Lee

Eruption LA (2018)
Production Company: 4 Mile Productions
Director: Sean Cain
Writer: Sean Cain

Hunter Killer (2018)
Production Company: Hunter Killer Productions, G-BASE, Hishow Entertainment
Director: Donovan Marsh
Writers: Arne Schmidt and Jamie Moss (screenplay); George Wallace and Don Keith (based on the novel "Firing Point" written by)

Indivisible (2018)
Production Company: Provident Films, Reserve Entertainment
Director: David G. Evans
Writers: David G. Evans; Cheryl McKay; Peter White

Let It Go (2018)
Production Company: unknown
Director: Stephanie G. Heim
Writer: Stephanie G. Heim

The Madness of Tellaralette Seville (2018)
Production Company: Nightpiece Films
Director: Al Carretta
Writer: Al Carretta

Union (2018)
Production Company: Bjornquist Films, Unionmovie
Director: Whitney Hamilton
Writer: Whitney Hamilton

Warfighter (2018)
Production Company: Fire Born Films, Fire Born Studios, TLG Motion Pictures
Director: Jerry G. Angelo
Writers: Jerry G. Angelo (original screenplay); Kerry Patton (screen contributing writer)

Welcome to Marwen (2018)
Production Company: DreamWorks, ImageMovers, Universal Pictures
Director: Robert Zemeckis
Writers: Caroline Thompson and Robert Zemeckis (screenplay)

Triple Frontier (2019)
Production Company: Atlas Entertainment
Director: J.C. Chandor
Writers: Mark Boal and J.C. Chandor (screenplay); Mark Boal (story)

Appendix B:
By the Numbers

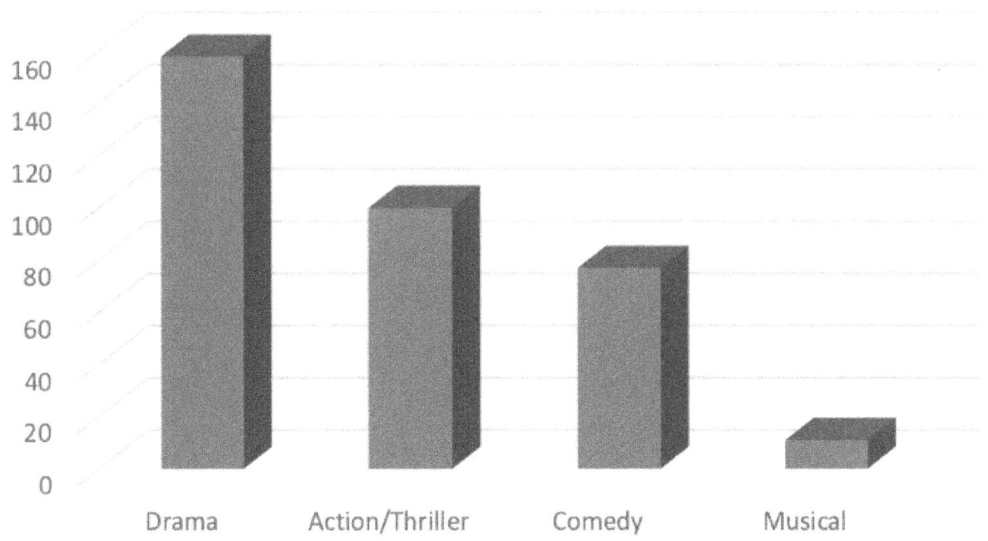

Broad categories for types of films included in this survey.

Appendix B

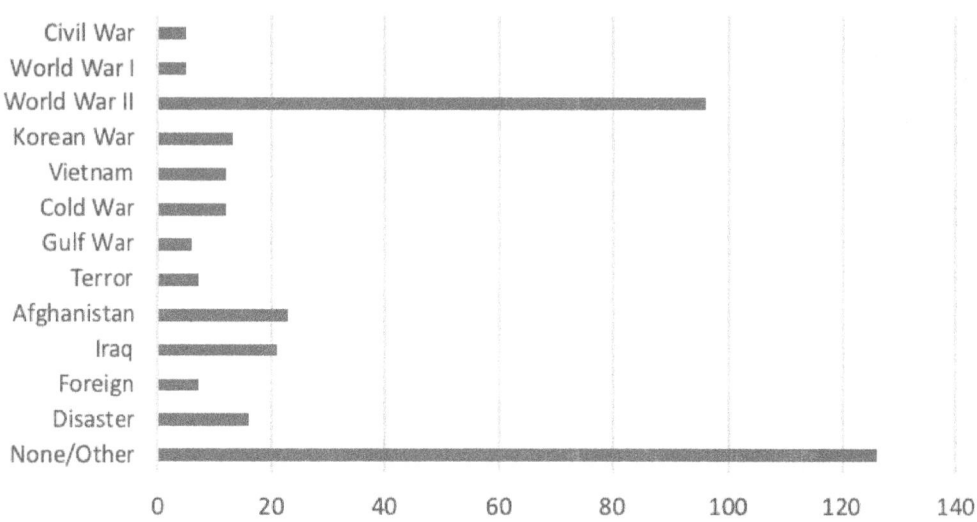

Number of depictions of military women in the Civil War and in each of the wars and conflicts of the twentieth and twenty-first centuries.

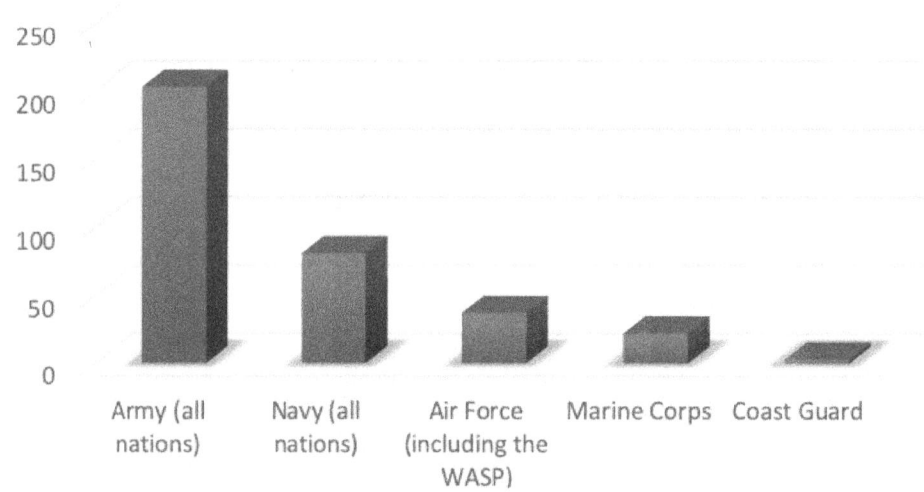

Number of servicewomen depicted for each branch of the service.

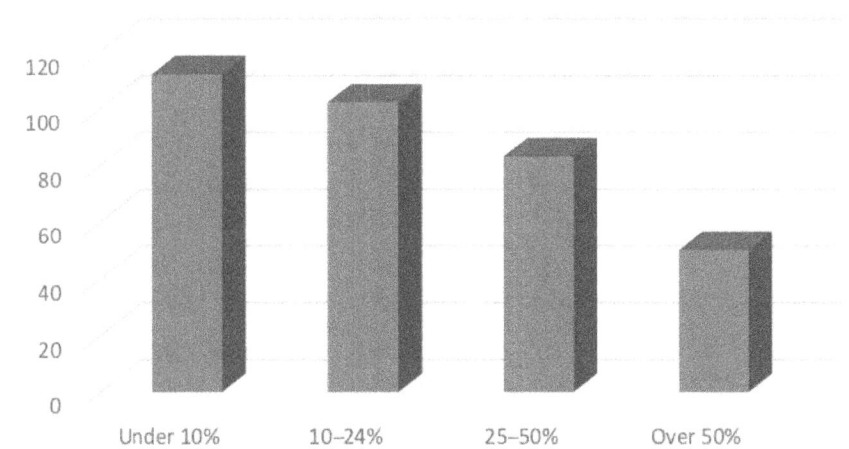

Percentage of time the primary female military character is onscreen. Almost 65 percent are onscreen less than one-quarter of the film's run time.

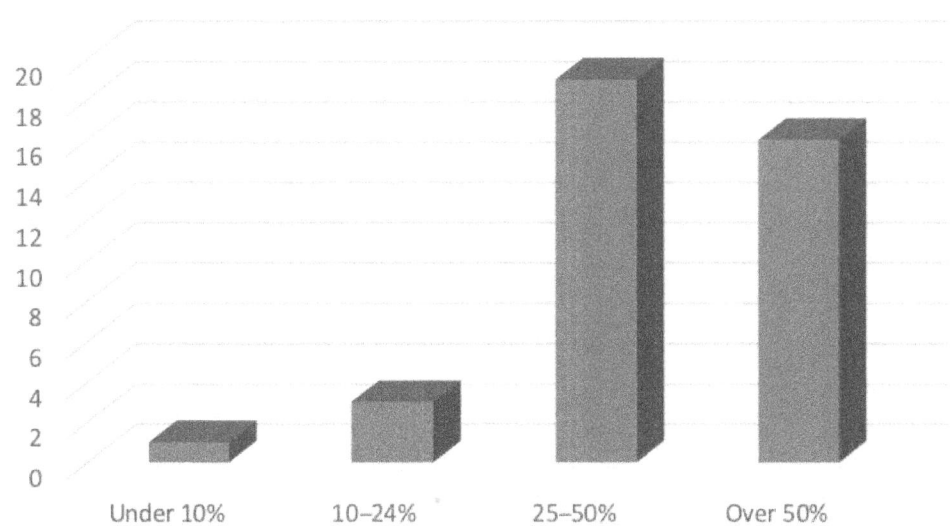

Titular characters fare better than most military women in film, with 54 percent garnering at least 40 percent screen time.

Chapter Notes

Introduction

1. Daniel Cohen, ed., *The Female Marine and Related Works* (Amherst: University of Massachusetts Press, 1997), 14.
2. "Women during World War I: Their Role in the Progressive Era," *Drawing America to Victory*, accessed February 18, 2019, https://history.delaware.gov/exhibits/online/WWI/Women-roles-ww1.shtml.
3. *Equal Rights Amendment: Guaranteeing Equal Rights for Women Under the Constitution*, United States Commission on Civil Rights, Clearinghouse Publication 68 (Washington, DC: Government Printing Office, 1981), 19.
4. Daniel Binns, *The Hollywood War Film: Critical Observations from World War I to Iraq* (Chicago: Intellect, 2017), 15.
5. Paul M. Edwards, *World War I on Film: English Language Releases through 2014* (Jefferson, NC: McFarland, 2016), 9.
6. Edwards, 18–19.
7. Michael S. Shull and David E. Wilk, *Doing Their Bit: Wartime American Animated Short Films 1939–1945* (Jefferson, NC: McFarland, 2004), 22. The ground-breaking animation provided a powerful, documentary-like depiction of the dramatic sinking of the Lusitania. It took 25,000 drawings to make the twenty-minute black and white short, significantly more than had been previously used in early animation.
8. Shull and Wilk, *Doing Their Bit*, 18–19.
9. Peter C. Rollins and John E. O'Connor, eds., *Hollywood's World War I Motion Picture Images* (Bowling Green, OH: Bowling Green State University Popular Press, 1997), 3.
10. Kimberly J. Lamay Licursi, *Remembering World War I in America* (Lincoln: University of Nebraska Press, 2018), 173.
11. Those two films are *Army Surgeon* (1942) and *A Shade of Gray* (2002). Two other films, *Shoulder Arms* (1918) and *She Goes to War* (1929), feature women cross-dressing as male soldiers, and *Today We Live* (1933) features an American woman in the British WAAC.
12. Donald Fishman, "The Cold War: Three Episodes in Waging a Cinematic War," in *War and Film in America: Historical and Critical Essays,* ed. Marilyn J. Matelski and Nancy Lynch Street (Jefferson, NC: McFarland, 2003), 44.
13. Shull and Wilk, *Doing Their Bit*, 4. The major film studios that produced animated features in support of the build-up to and during the war were: Warner Brothers (under the direction of Leon Schlesinger), Fleischer Studios (which by the end of the war became Famous Studios/Paramount), 20th Century–Fox (under the direction of Paul Terry), Universal Studios (under the direction of Walter Lantz), Disney, MGM, and Screen Gems/Columbia Pictures.
14. "Glossary of Military Acronyms," military.com, accessed February 11, 2019, https://www.military.com/join-armed-forces/glossary-of-military-acronyms.html. SNAFU is an acronym that stands for "Situation Normal: All Fucked Up." It is an indication of the lowest level of screw-up; TARFU (Things are Really Fucked Up) represents the next level, followed by FUBAR (Fucked Up Beyond All Recognition).
15. Michael Anderegg, ed., *Inventing Vietnam: The War in Film and Television* (Philadelphia: Temple University Press, 1991), 1.
16. Scholar Laura Horak closely examined thirty-seven silent movies that feature cross-dressing women, but she identified more than 400 possible titles. She was unable to examine the majority of them because they have been lost. Laura Horak, *Girls Will Be Boys: Cross-Dressed Women, Lesbians, and American Cinema* (New Brunswick, NJ: Rutgers University Press, 2016), 1.
17. Jill Lepore, *The Secret History of Wonder Woman* (New York: Vintage Books, 2015), 141. The rise of the film star system and the arrival of Jackie Coogan in the film *The Kid* (1921) sounded the beginning of the end of women playing boys in film, as noted by Horak on page 49.
18. Cohen, *Female Marine*, 23.

Chapter One

1. Thomas A. Edison, *Love and War* and *U.S. Troops and Red Cross in the Trenches Before Caloocan* (Thomas A. Edison Inc. Library of Congress, 1899), accessed July 20, 2017, www.loc.gov/item/98501279 and www.loc.gov/item/ 98501181. Thomas A. Edison Inc., which was headquartered in Menlo Park, NJ, played a pioneering role in the film industry. The studio of the prolific inventor made more than 1,000 films. Both films mentioned here featured actors playing American soldiers, Filipino brigands, and Red Cross nurses who are shown treating the wounded. Many of the civilian contract nurses

who treated American military men during the Spanish American War died as the result of the global flu pandemic; many of them are buried in Arlington National Cemetery beneath Frances Rich's sculpture *Nurses Memorial*.

2. Leslie Midkiff DeBauche, *Reel Patriotism: The Movies and World War I* (Madison: University of Wisconsin Press, 1997), 36.

3. Jeanne Holm, *Women in the Military: An Unfinished Revolution* (Novato, CA: Presidio Press, 1992), 9.

4. Daniel Budnik, *'80s Action Movies on the Cheap: 284 Low Budget, High Impact Pictures* (Jefferson, NC: McFarland, 2017), 2–3.

5. Julie Wheelwright, *Amazons and Military Maids: Women Who Dressed as Men in the Pursuit of Life, Liberty and Happiness* (London: Pandora, 1989), 7.

6. Stacie Robyn Furia, "Bombshells on Film Reels: How Women in Mainstream Military Movies Enact Hegemonic Gender Ideologies" (Master's thesis, University of Santa Barbara, June 2006), 6. Military nurses do not threaten this hegemony since their primary function is to provide aid and comfort to wounded men.

7. Horak, *Girls Will be Boys*, 66.

8. Richard Abel, *Americanizing the Movies and "Movie-Mad" Audiences, 1910–1914* (Berkeley: University of California Press, 2006), 119.

9. Horak, *Girls Will be Boys*, 13.

10. Jean Bethke Elshtain, *Women and War* (Chicago: University of Chicago Press, 1995), 103–105.

11. Ibid., 96.

12. Wesley Alan Britton, *Onscreen and Undercover: The Ultimate Book of Movie Espionage* (Westport: Praeger, 2006), 34. The other two films, *The Girl Spy, An Incident of the Civil War* (1909), also known as *Adventures of the Girl Spy*, and *Further Adventures of the Girl Spy* (1910), are no long extant. Gauntier starred as Nan in these films as well. Other lost films that featured cross-dressing Confederate women include *The Confederate Spy* (1910), *Little Yank* (1917), and *In the Fall of '64* (1914), which was loosely based on an incident in Nashville, Tennessee, where Ann Patterson helped free Confederate spy Thomas Joplin from a Union prison.

13. DeBauche, *Reel Patriotism*, 138. This move resulted in fewer films being produced annually since these longer films took more time to produce.

14. Dominick A. Pisano, "*The Dawn Patrol* and the World War I Air Combat Film Genre: An Exploration of American Values," in *Hollywood's World War I Motion Picture Images*, ed. Peter C. Rollins and John E. O'Connor (Bowling Green, OH: Bowling Green State University Popular Press, 1997), 67.

15. Confederate women frequently sewed flags and banners for family members to carry into battle, often using expensive clothing like wedding and ball gowns. For additional information, see Paula E. Calvin and Deborah A. Deacon, *American Women Artists in Wartime, 1775–2010* (Jefferson, NC: McFarland, 2011), 39–43.

16. DeBauche, *Reel Patriotism*, 38–39.

17. Cecil B. DeMille, *Joan the Woman* (1916, Paramount Pictures) and DeBauche, *Reel Patriotism*, 7. This film, DeMille's first historical drama, was based on Friedrich Schiller's 1801 play *Die Jungfrau ven Orelans* (*The Maid of Orleans*). The first film depiction about the French hero and saint, it was one of the earliest that can be categorized as spectacle, featuring complex battle scenes and hundreds of extras. The film was not initially marketed as a war movie, although as war loomed in Europe, more emphasis was placed on the militaristic aspects of the film. Isenberg noted that Farrar herself considered the film to the "the greatest of all pro-Ally propaganda" (193). See Michael T. Isenberg, *War on Film: The American Cinema and World War I, 1914–1941* (Rutherford: Fairleigh Dickenson University Press, 1981), 205.

18. Pisano, "*The Dawn Patrol*," 106.

19. Robert Baird, "Hell's Angels Above the Western Front," in *Hollywood's World War I Motion Picture Images*, ed. Peter C. Rollins and John E. O'Connor (Bowling Green, OH: Bowling Green State University Popular Press, 1997), 85–86.

20. Henry King, *She Goes to War* (1929, Inspiration Pictures).

21. Michael T. Isenberg, *War on Film: The American Cinema and World War I, 1914–1941* (Rutherford: Fairleigh Dickenson University Press, 1981), 213.

22. Aristophanes, *Lysistrata*, in *Great Books of the Western World Vol. 4*, ed. Clifton Fadiman and Philip W. Goetz (Chicago: Encyclopaedia Britannica, Inc., 2007), 824–845.

23. Isenberg, *War on Film*, 205.

24. The dark comedy was groundbreaking in its depictions of the hardships and irrational aspects of Army life experienced by soldiers on the front lines—constant bombardment, terrible food, and miserable weather. The film also introduced stereotypes that would continue in future war films—the bestial Hun, endangered women who need to be saved, the brave American fighting man. Many of the film's sight gags, such as the tree masquerade and use of limburger cheese as a weapon, were used by other filmmakers, as was the formula of focusing on the daily activities of the average soldier rather than officers.

25. DeBauche, *Reel Patriotism*, 196. The entire film, which is actually a dream, was released three weeks before the Armistice. Chaplin worried it would be seen as offensive; however, audiences embraced it, and, along with his fundraising efforts in support of the war, helped erase any stigma associated with Chaplin's lack of military service.

26. Hal Erickson, *Military Comedy Films* (Jefferson, NC: McFarland, 2012), 11.

27. Richard Fleischer, *Out of the Inkwell: Max Fleischer and the Animation Revolution* (Lexington: University of Kentucky Press, 2011), 50. Among their iconic animated characters are Ko-Ko the Clown, Popeye the Sailor, and Superman. Betty Boop actually began life as a "cigar-chewing, somewhat lecherous, piano-playing jazz hound named Bimbo," a response to the rising popularity of Mickey Mouse. Her popularity faded with the advent of the Motion Picture Production Code, which monitored films for "smut" and indecency. With the loss of her garter, longer skirt, and higher neckline, she lost her fun and spice, which eventually returned in the late twentieth century.

28. She is aided by Hugh's faithful servant, Old Ben, played by William J. Butler in blackface. She helps Old Ben save Hugh's money when the plantation house is burned, and upon Hugh's return, Old Ben tells Hugh of her heroism.

29. "Proud History," Office of Naval Intelligence, accessed June 23, 2018, https://www.oni.navy.mil/This-is-ONI/Proud-History. The Office of Naval Intelligence was established in 1882 under the direction of Lieutenant Theodorus Bailey Myers Mason. Instrumental in modernizing the Navy, it established the Countering Espionage and Sabotage Division in 1916, which was tasked to support domestic security operations by protecting American ports, harbors, and defense plants. After World War I, the investigation of espionage and sabotage was added to its mission. Lieutenant Junior Grade Cecil H. Coggers, a Navy physician who discovered a Japanese spy ring operating in the U.S. in 1935, wrote the official manual for conducting investigations which is still in use (with revisions) today.

Chapter Two

1. Judith Bellafaire, *Women in the United States Military: An Annotated Bibliography* (New York: Routledge, 2011), 1.

2. Katy Endruschat Goebel, *Women for Victory: American Servicewomen in World War II—History & Uniforms Series* (Atglen, PA: Schiffer Military History, 2011), 7.

3. Minnesota History Center, "Women in the Military—WWI: Overview," accessed November 30, 2018, http://libguides.mnhs.org/wwii_women.

4. *Ibid.*

5. Steven Jay Schneider, "Movies and the March to War," in *American Cinema of the 1940s*, ed. W.W. Dixon (Rutgers University Press: New Brunswick, NJ, 2006), 93.

6. Clayton R. Koppes and Gregory D. Black, "What to Show the World: The Office of War Information and Hollywood, 1942–1945," *The Journal of American History*, 64, no. 1 (1977), 89.

7. A total of 374, as asserted in Dorothy B. Jones, "The Hollywood War Film," *Hollywood Quarterly*, 1, no. 1 (October 1945), 14. Only five of these films, according to Jones, feature female units.

8. Jeanine Basinger, *A Woman's View: New Hollywood Speaks to Women, 1930–1960* (New York: Knopf, 1993), 463.

9. *Ibid.*, 478.

10. In 1977, Jimmy Carter signed Public Law 95-202 (91 Stat. 1433), *The G.I. Bill Improvement Act*, into law. Section 401 stated that "service as a member of the Women's Air Forces Service Pilots shall be considered active duty for the purposes of all laws administered by the Veterans' Administration."

11. Jeanine Basinger, *The World War II Combat Film: Anatomy of a Genre* (Middletown, CT: Wesleyan University Press, 2003), 205.

12. Basinger, *Woman's View*, 477.

13. *Ibid.*

14. Myra Macdonald, *Representing Women: Myths of Femininity in the Popular Media* (London: Edward Arnold, 1995), 13.

15. In contrast, of the 185 films released from 1986–2018, at least twenty-five feature servicewomen with children (there could be more, but for many films, marital/maternal status is not explicitly stated).

16. Proposed Executive Order, Regulations Governing Discharge from the Armed Forces of Women Serving under the Army-Navy Nurses Act of 1947 and the Women's Armed Services Integration Act of 1948. Cited in Mary V. Stremlow, *A History of the Women Marines, 1946–1977* (Washington, DC: GPO, 1986), 151.

17. Marcus Schulzke, "Kant's Categorical Imperative, the Value of Respect, and the Treatment of Women," *Journal of Military Ethics* 11, no. 1(April 2012), 30.

18. Germany did not actually begin utilizing women in a military capacity until 1943. See D'Ann Campbell, "Women in Combat: The World War II Experience in the United States, Great Britain, Germany, and the Soviet Union," *Journal of Military History* 57, no. 2 (April 1993), 314.

19. Schulzke, "Kant's Categorical Imperative," 28.

20. Evgeniy Sokurov, *Tsel Vizhu (See the Target)*, Grinsiti Studio, DVD, 2013.

21. Judith Stiehm, "The Generations of U.S. Enlisted Women," *Signs* 11, no. 1 (Autumn 1985), 166.

Chapter Three

1. President Harry S. Truman's Executive Order 10240, dated April 27, 1951, established regulations governing the separation from the service of "certain women serving in the regular Army, Navy, Marine Corps, or Air Force." See also Public Laws 84–585 (70 Stat. 285) from 1956, 85–155 (71 Stat. 375) from 1957, and 85–861(72 Stat. 1437) from 1958.

2. This statement was made in 1941 by Congresswoman Edith Nourse Rogers of Washington, quoted in "'Skirted Soldier': The Army's Gender Integration during World War II," Military.com, accessed January 18, 2019, https://www.military.com/history/skirted-soldiers-armys-gender-integration-during-world-war-ii.html.

3. William A. Taylor, "From WACs to Rangers: Women in the U.S. Military since World War II," *MCU Journal* Special Issue (2018), 83.

4. *Ibid.*, 84.

5. *Ibid.*

6. While most of OWI's initiatives occurred within the United States, they also had an international component for which psychological warfare against Allied enemies was the core function. See Lester G. Hawkins, Jr., and George S. Pettee. "OWI-Organization and Problems," *The Public Opinion Quarterly* 7, no. 1 (Spring 1943), 15–33.

7. Basinger, *Woman's View*, 477.

8. *Ibid.*

9. Steven Merritt Miner, "'Things Must Be Bad at the Front': Women in the Soviet Military during WWII," *MCU Journal* Special Issue (2018), 57.

10. Elizabeth Reis, "Impossible Hermaphrodites: Intersex in America, 1620–1960," *Journal of American History* 92, no. 2 (September 2005), 432.

11. Joanna Pawelczyk, "Constructing American Female War Veterans' Military Identity in the Context of Interviews," *Women & Language* 37, no. 1 (Spring 2014), 123.

12. Rose Weitz, "Vulnerable Warriors: Military Women, Military Culture, and Fear of Rape," *Gender Issues* 32, no. 3 (September 2015), 176.

13. D'Ann Campbell, "Women, Combat, and the Gender Line," *MHQ* 6 (Autumn 1993), 97.

14. At that time, pregnancy still required automatic separation from the military; that would not change until *Crawford v. Cushman* in 1976 (531 F.2d 1114 [2d Cir. 1976]).

15. Miner, "Things Must Be Bad," 55.

16. Melissa Herbert, "Feminism, Militarism, and Attitudes toward the Role of Women in the Military," *Gender Issues*, 14, no. 2 (June 1994), 26.

Chapter Four

1. France Winddance Twine, *Firearms, Feminism and Militarism* (London: Routledge, 2013), 38.

2. Yvonne Tasker, *Soldiers' Stories: Military Women in Cinema and Television Since World War II* (Durham: Duke University Press, 2001), 173.

3. Holm, *Women in the Military*, 206.

4. Susan H, Godson, *Serving Proudly: A History of Women in the U.S. Navy* (Annapolis: Naval Institute Press, 2002), 212. A total of thirty-six women Marines, nine female naval officers, 500 WACs, and 500–600 WAFs served in Southeast Asia during the Vietnam War, in addition to thousands of WAF and Navy nurses and medical personnel. A total of 286 nurses served onboard the hospital ships USS *Repose* and USS *Sanctuary*. Medical women were subjected to attacks while performing their duties in country; a significant number suffered from PTSD as the result of their service. The names of eight military women who died in Vietnam are listed on "The Wall" of the Vietnam War Memorial.

5. Karen Rasmussen, Sharon D. Downey and Jennifer Asenas, "Trauma, Treatment, and Transformation: The Evolution of the Vietnam Warrior in Film," in *War and Film in America: Historical and Critical Essays*, ed. Marilyn J. Matelski and Nancy Lynch Street (Jefferson, NC: McFarland, 2003), 154.

6. Sampson was honorably discharged and received a pension and a small piece of land for her service. She married, built a home, and raised a family after the war.

7. Rebecca Bell-Metereau, *Hollywood Androgyny* (New York: Columbia University Press, 1985), 704.

8. Interestingly, all of the male characters are listed with their ranks in the credits, but neither Midge nor Elvis is listed with a rank.

9. Tasker, *Soldiers' Stories*, 174.

10. *Ibid.*, 7.

11. Nora Ephron, "Yossarian Is Alive and Well in the Mexican Desert," in *Double Features: Big Ideas in Film*, ed. Nancy Carr, Michael J. Elsey, Louise Galpine, John Sniegowski and Mary Williams (Chicago: The Great Books Foundation, 2017), 8. Paula Prentiss' full frontal nudity in the dream scene created a great deal of controversy. The film, victim of mixed reviews and bad timing (*MASH* was released before it), resulted in financial losses and a short theatrical run.

12. *Ibid.*, 12.

13. Erickson, *Military Comedy*, 352–355. Based on Richard Hooker's experience as a medic during the Korean War, the film was a critical and box office success, despite its low ($34M) budget and use of second tier actors. The film was not popular with the military, however. It was banned on U.S. Army and Air Force bases, although not by the Navy.

14. Robert Lentz, *Korean War Filmography* (Jefferson, NC: McFarland, 2003), 226.

15. While her surname is O'Houlihan in the film, it was changed to Houlihan for the long-running television series.

16. Tasker, *Soldiers' Stories*, 177.

17. Maurice Yacovar, "The Bug in the Rug: Notes on the Disaster Genre," in *Film Genre Reader IV*, ed. Barry Grant (Austin: University of Texas Press, 2012), 313–314.

18. When the film became a popular television series between 1964 and 1968, the Seaview was listed as the world's first privately owned nuclear submarine, although the lead actors retained their military ranks and its cast was all male. The submarine's mission was officially listed as marine research, but secretly, it was to defend the planet from all threats, including extraterrestrials.

19. William Bradford Huie, *The Americanization of Emily* (New York: The New American Library, 1959), 17–19. The film is based on the novel of the same title, where Emily is described as being "aloof, self-assured, the carriage of cultivation.... [Her] face was piquant, intelligent, agreeably challenging.... Wheatfield hair, blue eyes, an English mouth—lips not thick or pouting but delicately curved under sensitive nostrils."

20. Gary Frietas, *War Movies* (Brandon, OR: Robert D. Reed Publishers, 2004), 212.

21. Kathy Schloeser, "The First Women of West Point" (October 27, 2010), accessed December 9, 2018, www.army.mil. Interestingly, the film *Women at West Point* is listed on West Point's "History of Women in the Military" website as an important event in women's military history. See www.usma.edu.

Chapter Five

1. Holm, *Women in the Military*, 384.

2. The Defense Advisory Committee on Women in the Services (DACOWITS) was established in 1951 by Secretary of Defense, George C. Marshall. The Committee is composed of civilian women and men who are appointed by the Secretary of Defense to provide advice and recommendations on matters and policies relating to the recruitment and retention, treatment, employment, integration, and well-being of highly qualified professional women in the Armed Forces. Historically, DACOWITS' recommendations have been instrumental in effecting changes to laws and policies pertaining to military women. The Defense Advisory Committee on Women in the Services, accessed April 23, 2018, http://dacowits.defense.gov/About/.

3. Godson, *Serving Proudly*, 250.

4. Holm, *Women in the Military*, 390–391, 406.
5. *Ibid.*, 416.
6. Godson, *Serving Proudly*, 253.
7. Mariette Hartley was not interested in starring in the television series, and her character was killed off in the pilot. The series did not sell, so it never came to fruition.
8. "Military Career Pay Chart," accessed April 30, 2018, https://www.navycs.com/charts/1942-military-pay-chart.html. The film specifically mentions that the women would receive flight pay. This would have been a significant enticement for many women. The most junior military pilots earned approximately $167 per month during the war, plus another 50 percent of their pay as flight pay. They would receive the same as male pilots, which was considerably more than they could earn in the civil sector.
9. Budnik, *'80s Action Movies*, 2.
10. Tim Walsh, *Timeless Toys: Classic Toys and the Playmakers Who Created Them* (Kansas City, MO: Andrews McMeel Publishing, 2005), 196–198. The G.I. Joe team began as a line of action figures created by the Hasbro Toy Company in 1964. The original team of twelve-inch male figures included the Action Soldier (U.S. Army), Action Sailor (U.S. Navy), Action Pilot (U.S. Air Force), and Action Marine (U.S. Marine Corps); the female Action Nurse was added in 1967. The figures' name comes from the generic term that refers to a World War II soldier. In 1982, the line was relaunched in 3.75-inch scale, complete with a backstory in which the "Joes" oppose the COBRA command's attempts at world domination.
11. Summersby was a member of the British Mechanized Transport Corps. She became a U.S. citizen and a WAC while driving Eisenhower, leaving the U.S. Army as a captain in 1947.
12. Theresa Kaminski, *Prisoners in Paradise: American Women in the Wartime South Pacific* (Lawrence, KS: University of Kansas Press, 2000), 242.
13. Jonathan Shay, *Achilles in Vietnam: Combat Trauma and the Undoing of Character* (New York: Scribner, 1994), 135.
14. Sharon D. Downey, "Top Guns in Vietnam: The Pilot as Protected Warrior Hero," in *War and Film in America: Historical and Critical Essays*, ed. Marilyn J. Matelski and Nancy Lunch Street (Jefferson, NC: McFarland, 2003), 117.
15. Hayden White, "Historiography and Historiophoty," *American Historical Review* 93, no. 5 (December 1988), 206.
16. *Ibid.*, 212. Ralph Donald and Karen MacDonald, *Women in War Films: From Helpless Heroines to G.I. Jane* (New York: Rowman and Littlefield, 2014), 120.
17. The film's sniper scene has been incorporated into the propaganda documentary shown at the Cu Chi tunnels outside of Ho Chi Minh City. The documentary also features newsreel footage of numerous women working in the tunnels, fighting against the enemy and caring for the wounded.
18. Eben J. Muse, "From Lt. Calley to John Rambo: Repatriating the Vietnam War," *Journal of American Studies* 27, no. 1 (April 1993), 91.
19. In reality, Hassan had only one child. Had she tried to enlist in the 1960s, she would have not been accepted, as it wasn't until well into the 1970s that married women were permitted to remain in the military or to have children and remain in the military.
20. Conchetta Hassan earned her wings on May 20, 1982. Twenty years later, at age 60, she was still serving as a CH-47 Chinook pilot.
21. Ron Steinman, *Women in Vietnam: The Oral History* (New York: TV Books, LLC, 2000), 18 and Holm, *Women in the Military*, 225–226. Between 1962 and 1973, 265,000 women served in the armed forces. While the official records are unclear as to the number of women who served in Vietnam, the Department of Veterans Affairs estimates that 7500 women served in country; 85 percent were nurses, all of whom volunteered for the duty. The typical age of nurses was 22–25, and many were not far out of school when they landed in Vietnam. Their training included combat related activities such as tent pitching, field sanitation, map reading, and disaster planning. Prior to 1965, there were a small number of Army and Navy nurses located in Saigon, Nha Trang, Son Trang, and Thailand. As the number of American military personnel increased, so did the number of nurses, including on the hospital ships USS *Repose* and USS *Sanctuary*. Because of the stress of their experiences and their exposure to the hazards of war, it is estimated that at least 25 percent of the military nurses who served in Vietnam suffer from PTSD.
22. Steve Neale, "Questions of Genre," in *Film Genre Reader IV*, ed. Barry Keith Grant (Austin: University of Texas Press, 2012), 198.
23. "Boot Camp," Today's Military, accessed May 4, 2018, http://www.todaysmilitary.com. The length of recruit training varies by military service: ten weeks for the Army, twelve weeks for the Marine Corps, seven to nine weeks for the Navy, seven and a half weeks for the Air Force, and eight weeks for the Coast Guard.
24. Carrie Peterson, "Separation Anxiety and Boot Camp: Why Basic Training Should Remain Gender-Integrated," *Law and Inequality: A Journal of Theory and Practice* 17 (Winter 1999), 139. By 1978, the Army, Navy, Coast Guard, and Air Force integrated basic training, although the Army returned to segregated basic training in 1982, lasting until 1994. The Marine Corps has steadfastly refused to integrate its recruit training, maintaining that "women are inherently more emotional and less physically and mentally capable than men and therefore can't handle the pressures of training alongside them." Kate Germano and Kelly Kennedy, "Why Co-ed Boot Camps Will Curb Sexism in the Marines," *New York Post* (April 28, 2018), accessed May 4, 2018, http://www.nypost.com.
25. Budnik, *'80s Action Movies*, 7. The film was so popular that in the fall of 1980, the television series *Private Benjamin* aired on CBS. Eileen Brennan reprised her role as Captain Doreen Lewis, and Lorna Patterson starred as Judy Benjamin. The series ran for thirty-nine episodes between 1981 and 1983 and was the fifth highest rated television show in 1980.
26. Tasker, *Soldiers' Stories*, 139.
27. Brennan won a Golden Globe and was nominated for an Academy Award for Best Supporting Actress for

her performance, as well as an Emmy for her performance in the television series based on the film.

28. Goldie Hawn received a Best Actress Oscar nomination for her role as Judy Benjamin, and the role rejuvenated her career. While many feminist scholars see the film as propagandistic and only marginally feminist, others have seen it as a positive portrayal of a woman who grows through her experience. In an interview, Hawn commented that the movie is "a statement about the patriarchy that still pervades our culture. The man is still considered the king and provider. Good little girls grow up to depend on that patriarch. I wanted to show that even a sheltered, pampered woman could find herself and become independent."

29. In real life, Quinlan's mother was a military supply supervisor, giving her personal experience with military culture.

30. Godson, *Serving Proudly*, 235.

Chapter Six

1. Holm, *Women in the Military*, 432.
2. *Ibid.*, 444. 30,855 Army women, 9.7 percent of the total Army force, served in the Gulf. 4,246 Air Force women (7 percent), 4,449 Navy women (4.2 percent) and 1,232 women Marines (1.5 percent) also served. The majority were active duty members, with approximately 13 percent of the total number of women being reservists.
3. Turner, 69.
4. Ian Zimmerman, "Furiosa: The Virago of Mad Max: Fury Road," in *Double Features: Big Ideas in Film*, ed. Nancy Carr, Michael J. Elsey, Louise Galpin, John Sniegowski and Mary Williams (Chicago: The Great Books Foundation, 2017), 148.
5. Sherrie Inness, *Tough Girls: Women Warriors and Wonder Women in Popular Culture* (Philadelphia: University of Pennsylvania, 1999), 24.
6. Tasker, *Soldiers' Stories*, 69.
7. "SAS: Women Allowed to Join for First Time," BBC News (25 October 2018), accessed February 25, 2019, https://www.bbc.com/news/uk45983882.
8. The phrase "Dead men can't dance" is an operator catch phrase, referring to the fact that if dead, an agent cannot complete a mission.
9. Holm, *Women in the Military*, 203. While female generals from other nations (primarily the USSR) have been depicted in action films, Burko's depiction comes more than two decades after the first American women were promoted to general. Anna Mae Hays, Chief of the Army Nurse Corps, was promoted to Brigadier General on June 11, 1970, and Elizabeth P. Hoisington, Director of the WAC, was promoted to that same rank moments later.
10. During this conversation, Goode mentions that they had been stationed together in Subic, a reference to U.S. Navy Base Subic Bay in Zambales, Philippines. Since both Goode and Watkins are Air Force officers, they more likely would have been stations at Clark Air Force Base, which was located near Angeles City, approximately forty miles northwest of Manila. Clark, Subic Bay, and Naval Air Station Cubi Point were all closed in 1991–92 when lease renewal talks with the Philippine government failed.

11. Meredith Guthrie, "Women in Hollywood Military Movies: A Cultural Textual Analysis of Films from 1980–2000" (Master's thesis, Bowling Green State University, 2001), 24.
12. "Forrest Gump (1994)," IMDb, accessed January 2, 2019, http://www.imdb.com.
13. Mary Lindell died in 1987 at the age of 92. She received a second Croix de Guerre for her heroism during World War II; her first was awarded for the nursing services she provided to men from both sides of the conflict during World War I.
14. Holm, *Women in the Military*, xiii.
15. William Shakespeare, *Macbeth*, in *The Great Books of the Western World vol. 25*, ed. William George Clarke and William Aldis Wright (Chicago: Encyclopaedia Britannica, Inc., 2007), 301. The second apparition tells Macbeth, "Be bloody, bold, and resolute; laugh to scorn/The power of man, for none of woman born/ Shall harm Macbeth." [Act IV, Scene 1, lines 79–80]. The second apparition is significant because it gives Macbeth a false sense of security and encourages his tyrannical behavior, allowing him to feel confident that he can maintain his position as king.
16. The film was adapted from the book *Trinity's Child* by William Prochnair.
17. Gary Freitas, *War Movies* (Brandon, OR: Robert D. Reed Publishers, 2004), 91.
18. *A Few Good Men* (1992), IMDb, accessed January 3, 2019, http://www.imdb.com and *G.I. Jane* (1997), IMDb, accessed January 3, 2019, http://www.imdb.com.
19. Tasker, *Soldiers' Stories*, 219 and Guthrie, "Women in Hollywood," 20.
20. The film's title is a reference to the term "G.I. Joe," which was used to refer to enlisted soldiers during World War II. The "G.I." stands for government issue and served to indicate that individual common foot soldiers were interchangeable, easy to substitute one for another.
21. Furia, "Bombshells," 61–62.
22. Guthrie, "Women in Hollywood," 90.
23. Basinger, *World War II Combat Film*, 228; Michele Vowell, "First Enlisted Female Graduates Army's Sapper Leader Course," (December 14, 2018), accessed January 4, 2019, http://www.army.mil; and "Woman Qualifies for Special Forces Training, Could Be the First Female Green Beret," (November 16, 2018), accessed January 4, 2019, http://www.npr.org.
24. Godson, *Serving Proudly*, 289. Under "Don't ask, don't tell," homosexuals were permitted to serve in the military but were forbidden from engaging in homosexual activities, which were seen as a threat to security and good order and discipline. Linda Hirshman noted in her book, *Victory: The Triumphant Gay Revolution* (New York: HarperCollins, 2012), that women were disproportionately targeted with accusations of lesbianism, often as a form of control. Female military members who rebuffed sexual advances from men were often accused of being gay and subjected to investigations which harmed their careers and reputations.
25. Margarethe Cammermeyer was born on March

24, 1942 in Norway and became a U.S. citizen in 1960. In 1961, as a nursing student, she joined the Army Nurse Corps, earning her BSN from the University of Maryland in 1963. She earned an MA in nursing from the University of Washington in 1976 and a Ph.D. in 1991. She served a tour in a MASH unit in Vietnam and earned a Bronze Star for her activities there, retiring from the Army in 1997. She was appointed as a member of DACOWITS in June 2010, and she and Diane married in 2012.

26. Both Zamora and Graham were convicted of first-degree murder and are serving life sentences for their crime.

27. This abstract was shown beneath the film's title in white letters on a black background.

28. The term "Tailhook" refers to the hook on the underside of Navy aircraft, used to stop an aircraft ("trap") when they land onboard an aircraft carrier.

29. Godson, *Serving Proudly*, 287. In all, eighty-three women were assaulted at the 1991 Tailhook Convention, twenty-six of whom were naval officers. Coughlin ultimately received $6.7 million in damages from her lawsuit against the hotel where Tailhook was held. Secretary of the Navy Garrett resigned, accepting responsibility for his leadership failure but admitting no personal wrong-doing. Admiral Kelso resigned from the Navy in April 1994, three months before his scheduled retirement.

30. Guthrie, "Women in Hollywood," 48.

31. The USS *Davenport* was actually a Tacoma class frigate (FF69). Launched on December 8, 1943, it was commissioned on February 15, 1945, decommissioned on February 4, 1946, and sold for scrap. An AOE, or fast combat support ship, provides logistics support to deployed ships at sea, providing them with ammunition, oil, and dry and refrigerated stores usually through vertical replenishment (vertrep) using CH-46 helicopters. AOEs, of which only four were commissioned, have a crew of 576 enlisted personnel and twenty-four officers.

32. The exact timing of their relationship is never explained in the film. Navy lawyers receive a direct appointment as lieutenant junior grade and accrue a four-year military obligation. They are typically promoted to lieutenant after one year of active duty. Since Dolan is still a lieutenant junior grade, it is probable that she has been on active duty for less than a year. It is possible that they met while she attended Officer Development School or at Basic Lawyer School, both of which are located in Newport, RI. "U.S. Navy JAG Corps," accessed January 5, 2019, http://www.jag.navy.mil.

Chapter Seven

1. *Women in the Army: Post 9/11*, accessed November 1, 2018, https://www.army.mil/women/history/.

2. See generally Christopher Graveline and Michael Clemens, *The Secrets of Abu Ghraib Revealed: American Soldiers on Trial* (Washington, D.C.: Potomac Books, 2010).

3. Jennifer K. Lobasz, "The Woman in Peril and the Ruined Woman: Representations of Female Soldiers in the Iraq War," *Journal of Women, Politics & Policy* 29, no. 3 (October 2008), 305–307.

4. "Women in the Military: Should Combat Roles Be Fully Opened to Women?" *CQ Researcher* 19, no. 40 (November 2009), 957.

5. Ibid.

6. Ibid., 962.

7. The list of top-grossing science fiction films with military women includes *Superman Returns* (2006), *The Incredible Hulk* (2008), *Avatar* (2009), and *Star Trek* (2009), among others.

8. Lawrence H. Suid, *Guts and Glory: Great American War Films* (Reading, MA.: Addison-Wesley, 1978), xiii.

9. Susan Linville, "The Mother of All Battles: *Courage under Fire* and the Gender-Integrated Military," *Cinema Journal*, 39, no. 2 (February 2000), 100.

10. Sarah Projansky, "Girls Who Act Like Women Who Fly: Jessica Dubroff as Cultural Troublemaker," *Signs*, 23, no. 3 (Spring 1998), 803.

11. Zimmerman, "Furiosa," 149.

12. Bellafaire, *Women*, 120.

13. Annette Kuhn, *The Power of the Image: Essays on Representation and Sexuality* (London: Routledge, 1985), 19.

14. Suzanne Bouclin, "Feminism, Law, Cinema." In *Women, Law, and Equality: A Discussion Guide*, ed. Kim Brooks and Carissima Mathen (Toronto: Irwin Law, 2010), 122.

15. *Dead Men Can't Dance* also has a female general in it (Grace Zabriskie as Brigadier General Burke). Overall, less than twenty-five of the 341 films surveyed show American military women with a rank of Major or above, less than 1 percent. In reality, women make up approximately 14 percent of all military officers with the rank of Major or above. See *2014 Demographics: Profile of the Military Community*, published by the Office of the Deputy Assistant Secretary of Defense (Military Community and Family Policy), under contract with ICF International.

16. A 2005 CQ Researcher report states: "Typically, men and women sign up for active duty or a Reserve unit for a set period. However, since September 11, 2001, stop-loss policies adopted by all branches of the services have allowed the military to keep personnel after their contracts expire." Pamela M. Prah, "Draft Debates: Is the Pentagon using a 'Backdoor' Draft?," *CQ Researcher* 15, no. 28 (August 2005), 668.

17. This could possibly be because this is a Disney Channel made-for-television movie.

18. In reality, the Constellation *was* on a tiger cruise on September 11, 2001. This film, however, does not purport to be based on anything that actually occurred during or immediately after that day. See Patricia Reily, '*So There We Were*': *Leadership Stories from the Men and Women Who Make the Navy Work* (Litchfield Park, AZ: Emergent, 2011), 113–114.

19. Theresa L. Geller, "Queering Hollywood's Tough Chick: The Subversions of Sex, Race, and Nation in *The Long Kiss Goodnight* and *The Matrix*," *Frontiers: A Journal of Women Studies* 25, no. 3 (2004), 14.

20. Campbell, "Women, Combat, and the Gender Line," 97.

21. Quoted in Sule Totkas, "Nationalism, Militarism

and Gender Politics: Women in the Military," *Minerva* 20, no. 2 (Summer 2002), 30.

22. According to the Army's Care Plan documentation, "All Soldiers who have dependents and are either single or part of a dual-military couple must have a Family Care Plan. The requirement for a Family Care Plan applies to both Active and Reserve Component Soldiers, regardless of grade." United States Army Combined Arms Center, "Army Family Care Plan," accessed March 17, 2019, https://usacac.army.mil/sites/default/files/documents/sja/familycareplaninfo.doc. In the film, McDermott put her mother down on her Family Care Plan, but she tells both Sergeant Jones and another unit member that her mother is not a viable option.

23. As with the Women's Air Forces Service Pilots, the Army's "Hello Girls" finally received veteran status with the passage of Public Law 95–202 in 1977.

24. Priscilla Forance, "Women and Arms: Portrayals through Film," *Minerva*, 1, no. 1 (March 1983), 81.

Chapter Eight

1. On February 19, 2010, then Secretary of Defense Robert Gates issued a memorandum to The Honorable Carl Levin, Chairman of the Senate Committee on Armed Services, stating that the Navy was "ready to implement policy changes to support a phased approach to the assignment of women to submarines."

2. ACLU, "Hegar, et al. v. Panetta: The Legal Challenge to the Combat Exclusion Policy," accessed January 16, 2019, https://www.aclu.org/sites/default/files/field_document/combat_exclusion_factsheet-plaintiffs-4-4-17-final.pdf.

3. The memorandum from then Secretary of Defense Leon Panetta, dated January 24, 2013, was sent to the Secretaries of the Military Departments and stated: "The 1994 Direct Ground Combat Definition and Assignment Rule excluding women from assignment to units and positions whose primary mission is to engage in direct combat on the ground is rescinded effective immediately."

4. Maureen Murdoch, Arlene Bradley, Susan H. Miller, Robert E. Klein, Carole L. Turner, and Elizabeth M. Yano, "Women and War: What Physicians Should Know," *Journal of General Internal Medicine* 21, Supp 3 (March 2006), S6.

5. See Craig Donegan, "New Military Culture," *The CQ Researcher* 6, no. 16 (April 1996), 364 and Ed O'Keefe and Jon Cohen, "Most Americans Back Women in Combat Roles, Poll Says," *The Washington Post* (March 16, 2011), Accessed January 15, 2019, https://www.washingtonpost.com/local/politics/most-americans-back-women-in-combat-roles-poll-says/2011/03/16/ABTereg_story.html?noredirect=on&utm_term=.1b775b769f54.

6. Stanley Rothman, Stephanie Powers, and David Rothman, "Feminism in Films," *Society* 40, no. 3 (March 1993), 68.

7. Lobasz, "Woman in Peril," 309.
8. Bouclin, "Feminism, Law," 121.
9. Lobasz, "Woman in Peril," 309.
10. Basinger, *World War II Combat Film*, 205.
11. Schulzke, "Kant's Categorical Imperative," 30.
12. *Ibid.*, 29.
13. Projansky, "Girls Who Act Like Women," 783.
14. Irene Hermann and Daniel Palmieri, "Between Amazons and Sabines: A Historical Approach to Women and War," *International Review of the Red Cross* 92, no. 877 (March 2010), 30.
15. *Stand Down Soldier, ArtMattan Productions*, accessed September 18, 2018, http://www.africanfilm.com/StandDownSoldierInt.html.
16. Magda Romanska, "Trauma and Testimony: Heather Raffo's '9 Parts of Desire,'" *Alif: Journal of Comparative Poetics* 30 (2010), 215.
17. Murdoch, et al, "Women and War," S8.
18. Yvonne Tasker, "Violence, Duty, and Choice: The Military Woman in Contemporary Hollywood Cinema," in *Women Willing to Fight: The Fighting Woman in Film*, ed. Silke Andris and Ursula Frederick (Newcastle, UK: Cambridge, 2007), 82.
19. Tracey Boisseau, *White Queen: May French-Sheldon and the Imperial Origins of American Feminist Identity* (Bloomington: Indiana University Press, 2010), 120.
20. Irene S. Vernon, "We Were Those Who Walked out of Bullets and Hunger: Representations of Trauma and Healings in *Solar Storms*," *American Indian Quarterly* 36, no. 1 (January 2012), 34.
21. Romanska, "Trauma," 215.
22. Elizabeth Swanson Goldberg, "Living the Legacy: Pain, Desire, and Narrative Time in Gayl Jones' *Corregidora*," *Callaloo* 26, no. 2 (May 2003), 447.
23. Elizabeth H. Stokoe, "Doing Gender, Doing Categorisation: Recent Developments in Language and Gender Research," (2003), 4, accessed January 16, 2019, https://pdfs.semanticscholar.org/6a32/af834946f4e4f-0196cc8ea01f2f3fd9ceabd.pdf
24. "Lion in a Box," accessed October 15, 2018.
25. Sheila Tobias, *Faces of Feminism* (Boulder: Westview Press, 1997), 171.
26. Hermann and Palmieri, "Between Amazons," 20.
27. Campbell, "Women, Combat and the Gender Line," 97.
28. Layla Alizada is the first and only Muslim-American actress featured in this survey.
29. GAO, *Women in the Military: Deployment in the Persian Gulf War* (1993), 40, accessed February 19, 2019, https://www.gao.gov/assets/160/153531.pdf.
30. Irene Jung Fiala, "Unsung Heroes: Women's Contributions in the Military and Why Their Song Goes Unsung" in *Women in the Military and in Armed Conflict*, ed. Helena Carreiras and Gerhard Kummel (Weisbaden: VS Verlag, 2008), 49.

Bibliography

Abel, Richard. *Americanizing the Movies and "Movie Mad" Audiences, 1910–1914.* Berkeley: University of California Press, 2006.

Ahlquist, Denise, Nancy Carr, Michael J. Elsey, Elizabeth Friedman and Mary Klein, eds. *Tube Talk: Big Ideas in Television.* Chicago: The Great Books Foundation, 2017.

American Civil Liberties Union. "Hegar, et al. v. Panetta: The Legal Challenge to the Combat Exclusion Policy." Accessed January 16, 2019. https://www.aclu.org/sites/default/files/field_document/combat_exclusion_factsheet-plaintiffs-4-4-17-final.pdf.

Anderegg, Michael, ed. *Inventing Vietnam: The War in Film and Television.* Philadelphia: Temple University Press, 1991.

Aristophanes. *Lysistrata.* In *The Great Books of the Western World.* Volume 4, edited by Dale H. Hoiberg, 824–45. Chicago: Encyclopaedia Britannica, Inc., 2007.

Baird, Robert. "Hell's Angels Above the Western Front." In *Hollywood's World War I Motion Picture Images,* edited by Peter C. Rollins and John E. O'Connor, 79–100. Bowling Green, OH: Bowling Green State University Popular Press, 1997.

Basinger, Jeanine. *A Woman's View: New Hollywood Speaks to Women, 1930–1960.* New York: Knopf, 1993.

———. *The World War II Combat Film: Anatomy of a Genre.* New York: Columbia University Press, 2003.

Bell-Metereau, Rebecca. *Hollywood Androgyny.* New York: Columbia University Press, 1985.

Bellafaire, Judith. *Women in the United States Military: An Annotated Bibliography.* New York: Routledge, 2011.

Binns, Daniel. *The Hollywood War Film: Critical Observations from World War I to Iraq.* Chicago: Intellect, 2017.

Boisseau Tracey. *White Queen.* Bloomington: Indiana University Press, 2004.

"Boot Camp." *Today's Military.* Accessed May 4, 2018. http://www.todaysmilitary.com.

Bouclin, Suzanne. "Feminism, Law and Cinema." In *Women, Law, and Equality: A Discussion Guide,* edited by Kim Brooks and Carrisima Mathen, 119–75. Toronto: Irwin Law, 2010.

Britton, Wesley Alan. *Onscreen and Undercover: The Ultimate Book of Movie Espionage.* Westport, CT: Praeger, 2006.

Budnik, Daniel R. *'80s Action Movies on the Cheap: 284 Low Budget, High Impact Pictures.* Jefferson, NC: McFarland, 2017.

Calvin, Paula E., and Deborah A. Deacon. *American Women Artists in Wartime, 1776–2010.* Jefferson, NC: McFarland, 2011.

Campbell, D'Ann. "Women in Combat: The World War II Experience in the United States, Great Britain and the Soviet Union." *Journal of Military History* 57, no. 2 (April 1993): 301–23.

———. "Women, Combat, and the Gender Line. *MHQ* 6 (Autumn 1993): 88–97.

Cohen, Daniel A., ed. *The Female Marine and Related Works.* Amherst: University of Massachusetts Press, 1997.

DeBauche, Leslie Midkiff. *Reel Patriotism: The Movies and World War I.* Madison: University of Wisconsin Press, 1997.

Defense Advisory Committee on Women in the Services. "About." Accessed April 23, 2018. http://dacowits.defense.gov/about.

Donald, Ralph, and Karen MacDonald. *Women in War Films: From Helpless Heroines to G.I. Jane.* New York: Rowman and Littlefield, 2014.

Donegan, Craig. "New Military Culture." *The CQ Researcher* 6, no. 16 (April 1996): 361–84.

Downey, Sharon D. "Top Guns in Vietnam: The Pilot as Protected Warrior Hero." In *War and Film in America: Historical and Critical Essays,"* edited by Marilyn J. Matelski and Nancy Lynch Street, 114–33. Jefferson, NC: McFarland, 2003.

Edwards, Paul M. *World War I on Film: English Language Releases through 2014.* Jefferson, NC: McFarland, 2016.

Elhstain, Jean Bethke. *Women and War.* Chicago: University of Chicago Press, 1995.

Ephron, Nora. "Yossarian Is Alive and Well in the Mexican Desert." In *Double Features: Big Ideas in Film,* edited by Nancy Carr, Michael J. Elsey, Louise Galpine, John Sniegowski and Mary

Williams, 5–16. Chicago: The Great Books Foundation, 2017.

Erickson, Hal. *Military Comedy Films.* Jefferson, NC: McFarland, 2012.

Fiala, Irene Jung. "Unsung Heroes: Women's Contributions in the Military and Why Their Song Goes Unsung." In *Women in the Military and in Armed Conflict,* edited by Helena Carreiras and Gerhard Kummel, 49–61. Wiesbaden: VS Verlag, 2008.

Fishman, Donald. "The Cold War: Three Episodes in Waging a Cinematic War." In *War and Film in America: Historical and Critical Essays,* edited by Marilyn J. Matelski and Nancy Lynch Street, 43–66. Jefferson, NC: McFarland, 2003.

Fleischer, Richard. *Out of the Inkwell: Max Fleischer and the Animation Revolution.* Lexington, KY: University of Kentucky Press, 2011.

Forance, Priscilla. "Women and Arms: Portrayals through Film." *Minerva* 1, no. 1 (March 1983): 81.

Freitas, Gary. *War Movies.* Brandon, OR: Robert D. Reed Publishers, 2004.

Furia, Stacie Robyn. *Bombshells on Film Reels: How Women in Mainstream Military Movies Enact Hegemonic Gender Ideologies.* M.A. thesis, University of Santa Barbara, 2006.

Geller, Theresa L. "Queering Hollywood's Tough Chick: The Subversions of Sex, Race, and Nation in *The Long Kiss Goodnight* and *The Matrix.*" *Frontiers: A Journal of Women Studies* 25, no. 3 (2004): 8–34.

"Glossary of Military Acronyms." Military.Com. Accessed February 11, 2019. https://www.military.com/hoin-armed-forces/glossary-of-military-acronyms.html.

Godson, Susan H. *Serving Proudly: A History of Women in the U.S. Navy.* Annapolis: Naval Institute Press, 2001.

Goebel, Katy Endruschat. *Women for Victory: American Servicewomen in World War II. History Uniform Series.* Atglen, PA: Schiffer Military History, 2011.

Goldberg, Elizabeth Swanson. "Living the Legacy: Pain, Desire, and Narrative Time in Gayl Jones' *Corregidora.*" *Callaloo* 26, no. 2 (May 2003): 446–72.

Graveline, Christopher, and Michael Clemens. *The Secrets of Abu Ghraib Revealed: American Soldiers in the Iraq War on Trial.* Washington, D.C.: Potomac Books, 2010.

Guthrie, Meredith. *Women in Hollywood Military Movies: A Cultural Textual Analysis of Films from 1980–2000.* M.A. thesis, Bowling Green State University, 2001.

Hawkins, Lester G., Jr., and George S. Pettee. "OWI—Organization and Problems." *The Public Opinion Quarterly* 7, no. 1 (Spring 1943): 15–33.

Herbert, Melissa. "Feminism, Militarism, and Attitudes toward the Role of Women in the Military." *Gender Issues* 14, no. 2 (June 1994): 25–48.

Hermann, Irene, and Daniel Palmieri. "Between Amazons and Sabines: A Historical Approach to Women and War." *International Review of the Red Cross* 92, no. 877 (March 2010): 19–30.

Hirshman, Linda. *Victory: The Triumphant Gay Revolution.* New York: HarperCollins, 2012.

Holm, Jeanne. *Women in the Military: An Unfinished Revolution (revised).* Novato, CA: Presidio Press, 1992.

Horak, Laura. *Girls Will Be Boys: Cross-Dressed Women, Lesbians, and American Cinema.* New Brunswick, NJ: Rutgers University Press, 2016.

Huie, William Bradford. *The Americanization of Emily.* New York: The New American Library, 1959.

Inness, Sherrie. *Tough Girls: Women Warriors and Wonder Women in Popular Culture.* Philadelphia: University of Pennsylvania, 1999.

Isenberg, Michael T. *War on Film: The American Cinema and World War I, 1914–1941.* Rutherford, NH: Fairleigh Dickinson University Press, 1981.

Jones, Dorothy B. "The Hollywood War Film." *Hollywood Quarterly.* 1, no. 1 (October 1945): 1–19.

Kaminski, Theresa. *Prisoners in Paradise: American Women in the Wartime South Pacific.* Lawrence, KS: University of Kansas Press, 2000.

Koppes, Clayton R., and Gregory Black. "What to Show the World: The Office of War Information and Hollywood, 1942–1945." *Journal of American History* 64, no. 1 (1977): 87–105.

Kuhn, Annette. *The Power of the Image: Essays on Representation and Sexuality.* London: Routledge, 1985.

Lentz, Robert J. *Korean War Filmography.* Jefferson, NC: McFarland, 2003.

Lepore, Jill. *The Secret History of Wonder Woman.* New York: Vintage Books, 2015.

Licursi, Kimberly J. Lamay. *Remembering World War I in America.* Lincoln: University of Nebraska Press, 2018.

Linville, Susan E. "The Mother of All Battles: *Courage under Fire* and the Gender-Integrated Military." *Cinema Journal* 39, no. 2 (February 2000): 100–20.

Lobasz, Jennifer K. "The Woman in Peril and the Ruined Woman: Representations of Female Soldiers in the Iraq War." *Journal of Women, Politics and Policy* 29, no. 3 (2008): 305–34.

MacDonald, Myra. *Representing Women: Myths of Femininity in the Popular Media.* London: Edward Arnold, 1995.

Miner, Steven Merritt. "'Things Must Be Bad at the Front': Women in the Soviet Military During WWII." *MCU Journal* Special (2018): 41–64.

Murdoch, Maureen, Arlene Bradley, Susan H. Miller, Robert E. Klein, Carole K. Turner, and Elizabeth M. Yano. "Women and War: What Physicians Should Know." *Journal of General Internal Medicine* 21 Supp 3 (March 2006): S5–S10.

Muse, Eben J. "From Lt. Calley to John Rambo: Repatriating the Vietnam War." *Journal of American Studies* 27, no. 1 (April 1993): 88–92.

Neale, Steve. "Questions of Genre." In *Film Genre Reader IV*, edited by Barry Keith Grant, 178–202. Austin: University of Texas Press, 2012.

Panetta, Leon. "Elimination of the 1994 Direct Ground Combat Definition and Assignment Rule." (January 24, 2013). Accessed March 14, 2019. big.assets.huffingtonpost.com/irectGroundCombatDefinitionAndAssignmentRule.pdf.

Pawelczyk, Joanna. "Constructing American Female War Veterans' Military Identity in the Context of Interviews." *Women & Language* 37, no. 1 (Spring 2014): 89–118.

Peterson, Carrie. "Separation Anxiety and Boot Camp: Why Basic Training Should Remain Gender-Integrated." *Law and Inequality: A Journal of Theory and Practice* 17, no. 1 (Winter 1999): 139–70.

Pisano, Dominick A. "*The Dawn Patrol* and the World War I Air Combat Film Genre: An Exploration of American Values." In *Hollywood's World War I Motion Picture Images,* edited by Peter C. Rollins and John E. O'Connor, 59–78. Bowling Green, OH: Bowling Green State University Popular Press, 1997.

Prah, Pamela M. "Draft Debates: Is the Pentagon Using a 'Backdoor' Draft?" *CQ Researcher* 115, no. 28 (August 2005): 663–70.

Projansky, Sarah. "Girls Who Act Like Women Who Fly: Jessica Dubroff as Cultural Troublemaker." *Signs* 23, no. 3 (Spring 1998): 771–807.

"Proud History." Office of Naval Intelligence. Accessed June 23, 2018. http://www.oni.navy.mil/this-is-ONI/Proud- History.

Rasmussen, Karen, Sharon D. Downey, and Jennifer Asenas. "Trauma, Treatment, and Transformation: The Evolution of the Vietnam Warrior in Film." In *War and Film in America: Historical and Critical Essays,* edited by Marilyn J. Matelski and Nancy Lynch Street, 134–58. Jefferson, NC: McFarland, 2003.

Reily, Patricia."*So There We Were...*": *Leadership Stories from the Men and Women Who Make the Navy Work.* Litchfield Park, AZ: Emergent Publications, 2011.

Reis, Elizabeth. "Impossible Hermaphrodites: Intersex in America, 1620–1960." *Journal of American History* 92, no. 2 (September 2005): 411–41.

Rollins, Peter C., and John E. O'Connor, eds. *Hollywood's World War I Motion Picture Images.* Bowling Green, OH: Bowling Green State University Popular Press, 1997.

Romanska, Magda, "Trauma and Testimony: Heather Raffo's '*9 Parts of Desire,*'" *Alif: Journal of Comparative Poetics* 30 (2010): 211–39.

Rothman, Stanley, Stephanie Powers, and David Rothman. "Feminism in Films." *Society* 40, no. 3 (March 1993): 66–72.

"SAS: Women Allowed to Join for First Time." *BBC News,* October 25, 2018, https://www.bbc.com/news/uk45983882.

Schloeser, Kathy. "The First Women of West Point." U.S. Army. Accessed December 9, 2018. https://www.army.mil/article/47238/the_first_women_of_west_point.

Schneider, Steven Jay. "Movies and the March to War." In *American Cinema of the 1940s,* edited by W.W. Dixon, 74–93. New Brunswick: Rutgers University Press, 2006.

Schulzke, Marcus. "Kant's Categorical Imperative, the Value of Respect, and the Treatment of Women." *Journal of Military Ethics* 11, no. 1 (April 2012): 26–41.

Shakespeare, William. *Macbeth.* In *The Great Books of the Western World.* Volume 24, edited by Clifton Fadiman and Philip W. Goetz, 284–310. Chicago: The Encyclopaedia Britannica, Inc., 2007.

Shay, Jonathan. *Achilles in Vietnam: Combat Trauma and the Undoing of Character.* New York: Scribner's, 1994.

Shull, Michael S., and David E. Wilt. *Doing Their Bit: Wartime American Animated Short Films, 1939–1945.* Jefferson, NC: McFarland, 2004.

"Skirted Soldier: The Army's Gender Integration during World War II." Military.com. Accessed January 18, 2019. https://www.military.com/history/skirted-soldiers-armys-gender-integration-during-world-war-ii.html.

Sokurov, Evgeniy, dir. *Tsel Vizhu (See the Target).* Grinsiti Studio, 2013.

Steihm, Judith Hicks. "The Generations of U.S. Enlisted Women." *Signs* 11, no. 1 (Autumn 1985): 155–75.

Steinman, Ron. *Women in Vietnam: The Oral History.* New York: TV Books, L.L.C, 2000.

Stokoe, Elizabeth. "Doing Gender, Doing Categorisation: Recent Developments in Language and Gender Research." 2003. Accessed January 16, 2019. https://pdfs.semanticscholar.org/6a32/af834946f4e4f0196cc8ea01f2f3fd9ceabd.pdf.

Stremlow, Mary V. *A History of the Women Marines, 1946–1977.* Washington, D.C.: Government Printing Office, 1986.

Suid, Lawrence H. *Guts and Glory: The Making of the American Military Image in Film.* Lexington: University Press of Kentucky, 2002.

Tasker, Yvonne. *Soldiers' Stories: Military Women in Cinema and Television Since World War II.* Durham, NC: Duke University Press, 2011.

_____. "Violence, Duty, and Choice: The Military Woman in Contemporary Hollywood Cinema." In *Women Willing to Fight: The Fighting Woman in Film,* edited by Silke Andris and Ursula Frederick, 78–94. Newcastle, UK: Cambridge, 2007.

Tobias, Sheila. *Forces of Feminism.* Boulder: Westview Press, 1997.

Totkas, Sule. "Nationalism, Militarism and Gender

Politics: Women in the Military." *Minerva* 20, no. 2 (Summer 2002): 29–38.

Turner, Karen Gottschang. *Even the Women Must Fight: Memories of War from North Vietnam*. New York: John Wiley and Sons, Inc., 1998.

Twine, France Winddance. *Firearms, Feminism and Militarism*. London: Routledge, 2013.

United States Commission on Civil Rights. *Equal Rights Amendment: Guaranteeing Equal Rights for Women under the Constitution*. Washington, D.C.: Government Printing Office, 1981.

"U.S. Navy Pay Grade Charts." America's Navy. Accessed November 12, 2018. https://www.navy.com/what-to-expect/military-pay.

Vernon, Irene S. "We Were Those Who Walked Out of Bullets and Hunger: Representations of Trauma and Healings in *Solar Storms*." *American Indian Quarterly* 36, no. 1 (January 2012): 34–49.

Walsh, Tim. *Timeless Toys: Classic Toys and the Playmakers Who Created Them*. (Kansas City, MO: Andrews McMeel Publishing, 2005.

Weitz, Rose. "Vulnerable Warriors: Military Women, Military Culture, and Fear of Rape." *Gender Issues* 32, no. 3 (September 2015): 164–83.

Wheelwright, Julie. *Amazons and Military Maids: Women Who Dressed as Men in the Pursuit of Life, Liberty and Happiness*. London: Pandora, 1989.

White, Hayden. "Historiography and Historiophoty." *American Historical Review* 93, no. 5 (December 1988): 1193–99.

Wicker, Foy D., Marilyn Maunch, Beverly Add Bendekgey, Kathleen M. Joyce, Julio Luna, David Moser, Dan Burton, Ann Calvaresi-Barr, and Kevin Perkins. *Women in the Military: Deployment in the Persian Gulf War*. Washington, D.C.: Government Accountability Office, 1993. Accessed February 19, 2019. https://www.gao.gov/assets/160/153531.pdf.

"Women during World War I: Their Role in the Progressive Era." Drawing America to Victory. Accessed February 18, 2019. https://history.delaware.gov/exhibits/online/WWI/Women-roles-ww1.shtml.

"Women in the Army: Post 9/11." Accessed November 1, 2018. https://www.army.mil/women/history.

"Women in the Military: Should Combat Roles Be Fully Opened to Women?" *CQ Researcher* 19, no. 40 (November 2009): 957–80.

The World War II Combat Film: Anatomy of a Genre. New York: Columbia University Press, 2003.

Yacovar, Maurice. "The Bug in the Rug: Notes on the Disaster Genre." In *Film Genre Reader IV*, edited by Barry Keith Grant, 313–31. Austin: University of Texas Press, 2012.

Zimmerman, Ian. "Furiosa: The Virago of Mad Max: Fury Road." In *Double Features: Big Ideas in Film*, edited by Nancy Carr, Michael J. Elsey, Louise Galpine, John Sniegowski, and Mary Williams, 145–52. Chicago: The Great Books Foundation: 2017.

Index

Numbers in **_bold italics_** indicate pages with illustrations

The A-Team 152, 190
Abbott, Bud 27, 39
Abu Ghraib 131, 148
Academy Award 7, 102, 116, 120, 169, 203–204*n*27
Ackerman, Leslie 83
Acosta, Allegra 170
Act of Valor 150–151, 191
action films 4, 7–8, 9, 15–18, 24, 28, 65–66, 80, 86–89, 91, 92, 93, 97, 105–110, 126, 132–136, 148–153, 171, 195, 204*n*9
Active Stealth 110, 187
Adams, Julia 58
Adlon, Pamela 110
Adrian, Iris ***45***
Affleck, Ben 143
Afghanistan 3, 9, 130, 147, 151, 156, 158, 162, 164, 167, 169, 170, 171, 172
Air Force 3, 6, 28, 29, 30, 52, 54, 55, 56, ***62***, 63, 66, ***68***, 69, 71, ***72***, 77, 85, 86, 90, 92, 94, ***95***, 105, 109, 115, ***118***, 119, 124, 126, 132, 134, ***135***, 138, ***139***, 140, 160, ***162***, ***165***, 166, 173, 201*ch*2*n*10, 202*ch*4*n*13, 203*n*23, 203*n*24, 204*n*2, 206*n*23
Air Force Academy 6, 124
Air Strike 135, 188
Airplane vs. Volcano 154, 191
Akune, Shuko 89
Albert, Eddie ***78***
Albertson, Jack 68
Alien 16
Aliens 16
Alizada, Layla 169, 206*n*28
All Hands on Deck 67, 181
All Quiet on the Western Front 7
Allied 149, 193
Allyson, June 53
Aloha 160–***162***, 192
Alone We Fight 153, 194
American Girl 169, 193
American Sniper 9, 160
The Americanization of Emily 80, 182, 202*n*19
Anderson, Mary 27–28
Andrews, Julie 80
Andrews, Naveen 116
Angel, Vanessa 90

Anlauf, Sally 90
Annabella 36
Annapolis 143–144, ***145***, 188
Annapolis (Naval Academy) 6, 84, 111, 114, 124, 125, 126, 143, ***145***
Apocalypse Now 9, 12, 65
Arden, Eve 41, 71–***72***
Arkin, Alan 72
Army 3, 5, 6, 9, 19, 21, 22, 23, 25, ***31***, 38, 39, ***40***–41, ***42***–43, 45–46, 48, 49, 59, 62, 68, 69, 83–84, 85, 89, ***90***, 96–97, ***99***, ***100***–102, 107, 111–113, ***112***, 123, 124, 126–127, ***128***, 129, 131, 132, 133, 136–***137***, 138, 143, 145–146, 149, 150, 152, ***155***, 157, ***160***, 162–164, ***163***, 166, 167, 168, 169, 170, 171, 173, 196, 200*n*24, 201*n*16, 201*ch*3*n*1, 202*ch*4*n*13, 203*n*10, 203*n*11, 203*n*23, 203*n*24, 204*n*2, 204*n*2, 206*n*22; hospital 16, 27, 31, 32–33, 38, 48–49, 50, 59, 65, 66, 77–79, 116, 153, 159; intelligence 48, 88, 110, 133, 146, 151, 164, 172–173
Army Nurse Corps 4, 15, 29, 49, 204*n*9, 204–205*n*25
Army Surgeon 35–***36***, 176, 199*n*11
Arthur, Indus 74
Arvidson, Linda 22
The Assault 166, 193
Atkinson, Linda 66
Avalon, Frankie 71
Aviation Officer Candidate School (AOCS) 102
aviator (female military) 4, 10, 11, 23, 28, ***29***, 56, ***56***, 57, ***57***, ***85***, 86–88, ***87***, 109, 148, 149, 171, 172, 173, 201*ch*2*n*10, 203*n*8, 203*n*10, 203*n*14, 203*n*20, 206*ch*7*n*23; Air Force 69, 92, 94–95, ***95***, 118–119, ***118***, 138, 139, 139, 160–161, 162, 164–***165***; Army 96, ***96***, 104, 106, ***128***–129, 135; drone pilot 149, 165–***166***, Marine Corps 135; Navy 102, 104, 108, 110, 111, 114, 125–126, 133–***134***, 141–142; Women Airforce Service Pilots (WASP) 28–***29***, 35, 173, 201*ch*2*n*10, 206*n*23
A.W.O.L. (2005) 146, 188

AWOL (2010) 158, 190
AWOL (2016) 158, 193
Aykroyd, Dan 90

Bacon, Kevin 140
Bainter, Fay 30
Baldwin, Adam 94
Barber, Gillian 124
Barker, Marcie 75–***76***
Barnes, James Jay 136
Barnyard WAAC 39, 176
Basic 136–***137***, 188
basic training 11, 19, 22, 23, 26, 28–***31***, 41, 46, 48, 57, 61, 62, 83, 90, 93, 94, 99–102, ***101***, 111, 113, 146, 167, 203*n*23, 203*n*24
Bassett, Angela 117
Battle Circus 53, ***53***, 179
Battle Flame 54–55, 181
Battle of the Coral Sea 48, 181
Beckinsale, Kate 143–144
Behind Enemy Lines (1987) 88, 184
Behind Enemy Lines (2001) 132, 187
Behind Enemy Lines: Colombia 132, 189
Behind Enemy Lines II: Axis of Evil 132, 189
Belkin, Jessica 168
Bell, Catherine 106, 155–***156***
Bennett, Elizabeth Ann 146
Bennett, Jonathan 151
Benton, Susanne 73
Berenger, Tom 109
Bernadette, Jamie 152
Bernsen, Corbin 115–116
Betty Boop 22, 200*n*27
Bezenek, Joseph 170
Biel, Jessica 133–***134***, 142–***143***, 152
Biggs, Jason 146
Binoche, Juliette 116
Birth of a Nation 7
Black Thunder 106–107, 186
Blackman, Joan ***67***–68
Blair, Janet 27
Blakeney, Olive 27
Blanc, Jennifer 107
Blanchard, Susan 102
Blood Stripe 12, 164, 193
The Bloody Child 117–118, 185

Index

Boardman, Eleanor 19–**20**, **21**
Bogart, Humphrey 53
Boller, Brent 136
Bomber's Moon 35–36, 176
Boone, Pat 67
Booth, Powers **118**–119
Booth, Samantha 140
Borgnine, Ernest 55
Bouman, Bonnie Lee 149
Bowen, Roger 74
Boxer Rebellion 5
The Boys in Company C 65, 183
Boys of Abu Ghraib 148, 191
Bradna, Olympe 35
Brady, Scott 54
Brand, Neville 49
Brandon, Sharon 109
Brazzi, Rossano 46
Breaking the Silence 166, 191
Breakthrough 47, 178
Brennan, Eileen 100–101, 203n25, 203–204n27
Brewster, Jordana 143, **145**
Bright Victory 47, 178
Bristow, Aidan 153
Broken Arrow 126, 185
Brooks, Lola 48
Browder, C. Stephen 168
Brown, Helen 47
Brown, Melanie 167
Bruening, Justin 157
Buck Privates 28, 39, 176
Buck Privates Come Home 39, 177
Burrows, Leigh 138
Butler, Gerard 150
By Dawn's Early Light 12, **118**–119, 172, 184

Cage, Nicolas **128**, 140
Caine, Michael 77
Calene-Black, Shelley 136
Calvert, Phyllis 34
Camp X-Ray 159–**160**, 191
Canova, Judy 41, 61
Captain Newman, M.D. 77–79, **78**, 182
Cardellini, Linda 163
Carlson, Dru Anne 105
Carmen, Julie 102
Carmine, Christianna 154
Carne, Judy 80
Carrell, Steve 157
Carter, Ash 6
Cassidy, Joanna 98–**99**
Castillo, Su 166
Catch-22 12, 72–**73**, 182, 202*ch*4n11–12
Caught in the Draft 28
Central Intelligence Agency (CIA) 88, 89, 105, 107, 150
Chalke, Sarah 105
Chaney, Lon 19, **20**
Chaplin, Charles 22, 39, 200n24, 200n25
Chapman, Marguerite 29
Chase, Chevy 90
Chasers 109, 185
Chastain, Jessica 161–**162**

Chau, Francois 94
Cheney, Lon 19, 20
Chesty Anderson, U.S. Navy 75–**76**, 172, 182
Chris, Marilyn 87
Christine, Virginia 30
The Christmas You Don't Know 169, 192
Ciccolella, Jud 129
Cinderella Goes to a Party 8
Civil War 3, 4, 7, 16, 17, 19, 22, 171, 196, 200n12; the Confederacy 17–19, 22, 23, 145, 200n12; the Union 17, 18, 22, 23
Clark, Spencer Treat 168
Clear and Present Danger 105, 185
Close, Glenn **123**–124, 140
Coast Guard 3, 5, 6, 11, 15, 25, 27, 86, 104, 105, 140, 149, 173, 196, 203n23
Coast Guard Academy 6
Cobb, Lee J. 69
Coburn, James 69, 80
Colbert, Claudette 31–**32**, 39
Cold War 8, 11, 12, 44, 55–63, 64, 65, 77, 85, 92, 93, 105, 118, 119n11
Cold Winter's Night 168, 192
Collins, Bianca 141
Colon, Mercedes 141
Colonna, Jerry 41
combat 5, 6, 9, 12, 16, 25, 41, 52, 64, 77, 82, 85, 88, 94, 96, 97, 104, 106, 107, 108, 113, 123, 125, 128, 129, 131, 134, 136, 142, 148, 158, 159, 162, 163, 164, 166, 167, 168, 169, 170, 172, 173, 200n5, 201n18, 203n18, 204n23, 205n4, 206n2, 206n3
Combs, Holly Marie 124–**125**
comedies 4, 8, 11, 15, 21, 22, 23, 28, 39, 42, 47, 54, 56–63, 66–77, 86, 89–**90**, 100–101, 110, **111**, **112**, **114**, **115**, 146–147, 171, 172
Command Performance 190
Commandos Strike at Dawn 35, 176
Conley, Darlene 77
Conway, Kate 153
Conway, Tim 69
Cooper, Bradley 152, 160
Cooper, Gary 23, 60, 146
Cooper, Scott 133
The Core 139, **139**, 188
Corey, Wendell 50
Corregidor 11, 32–**33**, 176
Corregidor, the Philippines 30, 32, 48
Costello, Lou 27, 39
Courage Under Fire 3, 12, 105, 106, 172, 186
court-martial 26, 52, 55, 60, 90, 97, 131, 137, 153, 158, 161, 165
Craig, Catherine 37
Crash Dive 106, 127, 186
Crash Dive 2: Counter Measures 127, 187
Crawford, Joan 23
Crosby, Bing 26
Crosby, Gary 58

cross dressing 4, 9, 10, 16, 17–19, 22, 23, 26, 27, 41, 42, 66, 67, 69, 158, 199, 200n12
Cruise, Tom **119**–121, 154, **155**
Cry 'Havoc' 3, 11, 30–31, 171, 176
Cueva, Isabel 169
Cullen, Brett 159
Curtis, Jamie Lee 102
Curtis, Tony 59, 60, **67**–68, 69
Cusack, John 147
Cutts, Patricia 48

D-Day: The Sixth of June 51, 180
Damon, Matt 161
Danger Beneath the Sea 138, 187
Danton, Donna 69
The Darling of the C.S.A. 17–18, 175
Dash, Stacey 113
David, Karen 132
Davis, Alysa 88–90
Davis, Jim 82
Davis, Judy 116, 124
Davis, Nancy 51
Davis, Viola 115
Daw, Renée 167
The Dawn Patrol 7
Dawson, Rosario 134–**135**
Day, Dorothy 30
Day, Laraine **31**
Day One 169, 192
Dead Men Can't Dance 107, 172, 174, 186, 204n8, 205n15
Deborah Sampson: Woman in the Revolution 4, 66, 183
Deepwater Horizon 149, 193
The Deer Hunter 9, 65
Defense Advisory Committee on Women in the Services (DACOWITS) 44, 85, 202*ch*5n2, 204–205n25
Defense Officer Personnel Management Act (DOPMA) 85
Delta Force 3: Killing Game 105–106, 184
De Mornay, Rebecca **118**–119, 172
Denier, Lydie 88
Dent, Catherine 138
Derek, John 49, 54
Desert Shield/Desert Storm 12, 104, 113, 117, 172
Devane, William 93
DeVito, Danny 113
de Viveiros, Eva 125
Devore, Dorothy 23
De Wilde, Brandon **81**
Dexter, Alan 46
Dick, Andy 111–113, **112**
Dickinson, Angie 77–79, **78**
Dietrich, Marlene 67
The Dirty Dozen: Fatal Mission 88, 184
Dirty Harry 65
disaster films 4, 48, 76, 77, 115–116, 126, 138–139, 153, 154
DiSparti, Joseph 152
Dixon, Joan 51
Do No Harm 168, 173, 193
Doc 167–168, 193

Index

Dr. No 65
Dodd, Claire 27
Donnelly, Ruth 50
Don't Give up the Ship 60, **61**, 181
Don't Go Near the Water 59–60, 180
The Doughgirls 41, 177
Douglas, Kirk 81
Douglas, Melvyn 34
Dowling, Constance 26
Down Periscope 113–**114**, 186
Drake, Alfred 27
dramas 4, 7, 18, 27, 28, 35, 38, 47, 52, 55, 67, 76, 77, 80, 81, 86, 91–97, 116–126, 139–146, 157–161, 166, 171, 172
drill instructor (DI) 96, 100, 101–102, 107, 113, **147**, 167
Drones 164, 172, 191
Drug Enforcement Agency (DEA) 128, 136
Ducey, Lara Thomas 153
Dudikoff, Michael 106, 107, 137
Duke, Patty 96
DuMond, Hayley 145
Dunne, Irene 35
Dunne, Stephen 61
Durand, Airisa 153
Duvall, Robert 75

The Eagle and the Hawk 7, 22
Eagle Eye 134, **135**, 189
Earthstorm 138, 189
Eastwood, Clint 93
Eden, Barbara 57–58, 67, 76, 101
Edison, Thomas 7, 15, 199*ch*1*n*1
Edwards, Elaine 54
Eichhorn, Lisa 94–**95**
Eilbacher, Lisa 102
Eleniak, Erika 109
Elite 154–155, 193
Ellison, James 35
Elwes, Carey 115
Emerson, Faye 30
Enemy at the Gates 140–**141**, 187
The English Patient 12, 116, 186
Ensign Pulver **79**–80, 182
Enter the Dragon 65, 88
Ermey, R. Lee 93
Eruption LA 153, 194
Eshaq, Mike 156
Esparolini, Presciliana 149
E.T. 86
Eubank, Shari 75–**76**
Ewell, Tom 62
Excessive Force II: Force on Force 129, 185
Executive Orders 5, 25, 201*n*16, 201*ch*3*n*1
Experiment Alcatraz 51–52, 178

Fabian, Ava 110
A Fair Rebel 22, 171, 175
Falk, Hailey 123
Farrar, Geraldine 19, 200*n*17
Fay, Meagan 101
Fenner, Shelby 140
Ferrel, Conchata 101

A Few Good Men 3, 12, 105, **119**–121, 172, 185
Fiennes, Joseph 141
Fire Birds (Wings of the Apache) 12, **128**–129, 184
Fireball Forward 65, 182
Firefox 93, 183
First Yank in Tokyo 34–35, 177
Five Gates to Hell 49, 181
500 MPH Storm 153, 191
Flight Nurse **52**–53, 179
Flight of Fury 132, 189
The Flying Missile 47, 178
Flynn, Colleen 105
Foch, Nina 55
Fonda, Henry 77, 146
Fong, Benson 49
Fontaine, Joan 28
Force of Arms 49–50, 178
Ford, Glenn 47
Ford, Harrison 126
Forrest Gump 116, 146, 185
Forrest, Frederic 106
Fort Bliss 163, 191
40 Days and 40 Nights 154, 190
Fox, Vivica A. 147
Foxx, Jamie 133
Foy, Madeline 54
Fradenburgh, Emily 151
Francis, Anne 60
Francis in the Navy 58–59, 180
Francis Joins the WACs 58, 179
Frazee, Jane 39
Frazer, Liz 80
Freedman, Sharon 168
Freedom Strike 107, 186
Freeland, Pete 2, 152
Freeman, Joan 66
Freeman, Mona 49
Friend, Philip 34
From Russia with Love 65
Full Metal Jacket 12, 93–94, 184
Fulton, Joan 39

Gable, Clark **33**–34
Gaffrey, Monique 141
Gale, Lorena 123
Garcia, Drea 166, 169
Gareis, Jennifer 135
Garner, James 48, 80
Garr, Teri 92
Garrison 136, 189
Gauntier, Gene 17, 200*n*12
Gaynor, Mitzi 46, 140
Gazzara, Ben 65
The Geisha Boy 60–61, 180
The General's Daughter 127–128, 186
George, Betsy Lynn 117
Gere, Richard 102
Germany 4, 26, 153, 201*n*18
Ghost Soldier 142, 189
Ghostbusters 86
G.I. Jane (1951) **45**–46, 178
G.I. Jane (1997) 3, 94, 119, **121**–123, 172, 186
G.I. Joe: Retaliation 152, 172, 191
G.I. Joe: Rise of Cobra 133, 172, 190

G.I. Joe: Spy Troops 133, 188
G.I. Joe: The Movie 89, 133, 184
G.I. War Brides 38, 42, 177
Gilhooley, Dana Lynne 147
Gillis, Ann 27
Gilmore, Margalo 46
Ginsberg, Ruth Bader 6
The Girl Spy Before Vicksburg 17, 175, 200*n*12
Gleason, Regina 54
Glover, Danny 138
Goddard, Paulette 31–32, 40, **40**
Godley, John 132
Going Under 110–111, 113, 185
Goldstein, Jenette 98
Gone with the Wind 24
Good Kill 164–**165**, 192
Good Morning, Vietnam 86
Gorshin, Frank 54
Gossett, Louis, Jr. 102
Gould, Barbara 57
Gould, Elliot 75
Grable, Betty 28
Grace Is Gone 147, 189
Grammer, Kelsey 113
Grant, Beth 138
Grant, Cary **42**–43, 56, 60, 146
Grant, Kathryn 59
Grauer, Ona 154
Great Britain 12, 18, 80, 87, 88, 116, 131, 186, 201*n*18, 202*ch*4*n*18; Army 23, 35, 51, 116
The Great Dictator 39, 175
The Great Escape 65
Great Guns 28
The Great Imposter **67**–68, 181
The Green Berets 9
Greenwood, Bruce 139, **139**, **165**
Greer, Jane 60
Gregg, Virginia 60
Gregory, Allison 154
Grenada 12, 85, 98
Grier, David Alan **115**
Grier, Pam 99
Griffith, Andy 57
Griffith, Melanie 102
Guantanamo Bay 159–**160**
The Guardian 140, 189
Gulf War 3, 104, 106, 116, 117, 118, 125, 129, 171
The Guns of Navarone 65
Guthrie, Lynne 75
Gutierrez, Eddie 167
A Guy Named Joe 35, 176
Guy X 146, 188

Hackman, Gene 98–**99**
Haines, William 19
Hale, Barbara 27, 34
Hale, Jean 69
Hall, Anthony Michael 109, 155
Hall, Frankie 93
Hall, Israel 167
Hamburger Hill 12
Hamilton, Joseph 54
Hamilton, Whitney 2, 145, 158
Hampton, Shanola 168
Hanks, Tom 116

Index

Harmon, Mark 98
Harrington, Cheryl Frances 110
Harris, Barbara Eve 107
Harris, Ed 141
Harris, Phil 49
Hartley, Mariette 86–**87**, 203*n*7
Hartman, Ena 69, 173
Hartnett, Josh 143
Hasfari, Hana Azulay 105
Hasso, Signe 40–**41**
The Hasty Heart 38, 178
Hawn, Goldie **100**–101, 204*n*28
Hayden, Russell 37
Hayes, Penny 91
Hays Code 9
Hayworth, Jill 81, **81**
Heafey, Jessica 138
Heche, Anne 144
Hein, Katie 144
Helgenberger, Marg 129–130
Hell on the Battleground 88, 188
Hellcats of the Navy 51, **51**, 180
Hellen, Marjorie 54
Hello Girls 11, 145, 206*ch*7*n*23
Hepburn, Katharine 55–56
Here Come the WAVES 26, 177
Hermann, Heather 168
The Heroes of Desert Storm 117, 172, 185
Herrera, Vanessa 152
Hespe, Olivia 165
Hitler, Adolf 8, 39
Hoffman, Connie 75
Hoffman, Isabella 113
Holden, William 49
Holliman, Earl 59
Holly, Lauren 113–**114**
Holsey, Trace Carter 108
Home from War 168, 191
Home of the Brave 142–**143**, 189
Homecoming **33**–34, 174, 178
homosexuality 2, 10, 12, 101, 116, 122, 123, 124, 137, 140, 151, 152, 157, 158, 204*n*24
Hope, Bob 40–**41**, 55–56, 57
The Horizontal Lieutenant 11, 70–**71**, 172, 182
Horn, Christine 149
Hoshelle, Marjorie 30
Hot Shots! 110–**111**, 185
The House with Closed Shutters 18–19, 23, 171, 175
Howard, John 51–52
Hughes, Laura Leigh 117
Humphrey, Mark 109
The Hunt for Eagle One 135, 189
The Hunt for Eagle One: Crash Point 135–136, 189
Hunter Killer 150, **150**, 194
The Hunters 47, 180
The Hurt Locker 9
Hussey, Ruth 37
Hutton, Betty 26
Hutton, Jim 70–**71**
Hyer, Martha 58–59

I Was a Male War Bride 39, **42**–43, 146, 178

Ice Quake 154, 190
Ike: Countdown to D-Day 139, 188
Ike: The War Years 91, 183
The Iliad 4
Immortal Sergeant 146
improvised explosive device (IED) 151, 160, 164, 169
In Harm's Way 80–**81**, 182
In Love and War 12, 48, 180
In the Army Now 111–113, **112**, 185
In the Name of Freedom 169, 190
In the Navy 27, 176
Indivisible 157, 194
Inflammable 12, 129, 185
intercontinental ballistic missile (ICBM) 68, 77, 85, 90, 93, 127
International Squadron 35, 176
Intimate Strangers 92, 183
Into the Sun 109–110, 185
Iraq 3, 9, 86, 108, 130, 131, 132, 142, 143, 144, 146, 147, 157, 162, 164, 169, 171, 172
Iron Angel 82–**83**, 182
Iron Eagle II 109, 186
The Iron Major 27, 176
The Iron Petticoat 11, 55–**56**, 180
The Iron Triangle 94, 184
Isbell, Tammy 138
Israel 66, 89; Army 66, 122
Ivers, Jan 166
Ives, Burl 79

Jack Reacher: Never Go Back 154–**155**, 158, 172, 193
James, Annie 46
Janssen, David 66
Japan 5, 9, 26, 31, 32, 33, 34, 37, 48, 54, 60, 69, 70, 71, 82, 91, 92, 143, 201*n*29
Jarhead 2: Field of Fire 151, 192
Jarvis-Bennett, Patty 152
Jenney, Lucinda 122
Jennings, Maxine 38
Jet Attack 54, 180
Jet Pilot 11, 56, **57**, 180
Joan the Woman 9, 19, 200*n*17
Johanna Enlists 19
Johnny Got His Gun 7
Johnson, Van 35, 39
Jones, James Earl 119
Jones, Tommy Lee **99**
Judge Advocate General (JAG) 40, 120–121, 205*n*32
Judgment at Nuremberg 64
Justice on the Border 152–153, 190

Karges, Sarah 168
Karyo, Tchéky 139
Kasch, Cody 159
Katon, Rosanne 75–**76**
Kaye, Danny 26
Keach, Stacy 92
Keep Your Powder Dry 11, 30–**31**, 177
Keife, Darren 159
Keith, Alexander 127
Keith, David 102
Kellerman, Sally **74**–75

Kelly, Gene 45
Kennedy, Douglas 53
the Keystone Cops 15
KGB (*Komitet gosudarstvennoy bezopasnost*) 89, 106
Khim, Leaphey 168
Kilmer, Val 136
Kingra, Deepti 170
Kirk, Phyllis 59
Kirke, Lola 158
Kiss Them for Me 56–57, 180
Kissin' Cousins **68**–69, 182
Knight, William 152
Knox, Elyse 27
Kongkham, Lynn 65
Korean War 3, 8, 9, 11, 44, 52, 53, 54–55, 56, 62, 63, 68, 69, 73, 82, **83**, 107, 171, 172, 202*ch*4*n*13
Kovacs, Ernie 70
Kravitz, Zoë 164–**165**
Kristofferson, Kris 130
Kruger, Otto 32
Kue, Choua 149
Kulp, Nancy 57
Kwan, Nancy 69–70, 173

LA Apocalypse 154, 192
Ladd, Cheryl **97**–98
Ladies Courageous 28–**29**, 177
La Flair, Brienne 167
Lake, Veronica 31–32
Lamar, Cachet 142
Lamont, Syl **78**
Landi, Elyssa 32–33
Langford, Frances 51
La Pier, Darcy 108
The Last Detail 109
Last Man Standing 155–**156**, 190
The Last Outpost 22
The Last Rescue 159, 192
Laurel and Hardy 15
Law, Jude 141
lawsuits 6, 42–43, 148, 202*ch*3*n*14, 206*n*1
Le, Ngoc 94
Lead from the Front 170, 193
Leave It to the Marines 61, 178
Lederer, Suzanne 91
Lee, Anna 35
Lee, Denise 142
Leigh, Barbara 77
Leigh, Janet 56–**57**, 59
Lemmon, Jack 57–59, **58**
Leodorescu, Cristina 132
Leonard, Queenie 28
Leslie, Joan **52**, 52–53
Lester, Nancy 145–146
Let It Go 168, 194
Lethal Woman 12, 96–**97**, 184
The Letter 168, 191
Lewis, Jerry 46, **47**, 60–**61**
Lewis, Mary 89
Li, Hiep Thi 107
The Lieutenant Wore Skirts **62**–63, 180
Lifeboat 27–28, 177
Lighte, Spencer 132, 152
The Lighthorsemen 7

Lightning, Crystle 142
Lion in a Box 167, 173, 193
Lions for Lambs 132, 189
Lipper, David 124
Lisi, Verna 69
Lone Star 126, 186
Lone Survivor 160
Lonergan, Susan 106
The Longest Hundred Miles **81**, 81–82, 182
Love and War 7, 15
Love's Deadly Triangle: The Texas Cadet Murder 124–**125**, 186
Lowery, Robert 28
Lucas, Josh 133
The Lucky Ones 143, 189
Luisi, James 96–97
Lynch, Jessica 142, 166
Lynn, Mara 61
Lyons, Katelyn 150

MacDonald, Kenneth 52
MacInnes, Angus 132
MacKenzie, Joyce 27
Mackenzie, Julia 91
Maclachlan, Janet 102
MacLane, Barton 60
MacMurray, Fred 40, **40**
The Mad Parade (Forgotten Women) 7
Madison, Guy 54
The Madness of Tellaralette Seville 165, 194
Mahaffey, Valerie 91
Malone, Dorothy 53
"The Man's in the Navy" 67
Mara, Kate 160–**161**
Marine Corps 3, 5, 6, 9, 11, 15, 19–**20**, 25, 37–38, 48, 61, 65, 82, 85, 93, 104, 108, 109, 117–118, 120, 125, 135–136, 137–138, 140, 144–145, 149, 151, 153, 155–**156**, 157–158, **158**, 160–**161**, 164, 165–166, 167, 168, 169, 170, 171, 173, 196, 201*ch*3*n*1, 202*ch*4*n*4, 203*n*10, 203*n*23, 203*n*24, 204*n*2
Marine Raiders 37–38, 177
A Marine Story 157–**158**, 190
Marini, Gilles 159
Marshall, Jennifer 149, 168
Marshall, Marion **42**, 46, **47**
Marshall, Penny 113, 139
Marshall, Skye P. 157
The Martian 161–**162**, 192
Martin, Andrea 48
Martin, Dean 46, 48
MASH 3, 9, 12, 72–75, **74**, 202*ch*4*n*11, 204–205*n*25
Mason, Mercedes 151
Mathews, Carole 54
Matthau, Walter 80
McAdams, Rachel 143
McClure, Doug 69–70, 82
McCollester, Maggie 168
McElhone, Natasha 146
McEnroe, Annie 98
McGuire, Betty 75
Mchale's Navy 114, **115**, 186

Mchale's Navy Joins the Air Force 69, 182
McHugh, Frank 37
McKay, Wanda 32
McNamara, William 109
McNeely, Helen 65
McQueen, Chad 108
McRaney, Gerald 138
Medford, Kay 79
Megan Leavey 160–**161**, 193
Melton, Sid 61
Memorial Day 151, 191
Menkes, Tinka 117
Merrill, Dina 60–**61**
Messing, Debra 114, **115**
Meteor Storm 153–154, 190
Michael, Patricia 91
Michaels, Dolores 55
Michaels, Dorothy 49
Mickelbury, Denise 96
Middleton, Sarah 150, **150**
Military Husband 169, 193
Military Intelligence and You! 146, 189
military police (MP) 57, 85, **90**, 98, 117, 136, 154, 166
Miller, Alissia 107
Miller, Brett R. 169
Mission Over Korea 54, 179
Mister Roberts 57–58, **58**, 180
Mobile Army Surgical Hospital (MASH) 53, 54, 73–75; **74**, 82, **83**, 123, 202*ch*4*n*11, 204–205*n*25
Modesir, Chloe 169
Modine, Matthew 94
Monáe, Janelle 157
Monaghan, Michelle 163
Montgomery, George 36
Moore, Deborah 110
Moore, Demi **119**–120, **121**–122, 123, 172
Moore, Margo 70
Moore, Melissa 110
Moore, Patrick 38
Morehouse, Jennifer 149
Morrison, Diana 144
Mortensen, Viggo 121–122
Moss, Rosie 169
Mosteller, Julia 89
motherhood (female military) 33–34, 92, 96, 101, 102, 106, 117, 123, 124, 141, 142, 144, 145, 147, 154, 162–164, 167, 168, 169, 173–174, 201*n*15, 203*n*19, 206*n*22
Mulan 12, 108–109, 174, 187
Mulgrew, Kate 93
Mumford, Eloise 164
Muni, Paul 35
Murga, Rebecca 2, 168
Murphy, Eddie 108
Murphy, Mary 57
Murray, Bill **90**, **90**
My Brother's War 145, 158–159, 188
My Own True Love 34–**35**, 178
Myra Breckenridge 67
mysteries 4, 24, 75, 98, 116, 127, 129, 134, 137–138, 156, 171

Namsploitation 88, 135
Naval Academy (Annapolis) 6, 84, 111, 114, 124, 125, 126, 143, **145**
Navy 3, 4, 5, 6, 11, 15, 24, 25, 39, 46, 50, **50**, 55, 60, 67, **67**, 75–**76**, **81**, 82, 86, **97**–98, 104, 105, 107, 109, 113–**114**, **115**, **119**–122, **121**, **125**–126, 133–**134**, 138, 144–**145**, **150**, 154–155, 161–**162**, 170, 173, 196, 201*ch*1*n*29, 201*ch*3*n*1, 202*ch*4*n*4, 202*ch*4*n*13, 203*n*23, 204*n*2, 204*n*10, 205*n*28, 205*n*29, 205*n*31, 205*n*32, 206*n*1; naval hospital 23–24, 46, 67–68, 97–98; naval intelligence 24, 48, 105, 107, 121, 127, 138, 201*n*29
Navy Blues 23, 175
The Navy Comes Through 36–37, 176
Navy Nurse Corps 4, 15
Navy Secrets 24, 175
"The Navy Song" 26
The Navy Way 28, 177
Navy Wife 23–24, 175
Neal, Patricia 38, 50, **50**, 80–81
Neal, Tom 45
Neill, Sam 116
Never So Few 47–48, 181
Never Wave at a WAC 11, 46, 62, 179
Newcomb, Virginia 159, 167
Nichols, Rachel 133
Nicholson, Jack 109, 120
Nielsen, Connie 136–**137**
Nilssen, Anna Q. 17–18
No Time for Sergeants 57, 180
Nobody's Perfect 69–70, 173, 182
Nolan, Danni Sue 47
Norris, Sarah 166
North, Sheree 48, **62**–63
North Korea 44, 82–83, 107, 138; Army 54, 134, 149
Not With My Wife, You Don't! 69, 182
Nowlin, Kate 164
nurses 3, 4, 5, 7, 8, 9, 10, 11, 12, 15, 19, 45, 47, 49, 52, 63, 70, 86–87, 97, 148, 171, 172, 174, 200*n*6, 202*ch*4*n*4, 203*n*21, 208; Air Force 6, 29, **52**–53, 54, 69, 176, 179; Army 4, 15, 26–28, 29, 30–32, **33**–34, 35–**36**, 37, 38, 46, 47–48, 49, 50–51, 53, **53**, 54–55, 57, **58**, **59**, 60, 65, 69, 70–**71**, 72–75, **73**, **74**, 77–**78**, **79**–80, 82–**83**, 91–92, 116, **123**–124, 151, 153, 159, 162–163, 167, 204, 205, 206; Navy 4, 15, 19–**20**, 23–24, **33**, 37–**38**, 46, 50, 51, 53, 65, **67**–68, 69–70, 80–**81**, 82, 86, 92, **97**–98, 127, 139–140, 143–**144**, 201*n*16, 202*n*4, 203*n*21; Red Cross 1, 3, 7, 22, 116–117, 171, 199–200*ch*1*n*1

O'Brien, Maria 101
O'Brien, Pat 37
O'Connell, Arthur 60
O'Connell, Joan-Carol 92–93
O'Connor, Carliene 149
O'Connor, Donald 58–59
O'Connor, Frances 140

O'Connor, Renee 144
The Odyssey 4
Off Limits 57–58, 179
An Officer and a Gentleman 102, 183
officer training 102; Officer Candidate School (OCS) 102; Officer Training School (OTS) 102; Reserve Officer Training Corps (ROTC) 102
O'Grady, Gail 125
Ogugua, Jade 149
O'Hara, Maureen 37–**38**
O'Leary, Matt 165
Olson, Jennie 170
Olson, Nancy 49–50
O'Moore, Patrick 38
On the Beach 48, 181
One Against the Wind 116–117, 185
One Kill 144–145, 187
One Weekend a Month 144, 188
Operation Delta Force 107–108, 133, 186
Operation Delta Force 3: Clear Target 108, 187
Operation Delta Force 5: Random Fire 133, 187
Operation Desert Shield/Desert Storm 12, 104, 113, 117
Operation Mad Ball 59, 180
Operation Pacific 50, **50**, 179
Operation Petticoat 60, 181
Operation Secret 179
Opposing Force (*Hellcamp*) 12, 94–96, **95**, 183–184
Our Man Flint 65, 69, 173, 182
Out of the Frying Pan, Into the Firing Line 8
The Outpost 7
Overall, Park 129–130
Owens, Patricia 49

The Package 98–**99**, 172, 184
Palestinian Liberation Organization (PLO) 66, 89
Palicki, Adrianne 152
Palmer, Betsy 57, **58**
Panetta, Leon 6, 148, 206n2, 06n3
Parachute Nurse 29–30, 176
Paradise Road 12
Paré, Michael 109
Parker, Jameson 83–84
Parker, Jean 28
Parker, Mary Louise 150
Patrick, Robert 88
Patriot Games 126, 185
Paul, Adrian 138
Payne, John 37–38, **38**
Pearl Harbor 143–**144**, 187
Pearl Harbor, Hawaii 25, 31–32, 37, 80, 140, 143
Peck, Gregory 27, 77–78
Pellonpää, Matti 153
Pennick, Jack 50
The Pentagon Wars 114–115, 187
Pepper, Cynthia **68**–69
The Perfect Furlough 59, 181
Perkins, Millie 79
Peters, Susan **31**
Petty, Lori **112**–113

Pflug, Jo Ann 74
Phifer, Mekhi 156
the Philippines 5, 30, 31, 32, 60, 82, 92, 137, 171, 204n10
Phillipe, Ryan 139
Phillips, Julianne 115
Pickard, Paris 158
Pickford, Mary 19
Pierce, Maggie 47
pilots *see* aviator (female military)
Pimenta, Neto DePaula 152
Platoon 9, 12, 86
Pleshette, Suzanne 60
Plotnikova, Svetlana 90
Polar Opposites 138, 174, 189
Pollack, Kevin 120
Porter, Don 39
Porter, MacKenzie 154
Powell, Dick 27
Power, Tyrone 28
pregnancy 6, 33, 63, 81, 202ch3n14
Prentiss, Paula 70–**71**, 72–**73**, 202ch4n11
Place, Mary Kay **100**
The President's Plane is Missing 12, 77, 182
The Presidio 98–99, 184
Presley, Elvis 45, **68**–69, 202n8
prisoner of war (POW) 30, 34, 36, 37, 48–49, 54–55, 88, 91–92, 116, 142, 159, 166, 169
Private Benjamin 12, 89–90, **100**–101, 172, 183, 203n26
Private Snafu 8, 199n14
Private Valentine 146–**147**, 189
A Private's Affair 57–58, 181
Prka, Tajana 164
Pro Patria 7
propaganda 7, 8, 9, 26, 65, 200n17, 203n17
The Proud and Profane 47, 180
post-traumatic stress disorder (PTSD) 8, 12, 34–35, 77, 92, 93, 117–118, 142, 157, 161–164, 165, 167, 168, 202ch4n4, 203n21
public laws 5, 6, 11, 25, 26, 42, 64, 201ch2n10, 201ch3n1, 206ch7n23
Pullman, Bill 111, 141
Purcell, Lee 87
Purl, Linda 83–84
Purple Heart Diary 51, 179
Purple Hearts 12, **97**–98, 183
Purviance, Edna 22
Pygmy Island 49, 178

Quicksand 137–138, 187
Quinlan, Kathleen 102, 204n29

Raiders of the Lost Ark 86
Rain 132–133, 187
Rakes, Kristen 148
Ralston, Vera 50
Rambo: First Blood 86
Ramis, Harold 90
Randall, Stacie 129
Randle, Theresa 135–136
Rangers (Army) 7, 89, 101, 129, 135, 136–137, 152–153

Reagan, Ronald 35, 51, **51**
The Red Danube 35, 178
Red Dawn 149, 191
Red Flag: The Ultimate Game 92–93, 183
Red Snow 54, 179
Red 2 150, 191
Reed, Donna 37
Reeves, George 31–32
Regan, Laura 142
Regeneration 7
Reinheart, Alice **62**
Remick, Lee 91
Remo Williams: The Adventure Begins 93, 183
Renaissance Man 113, 185
Repo, Lisa 116
Rescue Force 89, 184
Reserve Officer's Training Corps (ROTC) 102
Return 163–164, 190
Return of the Jedi 86
Revolutionary War 4, 65, 66
Ribisi, Giovanni 137
Rice, Elizabeth 159
Richards, Gabriella 166
Richards, Jeff 60
Richardson, LaTanya 126
The Road Home 167, 192
Roberton, Cliff 48
Rodriguez, Elizabeth 129
Rogue Strike 192
romance films 4, 22–24, 28, 34, 36, 46, 50–51, 53, 54, 59, 60, 84, 97–98, 128, 171
Romero, Cesar **72**
Rooney, Mickey 46, 57
Rosenthal, Carol 110
Ross, Katharine 77, 81–82
Rothery, Teryl 126
Royal Air Force (RAF) 28, 35
Roysden, Tiffany 152
Rush, Barbara 48
Rusler, Robert 135
Russell, Donnelle 132, 153
Russell, Rosalind 62
Ryan, Irene 61
Ryan, Meg 106
Ryan, Robert 37

The Sad Sack 59, 180
Sailor Beware 46–**47**, 179
Sales, Jeryl Prescott 162–**163**
Sampson, Deborah 4, 66, 202n6
Sanchez, Rosalyn 7
Sanchez, Stephanie 168
Sanders, John 156
Sarandon, Susan 91–92
Satellite Drop 170, 193
Savage, Ann 49
Savalas, Telly 88
Saving Jessica Lynch 142, 188
Savre, Danielle 151
Saxon, Pamela 126
Scarbrough, Jason 155
Schaal, Wendy 111
Schroder, Ricky 91
Schuck, John 74

Schukar, Tim 169
Scott, George C. 69
Scott, Ken 49
Scott, Randolph *38*
SEAL (Sea, Air, Land) (Navy) 7, 106, 127, 142, 149, 150, 154, 155
Seal Team Eight: Behind Enemy Lines 149, 192
Sealed Verdict 27, 178
Seattle Superstorm 154, 191
The Secret War of Jackie's Girls 86–88, *87*, 183
SERE (Survival, Evasion, Resistance and Escape training) 94–96, *95*, 107, 108, 122–123
Sergeant Deadhead 71–72, *72*, 172, 182
Sergeant York 146, 160
service academies Air Force Academy 6, 124; Coast Guard Academy 6; Naval Academy (Annapolis) 6, 84, 111, 114, 124, *125*, 126, 143, *145*; U.S. Military Academy (West Point) 6, 22, 83, 84, 127–128, 178, 202*ch*4*n*21
Serving in Silence 12, *123*–124, 172, 185
Seven Sisters 67
Seven Were Saved 37, 178
sexual assault 9, 28, 37, 47, 57, 95–96, 97–98, 116, 125–126, 127–128, 129, 138, 146, 154, 157, 159, 164, 165, 166–167, 193, 204*n*24, 205*n*29
A Shade of Gray 145–146, 187, 199*n*11
Shadows in Paradise 153, 190
Shakespeare, William 4, 16, 113, 204*n*15
Shatner, Melanie 108
She Goes to War 16, 20–*21*, 175, 199*n*11
She Stood Alone 125–126, 172, 185
Sheeler, Mark 54
Sheen, Charlie 110
Shepard, Sam 145
Shepherd, Hallie 159
Sheridan, Ann *42*–43
Sheridan, Tye 166
Shigeta, James 70
ships 19, 27, 60, 79, 86, 104, 107, 129, 202*n*4, 205*n*31
Shore, Dinah 26
Shore, Pauly 111–113, *112*
Shoulder Arms 22, 175, 199*n*11
Sibley, Sherry 118
Silo, Susan 69
Silvers, Cathy 110
Simmons, Beverly 39
Simpson, Jessica 146
Sinatra, Frank 47
The Sinking of the Lusitania 7, 199*n*7
Skerritt, Tom 94–95
Skirts Ahoy 46, 179
Skya, Sofya 153
Smith, Carol 87
Smith, Ida 146
Smith, Shawnee 107

Smulders, Cobie 154–*155*
sniper 93–94, 134, 141, 149, 151, 164, 165–166, 169, 203*n*17
Sniper: Ghost Shooter 149, 151, 165–166, 193
Sniper: Legacy 151, 192
Sniper: Reloaded 151, 190–191
So Proudly We Hail 3, 31–*32*, 171, 177
Soles, P.J. 90, *90*
Somers, Pamela Moore 132
Sothern, Ann 30
Sound Off 46, 179
South Pacific (1958) 46, 181
South Pacific (2001) 140, 187
Soviet Union 11, 35–36, 40–*41*, 54, 55–*56*, *57*, 88, 105, 111, 118–119, 127, 140–*141*, 150, 204*ch*6*n*9
Spanish American War 5, 7, 15, 199–200*ch*1*n*1
SPAR (Semper Paratus [Always Ready]) 5, 25, 27
Spartan 136, 188
Special Air Service (SAS) (British Army) 107, 204 *n*7
Special Forces 8, 89, 94, 107, *121*, 122–123, 129, 142, 172, 174, 204*n*23; Rangers (Army) 7, 89, 101, 129, 135, 136–137, 152–153; SEAL (Sea, Air, Land) (Navy) 7, 106, 127, 142, 149, 150, 154, 155; SERE (Survival, Evasion, Resistance and Escape training) 94–96, *95*, 107, 108, 122–123; Special Air Service (SAS) (British Army) 107, 204 *n*7
Spies Like Us 90, 183
Stand Down Soldier 12, 161–*163*, 192, 206*n*15
"Stars and Stripes" 20
Stateside 139–140, 188
Stealth 133–*134*, 188
Stefanson, Leslie 127
Stein, Andrea 111
Stephens, Rachel 57
Sterling, Robert 77
Stern, Ellyn 66
Stevens, Andrew 84
Stevens, Mark 53
Stewart, Elaine 46
Stewart, Kristen 159–*160*
Stockwell, Dean 114–*115*
Stone, Emma 160–*162*
Stop-Loss 139, 189
Storch, Larry *78*
The Story of G.I. Joe 27, 177
Stowe, Madeline 127
Stripes 90, *90*, 183
Strong, Leonard 54
Strudwick, Sheppard 59
The Submarine Kid 166, 192
submarines 6, 12, 48, 60, 76–77, 106, 108, 111, 113–114, 127, 131, 138, 148, *150*, 174, 202*n*18, 206*n*1
Suddenly It's Spring 40, *40*, 178
Sullavan, Margaret 30
The Sum of All Fears 132, 188
Super Cyclone 154, 191

Supreme Court 6, 43
Surface to Air 108, 187
Sutherland, Donald 75
Sutherland, Natasha 107
Swank, Hilary 139, *139*
Swanson, Kristy 110–*111*
The Swarm 77, 82, 183
Swit, Loretta 65
Swope, Tracy Brooks 87, 127
Swords and Hearts 23, 175

Tabassi, Leah 126
Tailhook 125–126, 205*n*28–29
Taking Chance 140, 190
Taking Fire 132, 153, 190
Tamminen, Jennifer 149
Tank Battalion 54, 181
Targeting 164, 192
Tars and Spars 27, 177
Tate, John 48
Taylor, Don 54
Taylor, Robert 51
Tea and Destiny 168, 190
Tedrow, Irene 47–48
Tell It to the Marines 19–*20*, 175
Ten Thousand Miles 193
Terminal Countdown (Y2K) 105, 187
Terry, Phillip *29*
Texada, Tia 136
Theiss, Brooke 137
There's Something About a Soldier 22, 175
They Were Expendable 37, 177
This Above All 28, 176
Thomas, Heather 88
Thomson, Dorrie 75–*76*
Three Brave Men 55, 180
Three Fingers 167, 192
thrillers 4, 24, 86, 98–99, 126–130, 136–138, *137*, 154–155, 156
Thunderbirds 49, 179
Tidal Wave: No Escape 115–116, 186
Tides of War (*USS Poseidon: Phantom Below*) 138, 188
Tiger Cruise 141–142, 188, 205*n*18
Time Limit 55, 180
A Time to Triumph 12, 96, *96*, 172, 184
To the Shores of Tripoli 37–*38*, 176
Today We Live 23, 175, 199*n*11
Todd, Richard 51
Too Young the Hero 91, 184
Torpedo Alley 53–54, 179
Totter, Audrey 54
Towne, Aline 51
Trang, Sophie 94
Travolta, John 126, 127, 136
Trevor, Claire 23
Triple Frontier 149, 194
True to the Army 41, 176
Tsao, Perry 142
Tucker, Forrest 51
Tucker, Jonathan 139–140
Turner, Lana 30–*31*, *33*–34
Twelve O'clock High 27, 178
2012 138, 190

Ulloa, Christina 169
Under Siege 105, 185
Union 158–159, 194
United States Military Academy (West Point) 6, 22, 83, 84, 127–128, 178, 202*ch*4*n*21
unmanned aerial vehicle (UAV) 164, *165*; drones 164–166, *165*, 172, 191
Up in Arms 26–27, 177
Up Periscope 48, 181
U.S. Troops and Red Cross in the Trenches 7, 15, 199*ch*1*n*1

Vallin, Rick 32
Van Camp, Marete 96
van Graan, Tanya 149
Veterans Administration (VA) 123, 124, 167, 201*n*10, 203*n*21
Vietnam War 3, 6, 9, 11–12, 64, 65, 73, 84, 85, 86, 88, 92, 93–94, *97*–98, 107, 116, 132, 167, 169, 171, 172, 202*n*4, 203*n*17, 203*n*21, 204–205*n*25
Vincent, June 61
virago 104–105, 106, 107, 108, 117, 122, 133, 151, 153
Virtuous 166, 193
Vold, Ingrid 88
von Zell, Harry 60
Voyage to the Bottom of the Sea 76–77, 181–182

The WAC from Walla Walla 61, 179
Wagner, Robert 48
Wahl, Evelyn 29
Wahl, Ken *97*–98
Wake Me When It's Over 11, 70, 181
Walken, Christopher 65
Walker, Robert, Jr. 79, *79*
Wallace, Dee 87
Walley, Deborah 71–*72*
Walsh, Loretta 4
Walt Disney Company 8, 12, 108, 146, 174
Wampler, Carrie 166
War on Terror 116, 135, 141; USS *Constellation* 141–142
War Stories 140, 190
Ward, B.J. 89
Ward, Fred 93
Warfighter 148–149, 194
WarGames 93, 183
Warhead (Prisoner in the Middle) 12, 66, 183

Warwick, Robert 30
Washington, Denzel 106
Washington, Sharon 140
Waterman, Felicity 107
Watson, Alberta 91
A WAVE, a WAC, and a Marine 27, 177
Wayans, Marlon 133
Wayne, David 59
Wayne, John 37, 39, 50, *50*, 56, 67, 80–81, 96
The Weakly Reporter 39–40, 177
Weber, Dreya 157–*158*
Webster, Bonnie 126
Weissmuller, Johnny 49
Weisz, Rachel 140–*141*
Welch, Raquel 67
Welcome to Marwen 157, *157*, 194
Welles, Orson 73
Wellman, Dorothy Coonan 27
Wen, Ming-Na 108
Wendel, Elmarie 111
West, Dorothy 18, 23
West, Kay 29
West Point (United States Military Academy) 6, 22, 83–84, 124, 127–128, 170, 172, 202*ch*5*n*1
Where There's Life 40–*41*, 178
White, Julie 140
White Feather 169, 191
White House Down 149, 191
Whitefield, Emily 133
Whitfield, Lynn 111
Widmark, Richard 55
Wilcox-Horne, Collin *73*
The Wild Blue Yonder 50–51, 179
Willes, Jean 57
Williams, Esther 46
Williamson, Fred 110
Willis, Bruce 150, 152
Willis, Christine 124
Wills, Anna Mae 154
Wills, Chill 58
Wilson, Chandra 126
Windtalkers 140, 188
Winger, Debra 102
Wings 7, 22
Wiseman, Michael 129
Withers, Grant 24
Withers, Jane 77
Without Reservations 39, 177
The Wizard of Oz 24
Women Accepted for Volunteer Emergency Service (WAVES) 5, 25, 26, 27, 48, 57, 60, 140
Women Airforce Service Pilots

(WASP) 28–*29*, 35, 173, 201*ch*2*n*10, 206*n*23
Women at War 30, 177
Women at West Point 83–84, 172, 183, 202*ch*4*n*21
Women of Valor 91–92, 184
Women's Armed Services Integration Act 5, 26, 44, 201*ch*2*n*16
Women's Army Air Force (WAAF) 28, 37, 86
Women's Army Auxiliary Corps (WAAC) 5, 11, 25, 39, 173
Women's Army Corps (WAC) 6, 8, 11, 25, 27, 30, *31*, 38, 40, 42, 45, 46, 49, 57, 58, 60, 61, 62, 69, 73, 173, 174, 201*ch*3*n*3, 202*ch*4*n*4, 203*n*11, 204*n*9
Women's Royal Naval Service (Wren) 28, 91
Wong, B.D. 108
Wood, Cindi *67*–68
Woode, Margo 82–*83*
Woodward, Tim 132
Wool, Breeda 158
World War I 3, 4, 5, 7, 8, 9, 10, 11, 15, 19–20, 22, 23, 24, 35–*36*, 116, 145, 171, 201*n*29, 204*n*13; RMS *Lusitania* 7, 199*n*7
World War II 5, 8, 9, 11, 12, 25–26, 30, 34, 35, 37, 38, 39, 40, 44, 49, 52, 53, 56, 59, 60, 62, 63, 64, 65, 69, 70, 72, 77, 78, 79, 80, *81*, 82, 84, 86, 87–88, 91, 105, 116, 153, 159, 171, 172, 203*n*10, 204 *n*13, 204 *n*20
Wray, Fay 24
Wright, Annabel 151
Wyatt, Jane 35–37, *36*
Wynter, Dana 51

A Yank in the R.A.F. 28, 176
The Yellow Birds 166, 193
Yellow Ribbon 168–169, 191
York, Kathleen 107
Young, Loretta 28–*29*
Young, Robert 23
Young, Sean 90, *128*–129
The Young Lions 48, 181
Your Mother Wears Combat Boots 89–90, 101, 172, 184
Your Roommate 166, 191
You're in the Navy Now 60, 179

Zabriskie, Grace 107, 205*n*16
Zarubeca, Shawne 110
Zeta-Jones, Catherine 150

www.ingramcontent.com/pod-product-compliance
Lightning Source LLC
Chambersburg PA
CBHW080804300426
44114CB00020B/2822